D1103921

Buddy Rich: One of a Kind
The Making of the World's Greatest Drummer

By Pelle Berglund

HUDSON MUSIC.

Published by
Hudson Music LLC
PO Box 467, Lavallette, NJ. 08735

Distributed by Hal Leonard Corp.
7777 West Bluemound Road
Milwaukee, WI 53213

Edited by Dr. Bruce Klauber and Joe Bergamini

Executive Producer: Rob Wallis

Design and Layout: Rick Gratton

Cover Design: Mike Hoff

Photos courtesy of Charley Braun

Visit https://hudsonmusic.com/oneofakind/ and enter the code/password BUDDY to access additional content from this book.

Printed in the U.S.A.

ISBN: 9781540064233

Library of Congress cataloging-in-publication data is available upon request.

CONTENTS

The whole idea of music is magic to me—that you can take all strange people that you've never seen in your life before, sitting in a theater, and in an hour's time make them friends, responding to you with their applause and attitude. And that's magic, to make three thousand friends in the span of an hour. Music is magic if it's played right, and if the people playing it are sincere. I think it does more to cover problems; you get people away from themselves when they become involved in music. If music could be the universal language, we wouldn't have quite as many problems if everybody were more dedicated to the arts, instead of politics, instead of all the uncertainty going on in the world. The only time you see people really settle is when they listen to some music. They sit down, and whether it's the sentimental value of a ballad or the excitement of an uptempo tune, it reaches everybody at the same time, and they walk out feeling great. If you reach each person for even one piece of music, that's magic.

Buddy Rich

FOREWORD

If you're reading these words, you're lucky. With thanks to Pelle Berglund for devoting seven years of his life to creating this biography, you're about to enter a world that doesn't exist anymore: 20th century big band and jazz music. *Before* the rock and roll era. A period of the American entertainment scene when bandleaders—trumpeters, trombonists, clarinetists, and crooning singers—made them the stars of the band.

That is, until the mid-1930s, when Gene Krupa came along. Playing with the Benny Goodman Orchestra, Krupa established the modern archetype of the swinging big band drummer, and in doing so made the drummer a "high priced guy." No one wanted in on that action more than Buddy Rich, a self-described washed-up 14-year-old former vaudeville child star. As a child Buddy sang, tap-danced, played a drum, kibitzed onstage, and did whatever he had to do to help put food on the table for his show-biz family. Then the Great Depression of the 1930s, changing public tastes, and the diminishing appeal of vaudeville shows left him out in the cold. But when he saw Krupa play the drums and then discovered the legendary drummer Chick Webb, Buddy knew he didn't want to dance, sing, or tell jokes. He just wanted to drum.

Man, did he drum!

As big a star as Gene Krupa was, the torch had been passed. Buddy, forever a Krupa fan, shifted Gene's drumming vocabulary into hyperdrive and along the way created an unparalleled musical legacy as arguably the greatest drummer of all time. As you'll come to learn through his story, Buddy Rich not only came to define the instrument he played, he *was* the history of American instrumental jazz performance. He was the ultimate in cool, a man who said he not only played up tempos, he "lived up"; a restless creature of his time who had one speed: *go, go, go!* No matter his financial ups and downs, Buddy remained at the top of the drumming game his entire life.

Throughout his life and career, whether they fought with him, loved him, cursed him, competed with him, fired him, or were fired by him; whether he frustrated them, infuriated them, dazzled them, charmed them, or confused them, everyone everywhere acknowledged the man for his singularly sensational drumming. There has simply never been a musician who matched him for his rhythmic dexterity, his musical cleverness, his personal cheekiness, his arrogance, confidence, and the breadth of his musical history.

He was also a sweetheart. Really, he was. A mensch, as my uncles would put it. I knew Buddy for about the last twelve years of his life, and he was always nice to me (even though I played that *"goddamn rock'n'roll"*).

Once I even made him laugh.

I believe it was the second time I was in his company. Buddy had just finished his set at the iconic Bottom Line supper club in Greenwich Village, New York, probably 1977 or '78. He blew everybody back in their chairs. Backstage after the show, crowded into a tiny dressing room were six star-struck drummers and Buddy. He was drenched, exhausted, exuberant, and ready to talk.

Court was in session.

At one point Buddy began talking to us about the mechanics of the ankle and foot; the manner in which they both work together to create power and drive. I don't know whether he studied this stuff or just knew it—but he was serious. The seminar revolved around whether one played the bass drum correctly—heel down on the pedal—or, as Buddy made it perfectly clear, incorrectly: heel up, slamming with the toe like a (god forbid) rock drummer. When Buddy finished with the mechanics of the lower talocrural joint, he went around the room asking us drummers what kind of shoes we wore when playing. His opinion: if you didn't wear a boot with a good sized heel, you were kind of a weak drumming specimen destined for oblivion. Truth be told, it was the late '70s, and the most popular footwear for drummers was sneakers, maybe sandals, and some drummers even went barefoot.

Buddy asked, we answered. The first guy said sneakers. Buddy sighed.

The next guy: loafers. ("What are you, a college kid?") Next victim: barefoot. ("Get the fuck outta here!") One guy pointed to his rugged looking Frye cowboy boots. Buddy kind of sneered. Finally he came to me. There I was. Time slowed down, my mouth was dry, and my hands were sweating. Understand, I'd worshipped the bandstand he played on for as long as I could remember. I didn't want to embarrass myself to Buddy or be embarrassed in front of the other guys—two of whom were pretty well known N.Y.C. studio cats. "You." Buddy pointed at me. "What about you?" I stammered, "Uh, well, Buddy, I wear (big pause) **boot-shaped-sneakers!**" Buddy laughed. "Good answer, kid."

I was in!

My passion growing up was drums. My father, who was born in 1909, *loved* baseball. For him, it was baseball all the time. I remember when I was a kid writing a book report on Lou Gehrig, the iconic New York Yankee, I asked him if he'd ever seen Gehrig or Babe Ruth play ball. He said, "Sure I did. But Max, I saw Ty Cobb and Cy Young play baseball. They were the greatest I'd ever seen!" I remember the look on my father's face when he spoke their names: admiration, respect, and joy as he shared with me the memory of seeing his heroes up close. That's how I feel about Buddy Rich. Of course, that doesn't make me unique, because anyone who ever saw Buddy Rich play the drums during the 69 years his presence graced us instantly knew that he was the greatest.

Buddy Rich *was* great, but it wasn't simply his drumming that made him so. As you'll come to learn in this wonderful book, Buddy was astoundingly resilient. He became an entertainer almost before he was able to walk, internationally famous as "Traps, the Drum Wonder." He was a six-year-old vaudeville show biz wunderkind known for his "trick" snare drumming, tap dancing, and singing, yet by the time he was twelve, the era of vaudeville and his parent's show biz act became extinct. The bottom dropped out of his career, and he looked at himself and what he saw was a veteran trouper and formerly famous, has-been child star. These were the Great Depression years in America. Jobs were scarce. You couldn't blame anybody for taking the short money route. Get a straight job. Grow up. Be *Bernard* Rich. That reality scared the you-know-what out of him.

Yet his situation motivated him. There'd be no nine-to-five for Buddy Rich. During what he described as among the bleakest periods of his life, going from "being a star to 'who cares,'" Buddy did whatever he could to stay in the business, help support his family, and hold fast to his drumming dreams. He danced, he sang, told jokes as an emcee. He suffered through the humiliating jobs and did not look back. Buddy clawed, pushed, and literally fought his way back in show business to become the jazz drummer he always wanted to be.

Buddy Rich was great because he never gave up.

I get that.

When Bruce Springsteen went his own way from the E Street Band in 1989, it was a dark time for me. Fifteen years as a member of one of rock's biggest acts, and suddenly it was over. It wasn't completely a surprise—but what a shock. Your work is gone, your personality is affected, your entire conception of yourself is upended. The map I used to escape the black hole of anonymity was what I knew from Buddy and the personal history of which he often spoke. I soon discovered firsthand the emotional, personal, and professional upheaval he'd experienced when his young career appeared over.

"Who cares." It's an awful feeling.

After the normal period of shock, grieving, all the phases you go through when the bottom drops out and you've got a family to feed (Buddy was a teenager; I was 38 with a two-year-old and a pregnant wife), I looked to Buddy's life, not his drumming, to help me get through it.

I got through it.

I've often wished I could have sought his guidance when our group broke up, but he was gone. I still have his phone number in my little red telephone book. For sure, his drumming always spoke to me; I'm sure his life wisdom would have as well. I'm sorry I didn't get to speak with him after I got the late night TV gig in 1993. I would have told him it wasn't just his drumming that helped me find my way back. It was his example of perseverance, his drive to get there and stay there, and his lifelong determination to always be better tomorrow than he was yesterday.

It's so appropriate that Buddy and Frank Sinatra were young twenty-something roommates on the Dorsey band. The stories are told here of how they fought like cats and dogs in the beginning. But they became life-long and devoted friends. They both did it their own way, so to speak. When you're a striver, it's never easy and not always fun. I learned from Buddy that no matter what else is going on in your life, whatever the road throws at you, when you hit that bandstand, *you bring it*. Period. Buddy's lesson: If you're not willing or able to make that commitment, find another line of work.

Decade after decade, mile after mile on the band bus playing those countless one-nighters he performed virtually until the end of his life, Buddy Rich brought it—he delivered. As you make your way through this fascinating and thorough work, *Buddy Rich: One of a Kind*, you will come to understand why Buddy Rich wouldn't have had it any other way.

— **Max Weinberg**
August, 2019

PREFACE

This is not a book about drums or drum technique. This is a book about Buddy Rich, the man. I have used many comments that Buddy made in interviews, and have been very careful to note where I found all the quotes. I have put everything in chronological order and tried to verify if he remembered correctly. He didn't always; many times he was wrong about the year, place or situation. Sometimes he didn't remember anything at all, for the simple reason that Rich never looked back—so I realized I couldn't completely rely on his versions. Thus, previously published articles and reviews became very important in my efforts to put everything in place. I have also interviewed musicians, arrangers, tour leaders, producers, authors and many others, all of whom helped me to clarify certain happenings.

My wish has been to show all of Buddy's different sides, not only the most frequently-shown image of the angry and sometimes ruthless drummer. Buddy Rich was so much more, and I hope the reader will better understand the pressures he dealt with all of his life. Wherever he appeared, the audience expected him to perform the best solo they had ever heard, and live up to the legend he had become: "the world's greatest drummer."

Buddy Rich. One of a Kind.
Pelle Berglund, Stockholm, December 15, 2017

CHAPTER 1

Fascinating Rhythm

Traps, the Drum Wonder, circa 1926.

It was March, 1919 and the husband and wife team of Robert and Bess Rich were once again out on tour. They took pride in always being on time, made meticulous preparations and demanded that new numbers were practiced carefully. Robert's old stage partner, Sam Wilson, had suddenly died only a few months previously, and Bess had taken his place in the act, so the extra preparations were especially important. They had also changed the name of their vaudeville act from Wilson and Rich to Rich and Rennard. It sounded quite French and exciting, and would be sure to tempt a curious American or two—or so Robert, often the one who decided the direction they would take, reasoned.

He wanted to develop the act even further, but that was easier said than done. There was something missing. They could definitely deliver a good quality show, but he was on constant lookout for that unique number that would make audiences flock to listen to them. Then something happened which would change their life forever.

They had arrived early in the morning at the Bijou Theater in Fort Wayne, Indiana, for a week's booking. The instruments had been delivered, and Robert was passing out the sheet music for a new number, written by him and his wife, to the musicians so everyone could rehearse. Everything was set up by 8:30 in the morning and the costumes were laid out. Their son, Bernard, called "Pal," barely 18 months old, was sitting in front of the stage watching, fascinated by all that was happening. The orchestra began to rehearse, but the drummer kept stopping and waving at Robert. Robert tried to ignore the drummer's attempts to get his attention, because the orchestra wasn't yet sounding good on the new chart, but to no avail; the drummer clearly wanted to tell him something. Growing impatient, Robert stopped the orchestra. The drummer immediately jumped down from the stage and gave little pal his drumsticks. "Play it again. Robert, look at your son!" he exclaimed. Everyone stared in amazement at Pal.

As the band began playing again, everyone could see that the boy followed the rhythm exactly. They all laughed in amazement. Intrigued, they stopped the music and changed the beat. It didn't matter whether they played in 4/4 or 3/4 time, the boy played with them easily. The musicians stood flabbergasted by the way little Pal could follow the orchestra's different rhythms. Immediately, ideas came to Robert's mind. Could he use Pal's talents in some way? Had they finally found something that would make them stand out from the other competing acts? He had his doubts; their son was so unbelievably young, and he couldn't put his boy through something that could possibly damage him for the rest of his life. Playing with the orchestra was one thing. Doing it in front of an audience was something entirely different.

Despite his hesitation, Robert let himself be persuaded by the band members and the producer that evening; Little Pal was allowed to be part of Rich & Rennard. The show would be a trial. They spent the rest of the day preparing as best they could. A snare drum and a bass drum were borrowed from a local music store and the band was given a short, new piece to play. It wasn't a random choice; patriotism was rampant after the end of World War I, and colorful parades and displays of nationalism were common. To exploit these feelings, Robert chose the patriotic song "The Stars and Stripes Forever," and dressed Pal in a white sailor suit. Everything was now ready for the show.

Robert and Bess Rich stood in the wings and hoped for the best.

***

Robert Rich was born December 2, 1886, in Albany, New York, to Jewish parents. His father was Russian and his mother came from Austria. Even in his early years, Robert knew that he wanted to be on stage, and when he was about 16 years of age, he made good on his wish to perform in public. At that time, he was working with a man named Reilly, and together they performed in clubs and small shows near Albany. Calling themselves Rich & Reilly, they made $5 an evening. Robert's part was mostly dancing. After completing their schooling at Albany Business College, the duo broke up and Robert went to New York alone, getting a job as a bookkeeper at a cardboard business. But he soon desired to return to the stage. He became a member of the famous Dockstader Ministrels, which was a recognized institution in New York with known names like Al Jolson, but he soon found himself feeling closed in and invisible in such a large organization. After a while he quit to join a smaller theater company. But even there his membership was short.

Instead, he started an act and learned to entertain an audience on his own. It was hard work and required meticulous preparation.

At the end of his teenage years, Robert performed with Sam Wilson, who had also belonged to Dockstader, and also left. This is how the duo Wilson & Rich was formed, and they quickly became quite popular. They each had their own distinct roles: Sam was the more organized and tidy person both on and off stage. He was also a decent singer. But the one who was most prominent and appreciated on stage was Robert, who had developed excellent comic timing, and he never failed to charm the audiences with his phenomenal, fancy footwork-focused step dancing and humor. Robert told author John Minahan: "Blackface, comedy, singing—in those years you had to do everything. If you got a job in a show and they wanted you to do a part, if they needed a Mick, they said, 'Can you do Irish?' And you'd say, 'Well, I can try it now, I'll tell ya that now, me lad, I'll be there if ya need me.' If they wanted a Dutch act, you could do it. Whatever they wanted, you had to do. I was a funny man; used to get a lot of laughs, too."[1]

At the beginning of 1906, Robert had met an attractive young lady named Bess Skolnik at a party at his cousin's house in Brooklyn, New York. She was only 17 years old at the time. They quickly fell in love and a year later they were married. A year later, Bess became a permanent part of the show when Sam Wilson died unexpectedly. With her clear, beautiful singing voice, she gave the performance a wider scope than before. They had two children in short order: daughters Marjorie (who was called Marge) and Josephine (called Jo). Robert loved both his daughters dearly, but he really wanted a son who he could somehow fit into the show. His wife Bess and daughter Jo were part of the act, but Marjorie had to stay home with Bess's parents. They continued to tour, and soon Bess was again pregnant. Robert's hope of a son was reawakened.

After a few months, Robert decided that it was time for the family to return home and live a more normal existence. They had long been looking for something that would give their careers a lift, but since nothing had happened, he believed that they couldn't carry on with their life of traveling and performing. By taking a regular job, Robert hoped their financial situation would become more stable. He just had to face facts, and after applying for a number of jobs, he became employed as a shipping clerk at the Wander Chemical Company.

On September 30, 1917, their third child was born in Sheepshead Bay, Brooklyn. This time Robert got his longed-for son, who was christened Bernard Rich and given the nickname Pal. It didn't take very long before they realized that their son was very special. He was hyperactive. He crawled, talked and walked early. And he was strong. Soon Robert discovered that his son also had rhythm in his blood. On one occasion during their numerous tours, the whole company went out for dinner. As they passed a music store, Pal stopped in his tracks. He pointed at the window and cried, "Me drum! Me drum!" He wasn't even 18 months old. It was the same when they went into a restaurant. If there wasn't any music, their son was inconsolable, but if there was music, he always picked up his knife and fork and played along.

"One time we went to the American Hall, which was the pride of the Loews circuit," said Robert. "We went to see a show, and there was a band appearing there. Pal was, oh, about 15, 16 months old, and we went in to see the band. We had two seats and he'd sit up on the arm of one seat and listen. We're sitting there watching the show, and the guy hits a blue note. Pal jumps out of that seat and he says: 'Oh, bad moggage! Bad moggage!' I could hardly believe it."[2] Time passed, and Robert continued his rather monotonous work as a clerk at the Wander Chemical Company. He wasn't happy there, and soon he found himself at a crossroads. He decided to start another show in the treacherous world of vaudeville, once again with his wife Bess.

It's not clear where the word "vaudeville" originated. Many believe that the theater form started somewhere in France in the 18th century, emanating from the word "vau de ville," said to be a name first given to songs written by Olivier Basselin, a 15th-century composer born in the town of Vau de Vire in Normandy. While this is possible, no one knows for sure. It could be that the word simply looked exciting in a program; it sounded French, and anything that came from France had to be classy. A typical vaudeville evening was often made up of a series of acts containing elements of either satire or parody, all independent of each other. There could be comedy skits, song and dance numbers, animal tricks, fantastic shooters from the Wild West who also did rope tricks, magicians and acrobats, or other types of acts. The acts in a vaudeville show were often based on 1880s entertainment performed in saloons, where there needed to be a variety of acts to meet the tastes of a demanding audience. Pop culture at the time meant that being able to perform an original, popular number could be the deciding factor for getting a job. The success of a performance often depended on whether you had an exclusive act; all the performers were striving to be unique.

Being an entire family on tour was very unusual. Usually, the father was in charge, but for the mother it was not so simple. If she got pregnant, she had to stay with relatives and bring up the child. The situation could be difficult if she happened to be the star of the show; a pregnancy could endanger the entire future of the show. Certainly some children could go along on tour, but this entailed other difficulties: Infants slept in a closet or a big suitcase. Later, when they were cute enough, they found themselves on stage and probably part of some number, or they just stood there looking as young as possible. Some children hated being on stage. Others thought it was great not to have to sit in a classroom. But one or two succeeded in carrying their family name to fame, becoming stars in their own right.[3]

At the Bijou in Fort Wayne, the Riches stood in the wings and worried about their decision to let their very young son perform. Robert was surely thinking that the audience would be kind to his little Pal. At the very least, he hoped that the audience would think his son was cute. Near the end of the show, Robert went out on stage with Pal and a chair. The orchestra got ready, and at a signal from his father, the boy began to play with his drumsticks on the chair. It was made of wood, so the sound of the rattling rhythm could be heard throughout the whole room. It sounded perfect. Little Pal charmed everyone. Then Robert brought out a real snare drum and let his son play along with "The Stars and Stripes Forever." The audience was mesmerized. They had never seen anything like this before. So that little Pal would know where he should stop playing, Robert had put a heavy "bum da–da dum–bum" at the end of the piece. It was a total success; Pal had performed for the first time in his life. At the age of 18 months, he received a huge round of applause, and the audience wanted more!

Robert Rich quickly realized that he could raise the fee for his act, but at the same time, he cared about little Pal's welfare. If he wasn't careful to look out for the boy, he could spoil his entire childhood. But he saw how happy his son was every time he was given a pair of drumsticks and a drum to play. Given Pal's obvious love of drumming, Robert decided to develop a new show with his son as the headliner. Before long, Robert decided that his son should have his own artist name. It had to be something that everyone could remember easily and wasn't too complicated. It had to stick out and be special. "Traps, the Drum Wonder" was born.

"We played various places and then his first set of drums was given to him by the Ludwig Drum Company in Chicago, in exchange for using his name on a line of their drums," said Robert. "They called it the Ludwig 'My Buddy' drum outfit. It was strictly for kids, and I think it sold for $31. But the drum set they gave him was a real good one, of course, and on the bass drum, which was almost taller than him, they had a big sign 'Traps, the Drum Wonder,' and then, under that, 'Using Ludwig Drums.'"[4]

Traps had come out of nowhere and became a star overnight. Later in life, Buddy Rich said, "I was a real showbiz kid. I wasn't exactly born in a trunk in some theater in Pocatello, Idaho. I was born in Brooklyn, not far from that great place Ebbets Field—but I lived out of a trunk all the time I was growing up."[5] Robert's fears that his son would be harmed by performing at such an early age turned out to be completely unfounded. Pal showed no signs of any anxiety at all. On the contrary, he enjoyed every time they came to a new place, a new theater and a new audience. "I started as a dancer, singer and drummer," Buddy recalled. "By the time I was two I was a permanent part of my parent's act. They'd bring me onstage dressed in a sailor suit or a Buster Brown collar and I'd play 'The Stars and Stripes Forever' on a drum. I had long, curly hair. I was the original Beatle." [6]

Robert changed the name of the show again, to Rogers, Bennett & Traps, probably to ensure the novelty of the show and so it would sound exciting. They won acclaim everywhere they went. Rumors of the talents of the musical child prodigy spread like wildfire. In 1921, *Variety* wrote,

"All there is to the act of Rogers, Bennett and Traps came right at the end of it. That was Traps, and that was enough. A nice looking boy in his neat sailor suit, this tour can go anywhere with him, but it's still wrong to have the kid in a three act. A boy of four who can drum in this manner should be heavily featured as a single. This boy Traps is the best novelty a vaudevillian could secure or buy, as such a thing could not be duplicated except by pure accident. Rhythm in a boy this young can't be taught. It's a gift." *Baltimore News*, the same year: "Traps, the tiny drummer of the fourth act, runs away from the other acts on the bill... he was well worth the price of admission alone." At a performance at Jeith's in Wilmington, Delaware, Traps got more applause and curtain calls than anyone else on stage the whole evening.

Robert clearly benefited from Traps' enormous success. Unexpectedly, however, he was contacted by the Geary Society, an organization in the entertainment industry aimed at protecting child stars from exploitation. They wanted to forbid his son from performing. At first, Robert ignored them, but soon he was charged, and news of it landed in the newspapers. There he was portrayed as a ruthless father who exploited his little son in vaudeville. Robert did everything he could to refute the accusations, but was ordered to pay a fine of $100. Although he reluctantly paid the penalty, the trouble continued. Soon the papers reported that the young boy had been taken off the stage at Loew's Yorksville. Robert tried to appease the judge by claiming that his son was unhappy if he couldn't play his drum. How could he stand in the way of his happiness? It didn't help; he was fined another $50. But they went on touring, probably because their income was exceeding the amount of the fines.

Robert ran into another problem he hadn't counted on. Bess suddenly became irritated that he put so much effort into promoting their son in the show. She felt neglected. Of course Pal was talented and of course he was a big plus in their act, but she felt that she should be prominently featured as well. [7] The show became a balancing act between seeing to it that Bess was happy and featuring Traps' extraordinary talents. It is easy to understand Robert's dilemma and how he felt. He had worked almost his whole life in vaudeville, hoping to have a hit act. Now he was on the verge of fulfilling his lifelong dream: a real chance to get on Broadway. It was time to use his talent for diplomacy so that he didn't miss the opportunity.

While vaudeville was losing popularity in the beginning of the 1920s, Broadway still dominated as the American theater world's epicenter. The rate of growth was incredible. Over 25 new theatres opened their doors through the decade, and audiences could now see hundreds of tragedies, sex farces, musicals and experimental shows of all kinds. Raymond Hitchcock was one of the biggest producers on Broadway. His specialty was musical revues, and it didn't take long for Robert to get wind of a new production Hitchcock was going to set up at the newly built Earl Carroll's Theatre. Among those at the subsequent auditions were Robert and his lively son, Traps. He was put through his paces and in just a few minutes the producers were won over. They signed a contract on the spot.

Pin Wheel Revue opened on June 15, 1922. The show was in two acts and featured Frank Fay, a vaudeville star who had gained fame as a comic actor, in the lead. It got lukewarm reviews. Most people thought the scenes were boring and hardly plausible. It didn't seem as good as was expected of a normal Hitchcock production. However, when little Traps went on stage, he played beautifully, and the audience was mesmerized. The week after opening, *Variety* wrote, "But the big surprise of the evening was Traps, the little boy who is actually six years old but looks like four, and who has been a hit in vaudeville the last few years. The whole act with this little boy playing was quite simply the highlight of the evening. He is very close to a great breakthrough and it will be surprising if he isn't offered a major role in some big musical." [8] *Billboard* said, "A little boy around four years old played the drums to the delight of the audience."[9]

Though it never led to long-term stardom on the vaudeville circuit, the Traps tour of Australia in the spring of 1924 was nonetheless one of the real highlights of Buddy Rich's career as a child performer. When all was said and done, the $750-per-week fee he received for the ten-week tour down under made him second only to Jackie Coogan—young star of Charlie Chaplin's revered 1921 film *The Kid*—as the highest paid child star in the world. The whole thing began when Robert heard that an Australian promoter was in the New York area. Robert contacted his agent, William Morris Agency honcho Abe Lastfogel, and insisted that Lastfogel bring the Australian promoter to their next job. Seeing dollar signs in his head, Lastfogel produced the agent, and before long, a contract was in hand for at least six weeks in Sydney, six weeks in Melbourne, and two weeks in Brisbane. Robert, Bess, Traps, and newborn Mickey left New York on April 24 on the SS *Ventura* (of the Spreckles Lines) destined for Australia. Sadly, when they arrived in Sydney on May 26, Bess fell violently ill, and after a hospital stay, it was determined she should return home with newborn Mickey. Bess was never again part of the act.

Traps performed before sold-out houses and received rave reviews everywhere. A newspaper article published in the *Brisbane Courier* on June 30, 1924, painted an accurate picture of what happened onstage at the Wintergarden Theater in Brisbane: "Traps, the five-year-old drummer from the United States, is a real infant phenomenon," said the *Courier*. "Possessing a genuine personality... the child indulged in witty banter in such a live fashion as to show that his was not an ordinary mentality. His work at the drums and tympani marked him as a musician of understanding. He wielded the sticks with dexterity remarkable for such young hands. Traps, at the conclusion of his musical turn, introduced a step dance, which showed him as lively with his feet as he was in wielding the drum stick." But despite the raves and full houses down under, calculating theater producers didn't see much potential in the act. Stateside assessment of the act's future was, said one anonymous agent, "Clever drummer. Bad buy, not recommended." On September 19, Robert and Traps headed home.

Traps' bad temper became more and more evident. He hated his sailor suit and his silly hairstyle. After returning from the Australian tour, the Riches were out for a walk when they met a couple of boys with their parents. All of a sudden the boys started to tease Traps about his silly appearance. Robert saw his son's reaction, and minutes afterwards he took him to a barber to get his hair cut.

Robert also did what he could to see that his son got through school. "He didn't go to any public school or anything," said Robert. "He was enrolled in a professional children's school, and he never attended that—maybe a few times—because we were on the road all the time. So they'd mail us the lessons and we'd do them. I'd teach it to him, and then have to send them in each week, and that had to be approved by the Board of Education. They'd send report cards and the other lessons every week, and we'd have to do them. When we were around here, I'd have a teacher come. Oh, boy he would fight them. He didn't want to study. But we put great big cards along the walls, and he became attracted to those, and he learned to spell and everything. One day she came out screaming, 'He never listens!' But he turned out okay. He could at least spell his name."[10]

At every new venue Traps studied the drums very intently. A drummer told Robert, "Your son stands in the wings and watches every single thing I do. When the last show is over and the lights come on he stands behind the drums and plays it all again. It's incredible."[11] Drumming legend Gene Krupa made the same observation, explaining, "When he was young he stood in the wings with his dad and watched all those fantastic drummers who played during the vaudeville era. They were unbelievable, every one of them, and he absorbed everything he saw. That's how he got his marvelous left hand."[12]

There were other challenges in the Riches unique touring life, including safety. Robert had to make sure nothing happened to his son, who had become the family breadwinner. An injury to Traps would destroy their source of income, so getting into a fight with other children could mean catastrophe. Buddy's daughter Cathy heard her father detail the situation. "My father was warned never to fight," said Cathy, "because if he broke an arm and couldn't work, it would be disastrous. One day, the local bully was taunting him and started chasing him down the block. Doing as he had been told, he started running towards home, screaming for my grandfather, who heard the commotion and was waiting on the front stoop. As my father ran up the steps, he was greeted by a fist in the face from my grandfather, who called him a sissy, and told him to never again run from a fight. At a tender age, lessons were already being learned about repressed anger and humiliation: mixed messages and isolation."[13]

Traps seemed to have taken this all in his stride and said later in life, "My father was a soft-shoe dancer and a blackface comedian, which embarrasses me now, but it was accepted then. He was from Albany. He was a liberal father, a good father, a good man. He was strong and nice looking and had a great sense of humor. When you stepped out of line you got a shot in the mouth and that straightened you out."[14] Unfortunately, the number of bookings began to decline, and it appeared that Robert had taken the act as far as it could go. His son played better than ever, had new clothes, a new hairstyle, new drums, and singing and step dancing had been added to the act. Nothing seemed to help, however, and their worry mounted. Robert feared that their largest source of income no longer had star quality.

CHAPTER 2

Enter the Jazz Scene

An older Buddy from the 1929 Vitaphone short *Sound Effects*.

America's economic bubble burst on October 24, 1929. Stocks fell sharply, with people panicking to sell as a result. Police were posted outside the stock exchanges and at the offices of stockbrokers who were overwhelmed by the sudden rush. In a single day, Black Thursday, a record of 13 million stocks changed hands and many stock exchanges closed due to the panic. Businesses and banks went bankrupt, people lost their jobs, and those with modest incomes had to leave their homes and farms when they could no longer pay the high interest rates on their loans. The live entertainment industry was hit very hard. Theater owners and producers saw their fortunes disappear, theaters closed, and productions were cancelled. Prior to the crash, there was a tremendous spike in productions on Broadway, but now the theater district faced hard times, causing theater owners like the Shuberts to file for bankruptcy. Some theaters reopened and featured burlesque shows, while several others became movie houses.

The film world had been threatened with falling revenues by the troubled economy, and in order to survive, film studios were forced to find other solutions. For example, Warner Brothers had been experiencing substantial financial problems as early as 1925. To revive the company, Sam Warner convinced his brothers; Harry, Albert and Jack; to invest in a new division called Vitaphone. Vitaphone's focus would be the talking motion picture, where a soundtrack would be recorded on a separate disc that would be played simultaneously with the moving pictures. The first films were shorts that featured vaudeville artists of the day. Eventually, feature-length movies were produced, like *Don Juan*, the first film to have a synchronized music score; *The Jazz Singer* with Al Jolson; and *Lights of New York*, which was the first all-talking motion picture. After a few missteps, "talkies" worked. At the end of 1929, shortly following the Wall Street crash, Warner Brothers showed a profit of $12 million.

The successes of talkies made it difficult for many vaudeville acts to find work. After all, audiences could now see and hear their favorite actors. Historian John Kenrick, author of the 1996 book *History of Musical Film: 1927 to 1930* and creator of the website musicals101.com, described the phenomenon, writing, "The big stars in vaudeville filmed their act on one occasion and then anyone who wanted to could see what they did at one single time. This hastened the inevitable end. When you think about it, if small theaters could offer the public the chance to see the biggest stars on the film screen for a nickel, why would the same audiences go to the same venue and pay more to see lesser talents perform?"

It was tough going for vaudevillians. Producers did what they could to find solutions, including the booking of vaudeville performers as "opening acts" for films. This worked in some places, while other theaters gave up and went over to only showing films. Some vaudeville acts did try to make it in films, with varying success, and the success of talkies had not escaped Robert. He figured if Traps and the act could be successful on an overseas tour, then they certainly could interest a film company in putting Traps on the screen. The kid was 12 years old, had mastered playing music, tap dancing and singing, and that should mean certain success. Robert strongly believed that talking pictures would be a golden opportunity for the act. "Jackie Coogan only made one film and became world famous," was Robert's rationale. "My boy has been working for a whole decade, but is still less known."

A film starring his son became Robert's goal, and late one Friday night in December of 1929, he felt ready to take the next step. Robert and Buddy walked from their home in Brooklyn up to the Vitaphone Corporation's offices on Avenue M. The mission was to make a film deal, and after some negotiation, he succeeded: Vitaphone agreed to film a short movie with Traps. The film's setting would be a music store, where all his son's talent and skill could be displayed. Murray Roth, a 26 year-old who had made a quick career in the world of short films by directing over 40 films in just the previous year, was chosen as the director. In addition, he was an established script writer, responsible for the screenplay of *Lights of New York*. Despite Roth's impressive credentials, Robert had no intention of relinquishing the right to control what his son would do on the film screen. He demanded control, and though no one knows exactly what argument he used—though we can guess that he emphasized that nobody knew his son's capacity and limitations better than he did—Vitaphone gave him the control he wanted.

February 17, 1930, was the premier for the short movie *Buddy Traps in*

Sound Effects at the Strand in New York, and it was shown before the main film, which that evening was *The Green Goddess*, with George Arliss in the leading role. The Warner Vitaphone Company marketed the short film with Traps using copy that read, "Buddy twirls his drumsticks, tap dances unbelievably, and sings amazingly well. He beats music out of chairs, paintings, pots and pans, glasses and everything imaginable. He is one of a kind!" It is also worth noting that this was the first time the name Buddy appeared in print. As for the film itself, Traps' playing revealed his musical prowess at the time. Though only the film soundtrack has been preserved (despite extensive searching by many film lovers and collectors) what can be heard is simply amazing. Buddy's snare drum playing was already nearly fully developed.

Reviews were mixed. *Variety* wrote, "Boy, hardly 14 with a decided talent for drumming plus rhythmic feet. Scene is a music shop. Trying out a new pair of drumsticks, the lad beats his tattoo on vases, glass, cans and all sorts of wooden, metallic or noise-giving materials. Distinct advantage of being the only boy performer off and on novelty; okay for any average program. When briefly attempting to sing, the result is pretty awful. Boy has a strained, unmelodious voice, possibly due to his early adolescent age."[1] "The performer in this musical novelty is a youngster who sings a little, dances some, and manipulates a pair of drumsticks all around the place," read the write-up in *Film Daily*. "He taps harmony out of a wide assortment of objects, from regular drums to bottles, cans, chair and whatnots. It is diverting, particularly because it is unusual and also on account of the youth and versatility of the artist."[2] *Motion Picture News* was also relatively lukewarm, saying, "Buddy Traps, a juvenile billed as 'the marvel drummer,' wields the sticks in a notion store, marching from counter to counter, up ladders and down, drumming to orchestral accompaniment on dishes, pans, vases and other bric-a-brac, ending with a clog dance and a song in a shrieky voice. It's a novelty that is fairly entertaining owing to the youth of the drummer, who has a good stage presence."[3]

Robert Rich probably had greater expectations of the film than anyone else. Yes, he had the chance to present Buddy to a larger audience, and although the audience response was mainly good, Buddy's star was faltering considerably. The situation was the same as prior to filming;

his son was too old to be presented as a musical child prodigy and too young to become established in the tough music industry. The short film, which had displayed all of Traps's talents, was actually no use, and just made it more evident that he was caught in the transition between child and teenager. To make a living, his son took any job he could get, and continued touring. *Billboard* wrote about his next step, reporting, "Buddy Traps, juvenile dancer, singer, comedian and musician, started an RKO tour this week in Toronto, going from there to Hamilton. The youngster is being exploited as 'America's Boy Wonder.' Jack Curtis agented him."[4]

Times were hard, and the Rich family was suffering. Jo Rich revealed just how bad things were. "There was just no money around," she said, summing up this situation. "This was 1931, and Marge and I were working an act, sending home every cent we could spare. The last week's work was cancelled. It was during the summer, and theaters were closing; they didn't have air conditioning at that time. We came home; we went to the hotel with our suitcases. We got into the elevator; we hear this music that's so loud that the walls were shaking. I said: 'God, somebody's got their radio on awfully loud.' We're coming up to our floor and the music is so loud we can't believe it. It's coming from our room. Open the door, here's 13 men, on the chairs, on the tables, on the floor —with Buddy with the drums—and they are rehearsing!"[5]

Marge Rich took up the rest of the story. "My father had got into a conversation with a young man who was on the breadline who told him a very sad story about how he'd come into town with a band, and the leader skipped with the money and left them all stranded. They were all from Pittsburgh, and they didn't have a nickel. Anyhow, while talking with him, my father got this fantastic idea: Here was a set band, brother's not doing anything, why doesn't he take his band and put brother up in front of it? Maybe he could get some work. All they needed was a few days of rehearsal and he could get them all booked! And sure enough, they did get work! Buddy's first band. But the guys said they only wanted to work long enough to get enough money together to make their fare to go back home."

Robert, who always had his head full of new ideas, succeeded in convincing the band that he could fix gigs for them and his son. He made a few calls and got the booker and agent Arthur Kraus on board with his project. Buddy Traps Rich and His Orchestra had several small performances out in the hinterlands before they turned their gaze towards New York. An unknown newspaper published an enthusiastic review of the band's appearance on a Broadway stage. "Since the advent of vaudeville on the Broadway stage, no feature act has received the marked applause that was given Buddy Rich and his band at last night's performance before a well filled house," the rave review read. "Youthful Mr. Rich and his group of musicians came to Broadway stage with the praises of successful past performances ringing in their ears, and they lived up to their reputation to the letter. The band started up its program with a medley of popular dance tunes, but it was the ability of the leader that put the band across. In the closing minutes of the act, Buddy Rich handed his baton to another member of the cast, and proceeded to demonstrate his ability on the drums. In the short time that he used the drumsticks, Mr. Rich did things with them that seemed almost impossible and still maintained a rhythm that sent the audience into prolonged applause."

That was the first time Buddy Rich was reviewed as a bandleader, and it was a sign of things to come. He gave direction, waved the baton, cued the boys, and took command. He got to feel what it was like to be in charge, standing in the center with fellows older than himself. They played a few more gigs, but not many. The musicians had made it clear right from the start that they were only going to play until they had enough money for their trip home. Even had they stayed, perhaps the mix of a band consisting of older, more experienced musicians with a 14-year-old leader just wasn't the right combination for show business success.

At this point in the young Buddy's life, things suddenly became alarmingly like what his own father had experienced around the turn of the century. When Buddy's first orchestra folded, he had to grit his teeth, put his ego on the shelf, and use his talents as best he could. Money had to come in from wherever he could find it, and any job was good enough. Author and jazz historian George T. Simon remembered seeing Buddy during this difficult, transitional period. "My brother and I took a boat ride up to Playland in Rye, New York," said Simon. "We had no idea there was going to be any entertainment. This kid was master of ceremonies. I had to go to the bathroom so I passed the backstage area. There I saw a kid with a pair of drumsticks, playing all sorts of fabulous things on a chair. Because of my interest in drums, I struck up a conversation with him. He told me he really was a drummer and what he wanted to do was work with bands. What he was doing was just to make money, he insisted."[6]

Much later, Buddy vividly and emotionally described to his close friend Mel Tormé how challenging this period had really been for him. He took every job he could find. As Buddy detailed to Tormé, "That was a hard part of my life, once having been a star to a 'who cares'? That was a tough transition for a kid to make. I had to go out... 'Good evening, ladies and gentlemen, a funny thing happened to me...' Bad fucking material! Bad material. On top of that, the brim (of my hat) pulled up, you know? Yuk, yuk, yuk! The embarrassment I was feeling—it lasted my whole life. To go out there in front was very tough thing to do, for a kid that was once something and now nothing. I was an opening act. 'Hey, look at me! I got a new hat.' You know? I go to Chicago to be an opening act, introducing Jackie Osterman—MC, right? And your act is smart jokes and one-liners, and they all suck. There isn't a funny line in the 18 minutes you're out there. You're dying—get me outta here—the audience is looking at you like, uh, get this bum off the stage. You're standing there doing bad material, trying to talk to people who don't want to hear you.

Buddy wept as he continued. "I even degraded myself low enough one time to be a stooge. You know what a stooge is? He's a guy who sits in the audience and has one-liners thrown at him. I stooged for a comic; you should know him because he's from Chicago. Roy somebody. Funny guy. Tough guy. Played all the tough joints. He asked me if I wanted to be his stooge for a week in a club in Milwaukee. I was staying at the Croyden Hotel in Chicago. I said yeah. I was 15 or 16. I was a stooge, not even human. You learn. I'll tell you what you learn. If you wanted to survive, you learned how to be humiliated in front of a lot of people. I did it, not for very long, up to the point where I couldn't take it anymore. I got ten bucks for the week. I took the gig because I needed the ten bucks!"[7]

The income Buddy made was of utmost importance for his family. But what he expressed here, in the mid-1930s, is that he was actually faced with his first major decision in life: To be true to himself, to avoid taking these terrible jobs, to be loyal to his instrument, and to try to develop his talent as much as he could. He loved playing the drums and the idea of concentrating on just that was now taking shape. The singing and dancing, at some point, just had to go by the wayside. He didn't dare tell his father, who placed great value on a vaudevillian's skills and just what a vaudevillian was. He would surely do everything he could to get Buddy to give up his plans to become solely a musician.

***

By 1933, there were 15 million Americans out of work. Many families were desperate, as their hard-earned savings had gone up in smoke. In response to the Great Depression, President Franklin D. Roosevelt introduced the New Deal: a series of programs, public works projects, and financial reforms that aimed to restore prosperity to Americans and put more Americans to work. With the economy in shambles, people wanted and needed a release. The American public went out more than ever, drinking, partying, dancing, gambling, and listening to music. As for Prohibition, club owners knew all about keeping spirits high and understood the connection between cheap drinks and lively music—especially the new and fresh music of the times, jazz.

Jazz clubs began to appear on what would become one of the most famous blocks of real estate in history: 52nd Street in New York City. This strip of clubs eventually became so well known that when a taxi driver was told to "drive to the street," he immediately knew the destination. Eventually, a visitor could almost experience the entire history of jazz there in a single evening. Trumpeter Pauly Cohen, who gained fame years later with Count Basie, recalled, "52nd Street. I was there every night until five in the morning. All the good jazz musicians were there. I enjoyed every second."[8] While the scene on 52nd Street was new to the general public, it wasn't new to African-American musicians. Billie Holiday recalled, "You could be dressed in white satin up over your ears, with gardenias in your hair and not a sugar cane in sight. And still it was just like working on a plantation. Take 52nd Street at the end of the 1930s and the beginning of the 1940s, for example. It was regarded as something especially out of the ordinary. Swing Street, it was called, and there was something happening in club after club. It was that 'new' kind of music, you know. And sure, you could call it new, for millions of Joes had never ever been up on 131st Street (in Harlem). If they had taken the trip there they would have heard swing music for the last 20 years."[9] Yet it was undeniable that 52nd Street had become the epicenter of the jazz scene in New York.

The Street was flooded with the new, popular music: jazz. There were hip places like Jack & Charlie's, the Onyx, Gay 90s, the Famous Door, Kelly's Stables, and the Hickory House. It was here that many of the big names would start their careers: Tommy Dorsey, Artie Shaw, Bunny Berigan, Joe Marsala, Sarah Vaughn, Art Tatum, Coleman Hawkins, Roy Eldridge, Fats Waller, Errol Garner, Maxine Sullivan, Teddy Wilson, Louis Prima, Pee Wee Russell, and later on, Charlie Parker and Dizzy Gillespie, to name only a few. Gillespie summed it up in his inimitable fashion: "52nd Street was my mother. I say mother and then I don't mean motherfucker, even if the Street was that too."[10]

Amidst his struggles, Buddy Rich became enamored with jazz. Listening to jazz on the radio, he carried away by the melodies and the beat. He thought it was liberating music and began to realize that playing this music, becoming a "real" drummer, and being respected for it, was his future. Playing the drums standing up, banging away on chairs and tables and whatever was nearby, tap dancing and singing; none of that felt like fun anymore. Vaudeville had nothing to do music, and he was ready to move on. One Wednesday evening in 1935, some friends took him to the Apollo Theater in Harlem to check out the the Apollo's famed amateur night. It was a dizzying experience. It was the first time he heard Chick Webb, and he would never forget it.

William Henry "Chick" Webb was a very special drummer. The small black man had been a hunchback from childhood due to tuberculosis, but he was lucky to meet up with a doctor who gave him some rather unique advice: Ease stiff joints by playing the drums. That interesting piece of medical info helped form the beginning of an enormously successful musical career. Despite his physical limitations, he began playing with giants like Duke Ellington and Johnny Hodges when he was only 17. Then he put together his own bands, and each one was one better than the next. One thing was for certain: Chick Webb's bands turned things upside down musically, especially in Harlem during the Depression. Chick became the star that everyone wanted to see and hear. He was a dramatic figure who influenced and inspired many, including Buddy Rich—and Buddy was sure that the day would come when he would lead a band as powerfully as Webb did.

There were other bands that made a strong impression on Buddy. He discovered a big band that he thought swung more than most. Glen Gray and the Casa Loma Orchestra was organized and led by saxophonist Gray, and became very popular, especially at colleges around the country. Several of their performances at the Colonnades, which was quite the elegant dancing and dining establishment within the Essex House hotel, were broadcast, and each time Buddy heard the band was on the air, he sat rooted in front of the radio along with his whole family in the living room, listening. Casa Loma was the first band that gave him a glimpse of what jazz was really all about. The orchestra was like a well-oiled machine, with the charts played by talented musicians who knew exactly what they were doing. This was also a band that could play any kind of jazz and were unique as an ensemble. Buddy naturally had his eyes and ears on the drummer, Tony Briglia.

Buddy described what he heard, saying, "Tony's playing ploughed straight through Casa Loma's brass section."[11] Briglia was in his 30s when Rich first heard him. He came originally from Canada and joined up with Casa Loma in 1929, when he replaced drummer Walter Urban. Briglia was a drummer with a brilliant technique who played with confidence and a visual flair that drew audiences' eyes to him. Buddy Rich was clear in his admiration for the band and for Briglia. "I had always loved the Glen Gray Casa Loma Band," said an enthusiastic Buddy. "They were so hot. And so hip! They wore tails at night. My ambition was to meet that band—and particularly Tony Briglia. He never played hi-hats, only press rolls on the snare drum! He was a bitch! I loved the way he played. Some of the tempos were so ridiculously fast, he had to be a speedball to play in the band. They used to broadcast from the Essex House every night around 11:30. I'd be sitting downstairs in our house, with a pair of brushes in my hand, ready to play. Kick it off, Glen! I played along with them. I was hot! I was hot! I played with the Glen Gray Band, because I knew all the charts. All of them! Go ahead! Kick it off! I got it! I want to play in your band!"[12]

There was another drummer who was totally changing the situation for drummers, and who also made a strong impression on Buddy at the same time as Briglia. This drummer believed that the drummer shouldn't only sit at the back as an accompanist; he should play long solos and sit featured on a high podium where everyone could see him. His name was Gene Krupa. This pioneer in the world of drumming would become a superstar and a legend.

Buddy Rich was tremendously curious about learning how to lead a band. Studying drummers everywhere, he listened, learned, picked up a little from each of them. Besides Gene Krupa, Chick Webb, and Tony Briglia, he studied Dave Tough's very special technique on the cymbals. That little man with the big power was also the one who inspired him most to play powerfully and with authority. Regarding Tough, Buddy later said, "His energy force was so strong that you'd think there was a 400-pound guy sitting up there!"[13] All these fine drummers had one thing in common: They were showmen who could impress when the occasion presented itself. They had grown up in the same show business-oriented environment as Buddy. If you didn't play so the audience liked you, you were doomed. If you didn't play a good enough solo, the juggler, dancer or the singer got the applause instead. And many of them played in the same place: on 52nd Street.

One of those who took Buddy to the Street was one-time Dorsey pianist Joe Bushkin. Bandleader Woody Herman, who remembered hearing about Buddy early on, said, "Shortly after we started at Roseland in 1936, pianist Joe Bushkin came in one night with a very young man. He took me aside and insisted, 'This kid is the greatest drummer in the world. You gotta take him for your band!' It was Buddy. 'I can't take him,' I told him. 'We have a cooperative band. It may carry my name. But the drummer and each guy in the group have as much to say as I do.' Joe was a little impatient. Then he shrugged and smiled and said, 'Well, then I'll take him over to 52nd Street and talk to somebody.'"[14]

Cathy Rich knew the story well. "When my father was 17," she said, "vaudeville was in its dying days, and there were few jobs. He was already a show business veteran who could sing, tap dance, and MC a show better than anyone. But he worried about what he would do next. He often told me stories of times when he would take the train to Manhattan to hear all the great jazz artists of that era. He began cultivating friendships within the jazz world, and word quickly spread about the kid who could play like no one had ever seen or heard."[15] At the same time, a demanding father was waiting at home in Brooklyn. Robert still thought Buddy should be helping to support the family, just like both his sisters did. At 18 years old, the truth was Buddy was not allowed to turn down the offers that came in; doing so could mean catastrophe for his whole family.

The Works Projects Administration was a unit established by President Roosevelt in 1935 as a part of his New Deal. The WPA was devoted to creating jobs for the thousands of United States citizens who found themselves out of work during the Great Depression. Four branches of the WPA were established strictly to benefit those in the arts. One of those branches was the Federal Theater Unit, which was specifically focused on unemployed performers who qualified for relief assistance. Evidently, one of those who qualified was Bernard Rich, who got a part in a WPA theater production called *Oh Say Can You Sing*? Whether or not Buddy knew the source of the job remains a question, but he joined the show on December 11, 1936, when it opened at Chicago's Great Northern Theatre. Among the numbers he performed here were "In Your Hat," "Grandma's Goin' to Town," "Swing Session" and "Mr. Hamfield Reminisces."

Local reviews after the opening were positive. Lloyd Lewis in the *Chicago Daily News* wrote, "Buddy Rich, a lively dancer, was much appreciated for his tap dancing."[16] Ashton Stevens wrote in *The Chicago American*, "Once again he demonstrated his various talents: singing, dancing, doing comedy, playing drums. The finale of that musical show featured Rich dressed in tails and a white tie, a handsome 20-year old, surviving." The show ran until December 31. On April 11 the following year, he performed at Loews in Montreal. *Variety* saw him there and reported, "Buddy Rich in tails and putting over a smart bit of tapping... working hard for less support than he earns."[17] He also appeared at the Roxy in New York on August 20, 1937, where another reporter noted briefly, "Trick drummer and hoofer, better at the latter."[18]

Performing just to survive was not good enough for Buddy Rich, and it's clear that he'd had it with vaudeville and what had become a hand-to-mouth existence. The lure of jazz and jazz drumming was growing stronger, and at this juncture, he was increasingly certain that he no longer wanted to be a trick drummer, a clever tap dancer, or an ex-child star. He wanted to be a drummer—a jazz drummer. Buddy was quite clear about it, saying, "Jazz, for some reason, affected me. Goodman's trio. Goodman's quartet. They were hot. When I stayed at the Croydon, I met the Condos Brothers, Nick and Steve, at the coffee shop there. We hung out. We used to play jazz records and dance to them. I learned a lot that way."[19] Still, he didn't dare take the plunge and tell his father what he was thinking. He had to wait for the right occasion, and in the meantime he continued to take jobs which he felt were meaningless.

Joe Marsala, an Italian-American clarinet player who first played guitar as a youngster, was born in Chicago on January 4, 1907. There was music in his family: his father played the trombone and his brother Marty played the trumpet. Joe began playing the clarinet when he was 15, but it took some time for him to be able to make a living as a musician. Of his early years, Marsala said, "I worked for a while shoveling cinders from a truck, then I started working at an office. I also worked as a salesman at a shoe store for $15 a week, and then at a factory that made rubber balls, and after that at a brass foundry, but I couldn't keep a job."[20] Bouncing from job to job, he ended up at a mail order firm, where he was placed in the music department. He started to fool around with a saxophone—on the job—and the boss fired him. After that, as a truck driver's assistant, he was involved in a horrific accident where he flew through the windshield. (This is what gave Marsala the facial scar visible in photographs.)

At night, like so many others, Marsala sat beside the radio and listened to jazz. On the weekends, he joined up with any band he could find, often playing for nothing. In the process, he developed his own style on the clarinet, after having listened to Leon Rappolo, Frank Teschemacher and Jimmie Noone. In 1929 he joined trumpeter Wingy Manone's combo in Akron, Ohio, and then the Harold West Orchestra. He returned to Manone, then got an offer to play a longer period at a New York City-based venue that would become legendary: the Hickory House. Manone ultimately left the band and Marsala took over as leader in May of 1936.

The Hickory House, at 144 West 52nd Street in New York, was opened in 1933 by John Popkin. Before gaining fame as a colorful club owner, he ran (unsuccessfully, thanks to the stock market crash) a perfume store. In 1933, Popkin and two partners hit on the idea of turning a used car showroom into a restaurant. A year later, he bought out his partners and turned it into what would become one of the major jazz rooms in the city. In an interview with journalist Whitney Balliett of *The New Yorker*, Popkin said, "In November 1934, I got the idea to bring in jazz. So I hired Wingy Manone who had the Marsala brothers with him and Eddie Condon."[21] Popkin's partners in the Hickory House were no great jazz lovers, according to a story Marsala told writer Leonard Feather. "After we had been at the Hickory House about a year," Marsala told Feather, "Jack Goldman, Popkin's partner, said to me one night, 'I can't understand how people like this jazz music. There's one guy over there who must really love it. He's been here every night.' I told him, that's Eddie Condon, you've been paying him a salary!"[22]

After becoming leader of the Hickory House's house band, Marsala was popular with musicians, and was one of the early leaders who freely booked racially mixed bands. He was a graceful and impressive player, and even though some judged him a typical Dixielander, there were also those who thought he was much more musically adventurous. Indeed, Marsala brought Dizzy Gillespie to a recording session in 1945. Marsala was clear about what he wanted to play, especially when it came to jam sessions, and believed that radio was killing creative music, since jamming was prohibited on radio. The Sunday afternoon jam sessions at the Hickory House, featuring his brother Marty on trumpet, Joe's wife Adele Girard on harp, Nat Chappy playing the piano, and Artie Shapiro on bass, eventually became a part of jazz history. Marsala recalled, "It was a funny thing. Here it was Saint Patrick's Day, and we opened that night with a harp in a jazz band. From that time on, we were in and out of the Hickory House for the best part of ten years. We started a series of Sunday afternoon jam sessions, which became a big deal."[23]

Count Basie, Art Tatum, Chu Berry, Roy Eldridge, Sidney Bechet and many others jammed with the house band, and since Marsala freely mixed both black and white musicians, there were some journalists who believed that it was Marsala, not Benny Goodman, who was instrumental in breaking down the racial barriers in jazz. Marsala himself agreed, saying, "No one had had an integrated band on all of 52nd Street before me. I never asked the boss for permission. I just did it." He began to make a big name for himself. Leonard Feather and the respected journalist John Hammond (then with *Downbeat* magazine) praised him. Feather went as far as to say that he thought Marsala represented "superlative musical creativity."

In August of 1937, pianist Joe Springer and drummer Henry Adler were playing at the Crystal Café on Church Avenue, near Rogers Avenue, in Brooklyn, New York. It was a club where crowds of musicians used to gather, including a young drummer named Irv Cottler, later Frank Sinatra' drummer. The band consisted of George Berg on tenor sax, Buddy Rich's friend Artie Shapiro on bass, and Adler on drums. What happened on one particular evening at the Café has been recounted in many ways, but Henry Adler's version seems to be the most accurate. "One night, Barney Salad, a kid I used to teach, came in. He had Buddy Rich with him. He said, 'This kid plays better than Gene Krupa.' So I thought, who is this big man? During the next set I played all my tricks. I figured that I ought to straighten this Buddy Rich cat out. I let him play the next set."

This was not the first time that someone tried to get Adler to notice Buddy. Freddie Gruber, legendary drum education guru and one of Buddy Rich's closest friends, recalled that Buddy's parents were frequent customers at the Crystal Café. Gruber remembered, "They were always saying: 'Can our son sit in?' Springer and Adler would always tell them no." This time, Henry Adler decided to trust Barney. He let Buddy have a try and gave the young man clear orders, saying, "You have to play quietly. Maybe you should play with the brushes instead." "I can try," answered Buddy. But Adler changed his mind. "Okay, play with the sticks then." After hearing Buddy Rich play for the first time, Adler was completely flabbergasted. "Who taught you to play?" Adler asked. "What are you talking about?" responded Buddy. "I want to meet the person who has given you lessons," said Adler. "Who taught you to hold the sticks like that?" This time it was Buddy's turn to be a little frightened. "Nobody has given me lessons. I have never taken lessons." Adler turned to George Berg and said, "You see. This is the way the instrument should be played."

Adler, who also owned a music store on West 48th Street, took Buddy Rich under his wing. He had never seen anyone play so well, and now he thought that the kid should learn to read music. "I felt that if he wanted to play numbers with large orchestras it was time he knew a little about notes," Adler said. "But there were a few hesitations about understanding what the notes meant. I remember that his father came to me one day and asked anxiously if this note thing would damage his son's musical development, and I answered, 'On the contrary, learning to read notes will help him earn more money.'" The week afterward he tried diligently but unsuccessfully to teach Buddy Rich how to read music. Adler was forced to admit, "As it turned out, he was the exception that proved the rule. He could do everything that we other drummers do, instinctively, and understand the essence of the arrangement—what should be played and stressed—quicker than any other note-reading drummer." Adler let the young Rich sit in with the band several evenings, and a few nights later, he wanted to talk seriously with him. Alder's plan was to introduce Buddy to Joe Marsala by way of using his connection to bassist Shapiro, who often jammed with Marsala.

One Sunday evening at the end of 1937, he took Buddy to the Hickory House, and when the band took a break, Adler approached Marsala. "I'd like to talk to you, Joe," Adler said. "I've got a young fellow with me that you have to listen to. His name is Buddy Rich." "A kid?" responded Marsala. "Maybe not so young," Adler explained. "He has just turned 20. But he's a genius on the drums. Won't you let him try a number?" "So he's really good?" Marsala asked. Pushing the issue, Adler replied, "Better than good. He's unbelievable! Just wait'll you hear him." Marsala gave in, saying, "Okay, he can play with us. One number just before we close at six o'clock."

Marsala then completely forgot about both Adler and the young Rich, who stood waiting patiently in a corner.

CHAPTER 3

Joe Marsala
and
His Chicagoans

Buddy Rich with Joe Marsala at the Hickory House, 1937.

They sat there week after week and Sunday after Sunday, just like Henry Adler himself made Buddy wait to play with him. Marsala kept ignoring them. Adler couldn't understand why Marsala had promised to let Buddy play and didn't seem like he was going to follow through. "Joe kept putting me off," Adler recalled. "He claimed there were too many important people in the audience. I told him that if you didn't let Buddy play, our friendship was over. He had to be heard. It's as simple as that."

Buddy Rich had almost total recall about that day. "On the fourth Sunday, at about 5:45, just before the sessions ended, Marsala summoned me," Buddy remembered. "I played 'Jazz Me Blues,' or something like that, and then Marsala said, 'Let's play something up.' In those days, I lived up. I started out at a very fast tempo on a thing called 'Jim Jam Stomp.' People were beginning to leave, but they turned around and started coming back in just as if a Hollywood director had given instructions in the finale of some crummy, heroic grade-B movie."[1]

One of those in attendance that day was a young Stanley Kay.[2] Kay, who would become Buddy's manager years later, remembered the scene. "When I got to the Hickory House that Sunday afternoon, I introduced myself to Buddy," Kay explained. "He knew I was coming. He was very nice to me. He got me a place to sit, and I had a Coke. All the guys who played in bands then—Eddie Mallory, Tiny Bradshaw and others—would sit in and jam. The jam session that day lasted from 3 to 6 p.m. As the session was winding down, Buddy still hadn't played. I was disappointed. But at about 5:50, Buddy climbed up and played 'Jim Jam Stomp.' It sounded like jet planes taking off. It was that fast. I said to myself that Sybil was right: the guy was better than Gene."[3]

The whole place went crazy and the audience wouldn't let the band off the stage. Marsala was impressed and asked Buddy if he would make the gig the next night. Buddy had to ask his father for permission. Explaining wasn't easy. He told Robert, "'Look, I'll be home very late. Mr. Marsala asked me to come back and play.' I was a kid. In those days, if you were a kid, you still asked for permission to stay out. They gave the okay. I don't think I'd ever stayed out till four in the morning before."[4] When he returned for the next evening's performance, it was clear that Marsala's regular drummer, Danny Alvin, was unhappy. Marsala didn't care. Buddy Rich played the entire second set, and when it was over, Marsala asked him if he wanted the job permanently. This time, Buddy didn't ask for anyone's permission. "I took the gig without asking dad's permission. I can't tell you how good it made me feel. He asked me if I could start in two weeks. I nodded. I never mentioned money. All I knew was I had the job. The $66 a week was secondary."

Buddy summoned up courage and finally told his father that his playing with Marsala wasn't temporary. He had been offered a steady job there and intended to continue as a jazz drummer. And if he wasn't allowed to take the job with Marsala, he was prepared to join whatever jazz band would have him. Robert was shattered and thought that Buddy was throwing away his whole career. "My pop couldn't understand my enthusiasm. He thought I was giving up my whole career to be what? A drummer in a band? I told him that's what I wanted. To a vaudevillian who didn't know that jazz musicians are pretty swell people, it didn't seem plausible."

After accepting his son's choice, each week Robert kept $56 of Buddy's $66 salary. Looking at what seemed to be the inevitable, Robert felt it was time for a serious talk. This, after all, was jazz, not vaudeville. "A week or two after I started at the Hickory House," as Buddy remembered it, "my father said he wanted to talk to me. I went home every night. I took the BMT at four in the morning and arrived at the house about 5:30. Today, I'd have to carry an automatic weapon. Pop and I got together one afternoon. He talked about drugs. He made me promise that I would steer clear of hard drugs and bad people and alcohol; that I would keep our name unblemished. You know, I went through my whole youth without ever smoking a cigarette. Never drank. I didn't start smoking until about twenty years ago. I kept my promise to him. I never got involved in anything. This was important to him."[5]

One of Buddy's later arrangers, John LaBarbera, remembered Buddy telling him about another issue. "Buddy supported his family when he was growing up. He was the star, after all. If he now decided he was going to play jazz, where the incomes could go up and down, this might mean a lot for the whole family. Naturally they were worried about the future." In Buddy's mind, the career change issue was resolved. "Eventually, my pop came to understand how I felt, particularly when he saw how much I enjoyed myself and that I was becoming a success. One thing you have to realize: My father always had my well-being in mind."

What Buddy didn't know was that Joe Marsala hadn't gotten rid of his "regular" drummer, Danny Alvin. Said Marsala, "I actually had Buddy on salary and kept two drummers for a while, because I didn't have the nerve to tell Alvin I hired somebody else. Buddy was a great jazz drummer right from the start. It didn't matter that he couldn't read music, because he had a phenomenal ear even then."[6] After two weeks, Buddy Rich became the band's regular drummer. Success was a fact. He was now a proud member of Joe Marsala and His Chicagoans, which meant that the Musician's Union was the next stop.

At the union hall, the local's clerk wanted to check to see that Buddy really was a musician and threw some sheet music down in front of him. Buddy Rich didn't know how to read notes. "I can't read that," he said. Maybe this clerk had heard about Buddy somewhere, as he asked, "Can you play a drum roll then?" Buddy played a perfect drum roll. "Give me those sticks and hurry down to the office with this paper. Pay your fee and get out of here before I get hell for letting you into the union."[7] Now he could call himself a card-carrying musician, and it was not a bad start. He was playing with a top band and also had the opportunity to study all the great musicians on 52nd Street. He didn't miss the chance.

Remembering the scene in those days, Buddy recalled that "every hotel in this city had a name band, plus every theater in this city at the same time had a name band. You had the Paramount, Loews State, Capital, the Strand, the Roxy, and Radio City in Midtown. Then you had the Astor Hotel roof with a name band. You had the New Yorker with a name band. You had the Statler Downtown, the Pennsylvania, the Edison, and the Taft, where Vincent Lopez used to play. There were a couple of hundred different musicians working in the city. It was really nice. And every band was different. That was 52 weeks a year. New York was New York. It was the Apple. You could go out at night, walk up and down 52nd Street and go from Hickory House to Kelly's Stables to the Famous Door. I mean, everybody was playing: name jazz musicians with small groups like Hot Lips Page and Roy Eldridge. There was music to be heard.[8]

"I discovered pretty quickly that you have to build up protection; an immunity to feelings. It was Dickie Wells, who was a club owner, Count Basie's trombonist, and a big man in Harlem, who gave me the confidence. One morning the Three Peppers, the intermission group at the Hickory House, took me up to Wells' place for a breakfast dance. A group named the Scotsmen were playing there, and they wore kilts. They had Teddy Bunn on guitar and Leo Watson on vocals and drums. They later became the Spirits of Rhythm. I'd never been to Harlem and I was worried because I knew they really played up there. The Peppers introduced me to Wells and he told me: 'I want you to play and if you don't, it'll be your you-know-what.' He wasn't very encouraging. Well, I played and it was a very exciting thing for me."[9]

Drummer Jim Chapin said he was there when Buddy Rich hit the street. "I had just begun to play drums. One night, after leaving the Savoy about three in the morning, I decided to try another Harlem spot called Dickie Wells'. I walked down the stairs into madness. A vibes player was playing a very fast tempo. It seemed as if he were riding a whirlwind created by a human dynamo who was playing effortlessly on a set of inadequate drums. It was Buddy Rich, all 19 years of him. He was well-known uptown. He'd already been a star in showbiz for 17 of those years. On this particular night, he was just sitting in."[10] "I came off the bandstand," said Buddy, "and Wells hugged me and said: 'You're my 100-year man.' Beautiful. From that time on it was straight ahead. For some reason, I've always had a great thing going with colored cats. No conflict—just with white cats."[11]

Buddy also saw Krupa and Webb, more than once and in top form, in Harlem. "I was fortunate to see a concert that was performed by the Chick Webb band and the Benny Goodman band in 1937 at the Savoy Ballroom in Harlem. Gene Krupa was with Goodman at the time, and he never recovered from the shock. He'd be the first to admit it, because he's a very honorable man. The Goodman band played 'Sing, Sing, Sing' for about an hour before it was time to close. Up until that time, Chick had just been coasting along, being merely magnificent. Benny had been pulling out all his flag-wavers. Finally, Gene did all his bits, and tore the place apart: people screaming, throwing kids out the window. There were two bandstands, like a movie thing, and when they finished, the first thing that Chick went into was 'Liza,' and that was up about double the tempo of 'Sing, Sing, Sing.' Chick Webb played a 20-minute solo—and Gene was looking for razor blades!"[12]

On November 24, 1937, Buddy Rich got an offer to take part in a real recording session. The popular group the Andrews Sisters were going to record some new material, and Stan King, bandleader Vic Schoen's regular studio drummer, couldn't make the date. Buddy, who just turned 20, was all nerves. He went to the Decca studio to record "Bei Mir Bist Du Schon," a Yiddish folk song that was adapted to the American swing market for the Andrews Sisters by Sammy Cahn and Saul Chaplin. The recording session for the song—which would become the theme song of the 1938 film *Love, Honor and Behave*—demanded a lot of patience from everyone involved. On top of that, the sisters didn't have much time for the session. They were making a movie at the same time. "I remember that date very well," Buddy remembered. "They came in dead tired after working and couldn't get anything right. We must have done 14 or 15 takes. Time ran out and we didn't do anything else."[13]

The Andrews Sisters, evidently, weren't the only ones at fault for the multiple takes. Vic Schoen remembered that Buddy's lack of reading ability was a problem. "I gave the kid a chance to go through the arrangement with me before we started. But it soon became evident that the rehearsal was going to be a near catastrophe when we found out that the drummer couldn't read notes. I had a new meeting with him afterwards to try to teach him how to play by reading notes. The whole meeting was very strained and the drummer more or less fled from the room. Buddy Rich was terrified of learning how to play from notes."[14]

The just-over-three-minute recording became a million seller, selling over 100,000 records within a few weeks of its release. Buddy Rich's drumming, in the end, was appropriate. The record itself, actually a "B" side at first, was magic, with sales getting a big shot in the arm per the efforts of the Andrews' manager, Lou Levy (no relation to the jazz pianist of the same name). Levy bribed certain record stores on Broadway to play it on loudspeakers aimed towards the street. No one had ever done that before. It worked. Maxene Andrews said, "All traffic was stopped and they played that song everywhere, and people said, 'Play it again, play it again!' All I wanted to say was, 'That's me, that's me!'"[15]

Buddy Rich had made his first recording. And it was a hit.

***

It was very cold that Sunday in January, 1938, and the evening's concert had been sold out for weeks. Though there were some doubts at first, the whole event had been worked out in detail months before by promoter Wynn Nathanson at the Tom Fitzdale Agency and concert impresario Sol Hurok. Jazz would again set foot in the hallowed hall known as Carnegie. In 1924, the so-called "King of Jazz" Paul Whiteman performed at Carnegie Hall, but the actual jazz content of the Whiteman band was minimal. The Nathanson deal was for a real jazz band: Benny Goodman's group, led by the reigning "King of Swing." Goodman himself was reluctant at first, as he thought his music wasn't meant to be played in a venue known for classical music. "The funny thing was that I was against the idea from the very beginning. Wynn Nathanson, who handled some of our publicity, came up with the idea and had to do some real fast talking before he convinced me. 'We will have a fiasco there!' I said over and over again. 'You will be a huge success!' answered Wynn. And Willard Alexander agreed."[16]

In December, 1937, the contract was signed and the concert would take place on January 16, 1938. Goodman started to prepare immediately, cancelling some future dates, and rehearsing daily—at Carnegie when possible—in order for the band to get used to the acoustics. There were a few new songs on the program, and plans to present something novel and rather risky for the concert stage: a real jam session. To be on the safe side, there was a note in the program that read, "The audience is requested to accept this jam session we're having as a pure experiment and in spirit, hoping that the atmosphere will help to establish it."

Goodman had come a long way since the initially disastrous but ultimately triumphant tour in the summer of 1935. Now he had the best musicians in the country with him, and in retrospect, many believe it was the best band Benny ever had. Among others on Benny's band at the time, including specially invited guest stars, were Lionel Hampton on vibraharp, Basie's Freddy Green on guitar, Count Basie himself and

Teddy Wilson on the piano, Harry James and Ziggy Elman on trumpets, Hymie Schertzer and Johnny Hodges on alto saxophones, guests Lester Young on tenor and Harry Carney on baritone, and visual thunder power on the drums courtesy of Gene Krupa. Duke Ellington was invited to participate, but turned the offer down. The plan was to play a concert in two acts with an intermission. The day before opening, Goodman had been asked: "How long of an intermission would you like?" Goodman responded, "How long does Mr. Toscanini have?"

The tickets sold out quickly, and even Goodman had to buy tickets from scalpers to get his relatives into the show. The scene was electric. Writer Irving Kolodin described it as a "vibrating hall," adding that "nearly all of New York had made up their minds to be there that evening."[17] Then it was finally time. According to Kolodin, Harry James stood at the edge of the curtain, looked out and was said to remark that he felt like "a whore in church." The edited version from Goodman or his press agents said that Harry looked out at the audience, glanced over the locale and said, "I feel like a schoolboy on a date with a waitress."[18]

Everyone, not surprisingly, had a case of nerves. The band took the stage, and Goodman emerged wearing tails and with clarinet in hand, took a bow, and counted off "Don't Be that Way." The band sounded nervous and stiff, and was anything but swinging. Gene Krupa knew it and decided to wake everyone up. When it was time for him to play his first break, he drummed for all he was worth and as fast as he could. That did it, and swing flooded the golden temple. The evening's final number was, of course, "Sing, Sing Sing," and the entire audience went completely wild, due in part to Krupa's solo, whose playing on the July 6, 1937, commercially recorded version of the tune is regarded as the first lengthy drum solo ever recorded.

The Famous 1938 Carnegie Hall Jazz Concert (as the album was called) became a part of history, musically and otherwise. It was one of the first times that black and white men played together on such an important stage, and, when released by Columbia Records in 1950, was the first time a double album was produced on vinyl. It sold over a million copies. Ultimately, jazz had broken through to the concert hall, opening the door for others to play in other hallowed halls. Swing was king, and all of

America, it seemed, was dancing.

A nearly 21-year old Buddy Rich knew Krupa's work well. How could he not? In spite of having seen how Chick Webb had "won" over Gene, he was deeply impressed by what he heard. He felt that a drummer must be seen and heard, and that a real drummer must be able to play in any combination and with the same drive. "One of the reasons Gene was so great was that he could do it all: blow the band out, come down front and play with a trio or quartet, then involve himself in a solo feature—no big deal. He knew that if you played with three or four guys, you kept things down and used brushes. You didn't step on the pedal. You played the pedal. You were subtle behind what was going on."[19]

Two days after the Goodman concert, Buddy Rich completed his second recording. This time he was a guest of Adrian Rollini, a creative musician who mastered many instruments, among others the bass saxophone, piano and xylophone. Rollini was a veteran player who had worked with Tommy and Jimmy Dorsey, Bix Beiderbecke, Jack Teagarden, Bunny Berigan and Benny Goodman. Buddy had been contacted by Rollini at the beginning of the year to play as part of the rhythm section on eight tracks. A recording with a big orchestra was in the making. Buddy would back Rollini's xylophone, and the singer on the date, Sonny Schuyler, a.k.a. Sunny Skylar. There were no nerves for Buddy in the studio this time out.

Back with Marsala at the Hickory House, he continued to enjoy his new life. Marsala was happy with his choice and the engagement was extended Sunday after Sunday. Buddy was paid well for doing what he loved—playing jazz—but the experience wasn't completely painless. After Marsala hired Buddy in the band, the owner Popkin kept insisting that he should fire him for playing too loudly. Marsala stood his ground and hung on to his new, energetic drummer, even if the other musicians in the band were not always happy with him. Pianist Joe Bushkin explained, "Rich was incredibly good at developing Danny Alvin's quite powerful way of pushing onward with the bass drum, until he began to play altogether too loudly behind my solos."[20] He may have been loud, but people were beginning to talk about this powerful youngster, including future jazz producer Teddy Reig. "I used to go to the Hickory

House and sit in the corner because I couldn't afford it," said Reig, who would later produce a number of artists including Charlie Parker and Count Basie. "I'd listen to Buddy there and then watch him go up and down 52nd Street and cut everybody on the block. He'd get more drummers fired than anybody. After a club owner heard Buddy, he'd get the idea that his drummer sounded like nothing at all."[21]

Traditional jazz pianist Art Hodes was one of the many who enjoyed the scene. "New York was a complete revelation from what Chicago was. One of the first places I visited was the Hickory House on 52nd Street, where Joe Marsala had the band. That was a 'price' job and Joe had a good group. Buddy Rich was his drummer and Marty Marsala blew trumpet. That's the first time I saw musicians playing for kicks with an audience and getting paid. You got to remember that in Chicago musicians played for acts or dancing. There was a social order in night clubs and musicians were pretty close to the bottom of the scale. Usually the showgirls, star acts, and MC were number one. Bartenders and waiters ranked next. Of course the bandleader rated, but not the sidemen. We became a notch above the wash room attendants."[22]

William F. Ludwig Jr., the drum manufacturer, was in the house at times. "I also saw Buddy at Hickory House and I was mighty impressed by his unbelievable technique," said Ludwig. Goodman's Harry James dropped by, and enthusiastically told the whole Goodman band, and especially the drummer Gene Krupa, about what he had seen and heard, saying, "Man, this kid over at the Hickory House is going to scare you to death. Wait 'til you hear him!" Gene Krupa remembers his reaction: "I was terrified."

Buddy Rich was getting respect. He was also looking for other playing opportunities. One of those opportunities was with the band of the master himself, Chick Webb. Webb's tenor saxophonist, Teddy McRae, remembered that Rich was petrified. "Chick let Buddy sit in the band. I think the band scared the shit out of him. I don't think he had ever before played in a band that played so loud and strong. Chick counted us in and he let Buddy play a lot of numbers. And he played well. Later Chick said: 'When I'm no longer around, keep this guy's name in your mind. Remember his name. Buddy Rich. He's going to be a great drummer one of these days."[23]

On March 1, 1938, Buddy Rich got another chance to record with an established artist. This time it was the jazz and blues singer Maxine Sullivan. Guitarist Carl Kress had helped Sullivan get a job at the Onyx Club on 52nd Street, a well-known spot that was also a frequent destination for those who wanted to jam. There she met orchestra leader Claude Thornhill. Thornhill was impressed with Sullivan's talents and wanted her to record some of his charts. Buddy Rich played on eight of the Sullivan/Thornhill sides, contributing what was needed and appropriate, with no nerves in evidence. He got his money and accounted dutifully to his father.

A week later, he got the opportunity to play big time: it was time for Joe Marsala's Chicagoans to enter the studio. On March 16, 1938, the band recorded four numbers. "Mighty Like the Blues" was a slow blues as the title suggests, with Buddy's playing very restrained. The second number was "Woo-Woo," which began with a Gene Krupa-influenced intro. The third, "Hot String Beans," was also slow, while the fourth and last track was "Jim Jam Stomp," the song that helped him land the job with Marsala to start with. On "Stomp," he could play at his fullest and he drove as hard as he could. "Jim Jam" was a fitting coda to his time with Marsala. Differences in opinion—likely musical opinion—arose between Buddy and some of Marsala's musicians, and it was time for Buddy to move on. Marsala liked him and didn't stand in his way. "Buddy was with me for about seven months," Marsala remembered. "We always got along fine. No personality problems. He was cocky alright, but with me this was more of an advantage than a handicap, because his self confidence became contagious. Like one time we played one of those concerts run by someone like Martin Block."[24]

On May 29, 1938, the Marsala band was booked at "The Carnival of Swing." The Carnival was an enormous festival in New York, a benefit for the New York Musicians Union Hospital Fund, organized by WNEW radio's Martin Block. Block's radio program, "Make Believe Ballroom," was a key showcase for swing artists and bands. The all-day, outdoor festival at New York's Randall's Island was considered to be the first outdoor jazz festival ever, and it featured around 25 name bands and swing combos, playing for an audience of more than 20,000 people. On the bill were the orchestras of Eddie Condon, Chick Webb, Count Basie, Benny Goodman, Duke Ellington, Woody Herman, and many more. Nearly six hours of swinging jazz would be played.

It was a day of joy. White and black musicians played together. Jo Jones was there with Basie. Jo played on Chick Webb's drums. As it was originally scheduled, Marsala would have a difficult act to follow. He thought he would have to follow the Goodman Quartet. "Buddy asked me, 'Are you worried?'" remembered Marsala. "I said, 'Well, this isn't any easy spot for us, you know. It's gonna be Benny Goodman up there!' He simply said, 'Don't worry, we're gonna wrap it up!' Even then, that's how confident Buddy Rich was." Joe Marsala didn't have to follow Goodman, however, because the King of Swing, who was one of the big headliners, cancelled his performance at the last minute. Apparently the King feared the outdoor fest's "unruly element" and was concerned for the safety of his band.[25] The mob howled its disappointment, but when Martin Block announced that Artie Shaw and His Orchestra would also play at the festival, everyone was cheering again. The King, it turned out, had nothing to worry about. The day after the fest, *The New York Times* reported that police and park officers had their hands full in protecting the players from "destruction by admiration," but hardly anyone got hurt.

Marsala's band received no featured billing, but they did do a good job. This was Buddy's first big gig in front of a huge crowd, and all the biggest bandleaders in the country could now see him, and for the rest of the day, he could stand in the wings to watch all his big jazz idols play. The band that was the biggest success at this event, according to those who were there, was Count Basie. Basie proved that big bands could reach the public at large without sacrificing the spontaneity that is the heart of jazz. This was not lost on Buddy Rich. Playing Dixieland jazz the rest of his life was not anything Buddy Rich really had in mind. Not when there were other giants like Goodman and Basie out there swinging. In June, 1938, he gave notice to Marsala, bound and determined to work with other bands. Buddy Rich's legacy with Marsala at the Hickory House? A "Jim Jam Stomp" burger.

Marsala would continue with his popular jam sessions at Hickory House until around 1947. For years, the club was a magnet for jazz musicians who loved to visit and to play there, including a trio led by pianist Marian McPartland that featured a young Joe Morello on drums. The Hickory survived bop and a lot of other things, but John Popkin just couldn't keep it going. In 1968, The Hickory House became the Pier 52 restaurant.

After Marsala, Buddy got a job at CBS in a radio show called "The Saturday Night Swing Club." The contract was for five Saturdays in July, 1938. Stanley Kay recalled, "It featured a studio orchestra directed by Leith Stevens. No one knew (Buddy) couldn't read music. The sheet music was put on his stand, and of course he couldn't tell the difference between a whole note and a quarter note. But he could hear. He listened to the arrangement once or twice and that's all that was necessary. He played it down as if he had written it himself."[26]

He often got to finish the show with a long solo, but this radio job was frustrating. Buddy actually made an attempt to put together his own little group at the Piccadilly Hotel Roof, filling in for Adrian Rollini's band. That didn't last long, according to Freddie Gruber. "Buddy's introduction to being a bandleader was at the Picadilly Hotel. They were playing on the rooftop of the hotel and the manager came up and requested that Buddy play a little softer on the bass drum, because they could hear it in the lobby. Buddy's response was, 'Bring my drums home. Nobody tells me how to play the drums. I'm leaving.'"[27]

There he stood. He had resigned from Marsala. He knew that he had been successful, that many important people had seen him both at the Hickory House and at Randall's Island. Surely, some big band would be interested in his services. He went home to his family and waited.

For the moment, the phone wasn't ringing.

Buddy Rich hit me between the eyes in 1966 when he released *Swingin' New Big Band*. My drum instructor had told me about Buddy Rich, and when I heard that album it blew my mind! I bought each new Buddy album as they were released: *Big Swing Face*; *The New One!*; *Mercy Mercy*; *Buddy & Soul*; *Rich In London* and on and on. In 1968, when I was 13 years old, I had my parents bring me to see Buddy for the first time at the Boston Globe Jazz Festival. I still have the program from that concert. My mom, who was fearless, somehow got me backstage to meet Buddy. He was very congenial and signed an autograph for me. A few years later, once I got my drivers license, I saw Buddy every chance I could. He played in the Boston area frequently and I was fortunate to see him numerous times. There is some voodoo that happens when you are in the room with genius. You can watch videos for hours but it never comes close to the life-changing experience of being in the room hearing, feeling and having your physiology altered by the music of the Buddy Rich Big Band. By experiencing Buddy in person it gave me an incredible example of the kind of energy and excitement I wanted to transmit to people coming to hear me play. I am grateful that I was born and grew up at the right time and place that I could be profoundly influenced by the greatest drumset player of all time.

Steve Smith

CHAPTER 4

Bunny Berigan and His Orchestra

Buddy marks time between leaving Bunny Berigan and joining Artie Shaw's big band at the close of 1938. Buddy's first appearance with Shaw was January 8, 1939.

Rowland Bernard "Bunny" Berigan was born on November 2, 1908. A powerful but sensitive player who wore his heart on his sleeve, he was called "Mister Trumpet," as he was the personification of his instrument. He had all the natural qualities, and like Louis Armstrong, who publicly and privately admired Bunny, he was equipped with an incredible physique. Both had big barrel chests, strong lungs, and iron lips. Berigan dressed conservatively, and with his little moustache, pointed nose, and glasses, he looked like a college professor. Above all, he was a brilliant jazz musician who constantly evolved, and a superior improviser who hardly ever repeated himself. He was rarely satisfied with his own playing; after a solo he might say, "I started off very well but then everything disappeared in a single cloud of shit."[1]

Berigan got his big breakthrough in 1935. Granted, he had made a name for himself among musicians and had been around for quite a while, but that particular year was the big year of swing, and it was as if Bunny was made to play that kind of jazz. He was the perfect player for the swing era, beautifully combining Bix Beiderbecke's melancholy tone and Louis Armstrong's raw passion. In June of 1935, he joined the Benny Goodman band, whose popularity was on the rise after the success in Oakland, California. Fletcher Henderson had just started contributing charts to the Goodman band, and with Bunny aboard, the Henderson orchestrations and other numbers in the Goodman book were imbued with a vitality they hadn't possessed earlier. He went along on Goodman's national tour, which had its triumphant finale at the Palomar in Los Angeles.

Bunny was restless and wanted to keep moving. To everyone's surprise, he quit his job with Goodman to work as a studio player at CBS radio. He recorded extensively during this period with a number of bands, including that of Tommy Dorsey. As a member of Dorsey's band in late 1936 and early 1937, several of his unique trumpet solos on Dorsey hits like "Marie" were such improvisational gems that they would later be transcribed and performed by Dorsey's entire sax section. Berigan also won the coveted 1936 *Metronome* magazine poll, receiving five times as many votes as the second place winner. Berigan was ready to step out on his own, and a year later, with backing from Dorsey, he formed his own outfit. Swing had now gained momentum and in March, 1937, the orchestra had its first performance. The band was made up of Berigan, Irving Goodman (Benny's brother) and Steve Lipkins on trumpets; Al George and Sonny Lee on trombones; Mike Doty, Joe Dixon, Georgie Auld and Clyde Rounds on saxophones; Tom Morgan on guitar; Hank Wayland on bass; and George Wettling on drums. This lineup had the group's first (and really only) hit: Vernon Duke and Ira Gershwin's "I Can't Get Started," a number taken from a show called *The Ziegfield Follies of 1936*, sung by Bob Hope, of all people. It became Berigan's theme song.

In mid-January of 1938, drummer George Wettling quit. Tenor saxophonist Georgie Auld recalled, "He had a beef with the pianist, Joe Lippman. We were driving along the highway. Lippman stopped the car, got out, and beat the shit out of Wettling, who had made an anti-Semitic remark. We left him there on the highway, in the middle of nowhere."[2] The band was booked to tour in New England with Wettling in tow, but rumors of the fight reached the papers, and Wettling was forced to leave for good. He was replaced by Dave Tough. On March 17, 27-year old John G. "Johnny" Blowers took over after Tough. Tough, a fragile but tremendously inventive player who was admired by one and all, wasn't an easy act to follow. No one knew this more than Blowers, who remembered, "Dave Tough was the most emaciated guy I ever saw, but my God, he had such tremendous power. I don't know where it came from. He was just a marvelous drummer."[3]

Blowers, who later became a studio giant as Frank Sinatra's regular percussionist, could also drive a band. He used a big bass drum that "reminded me of a cannon every time I pressed it," as he said. But his days with Berigan were numbered. Nearly three months later, on July 4, he played his final gig with the orchestra at the Raymor Ballroom in Boston. Blowers had received a better offer from the jazz violinist and radio personality Ben Bernie, who was leading a new band and had signed a long term contract with CBS radio to be the house band for a music quiz show. Berigan was happy for Blowers, and given his proclivity for partying, immediately organized a farewell gala. That could have been a disaster, as the band got Blowers so drunk that he missed his train the next morning. Somehow, he managed to find an acceptable excuse for Bernie.

The Berigan band was once again without a drummer. It was Buddy Rich's time. The actual date that he joined remains difficult to establish. Buddy told Mel Tormé that he went to one of Berigan's performances in Brighton Beach on August 8, 1938, where he visited Georgie Auld in his dressing room and told him that he was out of work and in an economic fix. He is supposed to have said, "I'm starving to death. I need a job." But in Doug Meriwether's book, *Mister, I Am the Band*, Buddy stated unequivocally, "That was an important milestone in my life, you don't forget things like that. Yeah, August 8, 1938. Georgie Auld drove over to our house and took me to the job at Brighton Beach. It was a hot afternoon and the bandstand was right at the beach. I think the first thing I did with them was 'The Prisoner's Song.'"

In Mike Zirpolo's Berigan biography, *Mr. Trumpet*, Auld confirmed that he indeed was involved in getting Buddy on the band. "I met Buddy first when I was 14 and he was 16. I got him into Bunny Berigan's band. We both lived in Brooklyn and Bunny was looking for a new drummer. He wanted to upgrade the class of the orchestra about then." Guitarist Dick Wharton had also joined the band around that time, and recalled, "Johnny Blowers had just left, and Georgie Auld was the middleman for Berigan when he convinced the young Buddy Rich to leave Joe Marsala and go over to Berigan. He must have understood what a great opportunity it was for him."

However it transpired, Georgie Auld and saxophonist Joe Dixon began a concentrated effort to get Bunny Berigan to accept their suggestion for a new drummer in the band. It wasn't that easy. Berigan was picky, and was very careful to make sure that the personal chemistry worked—and he had never heard of Buddy Rich. Saxophonist Joe Dixon said that Bunny "had to like you. If he didn't like you personally, he didn't want you in the band. He genuinely liked his musicians. We were his boys!"[4] It didn't make things any better when he heard that this Rich couldn't read music, but after a while, he softened up and invited Buddy to an audition. After the first number Buddy was going to get up from the drums, but Bunny held up his hand like a police officer stopping traffic and said, "Don't move! Stay right where you are!" He got the job on the spot.

When Buddy Rich joined Bunny Berigan's orchestra, it was a struggling band. The number "I Can't Get Started" had climbed to 10th place on the national charts, and as a band, it was ranked at number 30. Despite the success with a hit, it was difficult to create an individual style and to find a good follow-up to the hit record. However, in Buddy Rich's eyes, it was a big enough challenge to play in an 18-man band with good musicians and to be once again assured of a steady income.

Author Zirpolo cites Buddy Rich's first performance with Berigan—at Manhattan Beach in New York City—as early as July 5, 1938, and not in August as Rich later recalled. The venue was an amusement park with an outdoor stage, beside Coney Island. Guitarist Dick Wharton had good reason to remember, recalling, "Buddy played loudly right from the start and Bunny had to tell him to turn down the volume. But clearly Berigan liked all Rich's rhythmic figures and added several of (Buddy's) licks to the arrangement."[5] The booking at Manhattan Beach lasted a week, followed by two performances in Michigan and a week at the Fox Theater in Detroit starting on July 15. *The Detroit Free Press* wrote about the opening, "Berigan really flies in at the Fox with his trumpet and keeps the jitterbugs happy. There is a lively collection of talents that Berigan has with him on stage." Granted, there is no mention of Rich, but it is clear that he had given the band a lift.

After the Fox Theater, there was a performance in Syracuse and then the group went on to play a week at the Steel Pier in Atlantic City. At the same time, they were rehearsing for another show at a place called Casa Manana. In Robert Dupuis's book *Bunny Berigan: Elusive Legend of Jazz*, he writes that playing this show was not easy. "The rehearsal on July 24 was a mess," Dupuis wrote. "Jimmy Durante, Benay Venuta, Pat Rooney, and John Steel were on the bill, and the show required precision cueing for this mixture of singers, dancers, and comedians. Bunny could not cue well, and his key rhythm players, (pianist Joe) Bushkin and Rich, read with limited ability. Various participants reacted with ill temper." Dupuis' description of the happening is interesting, in that Buddy, though he couldn't read music, always had the unusual ability to memorize long musical pieces in record time, and he had done nothing but accompany different vaudeville artists since he was born. The problem was likely Bunny Berigan. He was good at reading music, but he wasn't great at leading an orchestra with a baton. Some of his band members thought that he couldn't even count off an ordinary downbeat.

Dick Wharton knew there was something wrong. "We drove back to New York City from Syracuse and arrived about four in the morning. Later the day after, we were supposed to rehearse for our coming show at Casa Manana, and it was a difficult rehearsal. The show we were to play in was rather complicated with a lot of variations and quick changes. Neither Buddy Rich nor Joe Bushkin could read music and Bunny wasn't used to leading an orchestra in this kind of stage show. It ended with everyone shouting at each other."[6]

In the end, the show seems to have worked for everyone. Tenor saxophonist Clyde Rounds maintained, "That show lifted the band back to the status they had enjoyed earlier. The show included artists like Jimmy Durante, John Steel, one of my favorite singers, Benay Venuta, and a relatively unknown Danny Kaye. The girls who danced in the show were so beautiful they distracted all the musicians! The guys were busier looking at the girls than at their sheet music! The place was packed and we got rave reviews. We thought we would be able to stay there a long time, but unfortunately it wasn't to be."[7]

Buddy Rich hadn't been in the new band very long before he got the surprise of his life. It happened at a rehearsal; Bunny Berigan informed the whole orchestra that he was going to hire a female vocalist. There were many who sighed at the news, especially Buddy, since he was not fond of accompanying singers and their endless ballads. As Buddy once said, "In those days, I lived 'up.'" At 1:00 in the afternoon one day, he came to what he thought was an ordinary rehearsal. Once there, he spied his sister Jo in the room. There was nothing odd about that. She often used to come and check out Buddy when he was practicing with different bands. He walked to his drums and started to tune them and set them up while the other musicians dropped in. When everyone was there, Berigan counted the gang off, and after two measures, Jo began to sing. She was standing with her back to Buddy. Suddenly, she heard the drumsticks drop to the floor. Berigan turned to Buddy. "You're not awake yet, take it again." They got through three numbers and Jo said thank you and left the rehearsal. Later, she got a phone call from Berigan's manager, who told her that she had the job. She was thrilled. In the evening, Buddy came home. He wasn't happy.

"Six or seven that evening, in he comes," said Jo. "I am flying. 'I got the job! I'm going to be on the road with you!' Buddy said, 'No, you are not.' 'What do you mean? I just got a call. I got the job!' 'I told Berigan that if you go on the road with the band, I won't.' 'Why? What are you doing to me?' 'You think I want my sister travelling on a bus with 18 musicians?' 'What do you mean? What do you have against musicians? You are a musician!' 'That's what I mean!'"[8]

After Buddy made Jo turn down the job, it went to Ruth Gaylor, who quickly discovered that she had joined a somewhat unusual band. Berigan had his own little way of testing his vocalists. A later drummer, Jack Sperling, said that Berigan wanted to play the role of a sort of father figure for the singer, and therefore he wanted to make her feel at ease right from the start. "Listen, you're with the band now," Berigan told Gaylor, "and with musicians around you're likely to hear quite a bit of rough language. So, just to get the embarrassment out of the way, sort of break the ice and get it out of your system. Let's do this: on the count of three we'll all yell 'fuck!' just as loud as we can. Then you've heard it, we've heard it, and nobody'll be offended. Then he counted 'one, two, three!' You know what happened? The girl shouted *'fuck!'* and everybody else was silent. Bunny liked that trick." [9]

Bunny Berigan may have been a talented trumpeter, but he was less than great as a bandleader. In contrast to Dorsey and Goodman, who both distanced themselves from their orchestras by being careful not to become too close with the musicians, Berigan didn't believe in discipline at all, and if anyone wanted to have some fun he was the first to join in. He drank too much and most of those around him regarded him as a true alcoholic. Artie Shaw was well aware of it. "Bunny couldn't handle a band," said Shaw. "He had no self-discipline. When he got in front of a band he would get worried, and then he'd start drinking. Pretty soon the men in the band lost all respect for him. It doesn't work. You have to present a kind of model for the men. You have to be the leader, meaning that you have to set the tone. You've got to do what you want the men in the band to do."[10]

There were days when he began the morning by calculating how much liquor he would need to get through the rest of the day. Fighting with agents, accountants, local promoters, and hotel owners made him nervous. He tried to find a balance in everything, without being very successful, so he worked, travelled, played, and drank even more. Georgie Auld said that "Berigan used to have a favorite expression when it was time to crack another bottle. 'Bring on the dancing team,' he would say to the band boy. The team was Haig and Haig."[11]

However, Berigan took his music seriously, and the only time he got upset was if someone didn't do their best. He accepted no less. Even Buddy realized this after a couple of performances. Berigan didn't care about popularity. Whatever the size or importance of the event, he played consistently at the highest level. Irving Goodman experienced the whole thing from the trumpet section. "Berigan was incredible at lifting the whole band when it was necessary. Everyone did as he asked, if only he showed what he wanted. His attitude was also fantastic. Even if we played in some little hick place out in the boonies he gave it all he had." Joe Bushkin agreed. "He managed his big band just like he looked after his little band on 52nd Street. He came in and played what he was supposed to, just like anyone else in the band. But he had no eye for business."[12]

On August 9, 1938, Buddy Rich made his first appearance on a record with Bunny Berigan and His Orchestra. Fifteen songs were recorded, based mostly on the material that Berigan had commissioned from the fantastic Fletcher Henderson, who was now writing for bands other than Benny Goodman's. On these tracks, it is clear that Buddy was more comfortable with Berigan than he was with Marsala, perhaps because the charts were simply more swinging. Though the recordings gained no great public popularity either on radio or the hit parade, bookings were plentiful and the band was popular in some circles. On August 14, the band started a week's engagement at Cincinnati's Coney Island Moonlight Gardens, followed on August 25 by a week at the Stanley Theater in Pittsburgh. After that, there was another week's booking at Detroit's lovely outdoor stage, Eastwood Gardens, where the band played until September 9. During the Eastwood stay, vocalist Ruth Gaylor left the band and was replaced by Jayne Dover.

At the same time, Berigan's drinking increased and the band members weren't able to stop him. It was getting so out of hand, that the band had to stop every 100 miles to buy a bottle of Old Quaker so Berigan could get through the trip. Several of the band members remembered that they all had to take turns sharing a hotel room with him, just to watch over him at night when he sat in the bathroom, wrapped in wet towels, wailing, "I'm dying, I'm dying, I can't breathe."[13] He neglected the band's business more and more, and began to mix up the bookings. On September 11, *Billboard* wrote a story about Berigan travelling to the wrong city, only to find the Gene Krupa band setting up on stage. *Billboard* made reference to Berigan's experience as "The Corrigan Twist," referring to Douglas "Wrong Way" Corrigan, the American aviator who was to fly from California to New York, but landed in Ireland.

Touring with Berigan was like touring with a rock band. Trombonist Ray Conniff, who later gained enormous fame on records and television with his choral group, the Ray Conniff Singers, was on the band briefly. He recalled, "It was a tight little band. Like a family with only rowdy boys, where Bunny was the worst of the bunch. And we took turns sharing a room with him. It was like one crazy party. You should have seen those hotel rooms! Spare ribs, liquor, and women in every corner!"[14] Though the band was on time for a two-week stand at Boston's Ritz Hotel beginning September 19, two days later the city was hit by a hurricane and large sections of Boston were wiped out. Over 400 people died and property valued at $460 million was destroyed. Naturally, the band couldn't continue, and though Berigan was able to collect a part of the contracted fee, the hotel cancelled all outdoor concerts after that.

One-nighters continued through September, followed by four Wednesdays in October at the Roseland Ballroom, but bad luck struck again. This time, the leader broke his foot at home and the four Wednesdays became two. As for the actual incident, band members Dick Wharton, Gus Bivona, and Joe Bushkin all remember that Berigan said that he had broken his foot while playing with his kids. At the time, Bunny said, "That sound of my foot breaking will be heard all over the country. Usually when I've had too much to drink, there was hardly anyone who saw or heard anything as long as the band sounded okay.

And now, when I fell and was sober, nobody is going to believe me!" Buddy Rich remembered it differently. "Bunny was one of the great drinkers of our time. We were doing a one-nighter in York, Pennsylvania, and when the curtains opened, Berigan came out playing his theme, 'I Can't Get Started.' He walked right off the front of the stage and into the audience and lay there laughing—with a broken foot. But he had the foot set and came back and finished the night."[15] Georgie Auld remembered, "He got it put in a cast and someone pulled a sock over it all and when some time had passed and it was time to take off the cast, he fell again— and broke his foot again!"[16]

None of this bothered Buddy Rich. His playing improved, as did his level of self-confidence. He was thinking about moving on. On October 26, 1938, Buddy Rich is said to have looked for a job as a drummer with Benny Goodman. Dave Tough was then in the drum chair as Gene Krupa's replacement. In Ross Firestone's book on Goodman, *Swing Swing Swing*, the author quoted Goodman trumpeter Gordon "Chris" Griffin as saying, "When Dave Tough failed to show up for Goodman's band's opening at the Waldorf Astoria in New York, he was fired and Buddy Schutz was brought in. Benny Goodman was dissatisfied and auditioned drummers in the middle of a whole mess of people. He even tried a very young Buddy Rich. We were down at Atlantic Beach for a week and this kid came in one night and sounded exactly like what Benny had just gotten rid of—and didn't want. He listened to him for about two numbers and said, 'Okay kid,' and that was the end of that. "He didn't want anybody as flashy as Gene Krupa."[17]

Obviously, Buddy Rich was keeping tabs on what was happening around him and waited for the right moment to move on from Berigan, when and if an opportunity arose. His next opportunity would not be with Benny Goodman.

It must have been a very tired Bunny Berigan who arrived back in Manhattan on Sunday, November 4, 1938. Whatever state he was in, there was still a mighty big task awaiting him. His band was to meet Erskine Hawkin's popular unit, billed as "The Twentieth Century Gabriel and His Orchestra," at The Savoy Ballroom. Hawkins was a very skilled trumpeter with a wide range, best known for his chart-topping hit

"Tuxedo Junction." Haywood Henry, the baritone saxophonist who played in Hawkins' band, recalled how the battle ended. "There were only three bands that stole the show from us at the Savoy: Duke's, Lionel Hampton's and Bunny Berigan's. Bunny took us by surprise. Usually, we'd prepare in advance by rehearsing or working over one of their specialties, just to make it more exciting. We didn't prepare for Bunny because we thought we had him. But Buddy Rich and Georgie Auld were with him and the house came down."[18]

Berigan's orchestra had a few successes here and there, one being that the October edition of *Downbeat* magazine named him only second to Harry James as "Best Trumpeter." After him, in third and fourth place, came Louis Armstrong and Roy Eldridge. Bunny Berigan was admired by everyone on the list. In 1941, Louis Armstrong was asked by *Downbeat* to name which trumpeter he admired most. "First I want to mention Bunny Berigan. There you've got a guy that I've always admired for his tone, his soul, technique, his phrasing, and everything else. For me, Bunny Berigan can do nothing wrong in music." Berigan probably thought that the award would mean better bookings and higher fees, but that was not the case. Instead, he decided to continue to record and rehearse. One of those rehearsals turned out to be quite special. Years later, author Mike Zirpolo spoke to Buddy Rich about it.

Cornering Buddy after a concert date, Zirpolo asked, "Mr. Rich, when did you hear Count Basie for the first time?" Buddy's face broke into a grin. "How did you know about me and Basie?" Zirpolo tried to answer, but was immediately interrupted. "I was with Bunny Berigan," Buddy explained. "We were in New York for a couple of days to rehearse. Bunny wasn't satisfied with how we played. So he broke it off and said, 'All you boys should go down to the Famous Door down on 52nd Street and see Count Basie's band there. That will do you more good than rehearsing.' So I went with Georgie Auld, Joe Dixon, Ray Coniff, and Joe Bushkin. We were all amazed by what we saw. They had such a fantastic swing. It was so light, so powerful. We were so impressed by Lester Young. All of us except Georgie, because he liked Herschel Evans."

Every important musician checked out Basie at The Famous Door. He was a total sensation there after the band had a hit with "One O'Clock

Jump," recorded the previous summer. At some point around that time, Rich sat in with Basie, and it became one of Rich's most treasured moments. Stanley Kay knew plenty about Rich's admiration for Basie. "Basie came over to him and said, 'I hear you're pretty bad,'" said Kay. "Buddy was humble, and Basie urged him to play in the band. I think Buddy was one of the few white guys who sat in who could really do what had to be done. He played the style perfectly."[19] Buddy Rich always spoke fondly of Basie. "I became good friends with Basie. He was the kindest and the most lovable person I have ever known. I met him for the first time when I was 18 years old. I met Jo Jones there, too, and we talked about the fact that their band hadn't many songs in its repertoire, maybe only four or five. Then it was a lot of 'You play those chords, and then that and that.' That was surprising."[20]

On November 30, 1938, nearly two months after Berigan and the band survived the Boston hurricane and Bunny's foot had healed, the band recorded again with a new vocalist: Kathleen Lane, who had sung with both Benny Goodman and Woody Herman. As for Jayne Dover, she had enough of the musicians in the band and their dirty language, and quit.

Georgie Auld told writer Leonard Feather what the atmosphere was like on the band bus: "Things were so rough that the chick with the band reached the point where she just couldn't take it anymore. One night there was only one seat left on the bus, and that was next to her. Johnny Napton, the trumpeter, wanted to take it, and she wouldn't let him. So he started cursing her out. She started to run out of the bus. 'I can't take this anymore!' she told Bunny. All this rotten language, this foulmouthed talk, I'm through!'

"Bunny, who has had one more for the road and then some, gets back on the bus with her and all the guys are seated in their chairs. He grabs the post beside the driver, starts banging on it with his cane and just about breaks the cane in half. He's furious. 'I've had it! All this language and the girl singer wants to quit the band, and you're hanging me up in the middle of a stack of one nighters without a girl singer! Now I want you to get one thing straight! (The girl is sitting there while he is saying all this.) The first fucking idiot that curses on this bus is automatically through!'

"Everybody on the bus started to laugh, so he catches himself and says, 'Well, I didn't mean to put it that way, but I am serious! I don't want to hear another foul word out of any of you as long as Jayne is sitting on this bus!' Well, we go about 250 miles and not a sound of anyone. The cats were even lighting their cigarettes real quiet because we knew Bunny was flipping. Along about daybreak, Joe Bushkin, our pianist, runs down the bus, stops by the driver and turns around facing everybody, including Bunny, and yells, 'I can't stand it any longer! Stupid fucking shit, you idiots, and every other word he can think of.' That was, without a doubt, the most frantic bunch of kids that were ever together."[22]

There were more incidents. Following this recording session, Georgie Auld got into a fight with Berigan in the studio, and left the band. "Bunny wanted me to play alto and tenor on the recording," said Auld. "I hadn't touched alto in a long time. I squeaked a couple of times. Bunny took his trumpet and threw it up against the wall, cursed me out, said: 'Blackie, you sonofabitch, you're doing the squeaking so we can go overtime.' It broke my heart."[23] Auld had seen enough and left. Back at the hotel, he ran into singer Helen Forrest and saxophonist Tony Pastor, who told them that their bandleader, Artie Shaw, was looking for him. Later that same evening, Georgie Auld joined up with Shaw's band. The next day he told Berigan about his decision. Bunny reacted just as badly as he had the day before: "If you move I'll knock your teeth out!" Then Bunny collapsed in tears, declaring that there would always be a place for him in his band.

Auld's departure meant Buddy's best friend in the band was no longer there, and that got Buddy thinking about his own situation with Berigan. "When I was around 18, 20 years old," Buddy explained, "I had a definite idea of how I wanted others to think of me. But I had two choices. I could do my own thing and go my own way, and be out of work. Or else I could go nearly my own way and continue working. So I compromised with myself, but not to the degree that I was dissatisfied."[24] The big band business knew all about Buddy Rich by that time. There were those who thought his drumming was really fantastic, but they also knew about his temper and, in some cases, it became a deciding factor in whatever interest they had in him. Harry James, who had heard Buddy with Marsala at the Hickory House and had played with Rich once earlier (in the beginning of 1937, when Rich sat in with a band playing at Bill's Gay Nineties Night Club), dug Buddy from the start. After that guest performance James had told everyone there, "That kid will be a great drummer someday."[25]

Harry James became a star with Benny Goodman, and like Krupa before him, became so popular that in December of 1938, he left Goodman and his $250 weekly salary behind to start his own band, a unit that was initially backed by Goodman. James was after Buddy Rich when he found out Rich was thinking about leaving Berigan and went to fellow bandleader Artie Shaw for advice. Shaw advised him against it, since he thought Rich was a typical Dixieland drummer, and that was surely not what Harry needed or wanted. James listened to Shaw and hired Ralph Hawkins as his drummer. Shaw, however, may have had an ulterior motive in his advice to Harry James.

Stanley Kay thought Shaw should contact Buddy Rich immediately. "I knew that Artie was playing at the Lincoln Hotel on 45th St. I also knew you could go upstairs where the lounge was, and when they opened the door, you could look down and hear the band play. There also was an area where you could see the musicians go into the alley on a break. When I saw Artie come out, he was in a good mood. So I said, 'Mr. Shaw, excuse me, I heard you're looking for a drummer. I know the greatest drummer in the world.' 'Who would that be?' he asked me. 'Buddy Rich,' I said. 'Oh, he can't play,' Artie said, waving me off."[26]

CHAPTER 5

Artie Shaw
and
His Orchestra

Publicity still from the one feature film that featured Buddy with the Artie Shaw band of 1939: *Dancing Co-Ed*.

Arthur Jacob Arshawsky was born on May 23, 1910 in New York City. He was a jazz clarinetist, orchestra leader, composer, and author who grew up in New Haven, Connecticut. As the story goes, the introverted youngster became interested in music, and worked at a grocery store at the age of 13 in order to save money to buy an alto saxophone. Three years later, he switched to clarinet and left home. Throughout the 1920s, he toured with any number of bands and orchestras. Success and respect came to him early. Having been exposed to symphonic music during his 1929 to 1930 tenure with Irving Aaronson's Commanders, by 1935 and now residing in New York, he had some specific ideas about what he wanted to do in music as a bandleader.

Perhaps more than anything, the enigmatic Artie Shaw loved to talk about himself.

"No one really knew who I was," as Shaw told the story. "Joe Helbock, the owner of the Onyx Club on 52nd Street, asked me if I wanted to play in a little band while they changed the instruments on the big stage. I accepted, and just for fun, I wrote a piece for clarinet and a string quartet, plus a little rhythm section. Nobody had ever done that in jazz before. After that I asked a few guys at CBS and NBC if they would play through this between some rehearsal breaks. They approved it, and I asked them to perform it with me at the Imperial Theatre."[1] The title of the piece was "Interlude in B Flat," and it became an immediate success. The combination of swing and strings was a winner and it didn't take long until several agents were flocking around him. They wanted him to start his own band, to be known as Art Shaw and His Orchestra (he was not yet Artie in the music world).

When he set out on the road with this band of unusual instrumentation, he met with tough opposition. The public had no interest at all in listening to any string arrangements. The Swing Era had taken off, courtesy of Goodman, Basie, Louis Armstrong, et al. and Shaw wasn't prepared to compete. When the band played at the Adolphus Hotel in Dallas, there were so few in the audience that the gig was cancelled. After another unsuccessful performance in New Jersey at the beginning of 1937, Shaw realized that if he was to have a chance of competing, he would have to put together a new orchestra that would play, said Shaw at the time, the loudest music in the whole world. Art Shaw and his New Music was a little more successful, and did participate in a number of radio broadcasts and recorded a few records.

On tour it was still tough going. "We went on the road in an old bus that we had bought from Tommy Dorsey," Shaw remembered. "His name was painted in large letters on both sides, a little weather-beaten but still readable. Before we had played and saved enough money to paint it over with my name, we had been stopped three times by the cops and accused of stealing the bus."

Despite the difficulties in making a breakthrough, Shaw didn't hesitate to employ a young, black singer as featured vocalist. Her name was Billie Holiday. She had just left Count Basie's band and Shaw wanted her because she was great, and because he could afford her. Bringing Billie along would prove to be a stroke of luck. After a few introductory performances, John Hammond, then writing for *Downbeat*, reported that Shaw was on the right track, writing, "Although Benny Goodman's recently revised band has something no other white band can touch, the combination of Artie and Billie makes me feel that Benny is going to have to watch out for himself."[3]

Then "Begin the Beguine" came along. The song was written by Cole Porter and released in the summer of 1938 as the B side of "Indian Love Call." Nobody figured that the flip side would be as popular as it was. As a result of "Beguine," things were beginning to happen for Shaw. Everyone loved that song, especially college kids. Trumpeter Bernie Privin was in the brass section when "Beguine" began to break. "I joined the band three weeks after 'Begin the Beguine' became available in the stores," said Privin. "Before I knew it, the band was the hottest thing in the country. The record was played everywhere. Because of it, Artie suddenly became a major celebrity."[4]

Artie Shaw was the reluctant, soul-searching celebrity. The audience didn't just want to listen to Artie Shaw's music. They wanted to see the band, and they wanted to hear "Beguine." This made Shaw anxious and he started to wonder if the success was worth its price. Artie Shaw, quite simply, was a man who did not enjoy success. He was a man who wanted to create good music, improve himself, and he was really not interested in whether people liked it or not. To him, music was an art form and something not to be fooled with. Who cared what the drunks in the audience liked? Whether he claimed to like it or not, slowly and surely, his orchestra hopped on the carousel of swing success without much of chance of climbing off. At the same time as "Beguine," Goodman had another big hit with "Bei Mir Bist du Schon," and Shaw felt he had to top it. They became inevitable competitors.

Hit records notwithstanding, there were still occasional bumps in the road, and the band didn't draw a crowd everywhere. One evening, Shaw learned a real lesson. The band was playing at the Lexington Hotel in New York, and during the break his agent called Shaw into his hotel room and said, "I got a lot of complaints, Artie, from the manager at the hotel." "Call him over, I want to talk to him," said Shaw. The manager said that "the band ain't doing a good job. Look at the room. Three people are eating dinner." "That's not my problem, it's your problem," Shaw answered. "Mine is to play good music." "You have got it wrong, kid. I am not running a concert hall here," said the manager. "I am running an establishment where we want people to come." Shaw responded, "What do you want me to do? Grab people and drag them in?" "That's exactly what you're supposed to do," the manager decreed. Artie Shaw never forgot that, and insisted, "If you should take off your pants and shit on the bandstand and people would pay to see you do that, I would hire you to shit on the bandstand."[5]

That was not Shaw's first encounter with the dark side of show business that, according to him, had nothing to do with music, and Artie Shaw being Artie Shaw, he couldn't get it off his mind. It wasn't easy having a black singer up front, either. However much he liked Billie Holiday, the situation became more and more difficult. In the end it was Billie herself who decided to leave. In October, 1938, the orchestra was playing at the Blue Room in the Lincoln Hotel in New York. The owner of the hotel refused to let her in through the main entrance, and she was instructed to get to the stage through the kitchen.

"I was billed next to Artie himself," Holiday recalled years later, "but was never allowed to visit the bar or the dining room as did other members of the band. I had to remain alone in the little dark room all evening until I was called on to do my numbers."[6] Shortly after this incident, she left the orchestra, and blamed it all on her manager. It didn't take long until there was a rumor spreading that Artie Shaw had fired her because she was black. Billie Holiday spoke up in his defense, saying, "There aren't many people who fought harder than Artie against the vicious people in the music business or the crummy side of second class citizenship which eats at the guts of so many musicians. He didn't win. But he didn't lose either." Shaw fired back, saying, "The press were on to me at that time. They said I fired her because she was black, conveniently overlooking that when I hired her she was black too!"[7]

On November 20, 1938, Artie Shaw landed a big contract to perform in a radio series sponsored by Old Gold cigarettes called "Melody and Madness." It was a half hour show on CBS and it didn't take long for it to become a hit. Shaw should have been pleased about that, but pleasing Shaw was difficult, as the seed that had been planted in him at the Lexington Hotel began to grow. The successes began to wear heavily on Artie Shaw. Not only did he continue to wonder constantly about the loathsome commercial side of the music industry, but he wasn't happy with how the band was stagnating musically. Even though he had matched Goodman in almost every way, it wasn't enough. Then drummer Cliff Leeman had to leave the band due to illness, and George Wettling stepped in. These were both fine players, audience hysteria around the band rose, and everything in the world of Artie Shaw should have been great. But "great" was never enough for Shaw.

Things began to change musically when Georgie Auld joined the band at the beginning of December 1938. Artie Shaw liked Georgie Auld, and thought he could help make a difference musically. "At the time that Georgie Auld joined the band," Shaw remembered, "there was a peculiar situation. I am by nature a compulsive perfectionist about things that I do and it gets to a point where it drives everybody nuts, including me. At that point, I had been developing that band for a period of three and a half years with a background of about twelve years of experience in what I wanted. I evolved in my own mind a very clear notion of what I felt popular music should sound like. I got to the point where the band was so trained and so disciplined it was practically a mirror image of myself.

Then suddenly I heard some of the men playing, and something was dead among the band. It didn't spark, it didn't come to life, and I felt there was an ingredient missing. About that time, I heard a guy named Georgie Auld play and everything he did stood in 180-degree opposition to what I believed music should be. There was a key factor. He knew precisely what he was doing and wanted to do, it wasn't accidental. I thought maybe if I injected that ingredient into what I had it would temper the band in a peculiar way."[8]

Triumphs continued. So did Artie Shaw's unhappiness. "When we got to the Lincoln Hotel in New York, it was complete bedlam on opening night. From that day I couldn't think straight. My life wasn't my own any longer. The newspapers were after me, autograph hunters, everything all at once, plus a lot of other stuff suddenly laid on my shoulders. The bigger the success, the more dissatisfied the band became. Georgie Auld joined the band for $125 (per week) and that upset the rest of the band, so they protested."[9] Regarding the amount of money the leader himself was earning, Shaw wasn't shy about admitting, "At the peak of that 1938 band, I was making $60,000 a week. It seemed insane. I began to ask myself: 'How can I be getting that kind of money when the first clarinetist in the Philharmonic only gets $150 a week?' It began to dawn on me that it was lunacy."[10]

Then there was the increased pressure of competition. Artie Shaw clearly understood that the band had to develop in order to survive and to compete with Goodman and the rest. He had to get a hold of the best musicians before anyone else did. Didn't he convince Auld to join him at the exact moment when Auld and Bunny Berigan were fighting? The next order of business was to find a skilled drummer who could replace George Wettling.

On December 1, 1938, Buddy Rich made his last recording with Berigan. He played out his two weeks' notice and was replaced by Phil Sillman. There were no hard feelings. Buddy Rich appreciated the time with the band, and for the rest of his life, he always said he was proud to have played with this legendary trumpeter. He not only appreciated the magnitude of Berigan's talents, but thanks to his time served with that band, he'd had the opportunity to show what he could do. He learned a huge lesson: to always do his best, no matter what the situation was. In several interviews years later, he expressed his appreciation for the time with Berigan. "His records don't show the enthusiasm of the band," Buddy believed. "It was a fun loving band, with music second. I was on the band six months. We had two one-week location jobs and the rest of the time it was one-nighters."[11]

In his own future band, he would even play an arrangement of "I Can't Get Started," Berigan's theme. The song had made a lasting impression on him. The tenor saxophonist, Jay Corre, soloist on the 1968 recording of the tune, recalled, "I had just started my solo when I happened to notice Buddy. He was playing the brushes and sat hunched over his snare drum, crying his heart out. Tears were running down his cheeks and landed on the snare. I understood right away that he was surely thinking of Berigan and the time they had spent together. Buddy's feelings affected my own playing, but that is a moment I will never forget."[12]

The reasons for Buddy's departure from Berigan's band were complicated. A steady job, even with an alcoholic bandleader, meant steady income, and steady income was important to Robert Rich, who was against his son going into the music business from the start. But making good music was of paramount importance to Buddy Rich. So was ambition. It was time to move on and to move up, and he likely relied on Georgie Auld to help him set things right again. They had a good history. The two first met after Buddy had joined up with Marsala. Auld was playing with trumpeter Roy Eldridge at Kelly's Stables, which was just a stone's throw from Hickory House. The two began to hang out. Though Auld was slightly younger than Buddy, he was very versed in the world of music—the playing side and the business side—and since he liked Buddy's playing so much, he didn't hesitate to lend him a helping hand when he could. In some cases, his help became crucial for Buddy's career.

After Auld had been on Shaw's band for a time, the bandleader confided to him that he wanted to completely reorganize the band. He wanted to turn it into a swing band, and it didn't take long until Auld started his campaign to convince him to hire Buddy Rich. Over and over, he proclaimed what a fantastic drummer Buddy was. Shaw answered that he didn't need a Dixieland drummer. Maybe that reaction was understandable, given that he only heard Buddy played live once, and that was at Randall's Island in May when Buddy was playing quasi-Dixieland with Joe Marsala. Georgie Auld put his foot down to Shaw about Buddy, saying, "If he's a Dixieland drummer, I'll play the next four weeks for you free of charge. Look, he can't read, but he'll do more for you than any ten drummers who can."[13] According to this version of the story, Artie Shaw listened carefully to Auld and agreed to give it a try.

But that's only one version of the "Rich joins Shaw" story. Would Shaw actually pay that much attention to Georgie Auld? While Auld's pleas might have played a role, it was standard operating procedure at the time for name bandleaders to be aware of which musicians were playing with which bands, and who was getting tired of the job, the money and/or the music. The fact was, Shaw knew everyone who Buddy Rich had played with previously, including his good friend Bunny Berigan. Tom Nolan, in his book *Three Chords for Beauty's Sake: The Life of Artie Shaw*, gives an example of their friendship, writing, "Art and Bunny hopped into bands at several clubs in Manhattan, and they shared a room for a while in sleazy hotels near Broadway that stood by jazz musicians. They shared everything: money, food, illegal liquor, marijuana, or whatever you can imagine."

It's clear that Artie Shaw knew exactly what he should do when rumors began to circulate that Buddy Rich was going to leave Berigan. "Buddy came around, I mean, I had been told about him. Georgie wasn't the only one; everyone knew about Buddy's playing." According to most sources, Buddy Rich got the job with Shaw in the middle of December. Mel Tormé and Doug Meriwether state in their books that Buddy not only auditioned for Shaw then, but that he also played on a live radio broadcast on Christmas, 1938. Buddy Rich's recollection of the exact time and date varied through the years. In several interviews he said that upon his return to New York, he got a call from Georgie Auld, who told him to come over to the Hotel Lincoln to sit in with Artie Shaw."[14]

But this doesn't tally with a recording made at the time. Author Mike Zirpolo listened carefully to "Jeepers Creepers," a radio aircheck recorded on December 25, and he doesn't think Buddy is on drums. "I have studied Artie Shaw for over 40 years," Zirpolo wrote. "One thing I learned about him early on: He was an absolute perfectionist. He knew how to rehearse effectively with a band, and he did it constantly. He only presented a musical work when he himself felt that it sounded good and when he knew that the orchestra could perform it exactly as he wanted it. It is highly unlikely that he would let some drummer, even one as unbelievable as Buddy Rich, who at that time was relatively unknown in jazz circles and who hadn't learned to play dynamically, play in a direct broadcast of a number that would be heard all across America. Remember, too, that Artie Shaw's own career had just started to take off. Would he risk everything going wrong just to test a new drummer?

"Shortly after Auld joined the band, he realized what was happening with George Wettling, that he was going to quit. He disclosed to Shaw that Rich wanted to move on from Berigan's band and convinced him to give him a chance. And since Shaw could offer Rich a better economic deal than Berigan, Rich informed Berigan that he intended to give notice. Rich tried out with Shaw at the Lincoln Hotel, but didn't play in any direct broadcast. He got the job right away, but was also informed that his first gig would be on January 8 the following year." [15]

That version sounds plausible. Given that Shaw actually went off on holiday to Cuba around this time, the orchestra, in Shaw's absence, was to have rehearsed under the leadership of arranger Jerry Gray. He let Rich sit in front of the orchestra and listen to each number. In the end, Shaw's anxiety about the young Rich not being able to read music proved to be unfounded. All Buddy had to do was to listen to a piece once to learn it by heart, no matter how complicated it was. Whatever the circumstances, it is clear that Artie Shaw tricked Stanley Kay when he stated that Buddy Rich couldn't play and waved him off with disinterest. He already had his eye on Buddy and had contacted him, which Kay soon discovered. "It turned out Artie was putting me on," Kay said. "He had already hired Buddy. A week later Buddy joined Artie's band. Tenor saxophonist Georgie Auld must have gotten him into the band. For years, though, I thought I had gotten Buddy that job. Buddy never told me what had happened, and it was a long standing joke between us."[17]

On January 8, 1939, Buddy Rich made his first public performances with

Artie Shaw and His Orchestra. Many of these were airchecks recorded from the "Melody and Madness" radio program, and upon careful listening, it was clear that this was a band that played incredibly well together. The addition of Auld and Buddy to the Shaw fold—musically, they were the absolute opposite of the other musicians in the band— helped change the sound of the orchestra virtually overnight. The result was a truly great Artie Shaw band.

Buddy Rich knew what he had to do. "I was quite clear about what my job was by the time I went with Shaw. I knew I had to embellish each arrangement, tie it together, keep the time thing going, inspire the players always to be better. My way was to keep the energy level up and push hard. This concept was strictly from Harlem. I learned from black drummers like Chick Webb, Jo Jones, Sid Catlett, and O'Neil Spencer. I was never a fan of white drummers, with the exception of Gene Krupa and Tony Briglia. They were just too bland. I loved excitement, fast tempo, lots of color."[18] Buddy's "way" was not every bandleader's "way," especially not the stubborn, demanding Artie Shaw. In the beginning, he had issues with some aspects of Buddy's playing. "When he first came in the band he used to throw everything he had into every chorus," said Shaw, "playing like the Czechoslovakian army. I taught him that it was better to start quiet, and then build up."[19]

It didn't take long until Shaw and the band members learned about Buddy Rich, "the man." Band vocalist Helen Forrest thought she sized Buddy up pretty quickly, explaining, "Buddy was my age when he joined the band, but he seemed much younger. He was a cocky kid who was afraid of being in the wrong. If someone told him how to do something, he'd tell them off. He threw his drumsticks at sidemen who messed up during a number on stage and threw his fists at some offstage."[20]

Not everyone in the band appreciated his hard, pumping bass drum played on every beat in order to strengthen the rhythm and give the band some bottom. Jazz writers and critics definitely didn't understand it, and gave him mixed reviews. The editor of *Downbeat*, George T. Simon, wrote, "Buddy Rich is a brilliant percussionist, he has tremendous technique, he's steady and he gets a fine swing, but, like so many drummers who've grown up in the Gene Krupa era, he's cursed with the misconception that the drummer is supposed to do more than supply a good background. As a result, Buddy in his enthusiasm plays too much drums, consequently breaking up the general rhythmic effect."[21] In reality, the musicians in the band were probably in shock from the start, as no drummer had ever played the bass drum so strongly in tandem with brass section. Suddenly, this young upstart from Brooklyn came in and kicked them thoroughly with his sharp accentuations. They just couldn't believe their eyes and ears, and deep down, they probably liked it.

Once more, Buddy Rich was experiencing the tough life of touring in a worn-out bus, with a schedule now even more stressful, and more packed with dates than he experienced with Berigan. The entire spring of 1939 was loaded with recording dates, the "Melody and Madness" radio series, playing and travelling. For several weeks of one-nighters in a row, they ate, slept, changed their clothes and amused themselves in the same bus with 16 other people. The band played for around five hours per night, often on crowded, wobbly bandstands, smiling all the time, and in some cases, playing for audiences that were hearing them for the first time. The job description was this: Be young, be strong, be full of rhythm, love the freedom and independence of a good jazz musician, cope with this life and the hardships along the way to the next meal, the next audience, the next dressing room, and the next city.

Buddy Rich remembered the life vividly. "Sitting in the bus in a snowstorm and putting newspapers in the windows to keep warm was one of the realities. Freezing in the cold months and fighting off bugs and sweating your butt off in the summer while travelling from town to town are not the kind of experiences that make for a feeling of nostalgia. I must admit, though, the large, appreciative audiences made you forget a lot of the inconveniences. I remember many a night getting off the band bus, after coming God knows how far, in unbelievable weather, and there it was: another ballroom, club, or auditorium. But the people who patiently waited for us got the juices going in me. Because they were so devoted, enthusiastic, you wanted to be great for them. You wanted to live up to their expectations."[22]

In some bands, the members grew very close to each other and they became a tight group. This didn't happen in Shaw's band, and he wasn't sure why. "The men began to treat me more as an employer than as a friend of theirs," he said. "I soon noticed that they were beginning to behave strangely toward me. I had occasionally gone out to eat with one or another of them when we were out on the road. Now I found a curious reluctance on the part of any of them to be seen with me."[23] Shaw believed Buddy's presence didn't help. "When Buddy started, the older musicians didn't like that he got so much applause. Instead of being a group of guys that were happy striving towards a common goal, they were all split up into small groups, and I began to get further and further away from my musicians."[24]

There were other reasons for Shaw's isolation. In time, Shaw was eating dinner only with his manager, because every time he tried to dine out by himself, he was besieged by fans. He understood that being a celebrity was a full-time job. People thought he was different. Everyone thought they had the right to stare at him and ask for autographs. He was placed on a pedestal and couldn't accept it. The enormously successful band that Rich had joined was led by a bandleader who hated his own popularity. He couldn't get used to an existence that meant that he couldn't leave his dressing room after the evening performance and go to the bus without being escorted by the local police. Artie Shaw peered constantly through the door and found a whole street full of young fans.

Artie Shaw hated being famous.

Buddy Rich loved it.

CHAPTER 6

Drummer
Without
a
Band

The Rich family home in Brooklyn, NY.

On January 23, 1939, Artie Shaw's band recorded the classic version of the song "(The) Carioca." Shaw didn't like the result. He wanted to completely redo it and asked the arranger, Jerry Gray, to work on it. Gray heard Duke Ellington play it first. "He was one of my idols," Gray said. "When I was a kid and he had a band called the Jungle Band. When Artie gave me the piece and asked me for a new arrangement, I jazzed it up."[1] When Buddy Rich got his teeth into that jazz number, he felt he finally got to show his drive and power and the audience went wild wherever the band performed it. When they arrived at the Strand Theatre in New York, it was a madhouse. People jumped up on the stage, the police were called, everyone was shouting, and fights broke out. The Artie Shaw band now knew what utter hysteria was like. With both "Beguine" and "Carioca" in the in their repertoire, the band's popularity was gigantic.

Georgie Auld couldn't forget what it was like. "They were dancing on top of tables," said Auld. "It was unbelievable. Never saw anything like it. One kid jumped off the front balcony and broke a leg. Every time we went into the theme, 'Nightmare,' we saw about 30, 40 kids jumping up on the stage. Security would have to come up and put them out."[2] Shaw, of course, took it personally. "Conditions were nearly unbearable. I was earning more money than ever, and I guess I nearly went crazy to boot.'"

The Strand was followed by a longer booking at the Palomar Ballroom in Los Angeles between April 19 and June 28. The band looked forward to some relaxation on a long location date, but relaxation was not to be. For opening night, nearly 9,000 screaming fans had bought tickets. Then, while rehearsing the day before, Artie Shaw collapsed and had to be rushed to the hospital by ambulance. Shaw maintained, "It was a strep throat at the start. After I left New York and went to California, the thing was finally brought to a climax by repeated overdoses of sulfanilamide, at that time still a new drug. In any case, I did end up with granulocytopenia, and almost lost my life. In all, I was some six weeks recovering, after passing out cold right in the middle of an opening night before a record crowd at the Palomar Ballroom, at that time the largest in Los Angeles—in fact, one of the largest in the world."[3]

Now he began to have serious doubts. "Why am I putting myself through this if I hate it? Was this what I was longing to do from the beginning? Is this worth dying for at the age of 28?" On June 16, 1939, Chick Webb, only 30 years old, died after a long battle with tuberculosis. He was buried in his home city of Baltimore, Maryland, and thousands of mourners were at the grave. Ella Fitzgerald sang for her friend and there wasn't a dry eye anywhere. Webb's death didn't go unnoticed by either Artie Shaw or Buddy Rich. Both respected the little giant immensely, and in Shaw's case, his reflections about life intensified, and now he wanted out. His agent, Tommy Rockwell, told him he could quit, but only "if you can write your memoirs and have enough cash." Naturally, he didn't, though he was pulling in huge amounts of money at the time. When he received information that the band was managing fine without him, it gave him something to think about while lying in his hospital bed.

The members of the band tried to cheer him up. Jerry Gray and Tony Pastor told him that everything was running smoothly and that they were looking forward to when he was back again. Artie answered morosely, "You can keep it. You can have the orchestra." He didn't really mean it, and understood that the timing wasn't right to leave. He had a contract with RCA and a deal to play at the fantastic Hotel Pennsylvania in New York City. Though he decided to follow through on the bookings, he also made up his mind that he would give it all up—when he had made a million dollars. Buddy Rich, on the other hand, was having a great time at the Palomar Ballroom. After every gig he went along to the hippest clubs, met the most beautiful women, talked to all the most important jazz musicians, and enhanced his reputation everywhere. He dressed smartly, became even more sure of himself, and knew that he could play anything and with anyone. He trusted his ear and his fantastic technique.

When Artie Shaw returned to the fold, the band landed a contract to appear in a Hollywood film called *Dancing Co-Ed*. Since MGM had been so successful with musicals, it was logical that the studio brass wanted to see if one of their new stars, Lana Turner, fit into this genre. They knew she was a good dancer, well-demonstrated in a "B" picture she did for MGM called *These Glamour Girls*. Now she hoped to get a bigger role in what would be her twelfth film, agreeing to play a college girl who has the chance to appear in a film as a replacement for a big dance star who got pregnant. In the other roles were Richard Carlson, Ann

Rutherford, and Roscoe Karns, all second tier players.

Since the film was made mostly to promote Lana Turner, the MGM also wanted to cast the hottest swing band in the country, Artie Shaw and His Orchestra. Plugging in the super-hot Shaw would certainly give MGM's publicity campaign a boost. Artie Shaw was supposed to play himself, and sure, it may have sounded easy. The question is why Shaw agreed to this project at all when he was in as bad shape as he was. He was a true musical idealist who claimed he was completely uninterested in earning more money. Evidently, the $50,000 offer sounded good at the time, even if he had to be embarrassed in front of the camera.

Shaw had never had stage fright before, but on film, the demands on him were altogether different than just introducing some songs with a couple of words. The problems began the very first day of filming, said Shaw. "The director was totally insensitive and I resolutely refused to deliver a line of dialogue beginning with the words 'hepcats and alligators.' I don't talk that way. I've got a radio program sponsored by Old Gold that's heard by 20 or 30 million people a week."[4] The director, S. Sylvan Simon, told Shaw in no uncertain terms, "The audience you play for is infinitesimal compared with the one that's gonna see this movie."[5]

After a few days of takes, Artie Shaw regretted that he had gone along with the whole thing, and tried desperately to buy himself out of the contract. He was turned down, as MGM had filmed too many scenes already. Shaw reacted by being surly towards everything and everybody. Even the star, Lana Turner, felt the draft. According to Turner, "Artie was despised on the set because of his arrogance. He never missed a chance to complain that it was beneath him to appear in a Hollywood movie." From that moment, he never said his lines exactly as they stood in the script. He talked the way he normally did, but the Shaw dialogue that remained in the final edit consisted of mainly of lines like, "Yeah, but..." Artie Shaw told gossip columnist Hedda Hopper of the *Los Angeles Times*, "I'm pretty awful as an actor, but I know it. I know a little about music, nothing about acting."

He did manage to get through the long filming days, though he was dissatisfied with everything, sour every day, and abrupt with his fellow actors, especially Lana Turner. Things got to the point where she even demanded to have her dressing room on the other side of the film studio so she wouldn't have to spend time with the surly Shaw. Still, she was attracted to him somehow. In some strange way they were actually drawn to each other, and that didn't go unnoticed by another person who had also fallen in love with her in absolute secret: the man behind the drums.

June was hectic otherwise. Shaw had not only contracted the band for *Dancing Co-Ed*, but even two film shorts, *Class in Swing* and *Symphony of Swing*, as well. Vitaphone, the producer of these featurettes, hoped that the these movies would cash in on the swing wave that was sweeping over the country, and made sure to include lots of jitterbugging. In both films, a proud Buddy Rich can be seen playing drums in a style similar to Gene Krupa's. Whether that was conscious or not from Buddy's side is impossible to say, but in front of the camera, there was a wonderfully self-assured young man on view who performed just as energetically as Krupa.

On September 1, 1939, Germany invaded Poland. Some in the United States were monitoring the chain of events, believing that a world war was imminent and inevitable. Some were not. The day after that historic event, it was business as usual for Artie Shaw and His Orchestra, who were booked to play at the Crystal Beach Ballroom in Ontario, Canada. Shaw drove in his own car and got there before everyone else. The rest of the band was to travel by train, but the train was late, and the band went on stage several hours later than scheduled. This did not please the local promoter, Tick Smith, who was furious. He wanted to deduct $400 from the contracted fee of $2,000. Shaw refused to let the band go on stage until the problem was solved, noting, of course, that there were over 2,500 people standing in front of the stage waiting for the band to continue. When the band didn't take the stage, things got ugly; the audience went wild and started to break windows. Sensing a riot, Shaw and the band, ensconced on the second floor, refused to let the band members go down to the stage. A week later, on September 8, Artie was stopped in the street by a fan asking for his autograph. He took pen to paper, only to find himself holding a summons in his hand. Promoter

Tick Smith had sued him for $10,000.

Things were getting crazy. Buddy Rich was playing in a band whose leader not only suffered from severe depression, but also was getting dragged into legal battles. The downward spiral continued. In November, Shaw was a sued by his record company's boss, RCA's Eli Oberstein, for $30,000. Oberstein claimed he had given Shaw professional advice on several occasions between April 27 and the end of May, 1938. The situation with the band was problematic as well, as some of the members believed that Artie thought he was better than others. One of those who bore the brunt of his anger was Buddy Rich, who began to make one demand after the other. Shaw wouldn't have it, saying, "That'll have to change. No prima donnas in this band!"[6] It began to feel like Buddy's time with Shaw was coming to an end.

Through various accounts of this period via writings published at the time and interviews years later, a clear picture of this period in Buddy Rich's history was emerging: Buddy Rich was beginning to see himself as the big star in the band. His unique manner of playing with the band was working. He shouted, pushed the band with his bass drum, and always played fantastic drum solos which drove the audience completely wild. This made a great impression, even on Artie Shaw, but the leader was interested in something else musically. Similar to Goodman's differences with of Krupa, Shaw thought that Rich was too prominent, too loud, and not playing for the band. Shaw wanted to develop the ensemble and the music, not conform to public fancies or help make the drummer a star. Shaw was a true idealist and put the whole picture first. Buddy wanted to shine.

Shaw tried dealing with Buddy, saying, "You know, it's just not working. You don't play with the band anymore. It's getting to the point now where it's like a drum solo accompanied by the band. You're going to have to tone it down." Buddy answered, "Man, I don't know how I can do that." Shaw pointed out, "You've got to learn, Buddy. You know, loud doesn't mean good. Sometimes a tremendous amount of energy can be propelled out through a quiet, understated thing." The advice was sound, but Buddy paid no attention to it. In the end, Shaw's band was on the way to catastrophe; a group of 16 members cannot exist successfully if the bandleader himself is on the way into a depression and complaining about his musicians at the same time.

Back in New York, the group was contracted to play at the Café Rouge in the Pennsylvania Hotel starting on November 14, 1939. The increasingly difficult bandleader gave an interview to *New York Post* reporter Michael Mok a few days prior, which became an accurate and widely-quoted record of how Artie Shaw felt during that time. "I hate the music business!" he told Mok. "I'm not interested in giving the people what they want. I'm interesting in making music. Autograph hunters? The hell with them. They aren't listening; only gawking. My friends, my advisors tell me that I'm a damned fool. They shout at me: 'You can't do that, these people made you.' You want to know my answer? I tell them if I was made by a bunch of morons, that's just too bad."[7] The day after the interview in the *Post* was published, Old Gold withdrew its radio sponsorship.

When all this happened, Buddy Rich had just turned 22 years old and was playing drums in the most popular orchestra in America. Yes, the band's leader was on the verge of a nervous breakdown, and though Buddy said years later he began looking for other jobs at that time, the truth was that he hoped, just like the rest of the band, that Artie would pull himself together and follow through on the tour they had started. Buddy Rich was undoubtedly worried about the future of the band, as he definitely didn't have any alternative plans at that moment.

When the band opened at the Café Rouge, with the public in a frenzy as usual, everything seemed to be fine. Four days later, everything wasn't fine. Shaw's nerves were fraying, and by the time he hit the bandstand, he was on the verge of exploding. The band made it through the first set. After the break, the band went on stand again, but without the leader. Artie Shaw had disappeared. "He left during the first set," Buddy clearly remembered. "He didn't show up on the bandstand. 'Where's Artie?' everyone was thinking. The room was packed. I sat down behind the drums and I waited. We all started to look at each other. Everybody in the brass section was looking at me. I'm looking at them." Several of the band members said some years later that they believed the hot-tempered Rich had said something thoughtless to the bandleader, and that Shaw was sitting in his room and refusing to come down and continue with the show. This was not true. In his book, *The Trouble with Cinderella*, Shaw wrote, "At the stage I was then in, any little thing would have been sufficient; and so, because of a slight unpleasantness with some idiot on the floor in front of the band, who was evidently trying to impress his partner by using me as a focal point for these witticisms, I suddenly decided that I'd had it. Instead of kicking him in the teeth, I walked off the bandstand."

In the British documentary film *Quest for Perfection* he spoke of his condition at the time and how tired he was of everything, saying, "I had struggled so long with public expectations that everything felt like an endless uphill battle. The public never learns." Helen Forrest, the band's singer at the time, told a different story. As Forrest saw it, "When we finished the set, Tony got a message that Artie wanted to see us in his room upstairs in the hotel. We all went up and crowded in, and there was Artie, bags partly packed, clothes strewn around the room, propped up in bed."[8] To his saxophonist, Tony Pastor, Shaw supposedly said, "I'm leaving the band." "Are you sick?" asked Pastor. "No," replied Shaw. "Just sick of the business. And I am finished with it forever."

The band just stood and stared at him. They couldn't believe it. "You've got a million dollars worth of bookings," someone said. "I don't give a damn about that," replied Shaw. "They could sue." "Let them sue. If I don't have a band, what're they gonna sue me for?" It got worse. Shaw called his lawyer, Andrew Weinberger, who told him, "What the hell do you mean by leave? You have a contract. You can't just walk away." "Can't I? I just did," Shaw told him.

A few minutes after the band left the room, Weinberger and the band's agent, Tommy Rockwell, stormed in. Shaw found himself in the cross-fire between the two of them, with both shouting and threatening a lawsuit for breach of contract. Nothing helped. Shaw's mind was made up. Still, the fighting continued all night. There were prayers, and there were drinks. Rockwell even tried getting Shaw back down to earth again with the help of a woman who was an expert in Christian Science and astrology. That did it. He ignored everything and said he was leaving. Rockwell threatened to take him to court. "You're welcome to do that," an agitated Shaw told his agent. "I am going to plead that I'm crazy. What court wouldn't believe that when I left my own band right in the middle of a performance and paid no attention to all their successes. That's what a madman would do, isn't it?"

Shaw left the hotel, got into his car and drove away in no particular direction. Later in life he explained his actions. "People don't understand that when you lead a band and are quite successful you are a prince," as Shaw saw it. "Wherever you go, people know you. And people don't just know you, they worship you, or else they think you're a crazy devil and laugh at you. It is a hopeless existence. When that happened at Café Rouge I called one of my best friends, Judy Garland, and I asked her if I should go back again. She answered quickly, 'No, you better stay out of this! Stay away! They are after you.' I did what she said and took off for Mexico to have a rest."9

Tommy Dorsey was sitting in his kitchen in New York discussing his future with his manager, Bobby Burns. Though he was recording some hit records, had a good band, and was having big successes commercially, he was still worried. Burns tried to calm him down by suggesting that Dorsey look back. Hadn't his career progressed since the big fight and split with his brother Jimmy at the Glen Island Casino? Hadn't Burns supplied him with good arrangements and fine musicians from the bands of Berigan, Marsala, and Shaw? You couldn't do much more, he felt. And Tommy Dorsey agreed.

The infamous split between the Dorsey Brothers took place May 30, 1935 at the Glen Island Casino in Westchester County, New York. Tommy and the orchestra had been there, and he had conducted the band as usual, counting off a tempo that seemed completely wrong to Jimmy. "Either we play the song properly or not at all," Jimmy said grimly. Tommy, who could see a fight coming on, shouted back, "All right, then we won't play it at all!" Tommy left the stage in the middle of a refrain and went back home to New Jersey. From that day on, the two brothers were bitter enemies, and lay in wait plotting against each other's careers. Not long after the split, Tommy had a hit with "The Music Goes Round and Round," which sold nearly 70,000 records and was followed by two other best--sellers. The record shows that Tommy and Jimmy earned their successes.

Thomas Francis Dorsey was born in 1905 in Shenandoah, Pennsylvania, into a family of four siblings. His parents were Thomas and Theresa; Thomas was a miner and a self-taught musician. Thanks to his music, he was able to bring in a little welcome money for the family. At that time, the churches in every little town all had their own little brass bands and Thomas led five bands at the same time, earning him the nickname "Professor." Tommy and older brother Jimmy, one year older than Tommy, often played in their father's orchestras and performed waltzes, folk dances, and two steps, learning the profession from the bottom up. Jimmy had an extra job in his younger years with a blacksmith, but that didn't last long; one day the sledgehammer slipped in Jimmy's hand and hit the blacksmith instead of the horseshoe. With Jimmy's career as a blacksmith over, the young brothers instead parlayed their musical experience to start a band together, called Dorsey's Wild Canaries. The Canaries were staffed with friends, and soon hit the road.

Every rehearsal was a strain for one and all. As Tommy remembered it, "It was no secret that my brother and I had more fights than a pair of newlyweds. But we are so different we can't help it. Take that orchestra we had together. There were always cliques in it and he and I were on opposite sides. I am a guy that wants everything to go well and quickly, even if I have to fight for it. But Jimmy wasn't so worried about if things were profitable, as long as we played well."

When the brothers' second orchestra broke up at Glen Island Casino, many in the music world were just waiting for the race between them to start. Tommy, who was longing to show his brother how things should be done, quickly pulled together his own orchestra and opened at French Casino in New York. Jimmy started another band at the same time and opened at the Roseland Ballroom just a few blocks away. When Jimmy also had the nerve to call his band the Original Dorsey Band, Tommy was ready to explode with anger, but he did the intelligent thing. He re-booked his tour plans and decided to take the band on the road in an effort to win over younger college students. It worked.

By way of the touring and radio broadcasts, Tommy's music was discovered, and the bookings streamed in. Ever restless, Tommy still wasn't satisfied. Refusing to stagnate, he was bored with the rather sedate music that the band performed, and wanted to modernize in order to get a share of the audiences that were going crazy for swing. Even the ever-sedate Glenn Miller had taken note and added several up tempo numbers to his repertoire. Dorsey talked to manager Burns about considering a new drummer, specifically the young Buddy Rich he first heard with Joe Marsala, and later with Artie Shaw at the Hamid's Million Dollar Pier in the summer of 1939 in Atlantic City. Dorsey thought Rich was promising, though his guitarist and sometimes arranger Carmen Mastre didn't agree. "For a few years, I kept Rich out of the Dorsey band, unbeknownst to him," Mastren admitted. "Tommy had heard a lot about him. He said, 'There's this kid drummer, Buddy Rich, with Joe Marsala at the Hickory House. Everyone says he can really play!' I told Tommy, 'He's still a young kid. You ought to wait before you talk to him.'"[10]

It didn't matter. The conversation in Tommy Dorsey's kitchen resulted in the phone ringing at Buddy Rich's home, with Bobby Burns on the other end. He said that Dorsey had heard him play and wanted to have him in his band. Buddy answered abruptly that he wasn't interested in playing in a band that was so strongly connected to Dixieland and ballads, and turned down the offer, though it sure looked like he was a drummer in search of a band at that point. After Artie Shaw's sudden departure, Georgie Auld tried carrying on as leader of Shaw's group, but that didn't appeal to Buddy, despite his friendship with Auld. Buddy had made his mind up, saying, "After Artie split for Mexico, I decided to relax for a while before getting back to work. The Shaw band continued without Artie up front. But I wasn't terribly interested in being a part of that."[11]

However it ended, Buddy Rich understood that he had learned a lot from playing with Shaw. Buddy concluded that "the Shaw band was a hell of an experience. I think Artie was a very dedicated guy. He taught me a lot about music, behavior on the stand, things in general. I liked what we did... the good tunes, the show music, even the pop tunes. The band always sounded good. Even the ballads had a pulse." In later interviews, his words about Shaw were not so kind (he called Shaw, among other things, "a complete idiot" when it came to Shaw's refusal to sign autographs for fans). In retrospect, he became dissatisfied with the music as well, saying, "He was always very difficult to work for. I probably would have left anyway even if he hadn't walked out. The music became boring. If you wanted to see him, you had to go through a manager. It all depended on what kind of mood he was in if he would see you or not."[12]

Buddy Rich decided to leave the Shaw band. He knew he had made a name for himself and that people were talking about Jo Jones, Sid Catlett, George Wettling, Dave Tough, Gene Krupa, *and* about Buddy Rich. He didn't want to get stressed about his next move, and chose to spend time with his family in Brooklyn. He enjoyed himself there. He slept in, ate his favorite food at Nathan's, one of the great places in Brooklyn, and just took it easy. The anxiety he had experienced a few months earlier had disappeared. "It seemed to me it was time for me to think about a few things," Buddy recalled. "I began to realize where I stood in the music business. It was clear that I had value to bandleaders."

It was during this time that the phone rang and Burns passed on the message about Dorsey's interest in having him in his band. Tommy, sitting in his kitchen, was furious with Buddy Rich. How did that young drummer dare refuse his offer? No other jazz musician in the whole country would refuse his offer! But maybe that just made him certain that it was this audacious young kid was just what he needed. He told Bobby Burns to offer him another contract. This time, he offered Rich fantastic money. Dorsey knew very well that Buddy had got about $60 a week with Marsala, and he had also a good idea of what Berigan and Shaw paid their musicians. Soon Rich received an offer of a mind-boggling $750 a week. Along with the offer, Burns also sent along a plane ticket to Chicago so that Buddy would be able to come and listen to the band when they performed at the Palmer House. This was big money. Buddy accepted and answered, "I'm prepared to give the band a chance."

The first meeting between Tommy Dorsey and Buddy didn't make history. Buddy flew to Chicago with his sister Marge and her husband, Carl Ritchie. By pure coincidence, Marge had received an offer to join a dance act there. They checked into the Croydon Hotel and Buddy went over to meet Dorsey and the boys in the band. It was an event that Buddy recalled clearly. "God, I remember that first day in Chicago so vividly," he said. "Tommy's manager, Bobby Burns meets me, and he says, 'You're going to love the band, we're making all the right changes, we're getting new blood, new life. Meet me downstairs in the Empire Room, we'll have dinner.' This is in the Palmer House. Okay, fine; went downstairs. Place was packed. People were dancing, everything. Band was terrible. I mean, it was a nondescript band for Tommy's playing. It was a dance band, because it played all those foxtrots. It had no individual sound. I heard about two or three tunes, I got up and left. Bobby Burns says, 'Where are you going? What's the matter?' I said, 'I can't play with a band like that. Are you kidding?' He says, 'Well, look, we're rehearsing tonight, we'd like you to play so you can get the feel of the band.' Okay, so I stayed. Stayed for about two or three tunes at the rehearsal, and I said, 'I'll see you.' I walked out."[13]

Out on Dearborn Street he ran into Marge and Carl again, and his refusal to join Dorsey made their jaws drop. "Dorsey doesn't play my kind of music," he told them. "I'm flying back to New York."[14] He had already phoned and told his dad. Everyone in Buddy's family thought he had absolutely lost his mind, telling him, "You're 22 years old, and you are telling Tommy Dorsey what kind of music to play?" Buddy answered as only he could: "That's right. I told him what to play and how to play it."

Buddy Rich commanded tremendous technical facility and from there used this gift to be one of the most imaginative musicians through the drum set of his time.

Bill Cobham

What Buddy said is so important about developing a touch on that instrument. Yeah, you got strings, you got brass, and you got woodwinds. A long time ago, we were sort of in the background. Then, of course, with the advent of Gene and Buddy and players like that, who brought the drums to the foreground, everything changed. Today it's very important to develop a touch. Because the cymbal is an instrument, the snare is a separate instrument, as is a tom-tom, a bass drum... When you're able to play 'em all, you got your own choir. Actually, a drummer has his own symphony you got soprano, alto, tenor and bass, you know. The first thing you listen for is a sound and what the guy is playing.

Louie Bellson

He was more than just a natural, he was a phenomenal technician, too. He knew the instrument inside and out. He took some really hip solos. I grew up watching him develop "Quiet Please." He was one of the guys who helped bring percussion out to the front. You know the old jokes: "Who's in the band? Three musicians and a drummer." Some guys really believed that. We had to endure a lot of that crap. So Buddy's talent, and that of Chick Webb, Gene Krupa, and a few others turned that around. It's much more than just keeping time for everybody.

Max Roach

(Interviewed during the *Burning for Buddy* recording sessions.)

CHAPTER 7

Tommy Dorsey and His Orchestra

One of the first publicity shots of Buddy after joining Tommy Dorsey, circa early 1940s.

For the moment, Buddy Rich had decided to forego what some saw as a coveted berth in the Dorsey band. Buddy and company were in the hotel, preparing to go back home, when the phone rang. Given that Tommy Dorsey was a bandleader who almost always got what he wanted, he wasn't through with Buddy Rich yet. It was Dorsey himself on the other end of the line, telling Buddy, "Listen now, I'm going to get Sy Oliver in to write our new arrangements. This will change the style of the whole band. Come on back." Buddy Rich knew very well who Sy Oliver was: a very highly respected arranger who had worked for Jimmie Lunceford and who had succeeded in revamping and energizing that band. Dorsey said that he was talking to Oliver about coming to his band.

This was also a turning point for Oliver, who explained, "Dorsey called me one afternoon about five o'clock and said, 'Buddy Rich has been hired. He's arriving in Chicago tomorrow. Can you do a number for him that we can rehearse tomorrow?' I said, 'Tommy, it's five o'clock in the afternoon. I'm in New York.' He said, 'You can do it!' So I wrote the damn number on the plane. It was called 'Quiet Please.' I landed in Chicago. Tommy picked me up and we went to the Palmer House. The piece was copied, rehearsed by the band, and Buddy played it on the job that night."[1]

Dorsey took a chance—he told Buddy he had Oliver aboard when he really didn't—but the gambit worked. Buddy Rich tried out with the band at the Palmer House. He liked what he heard, but at the moment, Dorsey wanted to talk about singers. "Sy says he heard a fantastic singer at the Sherman Hotel," said Dorsey. "I think I'll hire him too."[2] Buddy Rich wasn't a bit interested in which singer Dorsey had in mind. Buddy believed that singers generally just got in the way. But the prospect of Sy Oliver's arrangements, the offer of high wages, and the promise of featured billing all combined to clinch the deal for Buddy Rich. He said yes, and on November 24, 1939, he played on his first recording with Tommy Dorsey and His Orchestra. Only ten days after his last performance with Artie Shaw at Café Rouge in Pennsylvania, Buddy found himself in Chicago to record four numbers with Shaw's biggest competitor (aside from Goodman): "Losers Weepers," "Faithful to You," "Darn that Dream," and "Careless."

If Buddy Rich thought that the discipline with Artie Shaw was tough, he would soon discover that it was ten times worse with Dorsey, who led his orchestra like a drill sergeant. His militant management style combined with periodical alcoholic excesses made him extremely difficult to work with. He was known in the industry as a sly and calculating person who ran his orchestras with an iron hand. If a band member couldn't stand the lengthy rehearsals, Dorsey's short temper and his hard-as-nails manner of discipline, there was no point complaining. Quitting the band was the only option, but that sometimes wasn't easy, either. When bassist Billy Cronk tried to leave the band, he nearly got into serious trouble. Said Cronk, "I quit the band once and he got so mad at me he chased me three blocks, grabbed me, and put me up against a wall. He was much bigger than me, and said, 'Nobody quits the band, I fire them!' I took back my notice, and he threatened to fire me!"[3]

On December 31, 1939, Buddy Rich played his first live performance with Dorsey, also at the Palmer House. Unfortunately, the bandleader was sick that evening, so the orchestra was led by the 26-year-old guitarist, Carmen Mastren—the same Carmen Mastren who had advised Dorsey against hiring Buddy in the first place. Even Gene Krupa was in the audience. Krupa later explained to "Voice of America" radio host Willis Conover why he hadn't yet seen Buddy play. "The first time I heard Buddy play was in 1939 at the Palmer House in Chicago, when he had joined Tommy Dorsey's orchestra, and the only reason that I hadn't heard or seen him earlier was that I was terrified by all the rumors about him."[4] Gene Krupa, the very person who had paved the way for drummers to get the respect and the position they deserved on the stage, was now being challenged by a rhythmic monster that everyone was starting to talk about. The performance with Dorsey's orchestra went well for all. Buddy loved playing Sy Oliver's cheeky, uptempo jazz numbers. At the same time, he was a little apprehensive and curious about the singer who Dorsey saw at the Sherman Hotel.

Like so many other musicians of the time, trumpeter Harry James had wandered the long road. He had begun playing at the age of five, when he first learned to read music—and he could read anything. As a teenager, he ended up in Ben Pollack's band, and via several other paths in jazz he ended up with Benny Goodman in 1937. A year later, James was a big part of the famous performance at Carnegie Hall. In January, 1939, he left Goodman to start his own band. In his attempts to find some star artists, he asked Buddy Rich if he wanted to join up, but since Buddy had just left Berigan and received a good offer from Artie Shaw, he had turned him down—to Harry's great disappointment. Shaw had warned him off hiring Rich, and then taken him for himself instead. As the gentleman and veteran James was, he knew the rules of the game. In the end he managed to get a band together, and Harry James and His Orchestra played its first date in Philadelphia. After that, James went on tour and even got to meet Louis Armstrong in a so called Battle of Bands. Harry didn't realize until just before they went on stage that the other band was Armstrong's. If he had been nervous going on stage with Goodman at Carnegie Hall, this was ten times worse.

James remembered the night this way: "I was pretty nervous anyway. It took me an hour even to decide to play. I just sat there and listened, y'know. And Louis was just great that night, but it was quite an experience."[5] It went well, and Louis congratulated him afterwards on having a good band. But despite having some really good numbers in his book (like "Two O'Clock Jump," something of a copy of Basie's "One O'Clock Jump"), James hadn't yet had a hit. This worried him. In the summer of 1939, the competition between the big bands was fierce. It went extremely well for Shaw, Goodman, and Dorsey, but not for James, who had to lower fees to $350 an evening to get work. It was longer and longer between gigs. He decided to look for a male vocalist, and after having heard one that he liked on the radio, he looked him up in a club in New Jersey. But the owner of the Rustic Tavern in Englewood Cliffs didn't understand who he meant at first. "We haven't any singer here, but we have a master of ceremonies who sings a little," said the owner. Harry hung around to check him out anyway, and signed him up afterwards. His name was Frank Sinatra.

Things began to happen, albeit slowly at first. With Sinatra as vocalist, the band recorded "All or Nothing at All," which sold decently as a James title. Sinatra was billed in small letters below the James band on the original record label. When this recording was reissued by Columbia Records in 1943, it sold over 100,000 copies. Still, it was clear that James had made a smart move by hiring Sinatra. Female fans were beginning to take note of the skinny kid from Hoboken, and the band's fortunes began to improve—but not by much. Fees for the band were still lousy, and in December, James fell to twelfth place on the *Downbeat* trumpet poll.

At the end of the year, Sinatra was contacted by Dorsey, who had heard him sing with James at the Sherman Hotel. He made him an offer of $125 a week to sing with his band. Sinatra's wife, Nancy, was pregnant, and the offer was hard to refuse. Sinatra's problem was how to tell James he was leaving. James supported Sinatra from the start, and they had grown close over the past six months—and Sinatra still had a half a year left on his contract. At Chicago Theatre he worked up his courage, telling James, "Harry, it would have been easier for me to slash my wrists than say what I want to say now."[6] He told him about Dorsey's offer and what it meant to him. When Harry James had finished listening, he took Sinatra's contract, ripped it in half, shook Sinatra's hand and wished him the best of luck. He showed no sign of being angry, and seemed just to accept the situation as it was. Sinatra would remember this for the rest of his life. Before Sinatra could leave, Harry James stopped him in the door and said, "Well, if we don't do any better in the next few months or so, try to get me on, too."[7]

Frank Sinatra had his last performance with Harry James on January 25, 1940, in Buffalo and was replaced by Dick Haymes. Sinatra said later in life that when the James bus drove away, a tear ran down his cheek and he instinctively wanted to run after it. The rest of his life he called Harry "Boss," and joked about coming back to fulfill his contract. Two weeks after Buddy Rich joined up with Dorsey, the band's singer, Jack Leonard, was replaced by Frank Sinatra. Leonard was a good singer and a popular attraction in the band, having recorded more than 200 songs with Dorsey—with a bunch of them becoming hits, including "Marie." Officially, Leonard quit because he had enlisted, but this was not the case. As one story goes, Dorsey forced the band to rehearse without giving them a chance to have anything to eat for a long time. A starving Leonard sneaked out to get himself a sandwich, and was found out by Dorsey, who dressed him down. There was also talk about a salary dispute, as well as rumors that Leonard had plans to leave the band and work as a single, like Bing Crosby. No matter. Jack Leonard was out and became nothing more than a historical footnote. Frank Sinatra was in.

Buddy remembers very well how Dorsey introduced his drummer to Sinatra, saying, "I want you to meet another pain in the ass."[8] On February 1, 1940, Rich and Sinatra made their first recording with the new ensemble, and a month later they opened at the Paramount Theater. After a few introductory numbers, Dorsey went up to the microphone and announced, "And now ladies and gentlemen, our vocalist, Frank Sinatra." Suddenly, he stopped the intro to the number, and in front of an astonished audience, turned to Frank who was waiting in the wings, and shouted so loudly that the whole band heard him yell, "Go back there and comb your god damn hair!" Morris Diamond, assistant to the manager, Bobby Burns, was standing in the wings and was met by a rather embarrassed Sinatra rushing out, shouting, "Quick! Give me a comb!"[9] The band's former singer, Jack Leonard, was also in the audience, and when he saw what was happening, he smiled. Leonard had gone to the show with his friends to hopefully see the new singer make a fool of himself. But as soon as Sinatra began to sing, he and his friends slid further and further down in their seats. According to Sinatra, "I missed a little in a couple of songs, but the audience gave us a positive response. The whole band treated me quite indifferently. They loved Jack, and I think they said to themselves, 'Okay, we'll just see what he can do.'"[10]

The truth was that Sinatra was unbelievably good, as was the audience response to his fantastic voice and charm. Tony Bennett was one of those in the Paramount audience, and remembered it years later. "I went to see Frank Sinatra at the Paramount," Bennett remembered. "Tommy Dorsey was like the Wizard of Oz. He'd have Jo Stafford singing, Ziggy Elman on trumpet, and Buddy Rich on drums, all for the admission price of 65 cents. Every one of them would stop the show cold, but when Sinatra hit the stage, he topped them all. No one could follow him. The audience's reaction was pandemonium. You couldn't get near the Paramount when he was there."[11]

Buddy Rich was just as good, in several respects. At the Paramount, the bands on the bill also had to cut shows. In this case, one of the attractions was a knife throwing act from Europe. The number was set up with the knife thrower placing his wife on a spinning wheel. With appropriate, written accompaniment from the orchestra adding to the act's sense of impending dread, the thrower would toss knives at his spinning wife, barely missing her each time. It was of utmost importance that everything was synchronized musically. If the knife thrower missed, the show (and probably everything else) was over. When the knife thrower found out that the drummer in the band couldn't read music, he was horrified and wanted to replace Rich immediately. If the drummer couldn't read the chart correctly, his wife would be in mortal danger, he said. Tommy Dorsey calmed the man down, Buddy played the charts perfectly, and afterwards, the knife thrower ran up to Buddy, hugged him, and praised him to the skies.

Then it was time to hit the road. Frank Sinatra got on the bus and was looking for a seat. There was only one seat free, and it was beside Buddy—a loner like Sinatra. He sat down beside Buddy and they began to chat. With Dorsey and many of the traveling big bands, it was the custom that once a person sat in a particular seat on the bus, it belonged to that person forever. It was important to make the right choice from the beginning. "I like the way you sing," said Buddy. The ice was broken. They talked about where they had played, their childhoods, and about life in general. They bonded and decided to also share a room during the tour. Later, Sinatra asked some other band members why the seat beside Buddy had been free. Dorsey's description of Buddy seemed to be shared by the others in the band: "Because he's a pain in the ass. Nobody wants to sit with him!"[12]

More and more, old musician friends from all the bands Buddy Rich had played in earlier joined Dorsey. Bassist Sid Weiss came from Shaw's band, as did trombonist George Aurus and trumpeter Chuck Peterson. Then his old boss Bunny Berigan showed up on the band, having disbanded his own ensemble. Berigan wasn't in the best of health and still had a serious alcohol problem, but Dorsey had a soft spot for the trumpeter and really wanted to help him. With all these top musicians in the orchestra—and Sy Oliver as the arranger— things couldn't be better, and apparently, nothing could go wrong. But putting two similar, career-focused young men with the massive ambitions and large egos in the same orchestra could have unforeseen consequences. Dorsey would soon become aware of this.

The problems began after their first engagement at the Lyric Theatre in Indianapolis, Indiana, on February 2, 1940. Before the performance, Jack Egan, Dorsey's press agent, was told to enlarge the poster with Sinatra's picture on it so that the public would understand that Sinatra was the band's new singer. "After the first show in Indianapolis, Dorsey called me and asked how long it would take to have another blowup photo made," Egan explained. "I said I could possibly get it done overnight. He said 'Have one made of Buddy. Get one right away!' It seems that when Buddy saw Frank's picture in the lobby of the theater or on the outside, he wanted the same treatment."[13]

Jack Egan did as he was told and put up posters around the city with Sinatra's name in big letters at the top. This was quite unusual for the time, as few bandleaders had billed singers so prominently. While a great marketing tool, it would have repercussions, especially with the band's angry drummer. It would get worse. At a gig at the Meadowbrook Ballroom in Cedar Grove, New Jersey, three weeks later, Dorsey either happened—or decided—to have Sinatra's name larger than Buddy's on posters. Rich was furious, and told Dorsey how angry he was, but Dorsey tried to ignore him. Rich answered by speeding up the tempo in Sinatra's ballads and playing louder. The friendship between Rich and Sinatra was in jeopardy, and the irritation between them grew while the tour continued. The other band members couldn't do anything but wait for the inevitable confrontation.

At the same time that Buddy's irritation with Sinatra and Dorsey was growing, something happened after the premiere of the film Buddy had made with Shaw. The reviews of *Dancing Co-Ed* in *The New York Times* were lukewarm. They noted Artie Shaw's total disinterest in playing the role of himself, and wrote, "The idea is that Miss Turner is to win the coveted role, and though Mr. Carlson experiences a sense of ethical outrage when he discovers the plot, you know what love and a girl like Lana can do to a man's ethics. Leon Errol, Roscoe Karns, and Artie Shaw's orchestra work manfully to salvage their portion of the footage, but it's no use. Even old Artie seems to be unable to infuse a little life into the party."[14] Buddy Rich is not mentioned by name in the reviews, though he had a few good scenes and played with plenty of energy, though they were nothing like the memorable visual images of Gene Krupa that had appeared on the movie screen in the late 1930s.

Despite the lousy write-ups, Artie Shaw did glean some benefits from the film. A womanizer, Shaw called many of the actresses in the film to ask them out on dates. After being turned down by a few others, he finally decided to try his luck with the star of the film, Lana Turner. After some hesitation, she agreed to go on a date with him, despite his cool treatment during the filming. His words, like those of a swing-era Casanova, touched the highly regarded film star. "I'm sick and tired of these phony Hollywood females," was Shaw's opener. "What I want is a girl who could be happy with me alone." Lana answered, "That's exactly what I want: a man who has the brains to be satisfied with me only."[15] Artie Shaw proposed and she said yes. On February 13, 1940, they more or less ran away to Las Vegas and got married, much to Buddy Rich's chagrin. Perhaps Buddy's frustration is what led him to start dating a girl named Ruth Cosgrove. It didn't last long; they broke up and she later married comedian Milton Berle.

In March 1940, Benny Goodman's alto saxophonist Hymie Schertzer joined Dorsey's orchestra. He was rather surprised by the bitterness between Rich and Sinatra, noting that their nastiness towards each other affected the whole band. It was a very different first rehearsal for him, and Schertzer wasn't used to this type of thing, saying, "I had spent all that time with Krupa and those last few weeks when Dave Tough was breaking in with Goodman. I knew Tommy as a ballad player. The night I joined him, naturally the first thing we played was his theme, then immediately went into a loud uptempo number. Buddy Rich was the drummer, and he swung. A ballad was the next piece in the set. As we began to play I couldn't hear any drums. I looked around and there was Buddy sitting behind us with his arms folded across his chest. 'What about some rhythm, Buddy?' I asked. He looked at me as though I was nuts. 'Sorry, Hymie, I don't play ballads, only swing numbers.'"[16]

Wherever the band appeared, Tommy Dorsey and His Orchestra drew crowds of female fans who absolutely adored Sinatra. At every performance they stood at the front and swooned for the singer with the beautiful blue eyes and the divine, sentimental voice. Tommy Dorsey loved it all. "It was wonderful with all that sighing and moaning, but we also did every thing we could to make it popular," Dorsey admitted. "When Frank sang a song in some theater, he sometimes did some little trick with his voice so that the youngsters closest to the front drew deep drawn sighs. Well, I noticed that and said to the orchestra that as soon as a girl drew one of those sighs, the band should stop playing and sigh right back. This stimulated the audience to sigh even more."[17] Buddy wasn't happy about this. In spite of his fantastic solos, he felt he just wasn't getting the attention that Sinatra got, and Dorsey didn't know whether to laugh or cry at the situation. The ordinarily tough bandleader never took the two aside to talk things through. He made light of the matter, saying to the band, "This fight between my two prima donnas is really just fun!"

Sinatra and Rich continued to share a room, and to get on each other's nerves. Rich wanted peace and quiet in the room since he exhausted himself during every show, and he was annoyed by Frank's habit of cutting his toenails in bed. "Frank's only drawback as a roommate, as far as I was concerned, was the singer's penchant for cutting his toenails in bed. That damn clipper used to drive me nuts. Two in the morning. I'm trying to sleep. Frank's clipping away."[18] Sinatra was asked about this later in life, but he remembered nothing about that particular issue. His way of describing their relationship was slightly different, but not by much. "I was a reader," Sinatra explained. "I'd put the bed light on and read, and I'd hear the rustling, the moving around in the other bed, the shaking from one side to another, and I'd say, 'What's the matter, warm or something?' And he'd say, 'No, the goddamn light. Don't you ever sleep?' That went on for a while, but we had a wonderful time together for many, many months."[19]

The orchestra's successes, combined with a bandleader who at times drank too much, kept daily tour life interesting, on and off the bandstand. Jo Stafford liked Buddy. "I was one of the few people who got along with Buddy Rich," Stafford remembered. "He let me use his drums to make my bed. I remember his big bass drum. I'd put my feet up on that, with stuff over it, coats and things. I had a whole bedroom set up back there in the bus with Buddy's drums! The drums would fill up the aisle... part of me would be on this side of the aisle. Beer bottles rolled up and down the aisle."[20]   Buddy Rich remembered, "One time at a rehearsal, Dorsey couldn't find the harpist. He looked everywhere for her and his temper was up. Finally I told him to check the instrument case. There she was, inside, all curled up, sound asleep, drunk."[21]

Life on the big band road wasn't all fun and games. Dorsey was still a dictator and demanded complete obedience. One of those who found out what happened if you came too late to a rehearsal was Joe Bushkin."Tommy had strict rules about punctuality and exacted fines from anyone he caught arriving late for work," said the pianist. "Once, I had to pay up. The fine was that you had to buy booze for the whole band, which cost a lot of bread. Now, Buddy Rich was late for the first set nearly every night, but Tommy wasn't there and nobody ever finked on him. As it happened, I was always on time, except but twice. Once I was terribly late and that was when I had a fight with Buddy. When I appeared Tommy stopped the band and said, 'You used to play with us.'"[22] Bushkin learned his lesson and came on time after that.

On May 20, 1940, Tommy Dorsey recorded a song that would become one of his biggest hits. It was called "I'll Never Smile Again," and was once again a slow romantic number. This aroused conflicting feelings in Buddy Rich. Sure, it was a hit that everyone wanted to hear, and would bring in crowds. He also remembered the way Dorsey had talked him into joining the band with the promises of uptempo songs, swing, solos, and Sy Oliver charts with himself featured. Then along came that damned Sinatra with his romantic ballads.

The day after the recording session, the band began an eight-week stay at the Astor Roof atop the Astor Hotel in New York City. This is where the hostility between Buddy and Sinatra began to grow out of proportion. The whole thing began when Buddy told a young girl that she should go up to Sinatra and ask for an autograph. She stood there waiting until the performance was over, and then went up to Frank with her friends. He signed his name and mumbled something, then shouted, "Oh, thank you so much, now if I could only get three more from you I could exchange them for one of Bob Eberle's!" Behind Sinatra's back, Buddy Rich sat laughing. He thought the singer needed to be taken down a notch or two since he had begun treating the musicians like second class citizens after the success with "I'll Never Smile Again."[23]

The newspaper reviews of the Astor opening were by and large noncommittal, with *The New York Times* writing, "Buddy Rich, unmercifully trashing the skins, and in the meantime punctuating his efforts with some expert gum chewing; Frank Sinatra, singing the sentimental tunes." A few evenings later, everything came to a climax at the Astor. Exactly what happened has been described on many occasions, but the actual origin of the incident has only been explained by Buddy once, when Buddy was a guest on the television program of talk show host Mike Douglas. There he said, "Frank said some really humiliating things to one of the band's saxophonists who I felt didn't deserve it. I stood up for the guy and told him to stop."[24] Jo Stafford was sitting in her dressing room writing a letter home when Frank and Buddy came off the stage, completely furious with each other. She remembered, "They were shouting at each other, I don't know why. I wasn't listening so closely. Everyone heard when Rich shouted at Sinatra, 'You damned illegal immigrant!'"[25]. Then Frank took a large glass pitcher full of ice and threw it at Buddy. "He threw that mixer at me," Buddy recalled. "I just barely managed to get out of the way, and seconds later I was on top of him and hurt him. That was the end of the fight."[26]

Buddy exaggerated the whole incident slightly; the blows they exchanged were hardly knockout punches. Several of the band members were able to intervene and managed to hold them apart before the fight got out of hand. Some of those on the scene, however, maintained that if that pitcher had hit Rich it could have had serious consequences. Tommy Dorsey had to step in, and chose to send Sinatra home to cool off. Dorsey said, "I can manage without a singer tonight, but I need a drummer."[27] Sinatra lost face that night and went home, still very angry.No one in the band, not least Tommy Dorsey himself, had really understood how bad relations between Buddy Rich and Frank Sinatra were.

Everyone thought that the incident at the Astor Roof Hotel was forgotten by both of them, since they continued to share a room the rest of the tour, but this wasn't true. Relations between the two went from bad to worse, and through the following months they continued to harp at each other. In September, *Downbeat* magazine blared with the headline, "Buddy Rich Gets Face Bashed In," and reported that "his face looked like it had been hit with a shovel when he continued to play with Dorsey at the Astor Hotel. Nobody knows exactly what happened, but he must have met up with someone who was better with his fists than he was. His band members say that Buddy was asking for it!"[28] What actually happened was that Buddy went to nearby Child's restaurant after the first set of the evening, and that's where he got into an altercation. On the way back to the Astor, Buddy remembered, "Someone tapped on my shoulder and said 'Hey, Buddy Rich,' and very stupidly I turned around and a fist came at me and caught me right between the eyes. I fell down, the cat got on top of me and pinned my arms on my sides like this, and just beat the hell out of me for a minute. He really knocked me crazy. I went back to the hotel, and they stitched me up for the set that started at 10 p.m."[29] Buddy thought first that it was just a robbery, but it seemed too planned. He didn't want to get the police involved, as he had a hunch about who was behind the attack. In the end, he decided to keep quiet, keep a stiff upper lip and let it be.

Unlike Artie Shaw, Tommy Dorsey understood that upward trajectory in the band business meant getting into motion pictures. It wasn't enough to have high-paying performances and records that sold well. The audience was drawn to the movies, and in order to effectively compete, the Dorsey band had to be seen on the big screen. Though Shaw had hated every minute of speaking lines on film, Dorsey had no problem playing himself. In October, 1940, the band began filming *Las Vegas Nights*, a Paramount "B" picture in every respect, but one that guaranteed billing for Tommy Dorsey and His Orchestra. In the lead roles were Constance Moore, Virginia Dale, Bert Wheeler, and Phil Regan, and the premier was planned for March the following year.

At the same time, Dorsey's orchestra was contracted to play at the Hollywood Palladium in California for five weeks, from October 31 until December 11. Here, Buddy Rich met actress and comedienne Martha Raye, a year older than he. It wasn't long before the newspapers paired them together publicly. Raye was an entertaining, skilled and talented woman, whose underrated vocal talents influenced the likes of Anita O'Day, among others. She had just been in the movie *The Boys from*

Syracuse, and was a Paramount contract player. *Boys* was her 18th film since her big-screen debut six years earlier, and most of her roles had been comical, co-starring with the biggest names of the period, including Al Jolson, Bing Crosby, Bob Hope, and Charlie Chaplin. Buddy was attracted to Raye, the woman nicknamed "The Big Mouth," and they got on famously, having numerous things in common, including a vaudeville upbringing, and the fact that Raye had been a band singer, appearing onscreen singing with Benny Goodman in "The Big Broadcast of 1937," with Gene Krupa behind the drums. This made quite an impression on the young Buddy.

The real nature of the relationship remains a question, though different sources indicate that the romance was short and intense. Author Doug Meriwether indicated that they were just friends and nothing more. This seems credible, in that Raye was already married to the successful composer and conductor David Rose when she met Buddy. In the end, Rose left Raye for Judy Garland and Buddy and Martha Raye broke up. Evidently, Buddy compared every new girlfriend with Lana.

In the daytime hours, Dorsey's men filmed scenes for *Las Vegas Nights*, where Frank Sinatra performed the hit "I'll Never Smile Again," which, of course, drove the bobbysoxers crazy. In the typical Spike Jones number, "The Trombone Man is the Best Man in the Band," Rich was featured in an energetic, impressive final drum solo. The pay for the band's work in the film, however, was nothing to cheer about. As clarinetist Johnny Mince remembered it, "We got paid as extras, me, Sinatra, the Pied Pipers, and Buddy Rich, too. I think I remember it was $15 a day. Soon after we got to the studio, most of us were lying sleeping in a corner somewhere. There wasn't much that happened on a filming day."[30] The movie premiered on March 11, 1941, and the reviewers weren't kind. Bosley Crowther in *The New York Times* wrote, "The movie is so dull and awful that we refuse to name the people who appear in it. But they neither contribute or gleam to any greater extent so why should they be let off? Bert Wheeler shouts and shows off in the most peculiar way. Constance Moore, Lillian Cornell, and Virginia Dale do really nothing at all. They pose and stand in front of each other. Phil Regan wears cowboy boots and rattles off lines and Mister Dorsey plays his trombone and waves his limp hand."[31]

In the evenings, the band performed at Hollywood Palladium. As if there wasn't enough action happening, Bing Crosby contacted Dorsey asking for his help with yet a different film. Crosby and Bob Hope were filming a sequel to their hit movie *Road to Singapore*, titled *Road to Zanzibar*. Crosby wanted Dorsey's help with the music. Dorsey first turned down the offer, but then was convinced to change his mind, presumably because one did not say "no" to Bing Crosby at that time. In the end, according to the movie archives, the whole orchestra only appeared on the opening track, but when listening through the soundtrack, it is very probable that it was Buddy Rich who played the jungle drums in another scene. Despite what may have been left on the cutting room floor, to move a whole orchestra for one musical number less than two minutes long just goes to show the kind of money that Paramount was prepared to spend when they wanted to achieve the best result. Paramount wanted the hottest band to participate in the movie and Dorsey got the band's name exposed on film screens nationally once again.

Ever the astute businessman, Dorsey was smart enough to negotiate a better contract with the most prestigious motion picture studio of all, at least when it came to musicals, MGM. He demanded guarantees and big money. His reasoning was understandable. He was in demand, he understood that Sinatra was going to want more money, he knew that Jo Stafford might possibly leave the band to get married, and he was wondering how long he could keep Buddy Rich, an attention-getter wherever the band appeared.

In October, Buddy and Dorsey again had a disagreement about money. At two in the morning the night before opening, Rich telephoned band manager Bob Burns and said, "Hey, I just broke my arm!" After letting Burns stew for a while, he said, "Well, I didn't this time, but if those details about billing and money aren't taken care of by tomorrow night, I'm certainly going to break it."[32] Agreement again was reached, and Burns felt compelled to raise the subject with Dorsey and go along with his demands. Buddy Rich was now making $1,000 a week. For Buddy, it was never enough: Everything he earned, he spent just as quickly, and he paid no attention to paying income tax. Morris Diamond, Bobby Burns' assistant, put the money situation into perspective, when he explained, "Hey, Buddy was making that kind of money, and I was making $16 a week—it wasn't a living wage—and he was borrowing money from me at the end of every road trip! Whenever we came back to town, his father would be there and come up to me and ask: 'How much do I owe you?' And he paid me then and there."[33]

Filming movies during the day and playing every evening, combined with a lot of recordings, fine cars and dates with women here and there meant that Buddy Rich was living the good life. Where the rest of the world had been thrown into a world war (and with America worrying that the country would be forced into a war nobody wanted), Buddy was steadily climbing the career ladder. He had built himself a reputation as the best drummer in the country—many believed he was better than Krupa—and he didn't need to worry about a thing. Sy Oliver had noted his talent, done what Dorsey had promised and delivered one musical masterpiece after the other. Buddy Rich loved Oliver's fast, "killer-dillers" where he could show off as much as he liked—until those ballads showed up again.

Tommy Dorsey now had a singing group, The Pied Pipers, and he was planning to add a string section, which was the last thing Buddy Rich needed. Buddy hated anything that slowed down the tempo. He was so unbelievably energetic in his playing that he simply wanted to swing—and he wanted to swing on uptempo tunes, not play draggy numbers just to satisfy a singer gaining in popularity. The irritation between Buddy Rich and Frank Sinatra continued. After the close call at the Astor Hotel, a real fist fight between the two broke out. The other band members weren't sure what they should do to keep the two apart. When they played at Sweets Ballroom in Oakland, California, Rich and Sinatra began fighting in the parking lot; that time, Dorsey rushed in to separate them. His motive was selfish: he was afraid they would wreck their stage clothes. Another time it was Herb Caen, a popular columnist for the *San Francisco Chronicle*, who was witness to a fight backstage at the Golden Gate Theatre. Caen described the incident, writing, "Buddy was ramming Sinatra with his hi-hat, the cymbals that you play with your foot. Frank was screaming and swinging at him. Finally, Tommy broke it up with the help of a couple of guys in the band."[34]

Sammy Davis, Jr., then a young up-and-comer with the Will Mastin Trio and a major Sinatra fan, saw the band at Broadway Capitol Theatre in Detroit in October and remembered another incident. "Frank didn't like the way Buddy Rich played the drums when he was singing. When Frank sang 'This Love of Mine,' Buddy sat and talked out loud behind him. 'sh, shsh,' Frank tried, with the result that Rich replied 'Why is he saying sh?' Dorsey saw what was happening so he said to Rich, 'Settle down, Buddy.' It didn't help. Buddy started to play paradiddles on the drums. Then Frank lost his temper. He walked around the whole stage, out in the wings, and in again and hit Buddy on the jaw so he fell off the drums."[35]

How Dorsey could have accepted this warfare may be hard to understand, but in retrospect, Sinatra and Rich meant big business, and Dorsey would seemingly tolerate anything until it got out of hand. When it did, he would take them both off to one side and try to talk some sense into them. They nodded and said they understood, but a week later they were at each other's throats again. The situation was hopeless. Frank Sinatra described it later. "We both were two pains in Dorsey's ass. That's what we were in the band. Between Buddy complaining that the tempos were not quite right and my saying there weren't enough ballads in the library, we drove the old man crazy. But with all of that, he loved both of us. We really were the pets of the band."[36]

In 1941, Buddy won *Metronome* magazine's prestigious poll, and on January 16, he was asked to play on a special recording at RCA Victor studios in New York. There he recorded with the Metronome All-Stars: the magazine's poll winners, including Harry James, Tommy Dorsey, Ziggy Elman, Benny Carter, Coleman Hawkins, and two of Buddy's really big idols, Benny Goodman and Count Basie. They recorded two numbers: "Bugle Call Rag" and Basie's hit, "One O'Clock Jump." Buddy Rich, as usual, inspired the band.

The Dorsey band was ready to record again, but with a new addition. Buddy found out from *Downbeat* magazine, no less, that Dorsey had signed a contract with a new singer named Martha Frye. Rich reacted strongly to the news. "This was exactly what we needed: a new singer," he said at the time. He calmed down when Sy Oliver came up with some really swinging new charts; this always had a soothing effect on him.

Today, Tommy Dorsey's orchestra would have been looked at like bad boy rock stars. Think of it: different hotels and stages, beautiful women and lots of drinks every night, a lawsuit filed by Dorsey's wife against her husband, Sinatra arrested for jaywalking and Dorsey bailing him out, fellow bandsmen in a serious car accident, and Dorsey's escalating drinking problem, to boot. It was real rock star stuff.

It wasn't always a big party, what with constant rehearsals, new songs to learn, and long performances (most lasting several hours). In several interviews, Rich said that he hardly had time to change between brushes and sticks before the leader counted in a new number. There were light moments, however. The opening at the Astor Roof in New York on May 20 was especially memorable. Buddy Rich arrived in a newly purchased Lincoln Continental with Sinatra in the back seat. The band, now at its peak, was breaking records all over the place. The summer that followed was chaotic, and the pressure to remain number one was enormous. Sy Oliver expanded the repertoire with "Yes, Indeed!" which would become a big hit, and Dorsey was now rivaling Glenn Miller for the title of "King of the Big Bands."

In December of 1941, the band completed its first film for MGM, *Ship Ahoy,* starring Eleanor Powell, Bert Lahr, and Virginia O'Brien. Buddy Rich was featured in a blockbuster number, "I'll Take Tallulah," where he tap danced and more than held his own with the talented Powell. Buddy himself was happy with his performance. Not only that, he also played a tremendous drum solo in the big number "Hawaiian War Chant." On this song, Buddy explained to author Doug Meriwether, "The whole band was faking to the prerecorded soundtrack except me. I did it live! It would have looked phony any other way."

Buddy also won the *Downbeat* magazine poll that year as the best drummer. A personal development in November affected him more, however, when Artie Shaw and Lana Turner broke up. Buddy kept his eye on the gorgeous Lana, and when Tommy Dorsey got booked at the Hollywood Palladium once more, this time for a longer stay, he hoped Turner would show up to see the band. He knew very well that she loved swing music, musicians in general, and bandleaders especially, and Dorsey was a good friend of hers. Turner showed up on opening night, and when Buddy caught sight of her in the audience, he played so hard that sweat flew in every direction. She was really digging the music and Buddy took that as a sign that she liked him. Soon Lana, who had turned 20 and had already been married, started to date Buddy. Perhaps for her it was mostly for fun, but for Buddy it was dead serious. On December 6, 1941, after the evening's performance, at 2:00 in the morning, she invited Dorsey's whole band to her home in Westwood in the Hollywood Hills. There they enjoyed a late supper and drinks.

Lana Turner was an open, fun-loving woman who cared about people. Sure, she was a star—and knew it—but never let it go to her head. Buddy adored her. As the boys in the band played her new, white grand piano, Buddy couldn't take his eyes off of her. As the late night melted into morning, the party-goers began to drift off on Lana's sofas and beds, and everyone slept late into the next afternoon.

Suddenly, there came an unexpected knock on the door. Outside was Lana Turner's mother, tears running down her cheeks.

"Well," said Turner, "Don't you look happy!"

"You mean you haven't heard?" her mother replied. "For God's sake, turn on the radio! The Japanese have attacked Pearl Harbor. We're at war!"

I think I was one of the few guys who practiced with Buddy. One time in San Francisco, we were at the Shrine Auditorium and he was in Oakland with Harry James. We went back to the hotel, and it was late. He'd just got some new cymbals from Zildjian. It was 3 a.m. "Look at these," he says. Crash, crash, splash! I said, "Hey man, you're going to get us thrown out of here, Buddy!" "Screw 'em." Then he started pounding out some beats on the wall, and I'm thinking about jail. He takes out some sticks, "Whaddya think of these?" and all of a sudden it's 6 a.m. and we're banging out rolls. It was great. He'd say to me, "What do you think of so-and-so's playing?" I'd say, "Yeah, he's ok." Buddy would say "Oh come on, he sounds like he's rumbling down the staircase." I'd laugh and laugh at his honesty.

Joe Morello

I've heard him in every circumstance, and of all the drummers I've been around over the years, Buddy Rich is the consummate genius of the drums. He's like Tazio Nuvolari was with the racing car. He had complete control.

Mel Tormé

Buddy has something no other drummer had, or will ever have. I don't know how it came about and I don't think he does either. It doesn't matter.

Mel Lewis

CHAPTER 8

Love and War

**Publicity still from the movie *Ship Ahoy*, 1942
(Left to right: Buddy, Red Skelton, Eleanor Powell, Tommy Dorsey).**

On the morning of Sunday, December 7, 1941, Japan carried out a lightning attack on the American air and naval bases on Hawaii, Guam, and Manila. The city of Honolulu had been the focus of repeated attacks from the Japanese air force and it was quickly reported that a lot of damage had been done. The naval harbor at Pearl Harbor was hit especially hard, with the sinking of a large American naval fleet, and the bombs had set everything on fire. On the radio, President Roosevelt said, "The people of the United States have already formed their opinions and well understand the implications to the very life and safety of our nation. As Commander in Chief of the Army and Navy, I have directed that all measures be taken for our defense."[1] The same day, Japan declared war on America and Great Britain, and four days later, Germany and Italy lined up on the side of the Japanese. A Declaration of War was passed unanimously by the American Congress. Restrictions and rationing were implemented.

The Swing Era, as it came to be known, would never be the same. Many bands were hit immediately by the outbreak of war when leaders and bandsmen were called up to serve. Tours had to be rearranged, suitable replacements for drafted sidemen had to be found, and booking agencies found themselves with a whole set of new problems: Finding enough gas to fill the tour buses, and addressing the issue of whether or not people really wanted to go out and enjoy themselves in the middle of a raging war. Tommy Dorsey and His Orchestra was one of the few bands who remained at the top of the popularity heap, thanks to the two musicians who got more notice than the others, and who had so far not been called up: The world's best singer and the world's best drummer, who drew crowds wherever they went. The band also survived by getting longer location dates at venues like the Hollywood Palladium. At the Palladium, two soon-to-be hits were broadcast as a part of the "Spotlight Bands" radio series. Chuck Peterson's and Ziggy Elman's "Well, Git It!" and "Not So Quiet Please," a Sy Oliver chart that Buddy loved, were two flag-wavers. "Quiet Please" ended with a world class drum solo; a drum roll played as rapidly as a machine gun. The audience had never seen or heard anything like it. All this, together with the hit songs from the movie *Ship Ahoy*, combined to secure Tommy Dorsey and His Orchestra's position as the hottest band in the country.

After the Palladium, Dorsey had a two-month return engagement at the Paramount Theater. During this stand, Dorsey wanted to record "Sleepy Lagoon," a Harry James hit that Buddy hated but Dorsey loved (perhaps because of the challenging trombone part). "Lagoon" became a popular part of the set. At an eight-week stand at the Astor Roof beginning on May 5, 1942, Buddy Rich saw another side of Dorsey's leadership. One evening, Dorsey apparently had one taste too many, and couldn't play the high notes. Several musicians in the orchestra started to giggle. Dorsey fired them, one after another, loud and clear and right on the stage. Dorsey, who wasn't done with the tune yet, continued to miss notes again and again, and finally he had fired nearly the whole band—which couldn't stop roaring with laughter. Even the audience joined in. Dorsey gave up in the end and began laughing too. Everyone was back on the payroll the next day.

During the time the band was at the Astor, Buddy continued to go out with Lana Turner, and was spending more time with her. He followed her out to Hollywood, where she was playing in a new movie for MGM called *Somewhere I'll Find You* with Clark Gable. Smitten, Buddy repeatedly asked Turner to go with him to Tijuana, Mexico to get married. Lana didn't know how to handle the situation, as she didn't want to hurt him, and she didn't know how Buddy would react to a "no." Reluctantly, she said yes and headed off on the road to Mexico and matrimony. But she quickly had second thoughts, and while they stopped at a roadhouse for a quick bite, she rushed to the phone and called Dorsey press agent George "Bullets" Durgom. A man of great diplomacy who knew how to handle Buddy, Durgom talked Buddy out of the marriage, at least for the time being. Turner told Buddy that it just wasn't the right time.

Still, they continued to call each other, despite schedules that had Buddy playing with Dorsey at night and Turner filming with Gable by day. Lana agreed to visit Buddy's family. As Buddy remembered it, "One time, she called me and said she was coming in, and I said, 'Will you stay at the house in Brooklyn?' She said, 'Sure.' So I told my family, 'Listen, try to straighten up around the house and behave yourselves.'"[2] Buddy's sister Jo was a part of the welcoming committee. "We hear the car pull up," said Jo. "We look outside. They're out of the car, laughing hysterically.

Lana has dropped the engagement rings, and they're both down in the grass looking for them. They finally find them, we open the door, and here is this lady in a gray sweatsuit, no makeup, with her kerchief tied around her head, a little chubby, and she is gorgeous. Gorgeous—skin like a baby. Mickey looks at me, looks at Marge, looks at Lana, and says, 'You know, I've got two of the ugliest sisters in the world.'"[3]

Buddy Rich was happy man. Lana had given him a gold wristwatch with the inscription "Time for you always - L." At that time in his life, she meant everything to him. Word got around the neighborhood that Lana had come by to visit, and soon people were hanging outside the window or pretending to walk back and forth in front of the house in the hopes that she would come out. During the visit, Buddy described Turner as "so cool, so completely unpretentious, that when she'd go outside for a stroll or something, she'd wear old clothes, she'd stand around, sign autographs, talk with the kids; you know, absolutely nothing bothered her." She got to experience the Rich family sense of humor. They threw her in the shower with her clothes on, which is what they did with all their visitors, regardless of who they were. Despite the fun and games, the Rich sisters were worried about their little brother who was, after all, head over heels in love a with a movie star.

Unfortunately, there were warning signs that Lana wasn't just interested in Buddy. There had been photos in the papers of her with lots of different men. Buddy should have known something was going on, but everyone saw it except him. Jo Rich said, "He was the only one that didn't know about her. It was strange." After her catastrophic marriage to Artie Shaw, Turner was dating frequently and hitting all the clubs, earning her the tabloid title "Queen of all Nightclubs." *Liberty* magazine would later report that between her first and second marriage, she dated over a hundred men. How they verified this is anyone's guess, but at the moment, it appeared that Buddy Rich was one of her favorites. Marge Rich believed "it was a very serious romance. As a matter of fact, Brother thought she was going to marry him."

After staying with the Riches for six days, Lana was more or less ordered by her producers in Hollywood to get back to the set and film retakes with Gable. It was a tearful farewell, with Turner promising, "I'll call you as soon as I get there. We'll arrange the wedding." She left him with the rings in his hand and the watch on his arm. Two days later, early in the morning, she finally called and wanted to tell him the news before he read it in the papers. On July 17, 1942, Lana Turner had married the actor Steven Crane, claiming that the film company had made her do it. Buddy was devastated, and it took him a long time to get over her; afterwards he sought out women to date who looked like Lana.

Name bands had been gradually increasing in size over the years. In the early 1920s, bands grew from six to ten members. Ten years later, reed and brass sections grew from ten to 15. Dorsey had 30 players, including strings. Arrangers loved it, since it allowed them to do much more creatively with their charts. Dorsey's string section came mainly from Artie Shaw's orchestra, which disbanded when America entered the war. It didn't take long for Dorsey to offer them employment. (Shaw eventually put together a new orchestra that performed around the Pacific Theater for 18 months.) In addition to the strings, Dorsey also added a harpist and more singers. This, of course, meant more ballads, which Buddy hated. Still, the consensus of opinion today is that this was the best version of the Dorsey band. Sy Oliver's charts, many reworked for strings, were marvelous, and the soloists were the finest in the business.

It was challenging to staff Dorsey's band, and other bands, with good men, in that many of the best were being called up by Uncle Sam. Dorsey manager Bobby Burns joined the Air Force and was replaced by Arthur Mishaud. Trombonist Jack Teagarden, then leading a big band with considerable difficulty, had to watch as 17 of his men disappeared to the draft. Some of Dorsey's men were drafted as well. Tommy Dorsey did what he had to do, saying, "I was forced to put in a newcomer and pay him $500 a week—and that devil can hardly blow his nose!" Then, on August 5, 1942, Buddy Rich received his notice; Dorsey did everything in his considerable power to postpone the inevitable. He also knew that Sinatra wanted to leave the orchestra and set off on a solo career. Sinatra's ego was growing, and he was well aware of his position in the orchestra, sometimes thinking he was as big, or even bigger, than the leader. Once, when Dorsey was late to a rehearsal, Sinatra simply took over the conductor's baton. When Tommy came running in, out of breath, he was met by the comment, "Where the hell have you been?" "Sorry, I got held up in a meeting," replied Dorsey. "Bullshit," answered Sinatra coldly.[4]

September 3, 1942, was Frank Sinatra's last performance with Tommy Dorsey. Pianist and conductor Skitch Henderson remembered that "Frank left the band at the Circle Theatre in Indianapolis. I was with Jimmy van Heusen when the phone rang. It was Frank who said, 'Now that old goat has tooted his trombone for me for the last time. I'm leaving the band.'"[5] Through the years there has been much speculation about how Frank Sinatra got out of the ironclad contract he had with Dorsey. Dorsey, who told *American Mercury* magazine in 1951 that Sinatra "is one of the world's most fascinating men, but don't put your hand in his mouth,"[6] would insist that he was threatened. This led to the myth that the mafia lay behind the proceedings, fed years later by the infamous scene in *The Godfather* film. Maybe there were threats, but in later interviews Sinatra himself said that it was his own lawyer, who also represented the American Federation of Radio Artists, that made the deal to cut him loose. It was a $75,000 buyout, which ensured Frank Sinatra was contractually his own man. Still, the speculation continues today about what really happened.

Dick Haymes, who had replaced Sinatra in Harry James' band, became Dorsey's new singer. The evening before Sinatra was going to leave, Buddy finally asked him who had hired the gorillas that had jumped him outside of Child's during the Astor run. Sinatra admitted that he had asked some buddies from Hoboken for a favor. Frank and Buddy were able to laugh off the events by now, and wished each other well. A friendship was reborn.

On September 1, 1942, The Dorsey orchestra began filming another picture, *DuBarry was a Lady*, starring Red Skelton, Lucille Ball, and Gene Kelly. Without Buddy's knowledge, Dorsey saw to it that Buddy's draft papers disappeared. He wanted to complete the band's performances in this big MGM musical. Two weeks later, on September 15, Buddy Rich began his military duty in the Marine Corps. He told Mel Tormé that he wanted to fight for his country. "I really wanted to go. It was a pride of the country. Dig my attitude about it. When you saw a picture like *Wake Island*, and you watched a division of Japanese assault troops wipe out a small contingent of Marines when you're in the early 20s, you're thinking: 'How can they do that to us? Here I am, sitting behind a set of drums? I can't allow that! I gotta go out and do my thing.'"[7]

On the weekends he was free from military duty, spent every minute playing his drums. At the end of September, the 25-year-old Buddy played on the "Spotlight Bands" and "Treasury Show" broadcasts, and continued to play with Dorsey when called, as Tommy had friends in high places within the military. In October, he recorded the soundtrack to another MGM opus, *Broadway Rhythm*, featuring future California Senator George Murphy, Ginny Simms, and Lena Horne. Buddy insisted on not appearing on screen, since he absolutely did not want to run into Lana Turner at MGM, and wouldn't even eat in the studio's cafeteria. Dorsey used Maurice "Moe" Purtill in place of Buddy.

The following month, Buddy recorded the sound track to another MGM film, *Presenting Lily Mars*, where Judy Garland sang onscreen with the Dorsey band. After the recording, he took the train from Los Angeles to U.S. Naval Training City in San Diego, and from there, moved to Camp Pendleton, where he would be on duty for the next 14 weeks. At the end of 1942, pictures beckoned again, as he got an offer to put together an orchestra under his own name for a little Universal "B" picture called *How's About It*. The stars of the movie were the trio with whom he had made his first recording, the Andrews Sisters. Somehow, Buddy got time off from his military duty to do the picture without the intervention of Dorsey. The credits read "Buddy Rich and His Orchestra" and once again, he was featured in an extremely good drum solo. Around the same time, he also recorded a short solo for another Universal film, *Phantom Lady*.

Buddy then recorded with Benny Carter, the man who became one of the first blacks to write film music. "His regular drummer had left," Buddy said, "and I told him I would fill in until they found somebody. They played some complicated things, and I wasn't there that long to really get into anything. Yeah, Benny was a real gentleman."[8] Dorsey was not pleased with Buddy Rich's extracurricular activity, and when he got wind of Buddy's playing escapades, he was absolutely furious with him, saying, "Who the hell does he think he is? I own him!"

In the beginning of 1943, Buddy Rich found out that he had won *Downbeat* magazine's poll as the best drummer of 1942. With Dorsey on January 4, he began recording the soundtrack for MGM's *Girl Crazy*, starring Judy Garland and Mickey Rooney. Buddy's mind was on things other than playing; he thought that since he had been posted to Camp Pendleton, he would get a direct ticket to the other side of the Atlantic. Instead, the military took advantage of his celebrity, and he was hired to play at different movie premiers in Hollywood, including one at Grauman's Chinese Theater on March 3. He hated it. After these performances, which Buddy considered humiliating, there were fights, physical and otherwise, with his superior. Time after time, he went to his commander's office to see if he was on the list to be shipped overseas, but he never found his name there.

Buddy remembered that his captain's name was Rosenthal. "I remember his name because he was the only Jew in the entire Navy other than me," Buddy remembered with some bitterness. "I went to his office several times a week and insisted that they put me on the list to be sent across the Atlantic. I was accepted several times, but when it came to the highest authority, it was always denied."[9] There were more fistfights. "I wasn't at all used to hearing that Jews couldn't fight, Jews know nothing but how to make money, Jews started the war and so on. But after a couple of fistfights I never heard any more talk like that."[10] In July, he caught a break when he received permission to play in the band of tenor saxophonist Al Sears when drummer Chris Columbus couldn't make it. It was like a dream for Buddy, in that Lester Young was a part of the reed section. On the other hand, he refused an offer to play with the band Artie Shaw planned to put together to perform at military bases.

Despite all the fighting, Buddy advanced to the rank of combat rifleman and became a judo instructor. He was regarded as one of the best, but he couldn't stand the name-calling, the remarks about his background, his religion, or the trash talk about being a New York musician. In retrospect, it could have been that Buddy was thought of as a celebrity who needed to be put in his place. Later in life, he told author John

Minahan about an incident that stayed with him for a lifetime.

"So, I'm digging, and digging and digging, and I was tired and I was filthy and I was wet. You can't imagine how dirty you can get until you've worn the same boots and socks, and the same fatigues for five or six days without taking a bath or anything. I took my trench shovel off my pack, and I was digging, and the next thing I know, I heard, 'Dig faster, you Jew bastard!'

"And I got a kick in my ass and I went headlong into the hole. And that's all. All I know is, I had this trench knife—it's a knife and a shovel—in my hand, and I fell. I let go of the thing and I came up. I didn't know who it was. All I saw was a face in front of me, and I just really zonked it, and this cat went down. And it wasn't 20 seconds when I had two 45s right smack in my face, with the hammers back. Two MPs;[11] one on either side. This guy gets up and says something to the effect, 'You won't be out for a long time!' 'Fuck you, motherfucker!' And they ran me up in a Jeep, put me in the back with handcuffs and got me back. And I'll never forget the CO,[12] he was the only other Jew besides me in the whole fucking base.

"I was brought up to face a summary court martial. That's not like a general court martial, where you can go to jail for up to ten, twelve years, whatever they give you. This thing is just for minor offenses against military law. In a summary court martial it's just your CO and two lieutenants and they listen to you, the various reports of what took place. So, the articles read that at no time should you discuss politics or religion in the service, because you have too many opposing factions. The guys in my group told the CO what happened. He kicked me, hit me, and he called me a Jew bastard. They immediately shipped him out. He was a major."

Further, he told Minahan in vivid terms how, for 30 more days, he was forced to handle the garbage and trash, he had to clean the latrines and then be locked in a barracks for an additional 30 days. They shaved off all his hair, and he wasn't allowed to talk to anyone. Then he was put in a cell measuring a little over six feet across, with no furnishings whatsoever, only a small blanket on the floor. At night it was bitterly cold, forcing him to choose between sleeping on the blanket or putting it over himself for warmth. He received hardly anything to eat and lost several pounds. Then he was subjected to torture, as he was forced to stand on one leg until he couldn't do it any longer, at which point he was ordered to change to the other leg. The mistreatment also included sleep deprivations; they woke him up every third hour during the night. Finally, they searched him and planted cigarette butts that they then accused him of smuggling in. The military police were determined to break his spirit. In June, 1944, *Downbeat* reported the following news item: "BUDDY RICH TO GET DISCHARGE. Los Angeles – Buddy Rich, former Tommy Dorsey drummer, is set for a medical discharge from the Marine Corps. For the past nine weeks, Rich has been at the base hospital in San Diego. Relatives said he has been told to expect his release around June 1st. Friends in the music business here said Rich would probably organize his own band, following a short rest."[13] The question was whether or not Buddy had really injured himself or if the story was fabricated to avoid the truth about his time in the stockade and subsequent discharge because of it.

Buddy remembered, "They took me back to Los Angeles, and when you've gone that long without eating, you can't eat. Your stomach shrinks. My family, they were giving me all this beautiful food, and I couldn't eat. I swore that there wouldn't be one day in my life, ever, when I would do anything for any branch of the armed forces—except for the kids, who are doing the actual fighting." He would hate the military for the rest of his life. In several interviews many years later he vented his anger when he could, saying, "The whole military apparatus, God, how I hate it: 'Sir' here and 'sir' there; the whole disciplinary apparatus: to have to salute and take orders from guys who under normal circumstances wouldn't be allowed to set foot in your home!"[14]

While waiting for his discharge papers, Buddy went to the Hollywood Palladium (still dressed in his uniform) to hear trumpeter Charlie Spivak's band. In the second set, he sat in with Spivak on "Hawaiian War Chant," and listening in the audience was Dorsey manager Arthur Michaud, who offered Buddy his job back with Dorsey. They negotiated for a fee of $750 a week, sorely needed at the time, as he was completely broke after his time in the service. Buddy would be replacing Gene

Krupa, who was ready to reorganize his own big band after Dorsey helped him restore his reputation following a 90-day prison sentence for a trumped up drug charge. On June 6, 1944, the allied Western forces successfully landed in Normandy in northern France. The invasion, which had been carried out under the code name Operation Overlord, was the largest landing operation in history. This landing meant that the Allies could fight Germany from two directions. From the other direction, Russia attacked with full strength. People around the world were hoping that the world war would finally end.

On June 18, Buddy Rich was back with Tommy Dorsey and His Orchestra for a multi-week stand at the Casino Gardens Ballroom in California. A number of celebrity guest stars turned out, including Bing Crosby, Al Jolson, Judy Garland, and Sinatra. The reason for the large number of guest stars was simple: Dorsey invited them because he bought the place and was eager to establish it as an "in" spot. Wherever they went, Buddy was keener than ever to play, and every evening he played one magnificent solo after the other. Deane Kincaide, the saxophonist and arranger, liked Buddy. "I always got along well with Buddy," Kincaide recalled. "He has always had tremendous confidence in himself rather than conceit. One night at the Astor Roof in New York, Buddy took a solo that must have lasted 15 minutes. Every thing came to a standstill. Even the waiters stopped serving and watched."[15]

That summer, the band they made another movie for MGM, *Thrill of a Romance*, starring Van Johnson, Esther Williams, and the opera star Lauritz Melchior. As always, there was a lot of waiting and sitting around during filming, and the bandsmen tried to keep themselves occupied. Buddy organized jam sessions with Buddy DeFranco on clarinet, Michael "Dodo" Marmorosa on piano, Sid Block on bass, Ziggy Elman on trumpet and sometimes even Dorsey on trombone. Not everyone on the film dug the sessions. Clarinetist Buddy DeFranco remembered that "Lauritz Melchior was a well known opera star, kind of temperamental, and he didn't like jazz. He was very disturbed by our little jam sessions, and I also think his ego was bruised. He was probably disturbed that the movie crew would ignore the star and come over and listen to us and applaud. One day I guess he had enough of this and he walked over right in front of Buddy Rich and said. 'Have you had enough of that rotten music? I have.' Buddy looked at him and said, 'Fuck you!' as loud and clear as a bell. That was Buddy."[16]

Legendary lead trumpeter Al Porcino was also supposed to be a part of the band at the time the film was made. "I had played with Buddy Rich a month earlier when he sat in with us at a performance with Louis Prima at the Central Park Hotel in New York," said Porcino. "You know, Buddy was one of the most hated persons in the music industry at that time, just because you couldn't live with him on the road. His ego was incredibly big. Everyone made a lot of jokes about him behind his back, but nobody could deny what a great drummer he was. Whatever the case, I think I made a good impression on Buddy that evening, for suddenly the phone rang at my place and it was Tommy Dorsey, who wanted me to hop in as fifth trumpeter. It must have been Buddy who recommended me. I arrived at MGM studios and was met by Dorsey's manager, Arthur Michaud. I couldn't believe my eyes. When Dorsey then wanted me to play a solo, I couldn't do it. I'm really not that kind of a jazz player. I got Dodo Marmorosa to help me analyze the song. It didn't work. Dorsey wasn't satisfied. Finally the door opened and in stepped Ziggy Elman from nowhere and aced the solo on the first take. For years after that, Buddy said the same thing every time we ran into each other: 'Hey Jazz!'"[17]

It didn't take long before Buddy had a run-in with Dorsey again. On the way to a concert in Phoenix, Arizona, the road was lined with posters on telephone poles and buildings proclaiming that Tommy Dorsey was going to arrive with his previous drummer, Gene Krupa. This infuriated Rich. "I'm walking off. I am not going to sit here and play notes for another drummer." Tommy just turned around and looked at him, and said, "You better stick around, because if you don't, you're not going to get off this field alive!"[18] He meant it. When Tommy Dorsey tried to quit drinking cold turkey, it became hellish for the musicians, who were sometimes called to rehearse at 2:30a.m.—and with no overtime pay. Buddy DeFranco said, "When Dorsey quit drinking, which he did for about a year when I was playing with him, everything got worse. Everyone in the band hoped that he would start drinking again."[19] Sober or otherwise, Dorsey was a businessman, through and through. He fired people left and right as it suited him. Dodo Marmorosa had to go because he played a little too much bebop in his solos, and bop was something Dorsey didn't understand or like. At the time, neither did Buddy Rich.

However, Tommy Dorsey had bigger problems on the horizon. On August 4, 1944, what had to be the biggest scandal in Dorsey's life took place. His new wife, Pat Dane, had her birthday, and they were celebrating at the hotel. A Universal contract player who later gained fame as the creator and star of television's "Ramar of the Jungle," Jon Hall, put his arm around Pat. Dorsey became furious and knocked Hall down, causing him to bleed profusely. Complete chaos broke out, with the end result being a lawsuit against Dorsey. Booking agents were in a tizzy because Dorsey couldn't leave the state. It seemed a good time for Tommy Dorsey to stop drinking, which (at least) he tried.

In the fall of 1944, Buddy Rich and Count Basie were both in Los Angeles, as Buddy was filming there with Dorsey, and Basie was playing and broadcasting from a venue called the Plantation. Basie's drummer, Jo Jones, was called up for military duty. Count Basie remembered asking Buddy to "hop in" for Papa Jo. Buddy answered, "You're damn right I'll do it!" Buddy was hardly alone in his admiration for Basie. Nearly every drummer at the time knew what it meant to play with the man who helped define the essence of swing. Everyone looked up to him enormously, and for Rich, Basie was a God. Jo Jones described the Basie band as "an institution! It was like Notre Dame, it was like Vassar, it was like Oxford. It was like Eton."[20] Drummer Ed Shaughnessy, who would work with the Basie band live and play on several recording dates years later, had a good explanation why Basie and drummers always got along famously. "Basie's so great," said Shaughnessy. "He doesn't give you a million do's and don'ts. One time the engineer came out and said, 'I think we ought to have less drums.' Basie said, 'No, you do something with the mike. He's going to keep playing the way he's playing, because that's why he's here. Play it the same way, Shaughn. And do you your job, Mister. That's part of my band: plenty of drums.'"

Buddy Rich said playing with Basie was "such an honor. I was so proud that Count Basie asked me if I wanted to play with his band. I still get goose bumps just thinking about it." Indeed, for two weeks, Buddy went back and forth as often as he could to help Basie. If he had to run to get back to the movie, he offered to come back at night if necessary. "I got up at 6 a.m. and went out to the filming at MGM Studios," Buddy explained. "At 6 p.m. I went back to my apartment in Beverly Hills, changed my clothes and went to the Plantation and worked with Basie until 2 a.m. I guess I was back at my apartment around 4 a.m. Woke up at 6 a.m. and did it all over again." Years later, Basie said, "That's the reason why I love that cat and always will. He has done a whole lot of things, Buddy Rich really has. I'm talking about over many years, a whole lot of years. There's nothing he won't do for me. That's the way he has always made me feel about him. I don't even remember how it all started, but that's the way it still is today."[21]

Basie's orchestra was unbelievable during those weeks, and Buddy played some of his most fantastic solos. The band played an absolutely magnificent version of Basie's "One O'Clock Jump," and there was no doubt that the orchestra was very happy with the substitute drummer. According to Basie himself, this was the only time that the band came in on time and wanted to play longer than planned. "I look back on the stand at the Plantation with Basie as one of the monumental things in my life," a reverent Buddy Rich said. "It had nothing to do with my playing. Just the memory of performing with that band is important to me. That's all."[22]

Payment for Buddy's services was never discussed. On their last day together at the Plantation, Basie gave him a blank check and told Buddy that he could fill in whatever amount he wanted to. Buddy ripped it in half and said, "It was my pleasure." A few weeks later, a package arrived at Buddy's home containing a gold watch with the inscription, "To Buddy from the Count. L.A. Thanks." Now he could throw out the watch he had received from Lana Turner and instead put on this new one. He wore it with pride for the rest of his life.

Dorsey was playing the popular radio series, "Your All Time Hit Parade," and the band accompanied one star after the other. The group then did three days of recording for Victor in November of 1944, and one of the tracks recorded would become a gigantic hit: Sy Oliver's "Opus (No.) 1." The year 1945 began nicely for Rich and Dorsey. Buddy once again won the *Downbeat* magazine poll for the drummer of the year, and Mr. and

Mrs. Dorsey could kick up their heels and celebrate the court's dismissal of the Hall lawsuit; the judge ruled that Hall had to pay all the court costs and his own plastic surgery. Dorsey was again free to play in anywhere in the country.

Relations between Buddy Rich and Tommy Dorsey were still not great. Dorsey was sensing that Buddy was seriously thinking of leaving the band, in that his contract was nearing its end on May 29, and he was saying he was tired of being a sideman. Buddy knew the situation, explaining, "Bandleaders don't want drummers to get more attention than the orchestra or themselves. They want you to know that you are there, and that they want to feel your power. But they really don't want to hear you. If I did something that wasn't written in the notes they immediately reacted with 'What was that?' or 'Where does it say that?' I had so many problems, since I felt that what I did was right. And I continued to follow my instincts. For the most part, both Artie Shaw and Tommy Dorsey understood that it had little to do with making myself important. I was really trying to improve the numbers by playing with my energy. I guess that it has to do with the feeling I have for a certain song."[23]

He sought out Frank Sinatra to get some advice about the future. Sinatra was rehearsing for a new show in New York, and Buddy figured that no one knew better than Frank how to extricate oneself from "the dictator." As Stanley Kay remembered, "When Buddy came back from the Marines, I was with him and Frank at Toots Shor's bar in New York. I heard Frank say, 'Start a band. I'll back you up, and you're going to be so busy you'll pray for a day off.'"[24] Times were changing. The war was coming to an end, there was optimism in the air, and maybe the time was right for Buddy to become a leader. Musically, a new era was also beginning; many of the hipper returning musicians found bebop to be fresh and exciting, with its unexpected chord changes and new ways of thinking about rhythm. Eddie Laguna, who ran the Sunset record company, was one of those who was intrigued by the new sounds; he helped set up various jam sessions in Hollywood where bop and swing met. Despite the constant headlines predicting that Buddy Rich was going to leave Dorsey, Buddy stayed on, whether for contractual or economic reasons. Dorsey was telling the newspapers that his contract with Buddy would expire in

July the following year, but Buddy paid no attention what his contract said.

On June 9, Buddy went into Eddie Laguna's Sunset recording studios with pianist/vocalist Nat "King" Cole, trumpeter Charlie Shavers, tenor saxophonist Herbie Haymer, and bassist John Simmons. The sessions, produced by Laguna under the title *The Sunset All Stars* (released years later on a long-playing album called *Anatomy of a Jam Session*), were happily and effortlessly swinging. The guys had a ball. Someone suggested they play "All the Things You Are," but Nat Cole wanted to finish the session as soon as possible, since he wanted to get home to his family to watch some kind of parade. They agreed to jam, and the result was a six-minute, aptly-titled swinger called "Kicks." When the record came out (first as a series of 78s), Dorsey hit the roof. He threatened a lawsuit, but Laguna was smart enough not to put all the band members' real names on the label. Thus, Dorsey never sued, and whatever the case might have been, Buddy Rich didn't give a hoot what Dorsey thought about it. He later expressed great admiration for Nat "King" Cole, saying, "Nobody remembers that I recorded with him when he was one of the best jazz pianists, and hardly anybody ever realized how great a pianist he was. Not only his technique, but also his time thing; he was a real percussive player. I loved him."[25]

Despite the chilly relations with Dorsey, Rich still attended one of Dorsey's parties that summer. There, Dorsey's wife Pat Dane introduced Buddy to a young beauty by the name of Jean Sutherlin. Buddy, who had not had any kind of serious relationship since Lana Turner, felt both unsure and curious about the woman. While several sources indicated that this was where they met for the first time, the gossip magazines had paired them earlier that spring. Columnist Dorothy Kilgallen, then known as "Broadway's Voice," wrote as early as April that year (syndicated in the *Toledo Blade*), "Drummer Buddy Rich can't decide between Jackie Flynn, the Conover beauty, and Jean Sutherlin, equally dazzling. They both haunt his bandstand. Lana Turner once mooned over him too."[26]

Buddy fell in love with the 24-year-old Jean Connel Sutherlin, and on July 16, 1945, he married her in Los Angeles. She came from West

Virginia, where her stepfather, John Corbett, owned and managed a pharmacy chain. Her biological parents were Corrine and James Sutherlin. Their daughter had quite a history before Buddy Rich. A few years before Jean married Buddy, she was paired up with the eccentric millionaire Tommy Manville. In March, 1942, she was announced as his future wife (number six) in the newspapers. (Manville was known for quickly marrying the women he fell in love with.) There was even an official press photo printed of the happy couple on their engagement, but there was no wedding. One reason could have been the fact that when Jean called her mother to tell her about the upcoming wedding, her mother screamed that her daughter had gone crazy. Jean's mother is then said to have contacted one of Manville's friends and asked, "You know Tommy well, don't you? I need your advice. What should I do so my daughter can be rid of Tommy for the rest of her life?" The friend is said to have replied, "The best way for your daughter to be rid of him for the rest of her life is to marry him!"[27] Shortly thereafter, she broke off the engagement.

Jean thought she had found her life partner in Buddy Rich, and there were many who believed that the temperamental drummer would calm down now that he had settled down. According to the papers, they also had many mutual interests. She liked Basie, she loved to play golf and swim with her new husband, and both of them loved driving around in his car. They seemed very happy together, and he was more than happy to show his girl how he played the drums.[28]

Buddy may have been happy at home, but the tension with his boss continued all through the following autumn. Musically, no tension could be heard; Buddy Rich had probably not sounded better since he had entered the jazz scene with Marsala eight years earlier. In August of 1945, Buddy and Artie Shaw met for the first time since the bandleader left his orchestra and fled to Mexico. It was at a radio performance for the U.S. troops with a unit called the Jubilee All-Stars, featuring Basie, Lionel Hampton, Shaw, Les Paul, Illinois Jacquet, Dorsey, Ziggy Elman, and Buddy. On September 5, he went off to Columbia Studios in New York to record with Woody Herman's Herd. Woody's band was riding high in 1945, and Buddy replaced a sick Dave Tough, their regular drummer. Ed Shaughnessy, a fan of Tough and friend of Woody's, said, "When he stepped in there, the boys in Woody's band told me how good he was. Buddy was the only one who could match Dave's intensity."[29] The result was one of Woody's biggest hits, "Your Father's Moustache."

On October 12, Buddy recorded some V-Disc sides for the Armed Forces under his own name, *Buddy Rich and his V-Disc Speed Demons*, featuring Ella Fitzgerald. Also that month, he took part in the radio quiz show "Which is Which?" Other guests were Nat Cole, Dave Dexter, and Frank Sinatra. MGM released yet another film including Tommy Dorsey and His Orchestra. It was titled *The Great Morgan*, starring Frank Morgan, who had made a name for himself with *The Wizard of Oz*, but had no new Dorsey footage. Instead, *Morgan* used clips from *Ship Ahoy*.

At the end of October, 1945, Dorsey's orchestra again performed at the Paramount in New York, and once again (for whatever reason) Buddy was angry and disappointed. In the middle of the run, he left the stage and flew to his parents' house in Florida. A few days later he contacted Gene Lees, one of Dorsey's lyricists, and asked him to send his drums to him. Dorsey, who had anticipated the call, had bribed the hotel switchboard to send him a message when Buddy rang. Minutes later, Lees received a call from Dorsey, who wanted him to come to his hotel room and eat breakfast. Surprised, he went along, and after they had finished their coffee, Dorsey said, "That damned Buddy Rich called you and asked you to send him his drums, huh? Didn't he? The hell you're going to do it!"[30] The situation became intolerable for both men. Although he knew replacing Buddy wouldn't be easy, Dorsey realized that he would never manage the unruly Rich and decided to tear up his contract. The replacement was Alvin Stoller. Buddy played his two last gigs with Dorsey at the 400 Club in New York, and after that he was free to do what he wanted.

Alvin Stoller, then at New York's Commodore Hotel with Charlie Spivak, said he "knew Buddy wanted to leave Dorsey. Almost every afternoon I'd go to Tommy's rehearsals at the 400 Club. I kept coming back to sit in, and I was hired. It was a good thing for both Buddy and me. I got to go with a great band and Buddy was released from his contract and could go his own way."[31] Buddy Rich looked at it in another way. "When I left," Buddy said, "he hired Alvin Stoller. Stoller and I hung out together, and I guess Stoller had acquired some of my personality, because he gave T.D. such a rough time that Dorsey finally told him: 'There are three rotten bums in the world: Buddy Rich, you, and Hitler—and I have to have two of them in my band!'"[32]

CHAPTER 9

Buddy Rich and His Orchestra

Postcard/mailer advertising the new Buddy Rich Orchestra of 1946 opening at the College Inn.

During the 1940s, the newspapers loved to write about musicians who broke loose from their positions as sidemen and started their own bands. There was something romantic about a musician who left a secure economic berth to jump into the deep and risky waters of the band business. This was the case for Buddy Rich. There were daily rumors of him leaving Dorsey, but he hung on, probably for the $750 weekly paycheck. This time, he made up his mind and decided to take Frank Sinatra's advice to step out as a leader, and take him up on his offer to back the band.

In November of 1945, he looked up his old friend, headlining at the Paramount Theater. Sinatra was not alone in his dressing room. Another old acquaintance was calling on Frank. Fred "Tamby" Tamburro had moved back to Hoboken after having refused Frank's offer to be his personal valet the previous year. Now he had Frank Sinatra's ear and wanted $5,000 to buy a bar, as his financing plans had fallen apart at the last minute. He knew that his former singing partner was earning over a million dollars a year and he was sure that he would lend him the money. Frank flatly refused. A few minutes later, while Tamby was still there, Buddy Rich showed up and declared, "Frank, I'm going to do as you said and start my own band."[1] Sinatra kept his promise, wrote out a check for $25,000, and the two men hugged. An enraged Tamby, who was left standing there, grabbed Sinatra and pushed him up against the wall.

Buddy signed with the gigantic and influential MCA agency (also Sinatra's agency) to book the band, and he also changed managers. In place of his father, who was still managing him, he hired his sister Marge's husband, Carl Ritchie. With financing, a booking agency and management in place, his preparations began in earnest. The next order of business was to find an arranger who could write with Buddy's playing in mind. He made a good choice in contacting Eddie Finckel, who wrote a lot of modern-tinged charts for Gene Krupa, and was positive about writing for Rich as well. Some of Finckel's first charts were the cleverly-titled "From Rags to Riches," "Dateless Brown," "Quiet Riot," and "Rich-Ual Fire Dance." Describing their collaboration, Eddie Finckel remembered, "He was a wild guy, but I got along well with Buddy and there were never any problems. Actually, I wasn't around him that much except at rehearsals and the few times that I went to see the band play."[2]

Buddy also commissioned Billy Moore and Neil Hefti, who had written many arrangements for Charlie Barnet and Woody Herman; and Johnny Mandel, who wrote for Artie Shaw. The latter also joined the orchestra as first trombonist. When the repertoire was in place, it was time to contact the musicians, and a few weeks later Buddy's first big band was ready to hit the stand. The band personnel included Bitsy Mullins, Jimmy Pupa, Sid Illardi, and Paul Cohn on trumpets; Johnny Mandel, Earl Swope, Dave Sickles, and Sam Hyster on trombones; Tony Scott, Les Clark, Romeo Penque, George Berg, and Mike Blanos on saxophones; Sid Brown on bass; Tony Nichols on piano; Len Mirabella on guitar; and vocalist Dottie Reid. Rehearsals were booked at the renowned Nola studios on Broadway, and uniforms and music stands were ordered for everyone. There was a personality problem from the start, in that Buddy and alto saxophonist Tony Scott did not get along. Years later, Scott would say, "It took me only two weeks to dislike Buddy so intensely, and I hate him to this day."[3]

The choice of songs was also an issue. When Buddy was starting his project, bebop was becoming more and more popular, and several bands, notably Woody Herman's and Krupa's, were including some bop numbers in the book. Not Buddy Rich. He wanted to play the music he loved. It was his band! He had been playing other people's music for long enough. According to Johnny Mandel, "In 1946, Buddy was still thinking in terms of swing. He liked Benny Goodman's sound. Frankly, I can't even imagine Benny and Buddy in the same room together. They had such different temperaments. When I'd play bop in Buddy's band, Buddy would pound me on the chest with his finger and say, 'I hate bebop, I hate Charlie Parker.'"[4]

Though putting the band together took up most of his time, Buddy still played on other projects with musicians he loved. In the beginning of December of 1945, he recorded with Lester Young and Nat "King" Cole. On this series of magical recordings, later regarded as classics, Buddy demonstrated phenomenal brush technique—not without the influence of Jo Jones. Lester loved it. Prez maintained, "If you pay someone to play, you have to give that person an honest chance to tell his story."[5]

133

Playing with that caliber of musicians was an inspiration. Buddy listened and continued to learn.

Then he heard from Benny Goodman, who wondered if he could come and play with him, since Dave Tough had suddenly fallen ill again. Tough was a fragile, frequently unreliable soul who was sometimes not physically up to making the gig. Long into the night of December 19, Buddy Rich recorded three songs with his idol at Columbia Studios: "Lucky,' "I've Gotten Sweet on You," and the uptempo "Rattle and Roll." Buddy was aggressive and impressive. After the session, Rich received a check from Goodman. Benny, as was his wont, paid only union scale. Buddy was furious and wrote a sour note back: "I pay more for my shirts than this!"[6] Goodman never went on the record with his thoughts of Rich's playing on the session. Much later, in 1981, Mel Tormé met the famous clarinetist at a club in New York and took the opportunity to ask what Benny thought about Rich's playing, especially on "Rattle and Roll." Goodman was supposed to have answered, "Naw, naw, I didn't like that kid's playing. The only real drummer I ever had was Gene. Gene! He was the best!"[7]

On Christmas Eve, December 24, 1945, Buddy Rich and His Orchestra debuted at Valley Forge General Hospital in historic Valley Forge, Pennsylvania, a Philadelphia suburb. The performance was broadcast by Coca Cola, which sponsored the "Victory Parade of Spotlight Bands" radio series. Years later, the broadcasts were released as an album called *A Young Man and his Drums*, where a forceful and high-spirited Buddy Rich can be heard. Buddy must have been thrilled that night, after five years of plodding along with Dorsey ballads and strings. As to the actual recording of the night, he never saved a single copy of any record he made, and probably never listened to it. He never looked back—just ahead. The day after, the band continued with a week's engagement at the Terrace Ballroom in Newark, New Jersey. After three performances, Tony Scott was gone. Rich and Scott had very similar temperaments. Both said exactly what they thought at the moment, and confrontation was inevitable. A shouting Buddy put his foot down in the dressing room, telling Scott, "There is only room for one God on this band and I'll be damned if it's going to be you, so get out!"[8] Tony Scott was replaced by Al Kavisch.

Throughout January, 1946, the band continued to rehearse regularly at Nola studios. At one of those rehearsals, Sinatra came by. Maybe he wanted to hear what he had invested in, or maybe he was just curious about the whole orchestra. When he heard Buddy sing "Aren't You Glad You're You?" he suggested that Buddy should sing much more on stage, which he was happy to do. "I hadn't had any intention of doing any singing," Buddy said. "I've never sung anyplace before but in the shower. But I enjoy singing. I get a big kick out of it. We have 15 or 20 numbers in the book now that I do."[9] He also signed a recording contract with Mercury Records, followed by a five-theater tour: the Adams in Newark, the RKO Keith in Boston, the State in Hartford, the Earle in Philadelphia, and the Fox in Detroit. On opening night, Rich was in top form as usual and started the evening by saying, "You don't look like the same audience that was at the Terrace Room, but then again, you don't look like you've got that kind of money either." In order to hype the band, he appeared as a guest performer here and there, including Hildegard's radio show in New York, where he played with Harry Sosnick's house band. Everything seemed to be working. The band was getting glowing reviews, the papers and trades were impressed by his skill on the drums and the band's book, and the worry of being outmaneuvered by bebop calmed down somewhat.

Things were not so rosy at home. On March 3, the band played at the Palace Theater in Youngstown, Ohio. After completing the first set, Buddy got a phone call from his wife. Jean was desperate and accused him of never being at home, and said that he didn't care about her at all. The argument got worse, which ultimately turned into a suicide threat. In desperation, she took an overdose of sleeping pills. A worried Buddy made some quick phone calls, and thankfully, the police got there in time and took her to the hospital. They were able to save her life.[10] The friction between them had started right after their wedding. There was no honeymoon, as Buddy was occupied with rehearsals, recordings, and personal appearances with Dorsey. Rehearsals were particularly time-consuming, as the band had to frequently back guest vocalists on new songs. He had played on his own birthday in 1945, as well as Christmas Eve and on New Year's Eve. The following year meant new week-long engagements. He could hardly refuse; the band would fall apart. If Jean was happily married at the start, she certainly wasn't by this point. She had married a man who was never home, and even her suicide attempt didn't stop Buddy from continuing to tour. Only two weeks after the dramatic incident, he took his band to California for a six-week stay at the Palladium in Hollywood starting on March 19. Here he also took his brother Mickey on in the band, on tenor sax. If little brother Mickey thought he was going to get special treatment because of his relationship with Buddy, he was sadly mistaken. He was drilled just as hard as everyone else.

The orchestra's sound reflected Buddy's philosophy of swing music completely. Two LP albums of Palladium radio broadcasts, *One Night Stand with Buddy Rich*, were released years later; on these records Buddy's drive is clear. In March, he made a cameo appearance in a Republic picture called Earl Carrol's Sketchbook. Though the whole band gets billing, the Library of Congress maintains that Buddy, who can be seen on screen hidden among a string section, actually plays with a studio orchestra. The leading roles were played by Constance Moore, William Marshal, and Bill Goodwin. The film won no awards.

In the beginning of April, 1946 he also played on NBC radio broadcast with a group dubbed "The Jubilee All-Stars." This swinging, swing-meets-bop group featured Charlie Parker, Nat King Cole and Benny Carter, and the results could be heard years later on a couple of bootleg long-playing recordings. This was followed by a month's engagement with the band at the Panther Room at the Hotel Sherman in Chicago. This was an important date, and Buddy had to proceed carefully. He could no longer avoid bebop totally, so he contacted arranger Tadd Dameron, who wrote for Dizzy Gillespie (among others) and he decided to add some show biz-elements into the mix by adding singing and tap dancing into the mix. To handle all of this, he needed someone to play drums when he was singing, dancing, or fronting the band. Earlier, his trumpeter Bitsy Mullins had managed to accompany well enough on the drums, but Mullins gave notice and left the band on April 28, the last night of the Palladium job.

Stanley Kay detailed the scenario, recalling, "One day I got a call from Carl Ritchie, Buddy's manager and brother-in-law. Carl said Buddy wanted me to take the train to Chicago to join the band. I asked him, 'As what?' Carl explained that Buddy was expanding the act. He was doing more singing and dancing, and he needed a drummer to play when he wasn't behind the kit. I was so nervous heading out there. Man, I was going to be playing with and for my idol. When I got down there and climbed up on the stand, George Berg, a tenor saxophonist and the band's straw boss, had no idea what was going on. He said, 'Hey, kid, what are you, crazy? What are you doing?' I told him I was subbing for Buddy. He said, 'Get off of there. You trying to steal the drum set?' After a minute he finally realized why I was there. Buddy had never told anyone he was hiring another drummer."[11]

Kay, six years younger than Buddy, was offered the job of taking over the drums while Rich was singing and dancing. When Buddy had seen him play drums in his younger years, he said to Stanley's sister Sybil (who had performed with Buddy in his vaudeville days) that her little brother would never be a professional drummer. Though Stanley was awfully hurt by those harsh words, he made up his mind that he would do just that. He succeeded, and now it was Buddy himself who was offering him a place in his own band. At the same time, the breakup between Buddy and his wife Jean was made public. In May of that year, the powerful, syndicated columnist Walter Winchell wrote (published in a column printed in *The Morning Journal* newspaper, among many others), that "Mrs. Buddy Rich has left for a divorce."[12]

For Buddy Rich, it was straight ahead, and on May 24, 1946, Buddy Rich and His Orchestra opened at the Panther Room in Chicago with a very nervous Stanley Kay behind the drums. The two got along well, and Buddy would feel safe with him for years. William F. Ludwig II from the Ludwig Drum Company was there, and remembered that "the Panther Room in Chicago's Sherman House was a glittering room featuring animal motifs. Upholstery, artwork, menus, bar area: everything reminded one of panthers, those wild jungle beasts. Consequently, having Buddy open there with his new band was an extremely festive occasion. Opening night saw the place packed. The waiting line extended up the stairs into the main floor lobby above. The band was loud and great! The maitre'd and manager of the room was Ernie Byfield. He was a very important part of Chicago's entertainment scene, being also the manager of the famous Ambassador East dining room. One night I went with Buddy to see Ernie at the entrance, which was his customary post every evening. Ernie asked if Buddy could tone the volume down on the first set so the dinner guests could more easily converse. Buddy replied: 'Here. You take the fucking sticks and go lead the band and I'll act as maitre d' and seat the people.' I was stunned. The manager was making a simply request: tone the band down for the first set. Buddy's answer was to play louder than ever. Byfield was furious. He told me that Buddy would never play there again, and he didn't."[13]

After witnessing that outburst, Ludwig was a little hesitant to proceed with his real mission. He wasn't only there to watch and listen to Buddy Rich. His goal was to convince Buddy to leave Slingerland after his ten years with them and switch to Ludwig drums. His strongest argument was that Buddy would always be number two with Slingerland, since everyone knew that Gene Krupa was their foremost representative. At Ludwig he would be number one, and Ludwig could guarantee Buddy that all the marketing was already in place and that he would get first class treatment with them. The first class treatment even included the promise that each time Buddy was in the vicinity of Chicago, Ludwig would deliver a number of tympani for his show. He convinced Buddy to sign with them. "First, he was really uncertain," said Ludwig, "but after our second meeting, he agreed to sign. I didn't wait a second to write a letter to Slingerland telling them about Buddy's decision. At the next performance at the Panther Room, Bud Slingerland showed up. But it was too late. I had Buddy's signature."[14]

Things were still going relatively well for his orchestra musically, but there were economic issues. Sure, the band was getting great reviews and good bookings were coming in steadily, but generally, it was a financial struggle. His first stake from Sinatra was running out, barely six months after the $25,000 was received. He was being advised from all directions to gear his material more toward the public at large, as opposed to playing just what Buddy Rich liked. Some suggested more dance numbers. Others tried talking him into adding more bop. Buddy refused, but he privately worried that bop would overtake swing. Fortunately, Sinatra once more showed up in Buddy's dressing room. Having heard about Buddy's strained economic situation, he took out his checkbook again and gave Buddy another $25,000.

On August 8, 1946, Buddy Rich and His Orchestra opened for an engagement at the Aquarium Restaurant in New York that would last until mid-September. As always, there were new faces on the bandstand, and Buddy, now realizing the pressures his ex-bosses faced over the years, was forced to modify the band's direction, however slightly. He continued to add more singing numbers with himself as vocalist. Not everyone loved it. Swedish reporter Sten Jacobsson, who was in New York and saw the band at the Aquarium, wrote to all the Swedish jazz lovers: "The earsplitting sounds are produced according to the most modern recipe. The band is playing with an extra fine pep tonight since there are two radio broadcasts of a half hour each. They are playing great arrangements and solos, especially George Berg on tenor, Earl Swope on trombone, and Buddy Rich himself. But even so there is something personal missing in the band's style. They are playing an extremely talented big band swing, but unfortunately it is poured in the same mold as altogether too many orchestras today. I forgot to say that Rich has of late been attempting to launch himself as a vocalist without any great success"[15] (Note: Several of the Aquarium broadcasts were assembled years later on a vinyl recording called *That's Rich*.)

Buddy had hardly finished the engagement at the Aquarium when the Dorsey brothers called. They wanted him to come over to Tommy's place, Casino Gardens in California, where they were promoting an evening under the name of "The Battle of Dorseys." Buddy would be guest performer in Tommy's orchestra, which he accepted. In Jimmy's band, then one of the top bands in the business, Karl Kiffe sat behind the drums. Recording took place on two evenings, September 19 and 25, for an album later released under the same name.[16] However, it's still open to conjecture as to which band emerged the winner.

At the beginning of 1947, more reports about Buddy Rich's love life were showing up in the gossip columns. The always-alert Walter Winchell followed up on his surveillance of stars and wrote a small item that demonstrated that the media knew a little more about Buddy than what he believed himself. Winchell wrote, "Model Dorian Leigh tells chums she'll become Mrs. Buddy Rich. Is he melted yet from Jean Sutherlin?"[17]

Bebop's acceptance as a valid musical form was growing. The public and marketable face of the new music, which had nothing to do with the music itself, often focused on the appearance of the musicians who played it: the goatee, heavy framed spectacles, long cigarette holder, and beret. This bop thing was catching on. While the band business was still good, name bands could afford the luxury of adding more bop numbers to the book. When the established musicians were called up for service or retired, the new and younger talents got a chance, and by and large, these younger players wanted to create new music, not re-create the old. As time moved on, some of the older and established players were faced with music, and a music world, they didn't recognize. In some quarters, a cleft was created, though there were several exceptions, notably Coleman Hawkins, but there was no doubt that two camps were forming. On one side there were the swing musicians and on the other, the boppers.

The two camps sometimes didn't get along. The kings of swing, like Louis Armstrong, for example, said at the time about bebop, "You have all the weird chords that have no meaning at all, and people become curious just because it is new, but they soon tire because it is just rubbish—all of it—and you haven't any melody to remember and no rhythm to dance to. Everyone is poor again and nobody can get a job and that is the kind of trouble this modern mischief makes."[18] Drummer Dave Tough, who was playing with Woody Herman's orchestra at the time, and who was one of the few drummers who could play both big band and bebop, related an incident in 1944 on 52nd Street, where he and some others saw the Dizzy Gillespie/Oscar Pettiford Quintet, which was perhaps the very first bop ensemble. "When we walked in, those boys pulled up their horns and blew the craziest things," Tough reported. "One of them stopped suddenly and another one started without any reason. We could never decide when one solo ended and another one started. Then they all stopped all of a sudden and everyone left the bandstand. Those musicians scared us."[19]

Race was another issue. Some in the black, progressive music community were quite vocal about no longer wanting to play "white man's music." But there were white boppers, too, and some of them were tired of swing as well. The cutting edge innovator, blind pianist Lennie Tristano said, "Swing was hot, heavy and loud. Bebop was cool, light and quiet. The former bounced and panted onward like a worn out locomotive. The latter has a more refined pulse which is stressed more by mere hints. At those low sound levels many interesting and complicated accents can be added effectively."[20]

Dizzy Gillespie, whose singular image of the "hip bopster" often appeared in print, became something of the unofficial spokesperson for bop, and was often asked to detail how the whole new music started. As Gillespie explained it, "Some of us started to jam at Minton's up in Harlem in the beginning of the 1940s. There were always a lot of musicians who showed up who couldn't play at all, but still took six or seven choruses to show it. So, in the afternoons before the jam started, Thelonious Monk and I worked out some pretty complicated harmonies and in the evenings we played them to scare off the less talented guys. After a while we became more and more interested in the music we created and the more we experimented the faster our own style developed"[21] Buddy Rich was not yet among the converts. He freely admitted, "I like swing. I like the message it sends. But I don't understand this new trend that leads to really weird things. There is not a shred of melody. If you play a blues, you want it to sound like a blues, don't you? I will go on playing the music we are making now, contrary to all other bandleaders who say that jazz is on its way out."[22]

Dorian Leigh was probably the first woman who personified what is now called a "super model." She was an icon with her own style and class, and was the woman who stylistically defined the 1940s. Her face had graced the cover of *Vogue* magazine seven times during the decade. She loved to date—a lot. Among her dates, it's been said, were Dizzy Gillespie, photographer Irving Penn, singer Harry Belafonte, poet Robert Graves, and producer Sam Spiegel. There was an ugly rumor spread about her that she only liked to be seen with young, handsome, and broke men. She waved that away quickly, saying, "If I had to pay some bills to make that possible, it was only money and I happened to have it."[23] Now she was being paired up with Buddy Rich. Several sources indicate that they first met at a party that photographer Milton Green held for all his jazz friends. Dorian loved jazz and went along, and was attracted to Buddy at first sight. She enjoyed his company; he didn't smoke, he didn't drink or take any drugs, saying that he needed all his energy to play his drums.

He seemed perfect for her.

They fell for each other. "I was sure I was in love with Buddy," Leigh said at the time. "I envisioned him being a father to my two children and began to hope I would have a child by him as well. He seemed to be in love with me too, and, although he never told me in so many words, I assumed he wasn't married."[24] Their relationship began well. She followed along in the band bus everywhere, waited loyally for him at the edge of the stage, and she was introduced to Buddy's family just before Christmas, 1946. She was surprised when one of his sisters supposedly said, "The word Christmas is not mentioned in this house." In January, 1947, Milton Green contracted her for a photography session in Cuba for *McCalls* magazine. She would be away nearly a month and hesitated, thinking that her relatively new relationship with Buddy wouldn't survive that kind of long separation. She couldn't get him to come along on the trip because he had to play with his band. She was also aware that Buddy had received new financial help from Sinatra and now he was struggling even harder to keep the band solvent. Trying to convince him to take a breather, she said, "You're working tremendously hard!" and "You need a holiday for a change!" She was truly surprised by Buddy's answer. "Sure, you're right. I'm coming along," Buddy said, adding, "My band just folded."

Their first time on Cuba was pleasant for them both. Dorian often worked only in the early mornings, and in the afternoons they could lie by the pool and enjoy themselves with Milton Green and his wife Evelyn. During their stay, Buddy suggested that they should get married. She answered "yes," and they went to a church close to their hotel. The priest was a rather unpleasant man, and said he wouldn't consider marrying them since neither of them was Catholic. Besides, they didn't have a license to get married in Cuba. Not only was the priest correct, but Dorian also found out that Buddy was still married. The divorce from Jean Sutherlin had not come through. "We go through a ceremony, and then he tells me, 'My wife in California is going to use this against me to get a bigger settlement!'"[25] Back in the States, Leigh found out she was pregnant, and couldn't wait to tell Buddy the exciting news. Unfortunately, his response shocked her. "You know what this is? That's too bad!" said Buddy as he hung up the phone. She never dreamed that he would react in that way. Her pregnancy seemed to mean nothing to him, and he never even asked if she was going to keep the baby. She had a miscarriage some time later and the relationship was over.

The news of the pregnancy never leaked out to the press, but the gossip reporters did manage to find out that that they had gone to a priest to get married. They exaggerated the reports of the whole thing, declaring that they actually had been married there, but had had the marriage annulled after only a few days. This was not the case. Buddy and Dorian broke up when they got home to the United States, and the love affair had only lasted a few months. She thought that Buddy had shown his true colors. Time passed and after a few months, Buddy called her up without saying a word about what had happened. He only asked if she wanted to go out with him. Her answer was short: "I don't want anything more to do with you!"[26]

Buddy's attempts to save his band were in vain. New songs, new musicians, Sinatra's financial assistance, the flirtation with bop, more singing, more dancing; nothing had been enough. Generally, the band business was in decline, but what made the decision to disband particularly difficult was Buddy Rich's love for jazz. The truth was the money had literally run out, and in later interviews, Buddy revealed that he had lost over $250,000 in total. There was no alternative but to fold, and the only ones he kept on were Stanley Kay and his brother Mickey.

Buddy contacted Norman Granz, and the press lost no time in reporting the news. On January 29, 1947, *Downbeat* wrote, "BUDDY RICH DROPS BAND, JOINS GRANZ: Norman Granz, back here briefly following a trip to Mexico City to set future dates south of the border for his jazz concert unit, reported that Buddy Rich has dropped his band and will join the new Granz troupe in time for the opening event of the new tour, a date at Brooklyn's Academy of Music on February 6. In addition to Rich, the outfit is to include Roy Eldridge, Coleman Hawkins, Illinois Jacquet, Willie Smith, Buck Clayton, Trummy Young, Ken Kersey, Helen Humes, and a new bass discovery, Benny Fonesville." Buddy accepted Granz's offer to join the Jazz at the Philharmonic tour, beginning in February and at a wage of a $1,000 a week. Buddy was happy with the numbers, saying, "I joined up with Jazz at the

Philharmonic after I had dropped my band, and I managed to earn back a lot of the money that I had lost earlier."[27]

Initially, he looked forward to the tour and to playing with a fine lineup of musicians, but it wasn't long before his own taste in music collided with that of Norman Granz's. Buddy was irritated by all the non-structured jamming and the grandstanding that went on while he backed seemingly endless saxophone and trumpet solos. The very month after the end of the tour, he realized that he had to have his own band, where he could make the musical decisions and express himself the way he wanted to. He decided—again—to put together a whole new band. Who knows exactly why? Maybe he wanted to get past the episode with Dorian Leigh. He made other changes. He stayed on with MCA, but brought on Milt Ebbins, who also managed Basie, as his manager. Ever resourceful, Buddy managed to raise the capital for new stage clothes for everyone, new music stands, new arrangements, and everything else that was needed.

The band rehearsed all through March, and included several numbers that featured Rich's vocals with Stanley Kay back on drums. The first problem was musical. It was bop. It just wouldn't go away, and this time around, some of the hipper bandsmen were lobbying to play more bop. Buddy was still resistant to the new music. "The goddam beboppers," he said, pulling no punches. "The minute you got a few in the band, they'd want to throw out all the charts except for the bebop ones. The other guys in the band were always fighting with the beboppers."[28] In the end, he opted for a book with more dance numbers and ballads, at least in the beginning of the evening. As a performance progressed, the band would heat up with some jazz, and naturally, he couldn't let down his fans who all wanted to hear his incredible drumming.

On April 4, the new Rich band opened at the Arcadia Ballroom for a month-long stay. On the recommendation of MCA, he spent a great deal of time every evening at the front of the stage, singing, dancing, and talking to the audience. He used his experience from his youth, where he learned how to connect with the audience. An example from the time: A woman came up to the edge of the stage and asked, "Mr. Rich, would you dance with me? I've never danced with a famous bandleader before, and it would be a moment that I would never forget!" Buddy smiled and replied, "Gee, that would really be swell, but I'm the band's drummer and the only reason I'm standing up here is because I'm better looking than the rest of these guys!"[29]

Right after the opening night at the Arcadia, Buddy Rich took part in Art Ford's New York City-based "Saturday Night Swing Session" radio broadcast for WNEW Radio. This show was different than many of the others, in that nothing was rehearsed ahead of time. In front of a studio audience of about 200, the participants all improvised, and the songs and chats could be as long or short as they liked. Here, he was paired up with Ella Fitzgerald in a duet, "Blue Skies," later retitled "Budella" when issued on V-Disc. Buddy was really pleased to be able to sing with the First Lady, and on the recording—which has been preserved—the regard they both held for each other is clear.

About a month later, *Downbeat's* William Gottlieb reviewed the new band, and reported, "Several times throughout his career, Rich quit playing drums to be either a dancer or a singer, but ultimately he always returned to drumming. His vocal style has been compared to Mel Tormé's and Frank Sinatra's. Buddy Rich has a good chance of making a go of this venture, thanks principally to the growth of his own showmanship and a willingness to go along with trends. His orchestra will, however, have to acquire musical character and promotional knowhow before it will really click." Buddy replied in a comment in the same edition. "How right this review is," Buddy is supposed to have said (the suspicion is that it was written by Buddy's press agent). "I realize a band can be no more successful than its publicity. We shortly hope to get a good drum beater, and I don't mean a musician. We've already broken with manager Lou Mindling and now have Milt Ebbins, who also handles Basie and should know how to guide our orchestra. I certainly did learn my lessons with my last band. Long before we folded, I realized I couldn't make it playing (strictly jazz). But I was stubborn and wouldn't change. Now I'm sticking to melodic music played at low volume. However, we intend to feature standards. In that way, we can be pretty without being trite." If Buddy Rich actually said that, it had to have been one of the few times he actually agreed with a reviewer.

In September, he turned 30, and it was clear the band was in trouble. Al Cohn, who had replaced Allan Eager on tenor saxophone, was one of those who hung in with Buddy. "We were doing a week up in Boston," Cohn remembered, "and Buddy kept telling the band about this great Italian restaurant. He went on and on about how delicious the food was. Buddy, at that time, was especially pleased with how well the band was sounding, so he tells all of us one evening that after the last set to meet him at this restaurant. It would be his treat! All of us eat heavily and the check came—and no Buddy! Time passed, still no Buddy! Finally, we all had to chip in and pay the bill, but it wasn't easy, believe me!"[30]

By the time the band hit Spokane, Washington, Buddy informed everyone that he didn't have the money to transport everyone to the next engagement in Ione, Oregon. He contacted MCA and asked for an advance, but the agency turned him down, saying that Buddy already owed them $700. He missed the gig in Oregon, one of the few performances he ever had to cancel for that edition of the band. At another performance near Chicago, he called the band together, gave each man $5, and told them to get themselves to the next gig in Milwaukee. Back in New York, Buddy was in a foul mood and turned to the musician's union, asking them to sue MCA for holding back money he claimed was due to him. He won the suit, left MCA and went with the William Morris Agency. The touring continued, as did the endless one-nighters.

On October 21, 1947, the band played at Post Lodge in Larchmont, New York, about 18 or so miles from the city he truly loved. Hal Webman of *Billboard* magazine was there, and wrote a few days later, "Buddy Rich is still unquestionably one of the greatest drummers ever. He is blossoming out as a first rate rhythm singer and is now even making efforts to emulate the Mel Tormé type of ballad, warbling with moderate success. Rich clowns amiably in front of the band and wisely holds his drumming efforts to a minimum. And when they're required, the versatile Rich even can rack up a better-than-middlin' tap and soft shoe routine."

That fall, Buddy Rich also played with "Barry Ulanov and His All Metronome Jazzmen"on a radio broadcast. The mostly-bop band included Charlie Parker, Lennie Tristano, Fats Navarro, Allan Eager, and singer Sarah Vaughn. In December he played and recorded with "The Metronome All Stars," where Dizzy Gillespie, Buddy DeFranco, Flip Phillips, and Nat King Cole were members. In one number, they were all backed up by Stan Kenton's orchestra. As for Charlie Parker, Buddy's opinion of him had changed. He would never again speak poorly of him.

The band, now with MGM records, was contracted to record, but for some reason, MGM recorded only a sextet, made up of Tommy Allisson and Dale Pierce on trumpets, Mario Daone on trombone, Al Cohn on tenor sax, George Handy on piano, and Charlie Leeds on bass. Stanley Kay played the drums when Buddy's sang. Buddy hated the result, issued many years later on vinyl as *Rich Riot*. "Stupid! We should never have recorded," said Buddy. "People tell me that record is a collector's item! Why should anyone want to own it, much less listen to it? It wasn't me; it wasn't what my band was doing. Record companies just don't understand, man, they want you to be something you just can't be. Then they have the nerve to tell you that you don't sell!"[31]

He reorganized yet again. Allan Eager returned to replace Al Cohn, and the 21-year-old vibraphonist Terry Gibbs joined up. The latter would come to be very important for the orchestra's sound. The young Gibbs, who had a fantastic technique and understood both swing and bebop, joined after having toured with bassist Chubby Jackson, whose band was now on the ropes, without work. Gibbs signed with Buddy Rich for a wage of $15 a week, the same amount everyone else was making. The "new, new" Buddy Rich band snared a December 18 to January 7 booking at the Roseland Ballroom in New York City, to be followed by a date that Buddy was really looking forward to: a week's engagement at the famed Apollo Theatre in Harlem, beginning February 27, 1948. It was on this date that one of the legendary Buddy Rich stories began to unfold.

A few days before the opening at the Apollo, the band was sitting in the band bus, when Buddy turned to Stanley Kay and informed him, "We're going to the movies in the morning." "Buddy, I don't want to go to the movies," said Stanley. "I don't want to. I'm going to go to the gym and play handball." Buddy decided to come along, as did brother Mickey. It wasn't unusual that the boys did what they could to keep in shape. Buddy and Mickey used to jog or swim or whatever they could. Whatever they did, the story was always the same. Both wanted to win and they were always dead serious. They got to a handball court at the YMCA and started to play. Stanley Kay recalled, "Soon he ran into a wall, trying to make a shot with his left arm. As he hit the wall, he went, 'ahh, ahh.' I asked what was wrong. Buddy answered, 'I hurt my arm.' I said, 'Okay, go and sit in the sauna for awhile and come back to us later.' After a while he came back. 'It still hurts,' Buddy said." Kay took him to a doctor, who discovered that Buddy's hand was broken, as well as his arm—in two or three places.

Two days later it was opening night.

CHAPTER 10

Stubborn Guy

April 1, 1948, New York City: A broken arm fails to stop Buddy, who demonstrates his technique for songstress Jane Harvey and bandleader Alvy West (right) in the Green Room of the Hotel Edison.

On February 27, 1948, the Apollo Theater was completely sold out, and the sellout had nothing to do with rumors about Buddy's possibly bum arm. The fact was that other than Buddy's band and the bands of Woody Herman and Charlie Barnet, not many white bands drew audiences there. People rushed to buy tickets as soon as they heard news of Buddy's appearance, but the big question was how to deal with the issue of his broken arm. Buddy Rich's decision was to play every performance on drums, and he would play for the next three months with his one good arm. Stanley Kay helped him find a brown suit and a brown bandage to match the suit so the bandaged arm wasn't so noticeable. When Buddy and his friend Steve Condos did a tap dance number, Steve also wore a similar bandage so that everyone wouldn't stare at Buddy the whole time. It was actually only after the first number was finished, when Buddy went to the edge of the stage to say thank you, that the audience first became aware of the one-arm situation.

Mickey Rich knew better than anyone that there was no way Buddy was going to cancel the next six weeks of bookings while his broken arm healed, especially since two of those weeks were at the Paramount.[1] Apollo audiences were rarely shy, and cries of "It's crazy," "He's lost his senses," "It can't be possible," and "The man is a freak!" could be heard throughout the theater. Trumpeter Clark Terry summed it up by saying "Oh boy, I was there that day." So was Sammy Davis, Jr. "I saw him once at the Apollo Theatre and he had his arm in a sling," Davis recalled. "He played the entire show and his solos with one hand. In those days, they used to do a number where he would open up behind the curtain and after 16 bars, the curtain would slowly rise and a voiceover would say, 'Now, ladies and gentlemen, Buddy Rich and his band!' So, the Apollo Theater in Harlem, we all had our roots there, and if you were accepted there, you were accepted anywhere in the world. So this is what you heard: (imitates snare drum intro solo with voice) and so on, and when the audience realized that he was playing with his arm in a sling, it was pandemonium! It took 20 minutes and the whole music business knew about this."[2]

Buddy caused a commotion everywhere. All the papers wrote about it, and everyone was talking about Buddy Rich and how he could play all the songs with only one arm. The head of Paramount Theater, Bob

Whiteman, who had booked the band the following month and was not easily impressed, had to admit, "Everybody is talking about the band now." Terry Gibbs maintained that "it was one of the most fantastic things I've ever seen a drummer do." Jo Jones, who had also been at opening night, could only say, "If that arm heals, somebody ought to break it again." Later in life, Buddy commented on the incident several times and didn't think it was so remarkable. "It was a thing born out of necessity," he explained. "The band had been booked for months in advance, and with 19 people on the payroll, I couldn't very well just say, 'We'll be off for three months.' There was too much involved to cancel our bookings. It was just a matter of having to do it. What the hell's the difference anyway? If you can play with two hands, you can play with one. If you don't have any, you play with your feet."[3]

In March, 1948, Buddy's mother Bess died from cancer at the age of 59. Robert was brokenhearted, and Buddy also took her death very hard. He blamed himself for not having done enough for her. Marge, Buddy's sister, said, "When my mother died, brother kept insisting it was his fault. I told him he was crazy. How could her dying of cancer be his fault? He wouldn't listen."[4] While in mourning, he still continued to play with his broken arm. He didn't cancel a single engagement. In March, the band played at the Clique Club in New York. Several years later, the Clique became the legendary Birdland. The local promoter was jazz lover and historian Al Rose that had booked the band. "Buddy was there with his left arm in a cast," said Rose. "But despite a broken wing and everything, he was just as active in all the sets the whole evening. And he took part in all the marketing activities I had planned. I asked him if it was too strenuous for him and he answered, 'Everything has always been strenuous for me—even sex!'"[5]

March drew to a close with two week engagement at the Paramount. It wasn't easy, as the pace at the 3,600-seat Paramount was notoriously grueling, with five shows a day—and six on Sundays. Buddy drew great crowds. The Paramount's Bob Weitman came up to Stanley Kay and said, "Rumors say that Buddy's arm isn't really broken. If it isn't, tell him to keep the bandage on anyway." In *Billboard*, Bill Smith wrote about the opening, "Viewed as a package, the new show runs at an okay pace, with Buddy Rich the outstanding personality on stage. The band fronter has developed remarkably. As a skin beater he's always exciting to watch. With his left arm in a sling he becomes even more so. When he wound up with his 'Not So Quiet (Please),' calling for a drum solo, the applause was enthusiastic and wholehearted. Some of it may have been sympathetic, but most of it was due to a real talent."[6]

There was one story after the other about Buddy's unbelievable feat of carrying out a whole tour with one arm in a cast. Trumpeter Pauly Cohen remembered Buddy backing yet another knife-throwing act. "I played with Buddy at a theater where we were supposed to accompany a knife thrower who hit a twirling wheel with a woman tied to it," said Cohen. "Despite Buddy having broken his arm, he hit all the important places perfectly. It sounded as though he played with two hands. I've never heard anything like it."[7]

In May, the band arrived at the Regal in Chicago, another venue that booked mainly black bands and black performers. The Regal made an exception for the white Buddy Rich band, and it was the Regal's only exception. In Buddy's dressing room, he was warming up while Terry Gibbs and Stanley Kay looked on. Then Buddy got really irritated. "I'm getting tired of this shit on my arm. I can't take it anymore. I'm taking it off!" he shouted. A panicked Terry Gibbs told him, "You're crazy! You can't take it off! You'll break your hand again!"[8] Buddy was implacable. "Get out of my room!" he yelled, and then he chased them both out. Kay and Gibbs looked at each other and just shook their heads. Then they could hear how he was trying to cut open the cast. Seconds later, they heard Buddy banging a pair of drumsticks frenetically on something, probably a chair. Buddy was practicing as hard as he could. It couldn't be true.

"He took that cast off and played as though his arm had never been broken," said Kay. "I just stood there and said I couldn't fathom where it was coming from. It couldn't be possible. But that's what happened. "[9] Then Buddy went down to the stage and played with his left arm that he hadn't used for months. Gibbs had a hard time believing what he saw and heard, explaining, "Now, if I don't play or practice for four days, I sound like a child trying to learn a scale, like a real klutz. He played a drum solo on that show that I never heard anybody play, including him.

He did that just to show us he's Buddy Rich and no matter what, even with his left arm being in a cast for months, nothing was going to stop him."[10]

On July 6, Buddy Rich and His Orchestra opened at Hollywood Palladium in California for a five-week stint. During the stay, he was introduced to a woman by the name of Betty Jo O'Curran, and he fell in love. Marge Rich explained that "Betty Jo was married to dance director Charlie O'Curran. Betty Jo and I were very, very close friends. I invited her to Buddy's opening at the Palladium. That's how she and Buddy met. She was a lovely girl; very quiet. Buddy took to her instantly, and when she and Charlie split up, Betty Jo and Buddy began to live together."[11] They became a couple, but even though Buddy wanted to marry her, it didn't happen. In the beginning it was impossible, as Buddy's divorce from Jean Sutherlin still hadn't been finalized, but after some time, Betty Jo made it clear for him that she had no plans whatsoever to remarry. Marge believed that "Buddy was never a chaser. He really cared for this girl and wanted to marry her. She was the one who didn't want to get married. Buddy needed stability, marriage. 'Something of my own' was the way he put it."

July would be hectic for many reasons. Buddy replaced several members of the band. Among others, saxophonist Hal McKusick joined up and trombonist Johnny Mandel (who later would become a very successful composer and arranger) returned. Hal McKusick recalled, "I joined Buddy's band in California and played lead alto sax and clarinet at the Palladium Ballroom in Hollywood. It was an unbelievably good group of musicians. I remember that Johnny Mandel wrote some songs for Buddy quite early on. Buddy was an enormously enthusiastic bandleader. And I remember his right foot that pounded on with powerful beats. He drove the band incredibly hard."[12] The band continued touring around the country and returned to the Palladium, where they broadcast live on the radio once a week. Some found the life glamorous; some didn't. Terry Gibbs recalled a less-than-pleasant incident: Buddy used to travel in his new Cadillac between performances and Terry, whom Buddy liked, got to accompany him. During one of these trips, Terry told Buddy that the boys in the band thought they were just as good as Woody Herman's musicians. Why wouldn't he let them play more jazz solos? Buddy agreed and the next evening he was Mr. Nice Guy. They all were pleasantly surprised and played extremely well. This carried on during the trip, as Gibbs continued to suggest that one after the other be allowed to play a solo now and then, given that they all were so good.

In his book, *Good Vibes: A Life in Jazz*, Terry Gibbs explained how easy it was to get on the wrong side of Buddy, especially after his repeated comments that many in the band should be allowed to play even more solos. "On the fourth night," Gibbs wrote, "we were going through the Arizona desert. It was about four in the morning and it was pitch black outside. I started telling him again, 'You know, Buddy, the guys...' 'Wait a minute!' He stopped the car.'Listen! I don't want to hear your bullshit anymore! I'm getting tired of hearing all this from you. *Get outta the car!*' 'Get out of the car? We're in the middle of the desert!' I told him. '*I don't care! Get outta the car!*' Buddy screamed. I thought he was putting me on so I got out. Vroom! He drove away at 90 miles an hour. For the next ten minutes, which seemed like an hour to me, I stood there on the road, waiting for him to come back and pick me up. He never came back. I didn't know if the band bus was taking the same route that Buddy took. After an hour, the bus finally showed up. By that time, I was a complete nervous idiot."

In July 1948, the band starred in two film shorts. The first was a Universal picture called *Buddy Rich and His Orchestra*, where Buddy got to show off his singing voice in a few numbers, and was also featured in tap dance segment with Louis DaPron. The film ended with yet another fantastic drum solo, which was actually the only number he played live in the studio, as everything else was pre-recorded. The idea of starring in his own motion picture—of any length—must have warmed Buddy's heart. The second film was also a short in Columbia's *Thrills of Music* series. In that opus, Buddy tap danced with the great Steve Condos, sang a duet with Betty Bonney and played another tremendous drum solo in the number "Kicks with Sticks." These little films were not blockbusters, and in fact, the Columbia film is a rarity among collectors. But Universal and Columbia must have had their eyes on Buddy Rich, in that Gene Krupa, who had been churning out film shorts since 1939, had just been featured in two similar films: Director Will Cowman's

Drummer Man, and another entry in the *Thrills of Music* series. They all followed the same formula: Part music, part drumming, and part cornball entertainment.

The big band was managing to hang on, and after filming they embarked on a five-theater tour with stops at the Earle in Philadelphia; the Royal in Baltimore; the Howard in Washington, D.C.; the Regal in Chicago; and the Paradise in Detroit. There were discussions on the bus about the band's repertoire, and plenty of the sidemen continued to lobby for more bop. On the way back to California to complete the Palladium stand, the harping reached its peak. Hal McKusick was among the boppers. "By the time Buddy's band had reached Northern California, we were desperate," said McKusick. "So I called Jimmy Giuffre. I said he could write Buddy's entire book if he wanted to. I told him I'd even stay up all night with him copying his charts for the band. He finally gave in and told me to wire him money."[13] Although they may have been playing some new material by the fall of 1948, Buddy Rich and his Orchestra weren't living extravagantly. The touring was strenuous, with long stretches between jobs, drafty busses, six men sleeping in a hotel room at a time (some snuck in through the window), and terrible food the norm.

Terry Gibbs recalled that drugs were becoming an issue in the band, completely without Buddy's knowledge. On one occasion someone in the orchestra stole twenty capsules of narcotics. "All of a sudden, the door opened and the connection ran in," Gibbs detailed in his book. "He shut the door and pulled out a gun. Pointing to the right side of the room, he said ,'You three get over there!' Then he pointed at me to stand on the left side of the room. This all went down very fast. He called them all kind of dirty names. 'You dirty, so–and–so' and used every M–F word in the book. 'Okay, I'm not going to kill you but on the count of three, if you don't tell me where it is, I'll shoot you in the leg.' Then he pointed to the other guys. 'Then I'll shoot you in the leg, and then I'll shoot you. *One, two...*' He said it fast—he didn't wait. There was no pause in that sentence. Before he could get to three, the guys all said, 'Wait a minute! Wait a minute!' They panicked and got into a little huddle. While the guy was waving his gun up and down, one of them went into the closet and took out the twenty caps they had stolen and gave them to him.[14]

The next stop was the Avalon Ballroom in New York again for a nearly two-week engagement (Avalon broadcasts were later issued on the recording *Buddy Rich: Cool Breeze*), followed by a return to his beloved Apollo. To his friend Mel Tormé, Buddy described an incident that made a strong impression on him. It truly shows how popular and highly regarded Buddy Rich was in Harlem. "It's one of the great stories of my life," said Buddy to Tormé. "They had just delivered a new Cadillac. This had to be in 1948. For a couple of years, I had driven nothing but sports cars, as you know. I was appearing at the Apollo Theatre on 125th Street in New York. My band was only the second white band to ever appear at the Apollo; the other band was Charlie Barnet. The Apollo audience was a totally black one. Even though it was only 110 blocks from downtown New York, it was another world. The black audience appreciation was so much greater than the cats who went to the Paramount Theatre, it wasn't funny.

"Anyway, after the first show at the Apollo, I was told, 'Hey, they just brought your new car over. It's out in front of the theater.' I went out and looked it over. It was gorgeous. It had everything: radio and whatever was hip in those days. I went back inside for the next show, I guess it was the third show in the evening, and when I came back out (laughs), the car was totally dismantled. I mean, they took the radio out, the wheels off, everything. It was just left standing there like that. It looked like it had just been through one of Rommel's invasions of North Africa. I remember the cat who was the stage manager backstage. He was six feet eight; a black Kojak. He had a totally bald head, and he was mean. I went back to see him, and I said, 'Man, somebody's ruined my car; stripped it clean. Come look at it.'He looked at it and put his arm around me. Man, I almost sunk into the concrete, and he said, 'Don't worry about it. It'll be straight.' I moaned, 'Man, I haven't even driven the car. It's just been delivered.' 'Don't worry about it,' he tells me.'Don't worry about it? Man, that thing just cost me $3,000.'

"Anyway, I came out after the last show and the car was put back together. It was polished when they had delivered it earlier. It was Simonized in the three hours since I reported the theft. What happened was some of the cats did not know that the car belonged to Buddy Rich. When they found out it was my car, the car was put back in perfect shape;

better than when it was first delivered that day. I can remember going up to Harlem after that, to the Savoy or the old Renaissance Ballroom or Dickie Wells' club, and I could leave a thousand dollars on the seat of the car, I could leave my wardrobe in the car, my drums, and the word would get around: 'That's B's car,' and everything was safe. That was one of the greatest feelings, because I was accepted in Harlem, and to me that was the greatest acceptance of my career."

Jack Schiffman, owner of the Apollo Theater, loved Buddy. "Of all the white musicians who played at Apollo, there was no one who as beloved and popular as Buddy Rich," Schiffman remembered. "His act consisted of everything: quick wit, good singing and dancing, but just his style would have been enough to get standing ovations from our discerning audience. The way he got through every show by always standing front stage center made everyone think that they were watching a show where every little detail must have been rehearsed extremely well, not unlike an opera."[15]

Life on the road continued, as Hal McKusick recalled. "We travelled up the West Coast and played at different festivals in Oregon and Washington," said McKusick. "Then right across Canada where we finished off in Toronto. We passed Niagara Falls and were back at the Clique Club again. George Shearing and Sarah Vaughn played at the same gig. Buddy played as unbelievably well as usual, and the band was feeling really great."[16] Things may have been relatively good on the band, but that didn't mean that Buddy didn't explode from time to time. Stress was certainly a factor that this point, as he began to demand more and more of his musicians. He wanted everything to be in place and he definitely wanted to demonstrate that he was the leader. He was more and more understanding of why Shaw and Dorsey acted the way they did. They *knew* what it took to keep 16 musicians in line when they were on the road.

Philadelphia's Frank Palumbo was a big fan of Buddy Rich. When he booked them into the Clique Club, he had the band play at dinners and matinees, mostly because he liked Buddy so much. One night, as Palumbo stood listening to the band, he reacted to the volume and called Buddy over. In a friendly tone, he said, "Buddy, we have a little private booking with around 300 older women at the club tonight. Tell the boys to keep the volume down a little." That was the worst thing he could have said. "You may ask Buddy to do something," explained Terry Gibbs. "But nobody ever told Buddy what to do. When Buddy heard that, you could see the horns coming out of his head. Buddy said, 'Look, you run your saloon and I'll run my band.' Then I knew we were in trouble. I don't think ten minutes went by before three goons walked over to us, flipped their jackets open and we saw that each one of them was carrying a gun. I think we were out of town in about 26 minutes."[17]

Buddy started believing the band was on the road to nowhere. He was continuously lowering fees to get new bookings, and his sidemen were still making noise about the repertoire. He finally lost his patience. In January, 1949, *Downbeat*, always among the first of the trades to report changes in touring bands, confirmed: "Buddy gives boot to his boppers. Paving the way with a series of minor flare ups, Buddy Rich finally cleaned house and put his entire band on notice. Explaining that a certain element was taking the style of the Rich music into their hands, his firings backfired when it came time to board a bus to play at the Marine hospital on Staten Island. Not a single band member showed up. Buddy, anticipating this, had contacted Count Basie and Oscar Pettiford to work with him at the hospital as a trio." The "boppers" had made their position clear. Buddy countered with his own statement that read, "I like bop as well as any musician, but there are other things I want to play. These fellows want to play bop and nothing else. In fact, I doubt if they can play anything else."[18] As the finishing touch, Rich was voted as 1948's top drummer in the country by *Metronome* magazine. As usual, he ignored this completely.

Luigi Paulino Alfredo Francesco Antonio Balassoni was born July 6, 1924, in Rock Fall, Illinois. Anyone with such beautiful names had to be headed for success. Luigi was. He began playing the drums at the age of three, and like Buddy, he demonstrated an incredible musical talent at a very early age. As Louie Bellson, who first broke through when he beat out around 40,000 drummers to win the Slingerland-sponsored Gene Krupa Drum Contest, he would later become known as one of the first who developed double bass drums as an integral part of drum set, and as a drummer who would impress every bandleader with his ear, musicality, and abilities as a composer and arranger. Bellson had a good command of everything. His original compositions were stylistically advanced and had great feeling, leading Duke Ellington to once comment, "He isn't just the best drummer in the world. He is also the world's best musician." Ultimately, Louie Bellson was often ranked as among the three greatest drummers of all time.

This two bass drum thing intrigued Buddy Rich. Bellson was around 18 when he first had the idea. "I got the idea in 1938," as Bellson remembered it. "I was going to high school and drew a picture of a drum set with two bass drums. My teacher said, 'What are you doing?' I answered, 'It's a drawing of a new drum set, a whole new way of doing it.' I explained that most drummers only used one. But I have two. He answered, 'Keep working on that.' So he got me to continue. And then I tried to present my idea to different drum companies, but they thought I should take off with Buck Rogers to the moon. 'You're crazy,' they said. 'I know I'm crazy, but it's my idea,' I answered them."[19] Bellson didn't give up and kept going around to more companies and finally he got a bite. "I kept on looking for someone who believed in my idea and finally Gretsch agreed to make a set. It took a long time because they had never made a deal with me before so they didn't know anything about me. The first time I used the set was with a big band in 1946 when I played with Ted Fio Rito,[20] and it was just before I joined up with Dorsey. I took them along to him. He loved the idea because it made people look at the orchestra. He was the kind of bandleader who liked that."[21]

During the coming years, Dorsey and Bellson weren't shy about developing and exploiting the idea even more. Probably with a great deal of inspiration from the great Krupa, an eternal master at thinking up visual effects, Bellson and Dorsey came up with their own idea. Bellson knew that Dorsey "was a great man for theatrics, and he said. 'You know, this two bass drums idea is phenomenal. The only thing that bothers me is that when the ordinary layman sees you from the front, he thinks, 'How's he doing it? I see all those drums, but how's he doing it?' So I told Tommy I had an idea: a revolving platform. He said, 'That's it!'"[22] The next time Bellson played his long drum solo, the drum set turned, the audience gasped, and they were even more impressed by what they saw: Two bass drums that were also lit up from inside. As an added novelty, Louie put lights on the drumsticks. Audiences went nuts.

At the beginning of 1949, Buddy Rich was without an orchestra, but he still had a number of booking commitments that he had to fulfill. He must have wondered if he had made the right decision to disband, as there was really nothing wrong with the band. It was more and more difficult to keep everything together. Hal McKusick remembered the end, saying, "After the Clique Club engagement, there were fewer bookings and many of us remained in New York, as did I. It was a tough time for all big bands. I remember those days with Buddy with good feelings; I was lucky to have been there. It was a shame he had to break up the band because it was a very good big band."[23]

During December of 1948, Buddy made contact with guitarist Eddie Condon, whose NBC television program, "Eddie Condon's Floor Show," began to take off. In the beginning of 1949, he wanted to have Buddy guest on his show with his band. Buddy, who had just folded the group, put together a new one almost right away. The situation was challenging but gratifying. Having the entire band on television could help determine the future, but for the moment, his musicians were still bugged about playing swing, and his booking agency just wasn't able to deliver regular work. Buddy took up Condon's offer anyway, agreeing to broadcast from the Paramount Theatre between February 13 and March 8, 1949. This was Buddy's big chance to show off all his musical talents, and the two-bass-drum business that he was hearing about Bellson was starting to interest him more and more.

It wasn't surprising. It seemed that everyone was talking about that remarkable drummer Bellson, who did incredibly exciting things that nobody had ever done, and with a phenomenal technique. Buddy became noticeably aggravated. He knew Bellson well, but he couldn't understand what was so unique about his new drum set. Mel Tormé was booked in as guest star with Buddy's band, and at the rehearsal, he noticed a couple of extra big boxes. He asked Buddy about them and he got a short, abrupt answer: "Fucking Louie Bellson should learn to play one bass drum before he tries two!" The answer surprised Tormé, who knew very well that Buddy and Louie were very good friends. But Buddy had decided to put Bellson in his place, and had ordered two extra 22-inch bass drums.

He had also contacted Basie about lending him his chart on "Old Man River." The plan was to play a drum solo at the climax of "River," which was the perfect showpiece—Buddy remembered his early idol, Tony Briglia, performing something similar with the Casa Loma Orchestra as early as 1934. (A listen to the Casa Loma's recording of "Old Man River" shows a striking similarity to the Basie chart.)[24]

The very next day, at the opening, Buddy tested his idea on stage. When the closing number came, he played an "ordinary" solo on his drum set in the tune's first section, but at the end, the two bass drums were rolled to the front of the stage and Buddy performed an unbelievably fast solo on only them, with both hands held straight out in the air. It was unbelievable. He was playing everything he wanted to, but with his feet. The audience was shouting. They had never seen anything like it.

Swedish journalist Ted Warner wrote, "In the middle of February I flew to New York to meet my wife, and there we were lucky enough to get to hear the most amazing and fascinating (performer) in the way of music, namely Buddy Rich. His new band played at the big Paramount Theatre on Times Square. I can't find words to describe his technique and balance. I still can't believe that anyone can play the drums that way. I remember that my other colleagues at the paper said that he was fabulous with one arm when they heard him, can you imagine what he was like at full vigor? I was absolutely finished, groaning, sweating, crying and laughing in turns, so that my wife nearly had to carry me out on Broadway afterwards. The main number was 'Old Man River.' When the different soloists were all worn out, the king of kings began a solo that will surely go down in history. After about 15 minutes' display of the most fantastic imagination, the whole thing ended with him sitting on a drum stool with only two bass drums in front of him, and beginning to lay up a drum roll with his feet; even and precise until it sounded exactly as if he had done the same thing with the drumsticks on a kettledrum. This was followed by about ten minutes of footwork with various themes and paradiddles. Now I've heard all the top drummers in the U.S.A. and I'm not exaggerating when I say that Buddy Rich is more technical with his feet than all the others put together—even if they use both their feet and hands."[25]

Eddie Condon wanted to extend Buddy's contract several more months. Buddy didn't know what all the fuss was about—he didn't understand why there was such a hullaballoo around the whole thing. "I just got tired of hearing about Louie and his bass drums and how hard it was to play on them," Buddy said at the time. "I decided that if you were going to play on two then you should do it. But if you play on two in a drum set you can't play on your hi-hat at the same time. And if you don't play on your hi-hat you leave out the most important sound in drum playing. It is just a gimmick; nothing else. And I don't use gimmicks. I have no lights, no lighted drumsticks or any revolving platform. I don't want to be a clown or a showman. I concentrate on what I am playing, since I want to play well. And if you do something else that distracts you, if you have to think about how you're going to impress people, then you have to sacrifice your playing. I'm not going to do that. I have never done that."[26] Rumors of Buddy's phenomenal feet-only solo at the Paramount spread quickly. No one who was there could fathom how he did it. Even Stanley Kay, who had seen and heard plenty, was astounded.

In May 1949, however, everything finally came to an end. Buddy Rich was once again forced to face facts and disband his orchestra. At the remaining Condon shows he was signed for, he played as a guest with a few different groups. Buddy played in quartets, quintets, and septets, sang with Thelma Carpenter, backed Ella Fitzgerald, and even showed the actor Kirk Douglas—prepping for his role in *Young Man with a Horn*—how to hold the cornet (at Condon's own nightclub after the television show).

The question was what Buddy Rich should do now. Looking back years later, he said, "People advised me to cut the band down. I had nine brass, five reeds, and four rhythm. But I couldn't see it. I'm a very stubborn guy."[27]

This time there was no Georgie Auld nearby to help him out. The best drummer in the world was out of a job—again.

CHAPTER 11

Jazz at the Philharmonic

**Filming Jazz at the Philharmonic with
Bill Harris, Flip Phillips, Buddy, Hank Jones, Lester Young, 1949.**

Buddy with arm in a sling, 1948, with dancer Steve Condos.

With the demise of the big band era, the emphasis in the jazz world shifted to the virtuoso soloist. It made economic sense, to be sure, as many of the great big band players could now tour as soloists with their own small groups, or book themselves as singles fronting a local rhythm section. Whatever the nature of the booking, the soloist could play the way they wanted to play, whether swing, bop, or otherwise. Then there was the concept of the staged jam session, often presented in a concert hall, and featuring any number of star soloists of different stylistic eras on the same stage. Now and then there were stylistic collisions, but that just made everything more exciting—and profitable.

One of the most important jazz promoters who first saw the fiscal potential of the staged jam session was Norman Granz, a brilliant, forward-thinking, sandy-haired man, born in 1918 in Los Angeles. He quit his job as an apprentice film editor in MGM's foreign department to promote live jazz concerts, initially on a small scale, beginning around mid-1942. On July 2, 1944, he set up a charity event in his hometown, and presented greats including Illinois Jacquet, Nat King Cole, Red Callender, Les Paul, and J.J. Johnson all on the same stage. The evening was going to be called "A Jazz Concert at the Philharmonic Auditorium," but it got shortened by the newspaper typesetters to "Jazz at the Philharmonic" due to shortage of space. To the public, it became JATP. Granz organized the whole evening by borrowing $300 and taking all the risks himself. He had no need to worry. It was a tremendous success and the public just wanted more.

As the JATP franchise began to grow, a contract with Chicago-based Mercury Records was signed in order to issue recordings of the live events, and more and more well-known musicians wanted to join the Granz troupe. For the players, it was a fabulous, no-risk deal, and in the coming months and years, Charlie Parker, Lester Young, Ella Fitzgerald, Bud Powell, Flip Phillips, Buck Clayton, Coleman Hawkins and Gene Krupa, among various others, were signed.

Norman Granz became the most important jazz promoter in the United States, and never hesitated to mix styles and races: black musicians with white, bebop musicians with mainstream, jazz with Latin, and long instrumental numbers followed by beautiful ballads. This was JATP, and all Granz wanted was for everyone to play with their hearts. Naturally, his efforts had critics in terms of the music he presented, the cries of commercialism, and exploitation of big names. Granz could care less. He had more important missions in mind. "I felt that jazz could be used as a sociological weapon to fight discrimination," Granz explained early on. "The other was that I liked jazz and I liked the idea of presenting jazz, and third, I enjoyed the idea of making money on it."[1]

Commercial or not, Granz had the musicians on his side. He paid all of them very well, ensured fine hotel accommodations and meals at fine restaurants. On a six-week tour, an artist could make $5,000, compared with around $800 if they played the same length of time at clubs, and they were also free to express themselves on their instruments at first-class halls. Granz could be demanding from time to time, but he treated everyone well and insisted on respect for one and all. He didn't mind telling those around him, "I go crazy at concerts. I lose my temper every five minutes. I yell at every body. I am rude to people who pester me. Every concert has to go perfectly. If somebody goofs, he pays for it."[2] He also placed high demands on the audience, explaining, "I insist that the audience respect the musicians on stage, because when we started, the audiences weren't always used to listening properly. If anyone makes too much noise I stop the show. I even pass out instructions to them before the concert telling them how to behave."[3]

Granz' written instructions, titled "How to Act at a Jazz Concert," read thusly:*You know, it's becoming quite a problem to put on a good jazz concert today. It isn't the musicians, because they play the best way they know how, and it isn't 99 % of the audience because they come hoping to hear some good jazz and to have an enjoyable evening. No, it's that handful of exhibitionists who see fit to spoil the concert for everyone else, both the musicians as well as the rest of the audience. It's too bad because if these people could keep quiet, they'd not only please the artists and their neighbors sitting next to them, but actually would enjoy themselves more. After all, why pay good money to see great artists perform if you don't even listen to these artists? And if you're not interested in hearing these artists themselves, at least be considerate of the persons sitting next to you. Sure, it's OK to get excited and applaud and even cheer your favorite tenor man, or your favorite trumpeter on "Perdido" or" Cottontail" or "Flying Home," but why not keep quiet when the same artists play "Body and Soul" or some other beautiful ballad? After all, a jazz concert could become pretty boring if all you'd hear would be up tempo, loud numbers. JATP has a lot of variety in music to offer, so why not give us and your neighbors around you a chance to hear all the music we have to offer? Especially is this unfair to Ella Fitzgerald, Oscar Peterson, and the MJQ when they try to sing and play the pretty things for you? It isn't good manners to be shouting or talking when Ella is singing a ballad, or when Oscar is playing something very pretty. After all, the human voice and the piano are not like the trumpets and saxophones, and they simply cannot compete with audience noise. And believe me, you'll enjoy Ella, Oscar, and the MJQ more if you listen quietly. You can show your appreciation to the artist and applaud at the end of a number just as well as during a number, and I can assure you the artist will appreciate that gesture a lot more than you spoiling his solo. And another thing, shouting for numbers you want to hear isn't necessary. RELAX!* [4]

The concerts were sell-outs, but it wasn't all so easy for Granz and company. Racial prejudice was always in the background. According to Buck Clayton, who played trumpet on several of the early JATP concerts, "Norman was always a great fighter for equal rights, and sometimes he'd have to go to bat for us when we'd get to some city that put prejudice before anything else. Sometimes, when a restaurant would refuse us service, Norman would have us just sit there until they served us, no matter what happened."[5] If a local promoter wouldn't allow the performers to use dressing rooms in the theater—suggesting they change outdoors, which happened a couple of times—Granz immediately gave the simple order for the entire ensemble to pull out directly, leaving a very outraged promoter shouting that he would sue. Granz always answered, "Do that. I refuse to subject my people to this treatment."

In the fall of 1949, Buddy Rich found himself at a crossroads personally and professionally. Was he going to continue to live the life he had lived thus far, as a constantly-on-the-road "world's greatest drummer" and somehow successfully combine it with the normalcy of marriage and children? It was clear that he wanted to do both, but that didn't look possible at the moment. His relationship with Betty Jo didn't seem to be working. She still refused to get married, and he was constantly on the move somewhere, even without the big band. His nomadic lifestyle didn't strengthen their relationship. He continued working with the television Condon gang, sat in from time to time with Lester Young's quintet, and signed to do 13 weeks with Les Brown and His Orchestra. His time there was much appreciated by everyone. When he left, there was a cake and plenty of tears were shed at the closing party. Now on the table was an offer from Norman Granz. He wanted Buddy to be the closing act on his tours.

Granz and Buddy were not strangers. They had been introduced in 1945 while Buddy was still on the Dorsey band. The year after, on April 22, Granz saw Buddy sitting in the JATP audience at the Embassy Theatre and managed to get him up on stage. He jammed through two numbers, "JATP Blues" and "Slow Drag." Subsequently, he played a few Granz concerts and then agreed to go on a tour that didn't thrill him musically. Now he felt that he really had no choice; his economic situation was catastrophic after having closed down his orchestra.

Buddy signed up, and on September 18, Buddy Rich was again on Carnegie Hall's large stage in Chicago with Roy Eldridge, Tommy Turk, Charlie Parker, Lester Young, Flip Phillips, Hank Jones, Ray Brown, Oscar Peterson, and Ella Fitzgerald. It was the beginning of a three-month tour, and now, the company was more to his liking. "I think all of us played pretty much at the same level most of the time," Buddy said after the tour. "Sure, there were times when somebody was having an especially hot night, but with the great talent we had, you would have expect that. These were not like private sessions where you might show off or try to cut each other up. When somebody really was on, you enjoyed it with them, encouraged them. No man, there were no ego trips or reasons for them."[6]

With the start of this tour, the JATP enterprise got an even bigger commercial push. Ella Fitzgerald was a great success wherever she went, and with Buddy closing the show (often with his phenomenal solo on "Old Man River") the concert was framed beautifully. Prior to the arrival of Buddy and Ella, the rabble-rousing tenor saxophonist Flip Phillips was the star of the show. Now he was just one of the stars. Swedish journalist Ted Warner was again on the United States scene, this time for a JATP show at the Chicago Opera House. "On the whole it was nothing to brag about," Warner wrote,"but individually, Tommy Turk, Flip Phillips, Ella Fitzgerald and Buddy Rich shone. Especially Buddy (who) was pleasant, no stuck-up manners, but then he is a great artist. It was an experience, to say the least, sitting three meters from him, and watching how he worked with such ease and rhythm. He enjoyed himself, especially when Flip had his solo. Oh boy, what a backup!"[7]

The tour ended in November, and Buddy went into the recording studio for Granz. The impresario loved getting the right combination of musicians together and could spend hours choosing the players and the songs, booking a recording studio, supervising the session and listening to the result. Granz had good ears and he knew what he wanted. Buddy Rich respected that quality in Granz, saying, "He used to call me or Louie Bellson or whoever he thought would fit into the picture of the group he had in mind. This happened when Harry "Sweets" Edison was available, when Coleman Hawkins was there, the guys that even I liked to play with. But there were also occasions when I was busy with another orchestra somewhere else, and then he called somebody else. Granz quite simply had very good taste when it came to putting together a rhythm section."[8]

In October, a new project got started, and it was one that Charlie Parker wished for: recording with strings. "Parker nagged about strings," Granz insisted. "Everyone did."[9] Charlie Parker admitted that he "had been wanting to play with strings since 1941. Granz gave me the chance."[10] Parker may have been envious of of Gillespie, who had earlier experimented with a string section, but most probably he simply believed that playing on top of a string section would be a beautiful thing. Granz recruited Jimmy Carroll to arrange, and though Parker said he loved the charts and the very idea of playing with strings, when word got out about the impending *Bird with Strings* project, there were cries of commercialism, and the idea that strings don't swing. Lennie Tristano said that Bird told him, "He had done enough of his style of playing up until now. He wanted to develop in some other direction or try out something new. I imagine he was constantly reminded of that when everyone else tried to copy him."[11]

Even Parker fans were skeptical, but Granz and Parker could have cared less. Playing with strings was just another means of self-expression, they both reasoned. What was unsaid at the time, for the most part, was that a *Bird with Strings* project was a good means of getting Parker exposed to a wider audience in a kind of "crossover" project. Then there was the matter of the choice of Buddy Rich as the drummer on the session, which began on November 30, 1949.[12] Rich's style at the time, some maintained, was incompatible with that of Parker. The criticism was so vocal before the sessions began that Granz felt compelled to address the issue, though he did so after the fact, by writing the following text on the album cover for *Charlie Parker with Strings*: "There has been much criticism in the past leveled against Buddy Rich as a *loud* drummer without taste," the notes read. "But it would be hard for anyone to deny that Buddy's playing on this album is completely with good taste; as a matter of fact, I think his playing in this album clearly stamps him as one of the great drummers of all time."[13] Buddy Rich, still not a total bebop convert, answered the criticism directly in *Downbeat* magazine, saying "There hasn't been anything interesting in music except the so-called progressives, who come up with things which are absolutely above the listening intelligence of the average music lover and, therefore, have hurt the business itself. I'm from the old school. I'm a Count Basie and Benny Goodman fan. There's a lot of good stuff now, but more bad than good. Guys like Gillespie and Bird, it's their formula, and they play it great. But I think the guys that copy it are doing a very bad job."[14]

Norman Granz had not signed Buddy exclusively, and Buddy knew it. He kept his eyes open for other projects that appeared along the way. Then Tommy Dorsey called again. The Dorsey machine had once again changed character, returning to a simpler and more relaxed kind of swing—with a modernized book, to an extent—and was concentrating on a repertoire filled with some classic compositions from the likes of Cole Porter and Jerome Kern. Dorsey decided to record in the beginning of January 1950, and since the recordings were very important to him, he wanted Buddy on the date. He also needed Buddy for a crucial location date at the Shamrock Hotel in Houston, Texas, an impressive venue at the time that was important to Dorsey's post-war success and survival. The Shamrock was among the largest hotels built in America during the 1940s, and its opening was said to be one of the biggest social events ever held in Houston.

Drummer John Karoly was at the Shamrock. "Buddy used a mini set of drums that Ludwig had custom made for him," Karoly recalled. "They were secured to a platform that was pulled by ropes onto the dance floor directly in front of the bandstand. Buddy brought 'Old Man River' from his own band to feature himself and it was always a big crowd pleaser. On his final day, I was with Buddy while he was packing his drums, as Tommy's band boy had been given strict orders not to help him. When he had finished, we sat down at a nearby table to talk while Buddy smoked a cigarette. A few minutes later, Tommy approached Buddy and he got up to shake hands, which Dorsey ignored. He blankly handed him a check and said, 'This is the last one you will ever get from me,' turning his back on Buddy and walking away."[15] While Dorsey must have been very satisfied with Buddy's playing after the huge success of the engagement, he took pleasure in not showing it.

The big bands were folding. The decline, which began after the end of World War II, worsened by the day. The most well-known bandleaders were forced to close up shop, tour only on a part-time basis, or cut down to a small group. Buddy Rich, on the other hand, tried once more to put together a new big band in the spring of 1950, but didn't succeed this time, either. Count Basie and Woody Herman were advised to close down their bands and start small groups. Krupa kept a big band on with increasing difficulty until 1950, cut the group down a year later, and then gave it up completely in favor of touring with a trio. Duke Ellington was the only one who managed to keep his big band afloat, but barely.

In the spring, Buddy Rich jumped into the small group fray, sometimes fronting his own group, and sometimes playing the role of sideman with Flip Phillips, Charlie Parker's quintet, Bud Powell's trio, and again as a guest on Eddie Condon's television show. On May 16, he was back in the studio to record with Basie's superb small band, replacing the great Gus Johnson on four songs: "Neal's Deal," "Bluebeard Blues," "The Golden Bullet," and "You're My Baby." Buddy loved playing every minute with his idol. Clarinetist Buddy DeFranco said "Buddy Rich brought an important contribution to the group with the vitality of his drumming there." Another small group date continues to be mired in controversy. On June

6, Norman Granz put together Charlie Parker, Dizzy Gillespie, Thelonious Monk, Curly Russell, and Buddy Rich. Expectations from the critics around the country were high. This was, after all, a meeting of Bird, Diz and Monk. The result, *Bird and Diz*, became an album that absolutely exploded with inventiveness, but that wasn't enough for one English critic of high standing. Max Harrison, who wrote for the *Kings of Jazz* magazine, penned a stinging review. "Unfortunately the whole thing was sabotaged by the fact that the ensemble also contained a musician who stood completely outside the modernistic efforts, drummer Buddy Rich," Harrison wrote. "His presence doesn't compromise the music to any great extent, but it isn't pleasant to hear him play a solo after Monk."[16] Music historian Carl Woideck wasn't impressed either. "Norman Granz has one bad side," he wrote, "and that is his odd way of putting musicians together." Curly Russell, bassist on the date, called the choice of musicians "one of Norman's brainstorms."

Drummer Roy Haynes, said to be Parker's first choice at the time, was upset over often being cut out of Granz sessions at the last minute. "Bird was under contract to Norman," Haynes explained. "Before a session he'd show Norman the list of musician's he'd like to use. Everything would be alright until he got to my name. You mean you'd like to use Roy instead of Buddy Rich? The answer was on the paper, but Buddy always wound up on the date."[17] By the fall of 1950 Norman Granz could look back on a successful JATP tour. *Billboard* detailed the success, writing, "While jazz music, with the exception of a couple of metropolitan niteries, has fallen flat on its box office face across the country in recent years, Norman Granz, via his phenomenally successful Jazz at the Philharmonic concerts and recordings, has managed to parlay JATP into an institutional business venture which annually brings in well over $500,000"[18] Buddy Rich was a part of that tour and signed up for a new one the next winter. Granted, he had already begun to tire of the long jam session format, but economics forced him to continue. Harry "Sweets" Edison signed up as well, and that made it easier, since Buddy liked playing with him.

Around this time, Granz resumed his discussions with the Albanian director Gjon Mili about making a sequel to the acclaimed 1944 short film *Jamming the Blues*. Mili was a very successful photographer for

Life magazine and he had developed a camera lens that could photograph a person in movement so that every step could be viewed in real detail. Granz' goal with the new film was to increase his market by selling to theaters and television. At Mili's photo studio in New York, he gathered Charlie Parker, Coleman Hawkins, Hank Jones, Ray Brown, Lester Young, Bill Harris, "Sweets" Edison, Flip Phillips, Ella Fitzgerald, and Buddy Rich to perform in front of the cameras. The problem was that the studio wasn't equipped for live sound recording, meaning that the music would have to be recorded at a later date in a real recording studio. What was ultimately seen onscreen was a miming job, which didn't suit Buddy Rich at all. To make the miming process easier, some of the others made notes that helped them to find where they were in a song when the actual filming took place. When Granz viewed the final product, he wasn't satisfied with either Buddy's or Ella's performances. The miming job, especially when it came to Ella's lips and Buddy's movements, was lousy. The film was put into storage until 1996, when it was released under the title *Improvisation*, and it's an interesting piece of film. When Buddy does a drum fill, Charlie Parker is seen grinning, as he knew and understood that Buddy hadn't a hope of being able to memorize something he had recorded a month earlier. The result is still a unique film, in that it is the only filmed record of Buddy playing with Bird.

In October, 1950, Norman Granz started a new project. This time, he wanted Buddy to play with the Afro-Cuban All Stars, featuring Charlie Parker, Flip Phillips, and "Sweets" Edison guest-starring with the Latin stars Machito, Chico O'Farrill, and a Latin orchestra. Granz now wanted to have a go at producing Latin jazz, and with these musicians on board, everything looked good on paper. Parker's playing fit in beautifully with Machito and O'Farrill. Chico O'Farrill said it wasn't planned that way. "The original soloist was supposed to be Harry Edison," the great arranger remembered. "'Sweets' walked into the studio and he tried to play the solos, but it was a medium completely alien to his style, and he felt it and said, 'Look, this is not for me.' So that's when Norman said, 'Call Bird.' Somebody called him and an hour later he came over to the studio and asked, 'Where do I come in? Here? Oh, I see.' Bird: first take, perfect."[19] The recording was a shot in the arm for Machito, who was having some career difficulties at the time, something he blamed on the fact that he sang only in Spanish. But he thanked both Granz and Parker for carrying out the project. Machito recalled, *"The Afro-Cuban Jazz Suite in 1950 was our first artistic and economic success. After that, we were able to jump another hurdle in the market in the American community that would permit us to sing in Spanish."*[20]

Freda Josephine MacDonald was born on June 3, 1906 in St Louis, Missouri. She won her first dance competition when she was only 14, launching an incredible, international career. Josephine was a black, Franco-American singer who became best known for her erotic dancing and expensive designer wardrobe. The world would know her as Josephine Baker. In the following decades, she was successful in Paris, but she dreamed of an American tour, which she had never done. Baker's connection with the States began in earnest thanks to American night club owner Ned Schuyler, who first booked her (with considerable success) in Havana. Schuyler offered to both produce and promote her performances in America, and to facilitate this, enlisted the talents of Baker's close friend Shirley Woolf to organize the band that would back her in the U.S. Woolf chose Buddy Rich almost by chance, explaining, "I picked Buddy Rich because he and I were from Brooklyn. I didn't know he was the greatest drummer in the world."[21] Buddy put together a 16-man orchestra that included "Sweet" Edison, bassist Phil Leshin, tenor saxophonist Zoot Sims, and Stanley Kay to play drums behind Buddy on his song and dance numbers. On February 14, 1951, the show premiered at the Apollo for a two-week, four-show-per-day stand, sharing the stage with American entertainer Leo De Lyon. Lyon, born Irving Levin, was musical novelty performer who later became known for doing cartoon voices for the Hanna-Barbara studios.

Mel Tormé was there. "When the curtain went up at the Apollo in Harlem and she stepped onto the stage, the crowd's roar nearly burst the walls," remembered Tormé. "Buddy, of course, was a welcome 'regular' at the Apollo by now, and once again the patrons cheered him boisterously."[22] Zoot Sims recalled the gig as "a part-time band Buddy had at that time. I was a sub for Allan Eager. 'Sweets' Edison is the only name I can remember, but it wasn't a bad band at all. Josephine Baker put on a hell of a show and it was probably one of the few times Buddy was ever completely overshadowed by anyone who was on the same bill with him."[23]

After the Apollo, the package was booked for nearly a month at the Strand Theatre in New York. *Billboard* raved about the show. "If ever an act was worthy of a Hollywood superlative, this is it. The Buddy Rich band, apparently augmented with four violins for Miss Baker, was loud and rhythmic. While their show backing was first rate, the tympani—three men on one number—completely overpowered the brass and reeds. 'Old Man River' sounded at times that it might have been a well-written jump arrangement, but it required concentration to hear the brass while Rich pounded the skins."

In an interview later in life, Leo De Lyon was detailed in his recollections of the show. "Buddy Rich and Josephine Baker were from two different planets," said De Lyon. "Buddy Rich loved—adored—Josephine Baker. She was unlike anything he had ever seen in his life. The Buddy Rich Band would play the first number, something big and flashy. He had great soloists, a whole bunch of guys, very famous musicians, and he'd tear the place apart with this good band. Then I would come on and do my act, and then I would bring on Josephine Baker. Then she did a dance as part of her act. She did a Moroccan number where she came out with a fez. Stanley Kay, Buddy's backup drummer, would play this. Then Harry Edison would come forward and play some incredible jazz; almost Arabian but jazz trumpet stuff, and he would be blowin' while she would be dancing around him and the drummer and the whole thing. It became a real big part of the show. Finally, Buddy got so jealous that he decided he wanted to do that particular number with her. Sure enough, when he took it over, the number which usually ran about five minutes then ran ten or twelve, because the theater came apart! Buddy Rich—the way he played and carried on; Josephine went out of her mind with ecstasy! It was so perfect for what she was doing!"[24]

Josephine's clothing changes could take some time, and that meant that there were often demands on Leo to improvise; there were boos from the audience otherwise. Incidents happened; it was inevitable. De Lyon continued, "Because of traffic in New York City, I was once late for Buddy Rich's show on Josephine Baker's tour, and I ran the last two blocks. I didn't have time to change my clothes, and I hurriedly entered the theater to see Buddy Rich, the world-famous drummer, tap dancing brilliantly to fill time for my regular spot. Few people realize what an amazing singer he was, too."[25]

Buddy was happy. Baker was happy. There she was back in America, at the age of 45, singing her great numbers, "J'ai Deux Amours" and "Ave Maria," while wearing several of her most well-known stage costumes. She sang in five languages and made the whole Strand Theater feel like they were sitting in her personal boudoir. She shouted, "You make me so happy!"so enthusiastically to the audience that her manager immediately extended her tour with a fee of $7,500 a week. Musically, Baker and Rich were a perfect combination. But at the end of March, Buddy had to say no to continuing. His new booking agency, Shaw Artist Corporation, which had also organized Baker's tour, said they were unable to get out of his contracts with club owners who had already booked his new sextet on several dates. The Shaw agency was afraid they would be sued if he cancelled them. Josephine Baker was crushed, and the band that took over after Buddy, Louis Basil's Apollo house band led by Fred Stammock, was nowhere near the class of Buddy's band. The package was booked next at the Earle Theater in Philadelphia and Baker was worried about how it would go.

On March 26, 1951, Buddy Rich's sextet, consisting of Frank Galbraith on trumpet, Dave Schildkraut on alto sax and clarinet, Allan Eager on tenor sax, Cookie Norwood on piano. and Phil Leshin on bass, were booked at the High Hat Club in Philadelphia. Jonathan Haze, an actor who later appeared in a number of Roger Corman's "B" movies, worked as a band boy in his younger days. "I went along as a roadie for Buddy Rich's sextet," Haze remembered. "They were booked at the High Hat Club in Philadelphia, which was a little jazz club for blacks. At the same time, Baker was booked at the Earle Theater and, oddly enough, both acts opened on the same day. We set up the instruments and decided to go over to the theater and check on Baker. When we got there, tears were flowing. Her manager was running around. He was very nervous. Apparently, an earlier show had been a catastrophe. I mean, she was spoiled. She had been used to working at the big theaters backed up by Buddy Rich's band. She still had his music in her head. So Buddy made a new deal with Ned Schuyler to jump in and play the following days. It was a fantastic time. Boxers Joe Louis and Sugar Ray Robinson sat in the audience. It was unbelievable."[26] Ned Schuyler must have talked to

Buddy's agency about how important he was in Baker's show. The only likely scenario is that Shaw Artists had to pay the promoters who had booked Rich, an amount that was likely deducted from Buddy's fee, probably without him knowing about it.

Buddy Rich closed down the sextet, though it did very good business. "The Big Four,"also known occasionally as "Charlie Ventura's Big Four" (given Ventura's name value at the time) also starred pianist Marty Napoleon, bassist Chubby Jackson, and Buddy Rich. The four were truly "big." Ventura became a star with various Krupa bands; Napoleon, also a Krupa veteran, was a pal of Georgie Auld; and bassist Jackson came to fame with Woody Herman. These were four hard-driving players. They recorded four tracks together (Mel Tormé sat in on drums on one number while Buddy sang) which were released by Norman Granz, and settled in to a month long engagement at Club Silhoutte in New York. Once again, the Swedish reporter and jazz lover Ted Warner was there writing for his magazine in Stockholm.

"They opened at Club Silhouette and are still there playing for a full house every evening," Warner reported at the time. "Modern swing music has the seat of honor and that is exactly what suits most of the unmusical audience. The band swings like crazy and everyone who is there can feel it. I have heard some quartets made up of tenors with three accompanists and I have always been tired of them, because they fail to offer anything new, but in this case, you wouldn't even think it's the same setup."[27] The always-colorful Chubby Jackson said, "That was all we had: three in the rhythm section and one brass. But the pulse, sound and drive of the group could reach such heights! We answered each other all the time, glanced at one another and talked to each other through our instruments. Buddy Rich was the best of us. He was completely phenomenal—or a phenomenon?"[28] Business was fabulous, reviews were great, and fabulous offers, including another month in Chicago, were coming in. Buddy still wasn't happy. He had the big band bug again. He contacted Sinatra. According to Marty Napoleon, "Buddy had said he was going to quit (the Big Four) and be replaced by Gene (Krupa). Buddy was going to put together a new band that would be backed up by Sinatra. Gene came to check us out at the Preview Lounge in Chicago. We played a song called 'The Evolution of Jazz' and it ended with Buddy imitating Gene—with just his left hand. And it sounded just like Gene, and Gene was sitting there listening! After that he said it was impossible to replace Buddy. The others tried to convince him, but Gene just looked panic stricken!"[29]

On December 30, 1951, Buddy Rich had his solo debut on television on the "Peter Lind Hayes Show," where he played the drums and bongos with the Bert Farber Band and did a tap dancing number. The new 1952 version of Buddy Rich and His Orchestra had its premiere on March 26 at the Paramount, and the only musicians from his former orchestras were tenor saxophonist Allan Eager, alto saxophonist Dave Schildkraut, and bassist Phil Leshin. Jean Weeks was the singer, and at the Paramount the band shared the bill with June Hutton, Frank Fontaine, and the man who put the whole thing together, Frank Sinatra. The band continued to a long engagement at Rustic Cabin in Englewood Cliffs, New Jersey, followed by some dates in Canada, and a return to New York with some one-nighters.

During the same period, Norman Granz was expanding. He brought the JATP ensemble to Europe with all the best known drummers of the time in tow: Krupa, Jo Jones, Louie Bellson, and Max Roach. He would have liked to have had Buddy Rich, but Buddy was so busy with other projects and couldn't make such a tour. While Granz may have wanted Buddy along, he made it clear that he wanted Buddy Rich as a soloist. "Granz never came to hear us," as Buddy said at the time. "He had little interest in bands, especially mine, man. I don't think he ever had any intention of recording us. Besides, that was up to him, that was his business, not mine."[30]

Louie Bellson thought that Norman Granz was making enormous contributions to jazz, while Buddy, during the various times he was a member of the JATP cast, began to get more and more irritated by Granz's attitude. To Buddy, JATP felt like a musical circus. For whatever reason—musical, financial or otherwise—Buddy Rich was just plain bugged. Money-wise, Buddy was making a great deal of it and was spending it just as quickly. In the summer of 1952, he bought a new Jaguar. One night he came driving around the corner of 50th Street dressed like the star he was, with a beautiful woman at his side. He saw

Max Roach, who was winning many jazz polls at the time, on the sidewalk and shouted, "Hey Max! Beat this if you can!" [31]

Buddy Rich's relationship with Betty Jo completely collapsed. Ever since they had been introduced to each other by Buddy's sister Marge at the Hollywood Palladium in the summer of 1948, nothing had improved. On the contrary, as early as December of that year, gossip magazines were writing that Buddy was flirting publicly. One rumor paired him with actress Peggy Maley. *The Toledo Blade* seemed to have the scoop, writing, "Peggy Maley scolded Buddy Rich for not giving her enough attention. He left the club with her at four in the morning with his tail between his legs."[32] But these were only rumors. In the spring of 1952, Buddy and Betty Jo moved in together again after having lived apart for a couple of months. Now there were rumors of a wedding. In April, the *Syracuse Herald Journal* reported that Buddy had "gone someplace over a weekend to probably get married to his Betty Jo." In Stanley Kay's photo album are two photos identifying "Buddy Rich with his wife Betty Jo Brown."

Buddy's sisters claim they never got married, but married or not, Betty Jo and Buddy Rich were through by summer's end. The reason for the breakup was once again Buddy's nomadic life. He was single again and wondered if he would ever meet the right woman.

CHAPTER 12

Crossroads

Two views of Buddy with Harry James, circa 1964. Buddy would be in and out of the band many times from 1954 until he left for good to form his own band in 1966.

Eugene Bertram Krupa was born on January 15, 1909, in Chicago. Gene was the youngest of nine brothers and sisters and he came to the drums purely by accident. At the age of 11, his brother, Pete, got him a job as a chore boy in a local music store, and young Gene just wanted to play whatever instrument he could. He chose the cheapest, and that was a Japanese drum set that cost $16. He started to practice, played some little gigs along the way, and hooked up with a group of players who would become known as "The Austin High Gang," with ground-breaking players like Bud Freeman and drummer Dave Tough among them. He also began studying drums seriously with Roy Knapp, Al Silverman, and Ed Straight, who urged Krupa to check out drummers like Baby Dodds, George Wettling, and Dave Tough. But Gene's mother wanted him to become a priest. He was accepted to St. Joseph's College, a seminary prep school, and studied with the classically-trained Father Ildefonse Rapp, who taught him a good deal about the appreciation of music.

Ultimately, the lure of jazz was too strong, Krupa realized he was not cut out for the priesthood, and left the seminary around 1925 to pursue a career as jazz drummer. His first order of business was to join the Musician's Union. The second order of business was to check out Baby Dodds. "I kept coming back to dig Baby, always showing my appreciation for the extremely musical things he was doing," Krupa remembered. "It wasn't long before he sensed we had common ground for friendship. Our relationship lasted until his death. He was one of my main inspirations."[1] Gene Krupa was first with a lot of things. He is regarded as being the first to play a real drum solo, helped bring drums to the forefront as a musical instrument, and insisted that drummers be respected as real musicians. (Many bandleaders were used to saying their ensembles were made up of "12 musicians and a drummer.") Krupa helped change this attitude, and along the way, also facilitated developments in the actual drum kit, including his insistence on tuneable tom toms.

Gene's first recording, made in 1927 with the McKenzie Condon Chicagoans at Okeh Records in Chicago, was historic. On those sides, he was among the first to utilize the bass drum in a recording studio. The studio's engineer, Tommy Rockwell, was against it, saying, "I'm afraid that the bass drum and all the tom toms will make the needle jump off the wax and send it out the window." But finally he got it to work.

After that, there were more recordings with other artists, some jazz and some not. He got to know Benny Goodman early on, and when Benny revealed his plans for setting up a real jazz band, Krupa came to mind. Benny knew Gene was playing with Buddy Rogers at the College Inn in Chicago, so, really wanting Krupa on board, he sent his brother-in-law John Hammond to persuade Krupa to join up (Hammond was a talent scout, jazz fan, and writer). Rogers was a film star who parlayed his fame into fronting several bands—including playing 11 different instruments as part of his act—but he was no jazz musician. Accompanying him was not really Gene's cup of tea, but the job paid well. At the College Inn, Hammond approached Gene. "Just think what fun you'll have playing jazz every evening," he said, just as Rogers pulled out another instrument. "I'm coming," said Gene. Krupa joined up with Goodman and his fame increased by the week, with the climax of his tenure being the magical Benny Goodman Carnegie Hall Jazz Concert of 1938. Two months after that triumph, Krupa wanted out, once and for all. The reasons were mainly musical—along with Goodman's enormous ego. Wherever the band performed, the focus was on the matinee-idol handsome drummer, and the audience was demanding more of his wild and visual drum solos. In the end, it was too much for Goodman, who had created the band and that saw himself as the big star.

That wasn't the only explanation. "Their ideas about how music should be played were too different," Lionel Hampton claimed. "Benny didn't like all the crazy visual effects and the sensation that Gene tried to create. He thought it overshadowed the music. Gene thought that all the antics were only pure showmanship. I agreed with Gene, but I kept it to myself."[2] John Hammond had a similar theory, saying, "Contrary to what many think, Gene was not at his best during the Carnegie Hall concert. Benny took a new, hard look at him that night. Suddenly he came to the conclusion that the way he was playing disrupted the whole structure of the band."[3]

During a performance at the Earle in Philadelphia, things went completely off the rails between Gene and Goodman. The audience began to call more and more for the spectacular drummer, and when the curtain went up, it ended with Goodman and Krupa shouting at each other on stage. Krupa quit and was replaced by Dave Tough. This was coming on for some time, with Krupa admitting, "Managers had been after me for some time. Most of the major sidemen—Bunny Berigan, Bob Chester, Glenn Miller—had been approached. Big bands were big business then. I happened to be ready to hear what the managers were talking about. Ego certainly entered into it. Why be a clerk when you can own your own store?"[4]

Goodman, or his press agents, put a friendly face on the whole episode. Some wrote that Benny said, "Gene, I certainly don't want to stand in your way one bit. If you feel like starting your own band, go to it, and the best of luck to you!"[5] Krupa was big business; the agents knew that there were many who were after him, and in retrospect, convinced him to leave Benny Goodman at the right time. The Gene Krupa band, especially when joined by the likes of Anita O'Day and Roy Eldridge, was tremendously successful on every front: films, performances, radio and everything else. Gene was arrested in an infamous, blown-out-of-proportion marijuana bust in 1943; a trumped up drug charge that resulted in a nearly 90-day stint in jail. Upon his release, he tested the waters by playing with Goodman again for a while, then joined Dorsey, where he made his real comeback by replacing (coincidentally) Buddy Rich.

Many thought that Gene Krupa was best. Certainly, his showmanship, ability to project, his good looks, and the special effects turned on the general public, but it's important to remember that Gene Krupa always played with great feeling, integrity, and musicality. He was a living legend. He made the drums a solo instrument.

In August of 1952, Buddy Rich recorded again with Benny Carter, a Norman Granz session released as *Alone Together*. While recording this album, Buddy started hearing talk about who was the world's best drummer: Was it him or Gene Krupa? Ever the promoter, Norman Granz picked up on this talk, a bit of press agent-type nonsense (which he may have actually started, in that Granz was reportedly getting stacks of letters asking who he thought was the greatest). It was almost like jazz fans had formed two camps, similar to the Flip Phillips versus Illionis Jacquet tenor saxophone "competition" encouraged by Granz at JATP. On the one hand, there was Gene with his imagination, playfulness, and visual tricks, and on the other, Buddy with his fantastic technique. JATP fans, among others, were calling for "the title" to be resolved once and for all. Granz was intrigued by all the talk, and contacted them both about battling it out on stage in the next JATP tour.

It came to be billed as "The Drum Battle," and may have been the first such thing in history. On September 13, 1952, it was staged before a full and enthusiastic house Carnegie Hall. Having begun the previous evening in Hartford, Connecticut, this was the 11th edition of Jazz at the Philharmonic. The day of the performance, Buddy Rich came along in the afternoon to Carnegie Hall to set up his drums. Gene Krupa was already there, and had finished his preparing his gear. They greeted each other cordially, and began to work out the routine. Buddy thought, "I'll let Gene call the shots. He's older than I am and has been on tour much more." Buddy knew all about Gene's fame and the reasons for it, and he had no problem with that. Gene had a good idea of what should go down, and said to Buddy, "First we'll trade a couple of short solos, like four, eight, or 16 bars, then I'll play a long solo and then you play a long solo". Buddy agreed.

A short while later, while Buddy was sitting in his dressing room, Gene's wife Ethel walked by. Stanley Kay, on the scene again, recalled that "Gene's wife didn't know who Buddy was. She used to drink a little bit, and Buddy's door was open. She saw the name of Buddy Rich on the door and said, 'Oh, you're the hotshot one. My husband will tear you up tonight. He'll ruin you. Forget what he's going to do to you.'"[6] Needless to say, this wasn't a good thing for anyone to say to Buddy.

Showtime arrived, and Norman Granz went up to the microphone, introduced the participating players in the opening jam session, and eventually, the Gene Krupa Trio. The atmosphere in the hall was electric. After a superb set by a Krupa trio comprised of alto saxophonist Willie Smith, pianist Hank Jones and Gene, the duel began in earnest, and the crowd was already going nuts. When Gene started his first solo, Buddy was shocked. The whole wall behind him lit up and Gene's large shadow appeared. It didn't matter what he played; everything looked so incredibly impressive, and the audience went wild. Buddy wasn't prepared for the special effects or the response of the crowd. He remembered, "Of course I'd heard about this effect, but had never seen it in real life."[7]

When it was time for Buddy, ever the gladiator, to play his long solo, he didn't just double the tempo—he tripled it. Now it was Gene's turn to be shocked. He hardly knew what to do. Buddy looked in his direction and saw him pretend to drop his drumsticks behind the bass drum. He bent down, shouting to Buddy, "I can't play so fast! Please, go back to the ordinary tempo!" As the story goes, Buddy complied, and two became best friends from that moment. The truth was that everyone who was right in front of the stage had heard Gene's request, and the whole thing was pretty embarrassing for him.[8] Who won the evening? Norman Granz didn't announce a winner. The whole performance was typical for him: a duel between two fantastic musicians. Until then, trumpeters and saxophonists had been beating themselves up in duels on one JATP after the other, but with the entry of Krupa's and Rich's Drum Battle, the drummer's role as soloist was now right up there with the horns.

The review in *Downbeat* by Hal Webman a month later gave the display a four on a scale of five. "The high point, a drummer's duel between Buddy Rich and Gene Krupa, proved to be little more than an audience stimulator," Webman reported. "It brought pandemonium to Carnegie, and should produce the same sort of electrifying reactions across the country. Actually, the duel was hardly that, since Gene and Buddy never really did get going at each other."[9] In the end, Krupa knew very well that he had been out-played handily by Buddy, much in the same way that he had been bested by Chick Webb a few years earlier.

Gene Krupa, Buddy Rich and Norman Granz knew it was all showbiz, but at first, Buddy just didn't feel right about the whole thing. Stanley Kay remembered Buddy asking, "Why did I do this? I love this guy. I shouldn't have done that."[10] Reviewer Webman was right on one account. Wherever they went after opening night, they drew a full house and everyone wanted to see the drum duels. As time went on, Gene and Buddy began to enjoy the arrangement. After a couple of performances, they "knew" each other and played more for the show and less for the contest. Buddy detailed how they set things up, saying, "We didn't agree on any plan beforehand. If we had done that, everything would have been stiff and boring. We just went up on stage, watched each other, and both listened to the audience's reactions. Naturally there are a few who call for their favorites, but we just sit down at our drums and laugh. Then we start to play."[11]

Jack Egan, journalist and press agent, saw the two in action outside of JATP. "One scene during the JATP years comes immediately to my mind," Egan remembered. "It was opening night at the Bandbox, right next to Birdland on Broadway. As usual, the crowd pleaser was the drum battle between Gene and Buddy Rich. During the first show, Buddy played like a whirlwind. He was so damn fast and creative, all Gene could do was play some cute things on his little cymbal for fun and contrast. I went back to see Gene after the show. He said, 'Holy jeez, Buddy, take it easy out there, will you? I'm an old man!' Everyone in the dressing room broke up. Buddy smiled and pointed out that there was this chick in the audience he was trying to impress."[12]

In November of 1952, the JATP tour continued to roll across the country. The big jazz machine, with the drum battle as the highlight, was successful everywhere. Buddy and Gene were becoming friends and often travelled together. On the way to a performance at the Long Beach Auditorium in California they were talking about their usual topics: sports, music, life in general—and women. Gene couldn't stop talking about a woman he had dated for some time before he was married; he'd made a film in 1945 called *George White's Scandals*, and this particular woman had a small role as a showgirl. Her name was Marie Allison and Gene, quite the ladies' man in those days, continued dating her off and on even after he married Ethel. Gene and Marie hadn't seen each in quite some time, but as Gene rode along in the car with Buddy that night, he began to think about calling her up again.

Since the night in 1940 when Frank Sinatra left Harry James after a performance in Buffalo, the James band had gone through many changes. Like Basie, Herman, Dorsey and Shaw, James had to adapt to the demands of the time, and had been forced to make some difficult decisions. When Sinatra left him to join Dorsey, James lost his recording contract with Columbia Records, and had a hard time paying his musicians. He decided to go the commercial route, complete with strings and a repertoire of syrupy ballads. Audiences loved it. So did Columbia Records, where he returned to record a bunch of hits that included "You Made Me Love You," "Sleepy Lagoon," "I Had the Craziest Dream," and his theme, "Ciribiribin." James paid a price with the critics, who felt he had abandoned the world of jazz, but he didn't care. When he married film star Betty Grable in 1943, the focus of the whole entertainment world was on them. By 1945, Mr. and Mrs. James topped the list of the best-paid couples in America.

By the early 1950s, James was tiring of the formula, and the band business was not what it had been, so James wanted to change again. When he heard that Count Basie was going to set up a big band again after going the small group route, it struck a chord in him. Like Buddy Rich, Harry James loved Count Basie, and James' intent was to form a big band with a Basie-like feel. The immediate problem was finding a drummer with the power and dynamics to drive the band. James was a talented drummer himself, and had often hopped in as a substitute for Gene Krupa in Benny Goodman's band. Through the years he had admired Don Lamond and Louie Bellson, but his absolute favorite was Buddy Rich, who had turned him down years earlier when he chose to go with Artie Shaw. Rich could drive and lift any band, he thought. Author Lew McCreary believed he knew one reason why James dug Buddy's playing. "He had a heavy foot as a drummer, just the way Harry did when he played drums,"[13] wrote McCreary. This time, James was determined to hire Buddy Rich for his new band and put together an offer that no musician could resist.

Marie Allison and Gene Krupa were sitting at La Rue's restaurant at Long Beach, California. Marie was then engaged to actor Hal March, later best known as a quiz show host, but did agree to meet Gene. She wanted to know what the now-married Gene's intentions were. At the table, Gene continued to talk to Marie about Buddy, telling her that they had become really good friends on the tour that was underway, and suggesting that she come along to the evening's concert. "The fact is," Gene told Marie, "that Buddy is coming to pick us up and then we can get a ride with him."[14] Buddy drove up in a Cadillac with his assistant, and away they went. Gene and Marie sat in the back seat and she was struck by how young Buddy looked. He wasn't at all like she had imagined. Buddy couldn't stop staring at her in the rearview mirror for the whole ride. Marie wondered why he was acting so strangely.

When they got to the auditorium, Marie had to climb over a bag as she got out of the car. Buddy shouted at his assistant, "Why didn't you put that bag in the trunk? You made Marie uncomfortable."[15] She just laughed and said it didn't matter. On the way to the auditorium she asked Gene, "Tell me, which one of you is the best drummer?" "Well, suppose I let you be the judge of that," Gene replied. This put her in a very awkward situation. She had never seen this Buddy Rich play, and if Buddy actually was better, what would she say to Gene? Her fears were realized. At the performance she saw with her own eyes that Buddy completely outplayed Gene. In the dressing room after the show, Gene pressed her for her opinion. She lied. "No doubt about it, you are the best drummer."

Later, at a party in the hotel where the JATP cast was staying, Buddy's assistant approached Marie. Buddy wanted her phone number. "Oh, no, I don't go out with married men anymore," she answered. "Buddy's not married," said the assistant. "That's not what I've heard," said Marie. She knew that Buddy had been living with Betty Jo for several years and Gene had said that they were married. The assistant persisted and asked Marie if she had any girlfriends. "I have a million girlfriends." she said. "Can I get your number then so Buddy can call one of them?" She understood the trick, but still gave him her number.

The next day, Buddy called and asked her out to dinner. Once again, she politely refused, telling him that she didn't go out with married men. He explained that he had broken up with Betty Jo several weeks earlier, and that he had all his belongings in storage. She said, "I think it still wouldn't be fair to Gene. I mean, you are touring together. Let me call him and ask if it's okay." She called Gene. "Go out with him," said Krupa. "You'll like him. But, hey, don't marry him!" The same evening, Buddy and Marie ate dinner at the Tail O' the Cock. As they talked into the evening, Buddy wound up having too much to drink, and Marie had to drive his Cadillac back to her place. As they parted, Buddy asked, "Will you marry me?" She refused, since Buddy was drunk, but the next morning he called and proposed again. Marie still refused; she thought they ought to get to know each other first. Reluctantly, he agreed. She phoned Hal March and broke off her engagement with him, and Buddy and Marie started dating.

When Marie Allison met Buddy she was under contract with MGM as a dancer. She had a part in *The Pirate*, with Judy Garland and Gene Kelly in the lead roles, but felt that her career wasn't going very well, since she just wasn't moving ahead. Privately, she felt ready to settle down and get married again. In fact, when she broke off her engagement with Hal March, a one-year marriage to a football player named Mickey McCardle was behind her. Then she met the married Gene Krupa and everything became even more complicated. Now Buddy Rich had entered her life. She and Buddy quarreled a lot in the beginning. He wanted to know everything about her previous boyfriends and was quite the male chauvinist with her. At the same time, she was attracted to him, and they became a couple.

For three months, between January and March 1953, the Bandbox club became Buddy Rich's second home. He performed as often as he could in different combinations, from trios to quintets. In the beginning of March, Harry James' band also played there and James had a chance to really hear Buddy. He was speechless at what he heard, and was astounded at how great Buddy Rich had become. At the Bandbox, they sat in with each other's bands, and a determined Harry knew that he just had to have Buddy in his band. James used the Basie concept as bait, telling Buddy, "I'm going to put together a new big band. I'm going to play Basie's kind of music. I don't want to keep Bill Richmond. I have always known that sometime I just have to have you in my band, because for the first time, I'll have a drummer who drives me. Up until now it's always been me driving the band. But now I want you to do it. I need you, Buddy, and I'm willing to offer you a wage of $1,500 a week. You don't need to answer right now."

Buddy thought about it. He figured that he would make $35,000 in a year. Could that be right? Nobody had ever made that much money before—definitely not him. But Buddy wanted more, and as a part of the agreement, he insisted on featured billing, permission to wear whatever he wanted (as opposed to a band uniform), and the ability to record with others when the mood hit. James agreed to everything. It was one hell of a deal. The contract was signed and they shook hands. Buddy Rich was satisfied, Harry James was very satisfied, and Buddy Rich was now the highest paid sideman in the world. The day after signing with James, he went to a car dealership and bought the new XK–120 Jaguar he'd been looking at for some time.

Buddy and Marie were married on April 21, 1953, while Buddy was on tour with Harry James. During the courtship, Marie experienced "the real Buddy," and later admitted that his temperament could sometimes be challenging. She was a little uneasy, for instance, when he became jealous of a man who wanted to help her with her luggage at an airport and flew into a rage. She overlooked it, and explained to Mel Tormé, "Sometimes you're attracted to things you've never experienced before, be they good or bad. I had never known anyone that temperamental. But when he let all the barriers down, he was hysterically loving. Naive, wonderful, funny. That was the person I loved."[16]

Prior to the marriage, they sometimes carried on their relationship in secret when she visited him on tour, calling themselves "Mr. and Mrs." and using all kinds of different surnames. This carried on for six months until finally they took the plunge. Harry James was the best man, and Sal Monte, the manager of the band, was the witness. The wedding itself was a singular experience. "We had a Justice of the Peace who had a very decided British accent," as Marie recalled. "And it was just so weird for that part of the country that Harry, Buddy, and Sal were cracking up all through the ceremony. I was crying, because they were laughing all the way through my wedding ceremony!"[17] There was no honeymoon.

Buddy Rich left the Jazz at the Philharmonic tours and began making statements here and there about what he really thought about Norman Granz's JATP. The endless jam sessions gave him nothing musically, and he wasn't alone in thinking that. It was Dizzy Gillespie's contention at the time that "JATP was really not so very musical, because Norman liked placing two or three trumpeters at the front of the stage, dueling with each other. He himself stood in the wings, laughing. Sometimes it was funny. Norman had an odd sense of humor."[18] Pianist Hank Jones agreed. "Norman was more interested in presenting showmanship on the stage," he said. "That is why I finally quit."[19]

Buddy Rich was much more critical than Diz and Hank. In the June 1953 issue of *Downbeat*, one of the headlines blared, "Buddy Rich says JATP is Junk," with Buddy spilling his feelings about JATP in an interview. Pulling no punches, he said, "I don't want any part of Granz or his Jazz at the Philharmonic. You can make that plain. In the first place, it's not jazz. It's just honking and noise. He may be trying to prove something, but it has nothing to do with jazz, as I know it. This guy Granz talks about doing so much for jazz. What has he done? He takes top stars, Flip and Bird and everybody, and makes them play loud junk that he calls jazz. A lot of noise, not jazz. The people that he attracts to his so called concerts are the tipoff. Oh, they're all right, I guess. The kids are okay, but they get incited by Granz and his so-called jazz. They whistle and shout and make disturbances. One of these days musicians will have to face the facts that the music world needs some normality. The bopsters—and I don't mean Dizzy personally—set back music and jazz 20 years with their bad habits and foolishness. They gave all musicians a bad name." Buddy concluded that he was very happy to be with Harry James, making his final point clear: "You don't work for Harry James, you work with him. This is a great outfit."[20]

In the early summer, the James band made a film short called *Harry James and his Music Makers*. It was directed by film short master Will Cowan, who directed Buddy's 1948 short. Despite the lousy band business, films like these were still viable promotional vehicles, and the "new" James band began to take off. At the end of June, the band played at the Astor Roof and *Billboard* magazine reviewed them. "It was a stylish opening, and the dinner turnout was good, with music men, tourists and just plain dancers in attendance," they said. "James made a good investment when he added Rich."[21]

In *Downbeat's* August issue, Norman Granz, never one to back down from anything, replied to the somewhat unpleasant commentary made by Rich the previous month. "Rich is a great drummer, but a boor," said Granz. "Let me say at the outset that for many years I've regarded, in fact heralded, Buddy Rich as being one of the great drummers of our time; and I felt that each time I heard Buddy play, he played better than the time before, which is a tribute to his genius. Although Buddy has continued to grow in his playing, he has unfortunately remained an adolescent as a human being. It therefore pains me to write these lines about Buddy, but after reading what he had to say about JATP and me, I felt that I ought to say something to set the record straight."[22]

Buddy Rich may have felt a little lost at that time. He was playing with Harry James and saying that he was altogether happy there, but also recorded two albums outside of the band under his own name. *The Swinging Buddy Rich* received glowing reviews in *Billboard*. The other record was even more exciting musically for him, as he played in an all-star studio jam session with Buddy DeFranco, John Simmons, Freddie Greene, Benny Carter, Stan Getz, Harry Edison, and his idol, Count Basie. The album, *Jam Session #3*, was sort of an in-studio recording of what the JATP gang was doing live on stage.[23] What was perhaps most remarkable is that, despite the recent attacks in the magazines, both albums were produced by Norman Granz. Perhaps Buddy needed Granz's help. Perhaps he needed his money. Perhaps he owed Granz money.

Despite the public quarreling, Buddy kept coming back to Granz, even if it made Buddy angry to do so. Pianist Oscar Peterson, who was close to Norman Granz professionally and personally for many years, claimed that "Buddy Rich was a spendthrift and often didn't pay his bills, and often didn't pay his musicians either, when he was leading his own bands. At one point, Buddy drove to Granz' office in the new Jaguar he had just purchased. He didn't have enough money for gas. Granz, always known for paying musicians well, was getting tired of doling out funds to Buddy and turned down his latest request for an advance. Buddy threw a tantrum as only he could and said he was going to kill himself. With an accommodating gesture, Granz opened a window for him, and Buddy left in rage."[24]

Though bebop was never accepted by the public at large, by this time it had nevertheless become the accepted language of jazz improvisation. However, another genre was quickly emerging and threatening to take over all of pop music. Rock'n'roll was beginning to dominate the charts and the music world, partly due to the virtual overnight popularity of

Bill Haley and His Comets' "Rock Around the Clock." The song had actually first been recorded by the novelty group Sonny Dae and His Knights, and released on the small Arcade record label. But it was when Bill Haley made a cover of it in April, 1954, that it broke through nationally. Teenagers were latching on to what they considered "new music," although it was actually an outgrowth of the jump bands from the 1940s and even earlier blues styles. This thing they were calling rock'n'roll was becoming a headline-making cultural revolution that was, at the outset, mired in controversy. Some cultural alarmists believed that this type of "musical rebellion" actually caused juvenile delinquency and a multitude of other social ills. It was obvious, however, that controversial or not, rock was here to stay, and jazz musicians of every style were faced with some heavy competition.

The biggest threat to the musical status quo arrived in the form of Elvis Aaron Presley. In May of 1954, a 19-year-old Elvis returned to Sun Studios in Memphis for a second series of recordings. In the studio, he met guitarist Scotty Moore and bass player Bill Black, and during the following summer they released the single "That's Alright (Mama)." A few months later, Presley got himself a manager, the infamous Colonel Tom Parker. The following year, drummer D.J. Fontana, who would play for Elvis for 14 years, joined a band that was becoming hotter and hotter.

While rock was starting to make headlines and the Elvis phenomenon was growing, Buddy Rich was still at it, recording all over the place. On April 12 and13, 1954, he played on the Granz-produced recording *The Lionel Hampton Quintet*, with Hampton on vibes, Oscar Peterson piano, Buddy DeFranco on clarinet, and Ray Brown on bass. Buddy was seemingly everywhere in the mid-1950s. It's true that he loved the music, but he also needed the money; he had another mouth to feed. On May 11, 1954, Buddy and Marie had a baby daughter who they christened Cathy. Buddy was proud as a peacock and seemed to find a certain security and peace in a happy marriage and in fatherhood. Buddy's longtime friend, Jerry Lewis, became Cathy's godfather.

Family or not, the forever restless Rich definitely didn't ease off on performing or touring. He was always on his way somewhere. Marie, however, never felt that he didn't take his responsibility as a parent seriously. In several interviews, Marie and Cathy would insist that they never felt neglected. "I travelled a lot with Buddy before Cathy was born," Marie explained. "When she was born and then went to school, I couldn't go along as much. I stayed at home and looked after our daughter. I didn't want anyone else doing it. Buddy always called me every evening and did what he could over the telephone. The rest he looked after when he was at home. He always took two weeks off in the summer and four to six weeks around Christmas and New Year's."[25] Cathy described who made the decisions. "Mom was more the disciplinarian than he was," she said. "He was pretty soft when it came to things like that. You could just give him a look like 'Daddy' and he would give in. Sort of the opposite of what you would think. But you could only push him so far. He was definitely soft when it came to certain things, but if it was something that was really important, he would let you know it."[26]

Buddy's contract with Harry James expired on July 2, and three weeks later, he accepted an offer for a one-week engagement in the country where he had done his very first tour when he was a child: Australia. In later interviews, he explained his leaving Harry James by using the same excuse as he always had: billing issues, meaning that his name didn't get as much prominence as he had been promised.[27] He would, however, return to James several times in the future.

The Australian tour took place between July 23 and August 2, and was booked by the American promoter Lee Gordon, who had put together a gang of artists and musicians to perform 15 concerts in venues that included Sydney Stadium, Melbourne Stadium and Brisbane Stadium. Here, Buddy Rich would once again meet up with Artie Shaw, who was on the tour, as were Ella Fitzgerald and Bob Hope's popular comic foil, Jerry Colonna. Colonna and Rich arrived first, and were met by over 2,000 wildly enthusiastic fans. It was complete chaos, and the local newspaper, *The Argus*, reported, "While the pressmen tried to interview them, Rich started jamming on a couple of drums and Colonna on a trombone. Extra police were called into the airport where men, women and children tried to storm the plane as soon as it landed."[28]

Several days later Artie Shaw and Ella Fitzgerald arrived. Never at a loss for an opinion, Artie Shaw recalled, "I don't count that as a musical experience. I went there as the first of the American tourists, but they couldn't afford to bring the group. So I had to use Australian musicians, and they weren't too bad. I did the best I could, but I didn't get enough rehearsal time."[29] His displeasure can possibly be explained by a blow to his enormous ego. Shaw was met by only 15 teenagers at the airport. *The Canberra Times* wrote, "The whole thing was really an enormous contrast to the 2,000 who welcomed Buddy Rich and Jerry Colonna.[30] The tour was a financial loss for Gordon. Buddy gamely did his job, played his fabulous solos and went home.

Back home in the beginning of September, Buddy received a nasty surprise. He was contacted by a prosecutor at the Internal Revenue Service, a Leonard P. Moore of the Brooklyn Federal Court, who claimed that Buddy owed $13,074 in unpaid taxes for the past three years. He had 20 days to reply to the claim. This came at a time when Rich was thinking about starting another big band, this one to be backed by Jerry Lewis, who offered to put up the capital. *Downbeat* reported the news, writing, "The new Rich band will be organized here upon Buddy's return in October, with debut expected about November 15. Other than that, the enterprise is still in the formative stage according to Rich, who said 'Right now I haven't decided whether we'll have 8 or 18 men in it, but you can be sure they'll be the best in the business." [31]

It's likely that Buddy wanted to start another big band, but something made him change his mind, and he turned Jerry Lewis down. Maybe the spread of rock and Elvis bothered him, but more likely it was his tax problem—and the realization that leading a big band was difficult, financially and otherwise—that made him decide to choose an entirely different route. He accepted an offer to join a new orchestra put together by, unbelievably, the Dorsey brothers, Tommy and Jimmy, who had reconciled. Music business insiders were shocked. Explaining the deal, which had involved a very large check from the Dorseys, Buddy said, "They made me an offer that was just too good to turn down, not only from a financial standpoint, but because they are going to give me full billing with them as an 'extra added attraction.' I'm going to get the kind of presentation that I was supposed to get but didn't when I was with Harry James."[32]Buddy swore that both he and Tommy had settled down over the years, but from the first rehearsal the musicians could feel a tense vibe in the air.

Trumpter Pauly Cohen, who was on the scene, said, "I didn't think much about who was playing the drums. I was so concentrated on doing a good job. Everyone knew that Tommy Dorsey could kill you with his glance, so I kept my eyes on him. But I remember that Buddy once suddenly shouted that his pedal had broken. He swore at the guy who had set up his gear. He quickly got a new one. I understood that Buddy had a hot temperament. I did too, but I was careful not to get in an argument with him, because there I would have come out as the loser."[33] Trumpeter John Frosk, another bystander, recalled, "The night before Rich joined the band at Andrews Air Force Base, Tommy called us together. He wanted us to be real polite to Rich and not to get him agitated. Ten minutes before the first date we heard a crash. When Buddy saw the drums weren't set up right, he picked up the whole set and threw it down on the dance floor. The first day!"[34]

A notorious disciplinarian, Tommy Dorsey hadn't changed over the years. Between performances, the boys in the band would sleep in the bus, and sometimes hung their clothes out the windows. Dorsey hated things like this, so he followed them in his car and gave unannounced inspections. On the bandstand, the orchestra may have been billed as "The Dorsey Brothers," but it was always Tommy who called the musical shots, for better or worse. He drilled everyone the same way he had always done. If any musician seemed too tired, Tommy had the cure. Pauly Cohen remembered being exhausted in the middle of a tour. "Tommy tried to liven me up with some pills," said Cohen "I refused, but then took them—and suddenly I prayed to God that I would survive. Jesus! It was terrible! Tommy didn't say a word to me. Then when I wanted to quit the band, he chased me right around the block!"[35]

Ever since the day Frank Sinatra had praised Buddy's singing with his first big bands, Rich had been curious to see if he could further develop that side of his career. Bitten again by the singing bug, Buddy discussed this several times with none other than Norman Granz. Granz listened with interest and helped Buddy prepare for a recording session. He hired Howard Gibeling's Orchestra (Gibeling, also a composer, played trombone in Hal McIntyre's band), with the result being *Sing and Swing with Buddy Rich*, released on January 26, 1955. One side featured instrumentals with Buddy on drums (the "swing" part), but on the other ("sing") side, he asked his good friend Louie Bellson to take over the drum stool. After the recording, Buddy was more than satisfied. "I had never recorded vocals as I wanted to until this date," he said of the session. "This was the first time I got the feeling I wanted. It was wonderful and warm to sing with that group of fine musicians behind me. It was a great kick for me and even if nothing happens with the record, I'm very happy with the sides just for my own edification."[36] Reaction to Buddy's singing was mixed. Some thought there were similarities with Sinatra; others thought that his style was a little too light. The music from this album ended up on radio's easy listening stations, but a seed was sown in Buddy's mind, and he wasn't going to give up easily.

Soon, as had happened years earlier, it became apparent that Buddy wasn't happy with Tommy Dorsey. They got on each other's nerves. Returning to the Statler Hotel in New York City, the band played three sets a night for a month. Trumpeter Lee Castle fronted the orchestra for the first set, Jimmy Dorsey for the second, and Tommy finally joined them for the third. Buddy didn't like that. "Having the band together just for the final set never made any sense to me," Buddy said. "People spent damn good money to see that band, and they deserved more than just that."[37] At the end of one performance he suddenly threw his drumsticks in the air and shouted, "That's enough! I can't be nice any longer!"[38] He stormed offstage in anger as Tommy stood in the wings, laughing. Despite his displeasure and the occasional tantrum, Buddy stayed, and on January 1, 1955, Tommy Dorsey and His Orchestra with Jimmy Dorsey played at the Meadowbrook Ballroom in New Jersey. Here, they were also filming the television variety show "Stage Show," a summer replacement for the popular Jackie Gleason series. Gleason loved jazz, and he loved the Dorsey brothers. The very first evening of the engagement, Buddy was thrilled to accompany a man whom he greatly admired: Duke Ellington. Duke performed a medley of nine of his hits. In the coming programs, other guests were Nat "King" Cole, Patti Page, Johnnie Ray, and on March 12, the guests were singer Kate Smith, tap dancer Bunny Briggs, the singing DeMarco Sisters, and Count Basie. It was an incredible show.

On March 12, 1955, Charlie Parker was sitting in front of a television at the home of the well-known patron of jazz Baroness Nica de Koenigswarter, who was taking care of him in his critical illness. Bird was watching "Stage Show" on television, laughing at an acrobatic act on screen, when had trouble breathing and collapsed. He was dead within a few minutes. By this time, Buddy Rich had some to terms with bebop, musically and otherwise. He had great respect for Parker; he knew that the saxophonist hadn't lived an easy life, despite his enormous musical talent. For the rest of his life, Rich would only have good things about Charles "Yardbird" Parker.

The Dorsey job was getting to him. Buddy must have begun to realize that it took too much energy to play solely for money (and to simply satisfy the IRS). With the situation getting continually worse, he was beginning to realize it just wasn't worth the price. At an outdoor performance at Connally Air Force Base in Texas, the stage was invaded by a swarm of mosquitoes. Buddy bore the brunt of the bites, and his frantic waving to chase away the irritating insects was making a mess of the band's performance. Dorsey lost his patience and threw his trombone at Buddy. When the show was over, Buddy left the stage without a word to anyone. The next day, he called the trumpeter Lee Castle, who was also Dorsey's assistant, and gave notice that he wasn't coming back. When Dorsey heard the news, he shouted at Castle, "Tell him if he decides to change his mind, he won't have a drum set, I've just given it away to Rocky Marciano!"[39]

The situation settled down for a time. Dorsey wanted to have Buddy back and Buddy understood that he had to live up to his contract. In April at the Shamrock Hotel in Fort Hood, Texas, tempers flared again. They shouted loudly at each other right on the stage in front of an astonished audience. Once more, Buddy left the stage (this time before the show was even over), and went home. Dorsey called in Louie Bellson, who arrived a day or so later. To put it very mildly, Dorsey was not happy. It's been said that Dorsey was paying off a lot of Rich's debts and had paid out more money on those debts than would have been due Rich under his salary arrangement. Dorsey, whose pride had also been wounded, felt that he had been publicly embarrassed by Rich leaving so abruptly. As for the debt and financial issues, Buddy felt this was a matter for their lawyers to work out, and he thought that it was he who should be feeling embarrassed because he was forced to work for a man like Tommy Dorsey. He declared, in the end: "I should never have gone back to him!"

CHAPTER 13

DRUM BARBECUE

Publicity photo of Buddy Rich, circa 1958.

The phenomenon of American television gathered momentum in the mid-1950s, and one of the more popular formats was the talk show. They were relatively cheap to produce, in that content consisted mainly of interviews with celebrities plugging a new film, book or recording, combined with some comedy and a couple of musical numbers. Visually exciting and something of a name in the jazz business, it's not surprising that television producers kept their eyes on Buddy Rich. Though Buddy hadn't done any television since his appearances on "The Eddie Condon Floor Show" and "The Peter Lind Hayes Show" of December, 1950, he would soon hit the tube again.

This time it was the wildly popular comedy team of Dean Martin and Jerry Lewis who wanted him on their successful show, "The Colgate Comedy Hour." The June 5, 1955 episode first discovered in the television vaults by Buddy Rich curator Charley Braun featured Lewis and Rich in a drum duel. Thanks to social media and a number of drum videos, the segment has become a classic. Buddy and Jerry joked around with the help of some cute camera tricks. Buddy threw a pile of drum sticks over Jerry, who was sitting behind a ridiculously large drum set, and both delivered funny dialogue. All this nonsense ended with a furious drum solo by Buddy. It all was a roaring success with audiences, and it also caught the attention of network television honchos.

Aside from television, this was a busy period for him. He played again with Count Basie, and also recorded a new album under his own name, *The Wailing Buddy Rich*. In July, he played with Freddie Martin's orchestra in the short film *Melodies by Martin*, another Universal band short directed by Will Cowan. Then he was part of a trio with blind pianist Art Tatum and the unfailingly inspiring Lionel Hampton. This classic series of recordings didn't need a bass, thanks to Buddy's tasteful use of the bass drum. In August he was a guest on Steve Allen's popular "Tonight Show," and in the same month, he recorded the album *The Swinging Buddy Rich*. In September, he joined forces with trumpeter Harry "Sweets" Edison to record *Buddy and Sweets*, which would become one of Buddy's alltime favorites. Public and private animosity aside, all these recordings were done for Norman Granz.

Even as a new father, he was seemingly working everywhere; he had a family to support now. Buddy was back with JATP for a new tour in September and October; on these dates it was reported that he more or less wiped the floor with Gene Krupa in new duels at Carnegie Hall. In Downbeat, Nat Hentoff wrote, "The finale started with a long duel between Krupa and Rich. Buddy easily outmaneuvered Krupa without overworking himself."[1] Gene Krupa took it all in his stride, at least outwardly, in that Gene instructed his agent Willard Alexander, who also booked Buddy, that he was never to book him directly after Buddy's band. As time went on, the two drum giants became even better friends, and they made several recordings together, with the first studio effort being *Krupa and Rich*, a project that received surprisingly little attention in the jazz trades. On October 2, 1955, Buddy Rich made his last appearance with JATP, at the Chicago Opera House. At that show, he played one of his greatest solos, later issued as a recording and called *The Buddy Rich Explosion*. It was a powerful, beautifully paced solo from the first to last drumbeat.

A month later, he guested on the "GE Theater" television show, an anthology series hosted by then-actor Ronald Reagan and broadcast on CBS. Each episode was an adaptation of a novel, shortstory or magazine fiction. On November 27, Buddy Rich appeared with comedian Jack Carter and Broadway star Lisa Kirk, playing the small role of a bandleader named Johnny. He did engage in some serious dialogue with Lisa Kirk and played a 25-second drum solo during the 29-minute episode called "From the Top." Maybe it was the television experience, but Buddy was beginning to explore what he may have thought were more lucrative opportunities in show business. He really wanted to get into singing, and in several interviews, said that singing was "something I've wanted to do a long, long time. It isn't like a whim. I've had this singing thing in the back of my mind since—oh, since the days I was working in the same band with a pretty fair singer named Frank Sinatra. You know the band I mean. So I listened to Frankie and hope some of it might rub off on me. Nor is it merely a matter of proving a point. There's only so much that a man can express on a drum, for the rest, you have to use your voice."[3]

For three days, between January 4 and 6, 1956, Buddy recorded a new album where he didn't play the drums at all. *Buddy Rich Sings Johnny*

Mercer was produced (believe it or not) by Norman Granz, had Buddy backed by Buddy Bregman's Orchestra, and was released on Granz' newly-formed Verve record label—a consolidation of sorts of Granz' Clef and Norgan imprints. Norman, who signed Buddy to another contract, appeared to have liked the result and Buddy's singing, and wrote on the back cover. "As a drummer, Buddy Rich is regarded by many as the world's best. He knows what beat is all about. As a singer, he knows what interpretation is, what rhythm a song should have, how it should be phrased, and how the lyrics should be presented."[4] Norman Granz had spoken.

Though Buddy was planning how a possible singing career would work, for whatever reason, he still didn't think the time was right. He joined up once more with Harry James, who, at the time, had cut down to an octet. While he was in this group, Buddy Rich got to experience none other than Elvis Presley, performing on the same stage with James on April 3, 1956 on the aircraft carrier USS *Hancock*, which was lying at harbor in San Diego, California. The occasion was on television's "Milton Berle Show," and another guest was swimming movie star Esther Williams Her entrance on an enormous crane in front of all the Marines elicited huge rounds of applause. In the next segment, Buddy began with a short drum solo to introduce the James guest shot. On television, Buddy looked unbelievably strong, fast, and in better shape than ever. Both he and Harry James smiled at each other behind Elvis's back when they heard that he didn't have any written arrangements with him. It wasn't necessary. Elvis brought down the house. Buddy Rich had already been in show business for decades and could see what a magnetic force Elvis had become. He could also see that rock'n'roll was no fad, and that Elvis was just the beginning. If Buddy Rich had had misgivings about going in for a singing career, he was even more doubtful now—but he still kept it in the back of his mind.

On August 16, 1956, Buddy was back in the studio again, at Capitol Studios in Los Angeles. He was part of the rhythm section backing Ella Fitzgerald and Louis Armstrong on *Ella and Louis*. It was a memorable occasion for him, saying afterwards, "You are not really accompanying, man. You're a part of that entire mood. When I recorded with Ella and Louis, it was a dream. How many guys can sit back and say they've recorded with Louis Armstrong, Ella Fitzgerald, Ray Brown and Oscar Peterson at the same time? To be called for that thing is like being called for meeting the heads of the state. You're talking about people who have done more for that kind of music than anybody else, and there you are sitting in the middle of it. Now what better compliment is that?"[5] *Ella and Louis* and its follow-ups have become among the biggest-selling and most memorable recordings in jazz history.

The next day, he recorded a tribute album to his idol. With a band of 11 men, he went to Hollywood and recorded his favorite songs by Count Basie. Perhaps he felt it was about time, and gave the album the title *This One's For Basie*.[6] The record was reissued several times over the years with various titles, including *Big Band Shout*. Buddy Rich's praise and high regard for Count Basie lasted a lifetime. "Nobody else in the band business can move you like that," Buddy said. "I had the good luck to hear that band almost every night at Birdland, while we were at the Statler, and, believe me, anything this man does gets 25 stars if there is such a thing. All you have to do is say Count Basie to me, and I'm ready to travel, any time, any place, to hear this band!"[7]

The following year, Buddy re-tested the waters for a singing career. He recorded another vocal album for Granz, with Alvin Stoller (who replaced Buddy in the Dorsey band) in the drum chair. The title of Rich's new Verve record was a direct indication of his new path: *Buddy Rich Just Sings*. In the spring of 1957, he did more television work as an actor, appearing again as a bandleader, this one named Cozy, on the CBS Sunday night sitcom, "The Marge and Gower Champion Show."

The James band became something of a haven for him. In May that year, James was planning to put together a new big band that would feature charts that would channel the spirit and the feel of the Basie band. James knew no better drummer than Rich to do the songs justice. Though Buddy agreed to participate in a recording of Basie-like charts, the problem was that he was still under contract to Norman Granz. Harry was signed with Capitol Records. The solution was to present Rich as "Buddy Poor" on the record. Buddy didn't care what name was on the label, explaining, "I played many sessions with Charlie Parker and lots of others when I was contracted to another record company. I couldn't always use my name because of legal technicalities. I have made all kinds of recordings with great jazz artists. I played with Goodman, with Woody Herman and with Basie, and I didn't always get credit for it. As I said before, it was extremely exciting and enjoyable to play with them and that is really all that matters to me."[8]

Nobody was fooled. Everyone could easily recognize Buddy's tremendous drumming. James Hill, one of James' arrangers, loved Buddy's playing. "I had stayed up all night writing the drum part for 'Blues on a Count,' because I knew Buddy was gonna be there." Hill said at the time. "When Harry called it, Buddy threw the drum part on the floor. I didn't realize he couldn't read music. After he heard the band play it once, he had it all in his head, and he played it just great."[9] After the first day of recording. Harry James was so happy that he refused to change the black-and-white striped shirt he was wearing, and kept it on for the remaining time in the studio. (Like many other bandleaders, he was a bit superstitious.) James was really happy with Buddy, and when the record, released as *Wild About Harry!*, was issued, it really helped put James back on the jazz map again. The band was getting a good deal of radio airplay and was booked into several important festivals, although sometimes without Rich behind the drums; Buddy was off again in pursuit of a non-drumming career.

On May 8, 1957, Buddy Rich's quartet opened a week's booking at Larry Potter's Club in Studio City, California, along with a South American female trio called the Phantomaniacs. Buddy's act at Potter's club showed clearly how divided he was. He performed numbers where he showed off all his different sides, like in his "Traps" days. The evening opened with him just singing for the first half-hour, then he performed a comedy number with bongos, and after that, switched to playing on a pair of tympani, while quipping, "No risk of my audiences falling asleep!" He ended it all with a gigantic drum solo that left the audience breathless. The number was called "Drumocracy." Buddy wasn't happy with the result, and later explained, "I spent a lot of money with Nick Castle, yeah, a lot of money and I worked hard to make it something worthwhile. On opening night I died, man. When I got into my dance number, who do you think I saw sitting at a table? Mr Fred Astaire. I'd always been a big fan, seen all his movies, I felt awful, man. He came back to see me after the show and was very complimentary. He also played drums, so I had a set sent over to him and he was very pleased. We were never close friends, but I would see him every once in a while, and he would always stop and talk with me for a few minutes."[10]

After the show, he signed autographs as usual. Someone came up to him and made a remark that compared him with Krupa. Manager Carl Ritchie, his sister Marge's husband, was standing beside him and said to the reporter, John Tynan, "If anyone had said anything like that to him five years ago, Buddy would have hit him."[11] Buddy muttered something under his breath and signed his name. He received good reviews for the show, which should have resulted in more bookings at other venues in New York and Las Vegas. But nothing happened. As for the act itself, Buddy's future close friend Johnny Carson was at Larry Potter's club, and on television years later, described the performance as "the worst act I ever saw."

While cooling his heels, he recorded the live album *Buddy Rich in Miami*, featuring JATP cohort Flip Phillips on tenor sax, Peter Ind on bass and Ronnie Ball on piano. This album was also released on the Verve label and received high praise. He still couldn't make up his mind about what he was going to do about his non-drumming career, and performed a part of his Larry Potter's Club variety act, "Drumocracy," on Steve Allen's popular NBC television show on July 14. During the fall and winter, he was still drumming all over the place. He was a guest on "The Ed Sullivan Show" with James, and he appeared as a single on Patti Page's "The Big Record." Then it was off to tour in Europe with Harry James. The band visited West Germany, France, Belgium, Switzerland, Italy and Austria. After that tour, on November 19, he informed Harry that he wanted to move on other things and left the band again.

The last three years had been very hectic for Buddy Rich. Now hitting 40 years of age, it may have been a good time to take stock and look back on a sensational career: the Vaudeville era; playing in the bands of Marsala, Berigan, Shaw and Dorsey; touring with JATP; and performing with Charlie Parker and just about every giant of jazz. He had appeared in major motion pictures with the likes of Judy Garland, Red Skelton, Mickey Rooney, Esther Williams, Van Johnson, Lucille Ball, Gene Kelly, and Eleanor Powell. There were 15 recordings on the market under his own name, and dozens of recordings with legends like Nat "King" Cole, Goodman, Basie, Benny Carter, Louis Armstrong, Billie Holiday, and Ella Fitzgerald. Surely, he had to have had some feeling of satisfaction. But Buddy Rich was not a person who looked back. The fact was, he never saved anything he had made. "He didn't like talking about his childhood," according to Cathy Rich. "And when he did, he always referred to himself in the third person. Even to me. He never saved the records he performed on. Not one record. Not a video. He wasn't interested in what had been. He just wanted to move ahead."[12]

He did more television, appearing on "The Big Record" again, and in May of 1958, he guested on an episode of "Chicago Late Night," where he played a duet with Jo Jones. Buddy, who loved all innovative drummers, had an enormous respect for Jones, and always thought he learned something new from him. The respect was mutual. After this, it was another new jazz quintet that toured all over the country. The small group, Buddy said, was formed at the suggestion of his booking agency. His bookers advised him that if he had a smaller band he would be successful and, for once, earn some money. "They told me I could be a millionaire if I would just concentrate on having a small combo like they wanted," Buddy said at the time. "But no, there were never any regrets about that."[13]

During two days in April of 1959, the quintets of Max Roach and Buddy Rich recorded an album entitled *Rich Versus Roach*. Saxophonist Gigi Gryce, one of the bright names among young arrangers, had been given the task of writing the scores that would utilize all the men as one ensemble, but still leave space for the drummers to solo. For drummers, the highlight of the session was "Figure Eights," where swing's greatest drummer traded eight-bar breaks with the indisputable king of bebop. Their totally different styles of drumming were on display, and in retrospect, maybe the title of the album should have been "*Rich and Roach*," as this was no "battle," and there's no actual winner here. It's like comparing Van Gogh with Picasso.

He signed a new contract with Mercury Records, the company that released the project with Roach, for his fourth attempt at a vocal album.

In May, 1959, he recorded *The Voice is Rich*, where he is backed by Hal Mooney's orchestra. The reviews in *Billboard* were lukewarm: "Though Rich has no great vocal assets, he has a way of selling the tunes nicely. Makes for good, easy-listening material from which jocks can cull programming bands."[15] Buddy didn't take the criticism to heart. He believed in himself as a singer, but just like everything else, he had to have the right material and get the right backing. In the summer, he flew to the West Coast to play an amusing cameo as a bandleader in Jerry Lewis's new film for Paramount, *Visit to a Small Planet*. In the movie, Buddy is performing at a night club where the indomitable Lewis, who plays a creature from outer space, visits and is invited to play with him. The plot of the film isn't worth mentioning. Suffice it to say, it received no Oscar nomination.

Back in New York, big band fever struck briefly again, despite years of aggravation with his other large units. The band played some dates at the Club Mardi Gras in Wildwood, New Jersey; the Steel Pier in Atlantic City; and then at Birdland. The English drummer Kenny Clare was there. "I saw Buddy Rich at Birdland in July, 1959," Clare reported, "and I haven't stopped talking about it him since. Now everybody knows what I meant. Don't be discouraged, drummers. I've lived through it for the last eight years, and I only wake up screaming two or three nights a week now. He's the model for everything and everybody: the living proof that it can be done."[16]

Buddy was playing in top form, and he recorded a swinging, underrated session with this edition of the big band for Mercury with "Sweets" Edison in the trumpet section. But he was in pain. After a performance, he was walking home on Broadway near 52nd Street when he suddenly collapsed. He was taken to the Leroy Hospital in Manhattan where he was diagnosed with a kidney stone. It was removed and it he was told to rest. While others would have stayed in bed for weeks to recover, Buddy Rich was quickly back on stage at Birdland again, where he was booked for a longer guest stint between August 27 and September 17. He split the evenings with Art Blakey's Jazz Messengers and played as though nothing had happened.

After his final performance at Birdland, there was a celebratory cocktail party held at the New York Jazz Corner, and the entire music press was on hand. Buddy Rich had now made the decision to put all his efforts into his singing career. In order to make a dramatic announcement of his intentions, he found a pair of his drumsticks and, in front of one and all, burned them. "This is the new Rich who is standing in front of you," he said. Many of his fans and closest friends looked sad. *Downbeat* magazine was there as well, and Buddy spelled out his decision to them one more time, saying, "I can say so much more in 32 bars of singing than I can in a 40-minute drum solo."[17]

The singing act was prepared to the slightest detail. He kept on pianist John Bunch from his current small group, hired bassist Earl May and drummer Tony Inzalaco, and enlisted Lou Spence to write new charts for the accompanying trio. He rehearsed the rest of December in anticipation of an October 5, 1959 stand, booked by Willard Alexander, at a small but elegant club, the Living Room, on New York City's East Side. The title of the act, as released to the trades, was short and sweet: "Buddy Rich: Songs." The engagement was booked for three weeks. The audiences could tell that everything was well rehearsed. The songs did justice to his wonderful timing and phrasing, and his humor spiced up the evening. Given that this was a nightclub, there were some heavy imbibers in the house who didn't hesitate to shout, "Why aren't you playing the drums?" This happened several evenings in a row.

The reviews were mixed. *Variety* reported, "One of the world's best drummers, Buddy Rich, has beat his last drumbeat on his skins. Although his singing range is somewhat limited, there is a solid rhythmic feeling that adds to all the numbers. He uses his voice like a fourth instrument with the trio that accompanies him."[18] *Downbeat* wasn't as kind, writing, "He still has a lot to learn about singing. America is full of singers who can sing just as well."[19] Buddy was prepared for the criticism, and knew that he had to start again from square one. He even had his own psychiatrist with him that evening to boost his confidence. Everything had to take its time.

The day before the final performance at the Living Room, Harry James wanted to meet with Buddy. James wanted him to play with his band again after the first of the year for a long engagement at the Flamingo

19th August 1921. Variety.

NEW GERRY SOC RULE

Chrilden May Not Appear On New York Stage in Summer

The Society for the Prevention of Cruelty to Chrildn has passed a new ruling forbidding the appearance of Chriled in New York Theatres during July and August.

The Action was taken after the app earance of Rogers Bennett and Traps, with Traps a four - year old boy, at Loew Orpheum recently the society stepping in arresting the parents of the child who appear in the act with him. The couple were released on suspended sentence.

An additional ruling of the society make it prohibitory for children to appear for more than two performances a day.

1921 newspaper article detailing the arrest of Buddy's parents for violating child labor laws.

Buddy at age six, October, 1923.

The Toy Shop number of the Greenwich Village Follies of 1922

"Toy Shop" number from *Greenwich Village Follies* of 1922. Little Traps is next to the bass drum.

Top row, left to right: Leo Corday (Jo's husband), Mickey,
Carl Ritchie (Marge's husband), Buddy Rich.
Bottom row, left to right: Marge, Bess, Robert, and Jo Rich.
Photo credit: Shirley Shifrin

Publicity still from the movie *Ship Ahoy*, 1942 (Left to right: Tommy Dorsey,
Buddy, Red Skelton and Eleanor Powell). Notice clear view of Buddy's left
hand technique.

Buddy at age 20, 1937, performing in WPA show *Oh Say Can You Sing* shortly before he left vaudeville for the world of jazz.

A rare shot of Buddy with Bunny Berigan, 1938.

On the road with Berigan, 1938.

Buddy with Joe Marsala at the Carnival of Swing festival, 1938.

Buddy not long after he joined Artie Shaw in early 1939. While the cymbal and drum setup copied Krupa's, the bass drum shield art (the initials BR) was still a work in progress.

With the Artie Shaw band and singer Helen Forrest in one of the 1939 film shorts that featured the Shaw big band.

From the 1939 feature film *Dancing Co-Ed*.

Buddy hamming it up while with the Dorsey band, circa 1942.

The bewigged 1943 Tommy Dorsey band, outfitted for the film *Du Barry was a Lady*.

Newspaper ads for the newly-formed Buddy Rich Orchestra of 1945. Note that the "Will Mastin Trio" is on the bill. The trio, for many years, featured BR's good friend Sammy Davis, Jr.

Buddy onstage with the legendary Josephine Baker and comic Leo De Lyon (Irving Levin), 1951.

Posing in the early 1950s with a Ludwig kit.

Signed ad for Ludwig drums, circa 1951.

Betty Grable, Harry James, and Buddy, circa 1954.

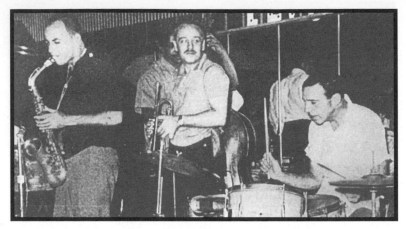

Buddy jamming in Singapore during tour of the Far East in 1961 with Sam Most, Wyatt Ruther, and Rolf Ericson.

Gene Krupa and Buddy Rich in the studio for the recording of *Burnin' Beat*, 1962. Though Krupa and Rich were both photographed informally in the studio, contractor and saxophonist Eddie Wasserman revealed that Buddy actually overdubbed his parts to tracks already recorded with Gene on them.

Rehearsing the brand new "Swinging New Big Band" in Las Vegas, 1966. Buddy listens out front while Bobby Morris runs the new charts down in the drum chair.

Buddy Rich and one of his biggest fans, Tony Bennett, possibly at the infamous Basin Street East engagement of November, 1966.

Comedy sketch with singer Buddy Greco, co-star of the 1967
television series "Away We Go."

Buddy in Nehru jacket, 1967.

Buddy, still endorsing Rogers drums, in action shortly after the formation of the 1966 "Swinging New Big Band."

Buddy, Benny Goodman, and Count Basie (Stanley Kay can be seen behind Basie) at Buddy's Place gala, mid-1970s.

Buddy and Sammy Davis, Jr., likely in England, late 1970s. The two worked together several times over the years, but their last projected tour of Europe never happened.

Buddy and Sammy Davis, Jr. press conference, London, 1978.

From "The Muppet Show," 1982.

Possible unused publicity photo, 1984.

Left to right: Frank Sinatra, Barbara Sinatra, Cathy Rich, and Buddy at the Concert for the Americas, Santo Domingo, 1982.

Marie Rich, 2019.

Hotel in Las Vegas. Buddy went to meet him, and James hoped to entice him by playing him a few Basie songs from his new "Basie book," but Buddy turned him down. He wanted to continue focusing on his singing career. Soon, however, he had to face facts when his booking agency informed him that there was very little interest in booking him as a singer. Then Mercury Records notified him his record sales were low, and that another vocal album was not in sight.

After the final evening at the Living Room, he was walking home with Mel Tormé, invited by Buddy that night to come and listen. As Tormé recalled, it was raining. Buddy was very quiet, but finally he asked what Mel thought of his vocal efforts. Mel answered, "Let me say it like this: I am not your favorite drummer and you aren't my favorite singer." Buddy nodded in understanding. They turned in on 52nd Street and observed that the street wasn't what it used to be. According to Tormé, they heard music emanating from one of the 52nd Street clubs, went in, and saw none other than Allen Eager, Buddy's tenor saxophonists from the second version of Buddy Rich and His Orchestra. The drummer with Eager was Max Roach. It didn't take long for Eager to notice Rich. They had sat down at a table and after awhile Mel saw that Buddy seemed very depressed. Buddy said. "Let's get the hell out of here."

Just as they got up to leave, Eager grabbed the microphone and welcomed Buddy Rich to the club. There was a round of applause, and Eager asked him to sit in. Buddy told him, "No man, I don't want to play." Then Eager began to taunt him openly, saying, "Hey, old-timer, come on up and make a jerk out of yourself! Let everyone see how corny you sound after hearing Max Roach!" Tormé wasn't sure he was hearing properly. Ever the wise-ass, maybe Eager knew how he could tempt Buddy to take the stage again. He knew very well from earlier days that saying Max Roach's name to Buddy was like waving a red flag. Tormé couldn't keep quiet. "Come on, king. Show them how to do it." Buddy turned around, went up on the stage, called for an up-tempo song—could have been "I Found a New Baby" or something based on that—and played a solo no one thought was possible. People flooded in from all directions and suddenly the club was full, just like long ago at the Hickory House, when his playing prompted a departing audience to turn around and come back in. Nine minutes later, he was still getting standing ovations.

Max Roach stood there with his jaw dropped. Of all the solos Tormé had seen his friend play, this was the most perfect he had witnessed. At two in the morning, they left the club and walked home. Buddy was still quiet.

Then he said, "Fuck singing! I'm a drummer!"

CHAPTER 14

Struggling on the Road

Buddy and David Lucas during Asian tour, 1961.

One of the most provocative television talk shows aired during the 1950s was one hosted by Mike Wallace, who would later best known as one of the reporters on television's "60 Minutes." In November, 1959, Buddy Rich was a guest on his show, "Night Beat." Wallace, master of manufacturing controversy on the tube in those days, wanted to pressure Rich the same way that he had done earlier with both Stan Getz and Gerry Mulligan, who had both confessed their narcotics problems publicly on his program. Buddy Rich didn't have those issues, but took the opportunity to deliver a salvo of what he maintained were bitter truths about the music scene of the time. He said rock and roll was played by idiots for idiots and blamed it for the declining interest in big jazz bands. He lashed out at America's disc jockeys for poisoning their listeners with rock, instead of leading their listeners towards good jazz. He explained that he hadn't any illusions about the audiences in jazz clubs. "With a few exceptions, only the musicians themselves understand what is being played," he declared to Wallace.

At the same time, he said he believed that the European jazz audiences were much more knowledgeable about jazz than stateside audiences. Afterwards, Wallace summed up Rich as one of the most colorful characters he had ever met. Especially amusing were his concluding remarks about different music personalities. He said that the Basie band was "the most wonderful band there is." Regarding Gene Krupa, Buddy told Wallace, "I respect him, but my idol was Chick Webb." About Frank Sinatra, he could only say, "The greatest!" And when asked about teen idol Fabian, he asked Wallace, "What's a Fabian?"

His singing career now history, it was back to jazz for Buddy, and he formed a swinging small group with Carmen Leggio on tenor sax, Willie Dennis on trombone and Nabil "Knobby"Totah on bass. While the band was touring, Buddy joked easily on stage about not being a singer any longer. If anyone in the audience asked him to sing a song he replied, "Go out and buy my last album, you'll love it."[1] When the band got to the Dream Room Lounge in New Orleans, Buddy wasn't feeling right. He felt stiffness in his fingers, mostly in his left ring finger, and two weeks later, the ache had gotten worse and spread to his whole arm. He had trouble breathing on stage during his solos, and sometimes he got a terrible stabbing pain in his chest, forcing him to lean against a wall for support. "I walked back to the Roosevelt Hotel," as Buddy remembered." I couldn't seem to get air in my lungs. I walked into the lobby and the desk was way down at the end. It looked like a mile away. When I got there, the night clerk said, 'Mr, Rich, somebody better go upstairs with you.' A bell boy came up. I drew a hot tub and sat in it until daylight."[2]

The next day he felt better. He could breathe again, and was in a good mood when the group flew to Atlanta to play at Top of the Stairs for ten days starting on December 9. Before the performance, he had promised to give a short speech at a Junior Chamber of Commerce luncheon. When he got there, he felt really awful again, and he had to be driven to the hospital. The doctor, Francis W Fitzhugh, Jr., examined him, and the results were alarming. Buddy was admitted immediately. He'd had a heart attack. He had just celebrated his 42nd birthday and had lived a fantastic life, but the stress and anxiety of maintaining an expensive lifestyle, and a diet rich with pasta, hot dogs, and other junk made him a strong candidate for a coronary. "I was told it was 20 years of anxiety, temperament, and unhappiness," Buddy said of the heart problems. "And I used to have terrible eating habits: three pounds of spaghetti at four in the morning after work, and then go to bed. Put all those things together and it tears you apart. Well, I am not a drinking man and I'm strong by nature, with good recuperative powers. I use my mental capacity to fight bad things off. I never wanted any part of sympathy."[3]

Buddy was in need of economic assistance. Even if it were true that the Dorsey brothers paid his tax debts up until 1956, he was once again on the IRS "hit list," and they were after him again. He was therefore overjoyed when the hospital bill was paid the same day he was admitted. It was his friend, the skinny singer from Hoboken, who again stepped in to save the day. "An hour after I was admitted here, Frank Sinatra sent me a big check," said Buddy. "He didn't know if either I or my band was working. He didn't know if I had enough money, either. He was always doing everything for me."[4]

In bed for five weeks, the doctors told Rich that he would never play the drums again. "Go home and rest for a year," they said. As a result, Buddy became depressed. He was a man who was used to reasoning that if you had a toothache, you went to a dentist and got it fixed, and then resumed your normal life. He figured that it would be the same with a heart attack: a couple doctor visits and a few pills, and life would go on. But he soon found out this was not the case. After a brief convalescence with Marie and Cathy in their Manhattan apartment, he contacted his booking agency, Associated Booking Corporation, run by Joe Glaser[5], and asked for help. "I'm ready to start playing again," he said. Glaser said no. He didn't want to risk being dragged into any insurance mess if something serious were to happen while Rich was up on some stage. Buddy thought about resuming his singing career or maybe buying his own jazz club. If he couldn't play, he at least wanted to be where jazz was being played, and he started negotiations to take over the East River Club in New York. Then he changed his mind and organized a new sextet.

By April, 1960, he was back. His plans to once again build a real big band were exchanged for a more realistic and easily managed sextet made up of himself on the drums, Irwin "Marky" Markowitz on trumpet, Seldon Powell tenor sax, Willie Dennis trombone, Dave McKenna piano and Earl May on bass. After two break-in gigs at the Village Gate in New York and at the Dream Bar within Miami's Johnina (where the live *Buddy Rich in Miami* date was recorded), he appeared once again before Birdland's appreciative audience on April 14. This time he was sharing the stage with Art Blakey's Jazz Messengers featuring Wayne Shorter. The infamous and oft-imitated master of ceremonies for the evening, Pee Wee Marquette, introduced Blakey with these words: "My ladies and gentlemen, on stage, the world's best drummer, Art Blakey!" Buddy just brushed it off by muttering in the wings and said, "Which Art?" Overall, Buddy took it in good humor; he was just happy to be back, and his temper was not in evidence that evening.

In the days before the engagement at Birdland, he had also recorded a new album for a Mercury Records jazz division called Emarcy, *The Driver*. Listening to this recording, it is impossible to fathom that the man behind the drums had had a heart attack five months earlier. At the time of the record's release he said, "You don't need to prove yourself to an audience. But you do need to prove to yourself that you are as good as you think you are. You want to be the best. And if so, then, man, be the best. How do you get to be the best? By constantly improving and challenging yourself. If I don't achieve something the first time, I am mad enough to try a second. I'll do it that second time because I was defeated the first—and I hate defeat."[6]

Another fantastic musician also played on the record; vibraphonist Mike Mainieri. Buddy had met him at Village Gate in New York. It was through a mutual friend's incessant pressure that the two hooked up. The friend was Pete Vuolo, and he called Buddy several times saying that he thought he should let Mainieri play with him. Buddy wanted no part of it, telling Vuolo, "The last vibraphonist I had in my band (Terry Gibbs) drove me crazy. I don't want another one." Vuolo didn't give up, and kept nagging until Buddy gave in and agreed to let Mainieri play the third set of the evening.

Buddy would never forget that night. "I was sitting at a table waiting to play the first set, when in walks this long haired, scraggly looking kid dressed in a zoot suit and carrying a set of vibes. I took one look and said, 'Uh oh,' but I told him to set up his stuff and wait until I called him. There was a hell of a crowd there. I had him wait three sets; I was hoping the crowd would thin out so it wouldn't be too bad if he didn't make it. Finally, I called him up on the stand and asked him what tune he'd like to play. He said anything would be all right. So I called up 'Broadway.' I figured all the young boppers would know that. He played the hell out of it. I figured it was a lucky break. I'd hit one of the tunes he knew. He did a ballad next, 'Tenderly.' To really appreciate what happened, you have to realize that the crowd was full of all those characters who hang out in the Village. Well, when Mike played that ballad, you could've heard a pin drop. The next set, I called a real fast tune. I wasn't through testing this guy yet. He played for 35 choruses and I couldn't wear him out and he never repeated himself! At intermission, I called him over to my table and asked him if he wanted a job. I could barely hear him say yes. My first instructions were to get a haircut and some decent clothes."[7]

Mike Mainieri also vividly remembered that evening, saying, "The week before, I had played at a club called the China Door. It was the worst in my life. A few days later I was at Birdland together with Buddy Rich. I couldn't fathom it. I was shaking like a leaf when he called me up. I remember that in the fast song, 'Cherokee,' he let me play over 40 choruses—he wanted to try and embarrass me—but I got through it all, got standing ovations, and afterwards he hired me directly at a wage of $90 a week. I even got to play on the recording of *The Driver* album."[8] The sextet became a septet when Mike joined up, and the band was a huge success at Birdland. After the stint there, Rich wanted to change things around again. Buddy was known for making wholesale changes from time to time, but in this instance, he wanted Manieri to carry the entire ball. "After Birdland, he fired the whole band, kept me, and I became a kind of vice conductor," said Mainieri. "Buddy just said, 'You put whoever you want in the band and write the arrangements. I don't care.'"[9] Those who made up the ensemble, besides Buddy and Mike, were John Morris on piano, Wilbur Wynne on guitar, Richard Evans on bass, and Sam Most on flute. For two days in October, 1960, the new ensemble went to Chicago and recorded an album for the Argo label, *Buddy Rich and His Buddies: Playtime*. Rich was in such a good mood during the recording that when the trumpeter Don Goldie from the Jack Teagarden Group happened to pass by the studio one day, just to listen for a while, he got to play on a couple of tracks.

In 1961, this version of the Buddy Rich Sextet was booked at the Cloister Inn, a hotel in Maryland, for a two-week engagement starting on January 9. On the opening day, the band also filmed a TV program for *Playboy* magazine magnate Hugh Hefner's television series, "Playboy's Penthouse." They performed three numbers, with Mainieri playing such a great solo that Buddy Rich felt he was playing in Mainieri's band. Hefner, a great jazz fan back then, booked a lot of jazz acts on the "Penthouse" series. Later on, Hef went the rock route, booking bands like Santana and Deep Purple.

In July, the band returned to Birdland. At the time, Norman Granz was back in New York and just happened see Buddy's new band there. Even if relations over the years had always been a little frosty between him and Buddy, he was always interested in new projects, and after having listened to the sextet, he offered to record the group, which resulted in the album *Blues Caravan*. A Swedish trumpeter, Rolf Ericson, played on this album and on the Birdland job. A swinging player who would be a part of the band on Buddy's next big tour, Ericson had played with many of the greats before he joined Buddy, including Woody Herman, Charlie Parker, Dexter Gordon, and even the Dorseys. Ericson was

Mainieri's idea. "It was me who invited him to play with Buddy,"[10] he said.

After one of the performances at Birdland, Buddy was visited in the dressing room by veteran comedian and author Joey Adams. Adams, husband of gossip columnist Cindy Adams, was pretty hot at the time. He asked if Buddy would consider bringing the band to join him on a four-month tour of Asia. Adams was honest about the trip, telling Buddy, "I must warn you, this is going to be a tough trip." Buddy responded, "Have you ever played one-nighters through Texas on a bus?"[11] He signed on, thinking that this would be an exciting trip; he'd visit countries he had never been to and play jazz for the Armed Forces. It sounded good on paper. Ultimately, it would be much worse than he could ever have imagined.

The International Cultural Exchange Service was a program created to facilitate and improve countries' understanding of each other through culture. With financing from the program, musicians, artists and painters who were invited to participate would travel to each other's countries. President John F. Kennedy was a strong supporter of this program, and for four months, the Buddy Rich Sextet was sent to Asia and the Middle East on the tour Adams described. As one of the first jazz groups to visit these countries, Buddy looked forward to showing the people in the East what jazz really was. Besides Buddy's band, the troupe was made up of singers, dancers, comics, jugglers, and other variety acts including the Four Step Brothers dance team, the singing Sylte Sisters, magician Celeste Evans, and veteran vaudevillian Chaz Chase, whose specialty was eating every object on the stage and beyond. More than 25 variety performers were in the troupe, all under the "supervision" of Joey Adams.

The whole production was estimated to cost the American government $160,000 (which would be equal to about $1.3 million in today's dollars) plus travel and accommodations for everyone. Buddy Rich's band got paid $2,050 a week that was divided among the band members.[12] It probably wasn't the money that made Rich choose to join up; more likely it was the excitement of visiting places where he had never played. The tour was to go to 13 countries: Afghanistan, Nepal, Thailand, Cambodia,

Laos, Indonesia, Singapore, Malaysia, Hong Kong, South Vietnam, India and Iran.

Before departing, Buddy and all the others had to be approved by the American authorities. There was no problem clearing him. "I've never been in jail. I mean as a non-visitor," Buddy said. "The CIA and the FBI investigated me before I made a State Department tour. Clean. The report said, 'The man doesn't even spit on the sidewalk.'"[13] On August 18, 1961, Buddy Rich, Mike Mainieri, Rolf Ericson, Sam Most, Wyatt Ruther, John Morris, and David Lucas (the latter added on bongos) set off for the adventure, and it was tougher than anyone imagined.

The first stop on the tour was Kabul, Afghanistan on August 23. Over 10,000 Afghans sat with their legs crossed, waiting excitedly for entertainment. Joey Adams was having cold feet while standing in the wings, saying "How do you get these bearded men into a good mood?" and "How can you tell if a woman in a burka likes what she sees on stage?" Then a storm began, and masses of sand drifted onto the stage. The stage manager, Jerry Bell, had to fight desperately to keep it away from the microphones. Buddy became very irritated when it got into the instruments, the dancers were having trouble breathing, and those responsible for communication between the United States and Afghanistan couldn't do anything but quietly watch. The show finally began, and the dancing, singing and comedy seemed to be going over well, but when Joey Adams told his jokes, but he thought he was bombing, as nobody laughed. He didn't realize that Afghans don't applaud like Western audiences. They had other ways of showing their appreciation. Pianist John Morris described one scene, saying, "At one of these shows, gun-toting Afghans from the desert appeared in a thunderous roar of horses and a cloud of dust to listen to the sextet's performance. They showed their appreciation by firing their rifles in the air all at once."

Joey Adams talked about the show in its entirety. "The cymbals banged. The horns blared. The Syltes sang, The Steps danced, Chaz ran on and off with assorted masks, and for a big finish, Flash McDonald, Prince Spencer, Buddy Rich and I—with our canes and straw hats—strutted around the stage á la George M. Cohan to the tune of 'Yankee Doodle

Dandy.' The closing act was Buddy Rich and his sextet. One hunk of our Western culture that's trickled through all the way from Basin Street to the Volga is jazz. The group opened with a swing version of 'Lulu's Back in Town' (from the Argo *Playtime* album), featuring Sam Most on clarinet, a man tagged by *Downbeat* as one of the greatest. This was followed by 'Misty,' with a solo by the award-winning, 21-year-old Mike Mainieri on vibes. The band concluded their medley of hit records with 'Caravan,' at which point they wound up the wild man of the drums, Buddy Rich, and let him go. And boy did he go! It was 'go' all the way. Buddy did a frenetic, frantic, hysterical ten-minute spot in which he massacred everything from the drums to the cymbals to the stage, the microphone, the piano and anything standing in his way. There was nothing that could follow this unless we blew up the stage altogether."

On the following days Buddy even played on the streets in Kabul. "I was doing a gig in the big market square in Kabul, Afghanistan," Buddy recalled. "We're the first jazz group to play in that part of the world. Some fierce looking guys from the mountains come galloping in on horseback, those long barreled guns slung over their shoulders. They sit in and play on fucking tree trunks, you know, with animal skin drumheads. That's been their instrument for over 500 years. That was unusual."[14] When they left Afghanistan, the group had been seen by over 40,000 people.

The tour continued to Bangkok in Thailand, where the group was to perform for the king and queen. Once there, a group of very serious-looking advance men showed up, who determined that the technical equipment, especially the lighting, was not up to King Bhumibol's standard. The "Royal Lighting Men," as they were called, scoured the country and finally were able to rent more lights from a crew on location filming *The Ugly American* with Marlon Brando. The group had also been delayed in traffic coming from the airport, so when they got to the hotel, they were stressed. Even at this early stage, it was evident that Rich was becoming irritated by these inconveniences.

After a minor incident where Buddy's laundry went missing, the sextet played in the king's private theater for 300 specially invited guests. Suddenly the king himself came onstage. Joey Adams explained, "The king is a jazz buff who has jammed with that other king, Benny Goodman, and really knows his way around a clarinet. He not only talked jazz with us, he brought his own private band onstage for a giant jazz session with Buddy and the boys. His Majesty tootled a couple of solos and even played some of his own compositions. So hipped is he on jazz that his son, the Crown Prince, besides learning reading, writing and royalty, is also taking clarinet lessons."[15] They left a very contented King, who immediately sent a letter to President Kennedy, thanking him for the fine entertainment.

Next was a mini-tour within Thailand to the cities of Chiengmai, Udorn, Hua Hin, Lopburi, Korat and several smaller locales. On this leg of the tour, Adams was beginning to feel that Buddy Rich was not an easy person to have around. Adams' side of the story was that Buddy didn't want to travel with the rest of the company and always showed up at the last minute before he was due on stage. What irritated Adams most was that Buddy was always quarreling with the others in the troupe. On one of the bus trips, he supposedly punched a guy while a worried Adams looked on. Percussionist David Lucas, however, said things didn't exactly transpire this way. "Joey Adams is exaggerating a lot," Lucas believed. "Buddy was not physical in that way. Buddy didn't suffer fools. He confronted people directly when he felt something was wrong. One time I got in a fight with a man in the troupe. He was a trouble maker. I told Buddy about him, and Buddy walked up to him and said, 'Don't you ever mess with my band members like that!'"[16]

Next on the tough agenda was a flight from Udorn to Katmandu in Nepal. At the airport, the troupe checked into a hotel overnight. A good rest was not on the itinerary, as the musicians fell ill from dysentery. Mainieri said, "We had the Kabul trots. We were shitting for months." Buddy tried to help by getting his hands on some better food. He went into the city and came back with some cans of preserves. Then things began to get out of hand. "After combing the town, Rich came up with a can of peanut brittle he scrounged out of some local grocery store," Adams remembered. "We couldn't wait to open it. It may not sound like much, but at that very moment it was more exciting to us than caviar and champagne wrapped in mink. The can had a key to open it, like a sardine tin does. Because of the heat, Buddy's hands were sweating and the key broke in half. In his anxiety to get at the peanut brittle he ripped away the top of the can, and at the same time he ripped away half of his thumb. The blood just gushed in torrents from his million-dollar drumming hand." They managed to find a doctor who could stitch him up so he could play again. David Lucas again maintained that Adams was stretching the truth. "The wound wasn't that big and they never took Buddy to any hospital to get stitched," Lucas said. "If that had happened, I should have seen it, because I was with Buddy all the time."[17]

After several days of hard touring in Nepal, they flew to Phnom Pehn in Cambodia, where they played for Prince Norodom Si Hanouk and received medals from the Queen Mother. On October 5, they landed at the airport in Vientiane, Laos, where they played at hospitals, schools and in other informal settings. Traveling together under tough circumstances, the troupe began getting close to each other, and there were some lighter moments. David Lucas remembered, "We were sitting in a hotel room in Laos: Buddy, me and the three Sylte sisters. We were doing a jam session on every playable items we could find—table, chairs, bottles, suitcases—Buddy was playing with two hair brushes on a pad. That was the best session you could imagine!"

By the time they arrived in Djakarta, Indonesia, the fun had ended for Buddy Rich. He was tired of nine-hour bus trips on bad roads, scruffy hotels, and nights in crowded tents surrounded by swarms of mosquitoes. Joey Adams kept asking everyone in the troupe to do more and more interviews, photo ops, publicity, informal performances, and other things. Most of them thought it was fun, but Buddy didn't. Naturally, Buddy had every right to demand that he only play according to what the original contract dictated, but there was also the aspect of international relations. At every stop, the town honchos always wanted the troupe to play more and more performances, less the troupe be reported as "difficult" to American government. Adams had a difficult time constantly handling these challenging and sensitive situations. "Each one of our troupe had his own problem," Adams said. "There were 25 plots going on at one time. I had to be the mother, father, and target for the whole crew. It was my job to keep everybody happy. Win, lose, or draw blood, I had to try to pacify the troupe, please the Embassy, work harmoniously with USIS,[18] cater to the big shots in each country, and report to Washington."

Djakarta in Indonesia was next, and things would become even hotter. When they arrived, they were all asked to come to the Radio Indonesia radio station. Most of those in the troupe were happy for the invitation, but not Buddy, who felt that this was going past the limit. The American ambassador there tried to explain how important it was for them to visit the radio station, but Buddy refused. In his book, *On the Road for Uncle Sam*, Adams described how things began to get really rocky between him and Buddy. By that time, he was so irritated by him that he always called him "Bad Boy." "We'd been having trouble with him straight along," wrote Adams. "He refused to come to official functions. If he did show up, sometimes he'd come in Bermuda shorts and sneakers to show his defiance. He refused to wear ties and jackets when the weather was hot. He caused strife within the company by picking fights, challenging members of the cast and hurting some of them professionally onstage. He made impossible demands for cars and living quarters."

Adams had a bunch of other claims, and maintained that he bent over backwards for Buddy, calming him down, giving him special treatment because he knew how much he meant to the show as a whole, looking after him when he was sick, and being sympathetic to him when he was homesick. When Buddy complained about the food, Adams' wife made special meals for him. Adams also said he loaned Rich money, and when Buddy didn't like his room, he got to stay in Adams' room together with his wife. Nothing helped. Meanwhile, the others in the troupe wondered why he treated Buddy this way, and their respect for Adams disappeared. They thought he was afraid of Rich. One of Adams' best friends in the cast came into his hotel room one day and said, "Why don't you fire him? Can't you see what is happening? Everyone is turning against you!" Before the inevitable confrontation, there was a memorable performance for Prince Sukarno. Magician Celeste Evans explained why that night was memorable. "I remember the prince kept insisting on holding one of my
doves," Evans recalled, "and one of them pooped all over him."[19]

The levity was short-lived. On the evening after the show, Joey Adams called them all together in the Dharma Nirmala Hotel. Adams, clearly nervous, said, "We are here for one reason: to bring friendship," Buddy Rich interrupted him, saying, "Are you going to start that love crap again? Are you going to tell us some more about how we should all love each other and about having harmony and friendship and affection and all those other tinny phrases you throw around?" "Don't mistake goodness for weakness," Adams replied. Then he told them again about Radio Indonesia's wishes and how important it was for the relations between the countries. Buddy reacted by pulling out his contract. Joey Adams told him what he could do with it. "Fuck!" shouted Buddy, puffing quickly on his cigarette. "If anyone here doesn't want to cooperate in the Indonesia-American effort, you can take the next plane back to the States," Adams exclaimed. "I will even pack your bags and make your sandwiches."

Rich reluctantly continued the tour to Singapore and Hong Kong. David Lucas again contradicted Adams on these events, explaining, "Once again Joey Adams is not telling the truth here. Joey never dared to talk to Buddy like that. Buddy didn't demand things that weren't in his contract and he surely didn't complain all the time. Remember, he had toured since he was a little kid. I was his roommate on this tour and I never heard him say things like that."[20]

In the beginning of November, the ensemble reached Saigon in Vietnam, the ninth stop on the tour. It wasn't the best time to go there. Battles raged around the town and a grenade had been thrown at the U.S. Ambassador four months earlier. Adams feared the show would not take place. Performances were delayed by bomb squads, and police patrolled the theatres. But the Joey Adams Vaudeville Troupe went in and did their job, and on opening night, Buddy Rich was a success again. The *Times of Vietnam* newspaper wrote, "The troupe opened before a large and enthusiastic audience with a program featuring American songs, jazz music and many variety numbers. Buddy Rich, world famous drummer, dominated the show with his skills. 'The equal of which has never been seen here before,' as one spectator put it."[21] Flutist Sam Most agreed. "Every time Buddy played a drum solo, it was a guarantee that the crowd would go wild."[22]

By now, Rich was tired of the tour and wanted to go home. Continuing to India for one more month's travelling under these conditions did not appeal to him at all. He was also tired of Adams accusing him of one thing after the other. If he had been given special treatment, it was nothing compared to what Adams himself had received, according to Rich. This was all written in reports sent home to the U.S. government. There it stood in writing: "Congressional testimony revealed that embassies found Adams difficult. He demanded a personal photographer, driver and VIP treatment in general."[23] After the last show in Saigon, Rich called in Mike Mainieri and said, "Mike, we're going back, you and I. We're getting out of here tomorrow. We'll leave the band, go back to New York and start another band." Mainieri, who had hired the other band members, replied, "Buddy, we can't leave the guys here." "You're right," Rich replied.[24] The next morning, the band left the hotel without paying their bill. At the airport, chaos broke out, with Adams and Rich getting into a fist fight. Government reports claim that Rich gave Adams a punch on the jaw and took another plane home.[25]

With Buddy Rich gone once and for all, Mainieri took over the role of leader. Artistically and musically the group coped, but economically, they were worse off, since the American government froze their wages due to Rich's outburst. Mike Mainieri helped the show go on. "I played the drums for the rest of the tour, billed as Buddy Rich," he said. Pianist John Morris summed it up, saying, "Buddy was fighting with Joey Adams all the time, and he finally just bugged out and left the tour early." Buddy cleared out so fast he left his cymbals, drums and cameras behind with Mainieri, who was not happy with the situation. "I was so pissed off. I sold off Buddy's cameras and gave away most of his cymbals. He wanted to kill me," Mainieri recalled. David Lucas continued to take Buddy's side after the fact, and believed "it was Joey Adams who was the weakest link in that chain. He was no leader of the troupe. I also left the tour before Buddy. When we came to Teheran, Adams was disrespectful against me and that was it. I took the next plane home. Buddy and I stayed friends since then."[26]

On November 29, a wire service item appeared in several stateside newspapers that read, "Drummer Buddy Rich is back in the US, but his band is still touring Asia with Joey Adams' troupe." When the band finally got home in December, Buddy wanted to continue playing with them, but they put their feet down and said he had to pay them first. Apparently, they got about half of what they were due, but were still prepared to play with Buddy. There was, however, an abrupt change in plans. Buddy's doctors wouldn't let him play. He had lost altogether too much weight on the tour and was ordered to do what he hated most: rest.[27]

The Asian tour had not been what he had envisioned. Touring under such arduous circumstances was possibly too much for the 44-year old Rich. He had handled playing long, late sessions with Marsala, Shaw and Dorsey, but touring in unbearably hot temperatures often without drinkable water, sleeping in tents with snakes crawling around his head, and being constantly worried if the band's instruments would get there in time was simply too much. He was deeply impressed by the hospitality of the people they met, but strongly upset by the misery he saw everywhere. In later interviews he summarized the whole Asian tour. "Sure we were treated beautifully," Buddy said. "But that was the worst experience of my life, man. I'd never seen so much poverty, filth and starvation. It made you sick inside wherever you went. People dying on the streets, babies, little children crying for food and needing medical help, it tore your heart out."[28]

Harry James and His Orchestra were playing at the Driftwood Lounge at the Flamingo Hotel in Las Vegas. Between sets, James wanted to talk to his orchestra in the dressing room. "Buddy Rich, the world's best drummer, has called me," James told them. "He wants to play with me again and I have said that he is welcome."[29] Buddy made his customary demands: high salary and featured billing. James agreed to his terms and gave him $1,500 a week, meaning that Buddy Rich was now the highest paid sideman in the music business, a feat that qualified for a long-standing place in the *Guinness Book of Records*.

It was a rather content drummer who was relaxing in his family's new home; a bungalow in North Miami Beach which Buddy had bought a few years earlier. The whole family badly needed to get away from the stress of New York. Thanks to the move, Buddy also got closer to his father, Robert, who had remarried and lived nearby. Buddy simply couldn't relax for any extended period of time, though his doctors had ordered him to slow down, and Marie and Cathy were always concerned about his pace and his restlessness. Buddy paid no heed to the doctors' warnings and flew to New York to record a new album with Gene Krupa. From the beginning, the album *Burnin' Beat* was intended to be recorded simply as a small production, but Norman Granz, who was once again behind the whole project, wanted something bigger. A good-sized band was contracted for the session by Krupa's saxophonist at the time, Eddie Wasserman, and the result was a wonderful session, with the intensity between Buddy and Gene shining though. The truth, however, at least according to Wasserman, was that Buddy and Gene never played at the same time in the studio, and that Buddy—at least on a number of the tracks—overdubbed his parts. Regardless, the recording stands as a memorable meeting between two giants.

While Marie and Cathy continued to worry, Buddy insisted that playing made him feel better. He gained weight and carried on as usual. At the Flamingo with James, he was happy when he saw his name in big letters on the marquees. The promises about "featured billing" had been kept. He told Harry James, with some sense of relief, "I'll never leave this band again. I'm very happy to be back; it's like coming home."

Buddy Rich was playing better than ever, but started thinking that life shouldn't be just about playing drums. Wanting to keep in shape and improve his health somehow, he took up golf. He wasn't especially good at it, but at least he was getting some exercise. "Dad loved to play golf," Cathy remembered, "but he didn't really have the patience for it. One morning when we were living in Las Vegas, he was part of a foursome playing at the Tropicana golf course. By the time he got to the 18th hole, he had played so badly and was so furious at himself that, after he had hit a ball into a pond, he picked up his golf bag and heaved it and all his clubs into the same pond. Then he turned and started walking back to the clubhouse. The others in foursome looked at him disappearing over a small hill. All of a sudden, they see him coming back. He walks past them, a calm look on his face, goes to the edge of the pond, rolls up his pants, wades in, fishes around for the golf bag, finds it, lifts it out of the water, and removes his car keys from the bag. Then he lets the bag drop back into the water and, without a word, walks by his friends once more and makes for the clubhouse. It's like a scene out of a Chaplin movie."[30]

On May 9, 1962, Buddy was playing golf with singer Billy Eckstine at

Paradise Valley in Las Vegas, when he started to pant and grab at his chest. He was having another heart attack. Eckstine drove him directly to the club house and shouted for help, and Buddy received care from two doctors who had just finished playing their rounds. As he was lying there panting, Eckstine said to Buddy, "You'd do anything to win a hole. Wonderful." Buddy was later moved to hospital where the doctors wanted to admit him, but Buddy wanted no part of it. As Cathy recalled, "When he told them in no uncertain terms what they could do with their hospital, they hid his clothes so the temptation to leave wouldn't be so great. If you knew my father, you'd know that hiding his clothes would never stop his escape plans. He waited until the middle of the night, and, dressed only in his hospital gown, made his way across the desert, barefooted, to Harry's house, where he collapsed."[31]

He recovered quickly this time, but the episode showed that he hadn't learned anything from his body's warning signals. He continued to live the life he had lived, changing nothing about his lifestyle. The situation was not made any better by his IRS woes. In addition to continuing to pursue him for back taxes, they were looking into the ownership of his Florida home and demanding that he increase his payments to pay off old debts and get caught up for the preceding year. Buddy didn't seem to care. Self -confident as ever and never looking back, he continued to forge ahead, with his high salary from James providing at least some sense of security. For the rest of 1962 and the entirety of 1963, he played with Harry James at the Flamingo Hotel in Las Vegas. Always on the move, he was in and out of the band several times via the formation of some swinging, short-lived small groups, but each time, a patient Harry waited with open arms and welcomed him back. Through the years, ever since Harry was best man at Buddy's wedding, they had become very close friends. Countless times he had stepped in, financially and otherwise, when Buddy had problems.

Given that the James' band second home was Las Vegas, it seemed appropriate that Buddy move the family there. In the summer of 1963, the Riches moved to Nevada to live permanently, and it was in Vegas that Buddy's great interest in UFOs grew. His belief in extraterrestrial life was serious, and he bought masses of magazines and other literature on the subject. He declared that he had witnessed something unexplainable while on a trip between Las Vegas and Los Angeles in the summer of 1954. "I was appearing with my band in Atlanta, Georgia," remembered Buddy. "My brother was right beside me in the front seat of our sports car. We were driving along, on the way to do a show, when I happened to glance through the windshield of the auto and saw two brightly illuminated objects coming out from behind the dark side of the moon."[32] The brothers stopped the car to get a better look, and saw some objects doing figure eights in front of their astounded eyes. They seemed to be playing tag with each other and were making incredible turns at impossibly high speeds. After a few more minutes, the objects shot straight up and disappeared into the starry sky. Buddy called an Air Force base close by, and was told that they had received over 500 calls reporting the incident, but that their radar indicated that nothing was flying in the area at the time. Buddy, however, felt convinced of what he had seen.

At first he enjoyed debating this with others who weren't as convinced about UFOs as he was, but later in life he would become much more restrained and quiet about it, especially with the press. Interviewers would often ask, "What about that rumor that you were visited by extraterrestrials?" Buddy would reply, "Rumor? I won't talk about that." When reporters would persist, Buddy would explain, "People wouldn't understand. It's a very personal thing. It leaves one open to ridicule, and I rather not get involved in that. I'd come off sounding like some fucking nut."

Although Buddy had a safe and secure position with Harry James, he knew there was more for him to do in the world of jazz. The urge to drive his own big band was always in the back of his mind, but while these thoughts were percolating, he did experience his share of excitement while with James, including a successful tour in Japan in the spring of 1964. The Japanese fans treated both Harry and Buddy like royalty. They recorded a fantastic televised concert there, and Buddy would visit this country several times in the future. Buddy and Louie Bellson also travelled to Japan on tour and recorded an album (reportedly at their own expense), the vastly underrated *Are You Ready for This?*, where the two drum greats were backed up by George Kawaguchi's Japanese big band.

World travels were the norm for the Rich family, but some civilians had different views of what "normal family life" was. Marie Rich remembered one story in particular. "The summer before Cathy entered first grade, we went to Japan," Marie remembered. "When she started school, the teacher asked all the kids to write about what they did over the summer. Cathy wrote that she had gone to Tokyo, Hong Kong and Australia. So the teacher reads it and sends a note home to me and Buddy that says, 'Your child has a very vivid imagination.' So Buddy went down to the school and said to the teacher, 'If my daughter tells you she was in all those places, then she fucking was!'"[33]

More recording sessions took place the following year. Buddy recorded two albums with James—*Green Onions and Other Hits* and *The Ballads and the Beat*—that demonstrate rock creeping in, however slowly. Some of the orchestra's concerts were filmed for television. On May 1, 1965, the band was in the WGN studios in Chicago to record two 20-minute programs in the series "The Big Bands." Others in the lineup included Woody Herman, Stan Kenton, Lionel Hampton and Count Basie. On July 3, Buddy took leave from James again and was temporarily replaced by Alvin Stoller. Buddy had been invited to play at the Newport Jazz Festival and while there, he put on a performance that went on the record as his best solo ever, according to his faithful fans and even himself.

The Newport Jazz Festival is the oldest, and in many ways still the most prestigious, of all the outdoor jazz festivals. With a seating capacity of 18,000 at their "Festival Field," Newport booked the top names in the business. In 1965, the headliner was none other than Frank Sinatra, backed by the Basie band. Buddy Rich was booked for several performances: He was to play during the day in a "drum spectacular," billed in the Newport program as a "drum workshop," with Jo Jones, Elvin Jones, Roy Haynes, Art Blakey and Louie Bellson, all backed by pianist Billy Taylor's ensemble. Buddy was unusually fired up that day. After the others had performed, Buddy took the stage and performed a drum solo. The awed audience witnessed a defining moment of unmatched virtuosity and utter mastery of the drums, and they responded in a frenzied ovation.

Buddy himself remembered that particular solo, a rarity for him. "When those other cats were all done, I sat down behind my drums and began. I'm telling you, I did things that day I didn't even know I was capable of playing. I mean, I actually astonished myself! When I was finished, I laid the sticks down on the large tom, stood up, and walked off. I had said it all, man, like I never said it before—or since." Dan Morgenstern wrote in *Downbeat*, "If nothing else of value had happened at Newport, it would have been enough just to see Buddy Rich. The audience's standing ovations felt as though they would never end. He is without a doubt the greatest drummer who has ever lived."[34] Later the same evening, he played once more at the festival, this time in the wind and the rain, and as part of Indiana University Septet. For Buddy, the show went on, and stagehands held an umbrella over him during his portion of the program.

Soon he was back at the Flamingo with James, back to business as usual—and nightly accolades from adoring fans. Praise abounded from everyone who was there. Trombonist Phil Wilson said, "I was playing with Woody Herman in Las Vegas, and sometimes our drummer, Jake Hanna, and I went over to the Flamingo to see Buddy Rich with Harry James. The band was fantastic, and you could see Buddy play like you and I wish we could play. We were overwhelmed. Two words sum up Rich: power and inspiration. He looked so content with what he was doing. It was like he didn't want to be anywhere else in the world."[35] But things weren't what they seemed. As soon as he had some free time, he met with Irv Kluger, the drummer who played in the house band at the Flamingo, who he knew since his days with Shaw and Dorsey. The subject of their discussion was repertoire—the songs Buddy wanted in the band book for a new Buddy Rich big band. Buddy had no financing for such a project, but he didn't care, and forged ahead at full speed with his plans.

On February 11, 1966, Buddy Rich and Gene Krupa appeared on "The Sammy Davis Jr. Show" on NBC-TV. Gene and Buddy again performed their drum battle, which was the first Krupa/Rich drum duel ever televised. On the show, playing on drum sets facing each other and accompanied by George Rhodes' orchestra, they had some nice exchanges with each other on "Cute" while backing Davis Jr.'s tap dancing. Then it was into a cleverly arranged medley of Gene and Buddy's two old feature numbers, "Sing, Sing, Sing" and "Hawaiian War

Chant." Here, Krupa showed that when it really counted, he could project the visual playfulness that was always his trademark. Buddy tried to play as usual but seemed to be restrained by something. Still, the usual smile was there, and he loved being with Sammy Davis Jr., who was his good friend. Buddy and Sammy had both grown up in the world of show business; they understood each other.

Buddy went back to Vegas and rejoined Harry James at the Flamingo, but not for long. By April 21, he had made up his mind, and after the show he pulled Harry aside backstage. Buddy told him that he was leaving the band. James wanted to know why. Buddy answered honestly, saying, "I'm tired of playing 'Sleepy Lagoon' every night."[36] He went home and woke Marie at 4 a.m., saying, "Guess what happened?" Marie responded, "What?" "I'm going to organize a new big band."[37] Later, Buddy said he'd never seen Marie jump out of bed so fast.

Incredulousy, she asked, "You're going to do what?"

He was put on earth to play drums.

Stanley Kay

Give him a long drum solo and he'll just blow the place up.

Joe Morello

Buddy Rich is just incredible. He's a great, fantastic player. If it can be done on a drum, he can do it. I've heard people say he doesn't swing. I think he swings. I used to practice with the things he does. I've heard it said he's not subtle. I've heard him be so subtle, so gentle. This man can play.

Ed Thigpen

That damn fool knows the instrument.

Jo Jones

CHAPTER 15

The Swinging New Big Band

Playing Rogers drums with his new big band in 1966.

There weren't many swing-era bandleaders who were still on the road and touring with big bands by 1966. Only James, Basie, Ellington, Woody Herman, and the Glenn Miller ghost band franchise were still around, and survival was a challenge for all of them. For Buddy Rich to start a big band when the Beatles, Rolling Stones, and all the other rock groups were dominating music (and the popularity of jazz was on the decline) made many wonder if Buddy had completely lost his mind. Marie Rich believed that the timing for such a venture was all wrong, though it didn't really surprise her. Many were the evenings when Buddy had come home complaining, "I'm going crazy. I can't keep playing what I do now." At the same time, she knew that if he had decided to do something in music, she couldn't stop him, however much she wanted to. He only listened to one person—himself—and if he felt he had to follow his heart, he would do so at whatever price. His other forays into the world of big band leadership had cost him piles of money, a broken arm, and two heart attacks. Now he was going to start another big band.

There was only one person who understood Buddy: Harry James. When Buddy told him of his decision at the Flamingo Hotel, James immediately organized a farewell party and he and everyone there wished Buddy well. It hadn't escaped James how much Buddy had developed in recent years (Buddy had learned the James band book in record time), and he knew the day would come when Buddy Rich would want to strike out with his own band, with specially written music that would display his tremendous drumming skills. Harry James also had a pretty good idea of what Buddy wanted musically, and he knew that the time had come for Buddy Rich to step forward into the limelight he deserved.

Rich was preparing himself extra carefully this time, and had contacted arrangers Oliver Nelson, Bill Holman and Bill Reddie, who were given strict orders not to submit ballads or dance songs. He not only wanted songs that were tailor made for his unparalleled technique, but modern-sounding charts that should also appeal to a young audience. Otherwise, Buddy believed the band would soon go under again. Buddy felt he had a handle on the pulse of the market, and took the advice of Harry James' agents, ICM, to heart. ICM told him that if his band was prepared to play modern rock music, but with a jazz approach, it would very likely stand out. The concept didn't work especially well for James, but Buddy Rich felt ICM was on on the right track for his band. As always, he was lacking financing, and this time around, it wouldn't be easy. It was no secret that his own economic situation was not great, and he couldn't bring himself to contact Sinatra again. There had been others who had offered.

Buddy Rich talked about one of the offers. "One day there was a knock at my door," said Buddy. "A man was interested in backing my new band. He said to me, 'You have to forget who you are and who you have been. That isn't important. All that stuff about you being a good drummer. Forget it. Start fresh from the beginning. Be commercial and start earning a little money.' I told him to go to hell." He decided to go it alone. It was either sink or swim. When choosing the members of his band, his original intention was to use only young, hungry musicians who wanted to play the new music, but there were some well-known veterans in the first lineup. Tenor saxophonist Jay Corre was the only one who Rich took from Harry James' group, and Sam Most and John Bunch had played with Buddy many times before. Bassist Jimmy Gannon and reedman Eddie Shu, who were also in the early lineup, came from Krupa's small groups. Trombonist Jim Trimble became the band's manager.

Buddy knew that Las Vegas audiences were hard to please when it came to jazz. In Vegas, artists, bands, and orchestras were expected not only to perform at the best of their ability, but they had to embody the essence of commercial entertainment. The equation was simple: Please your audience, or disappear—and Buddy Rich knew this very well. Still, the band's opening night at the Aladdin Hotel would end in total catastrophe. Standing in the wings on Friday, May 13, 1966, it was time for "The Buddy Rich Show," and Buddy was more nervous than usual. Perhaps he was wondering if the band could have prepared more, even though Buddy rehearsed the group much longer than he was used to. He had also gone along with the arrangers on one point; to make things more relaxed and commercial he had taken on a singer named Susan Maro, who spent some time with the Les Brown band in the late 1950s, and her name was featured in the marketing. Buddy had good songs on his set list, he had handpicked the musicians and the place was packed with important people and stars. He had done everything he could do. What more could anyone ask of him? When the band began, it became obvious that Buddy Rich had paid no mind to offering the audience anything light, simple, or commercial. He played the program he had rehearsed from the beginning, and Susan Maro only got to sing two or three songs. Then Buddy went into swinging overdrive, and the management of the Aladdin Hotel couldn't believe their eyes and ears.

Buddy took great delight in both the music and the fact that he had delivered, at the very least, the totally unexpected. He had chosen his own path for his entire life. What made agents, casino owners or anyone else think that he would change, now that he had started a new orchestra under his own name (for the second time)? Nobody should expect it! Nobody! He ended the evening with yet another fantastic solo. *Downbeat* magazine, who followed him constantly and wouldn't have missed his opening for the world, wrote, "The climax of the whole show, which we all could expect, was a solo by the leader of the band, accompanied by Bobby Morris—who was hired in as second drummer to back up Susan Maro—on the congas and bongos. As a big band drummer, Rich probably has many equals, but as a soloist he is one of the greatest of all time."

Unfortunately, however, performing the program without taking the slightest consideration to the wishes of the hotel owners had its price. Buddy Rich never forgot that night. "As a matter of fact, we played a hotel in Las Vegas, I think we are the only band to have been cancelled the opening night. It's true. We played the Aladdin Hotel and the pit bosses came back, complaining to the main man that we were making too much noise for the gamblers. As you can tell, the band is very quiet and very soft, and lovely to dance to. We were booked for four weeks, they paid me off and we finished that night."[1] Buddy didn't let this get him down. Everyone got paid for the whole engagement, but it was clear he had to regroup so he could continue paying his musicians their wages. This time, help would come from an entirely different direction.

Sammy Davis Jr. was a good friend of Buddy's. They enjoyed each other. Given that they had grown up as child prodigies in the vaudeville era, both sang and tap danced, and Sammy was quite a good amateur on the drums. Buddy always laughed when he saw him play because he looked so funny. Davis, performing at the Sands in Vegas at this time, knew what a good band Buddy had, and he invited them to back him on his next record. Buddy accepted straightaway, and on June 19, 1966, the tape recorders were turned on at the Sands to capture Buddy Rich and His Orchestra under the direction of Davis' conductor George Rhodes. Buddy and his group accompanied Sammy Davis Jr. on several classics, including "Come Back to Me," "What Kind of Fool Am I," and "Please Don't Talk About Me When I'm Gone" in front of a specially invited audience. The incredible atmosphere in the venue is preserved on the album.

Davis Jr began the recording by saying, "For all of you sitting at home maybe listening to this record, I want to say that this is an extremely special evening for me. We are recording now, if I look at my watch it is a 5:15 in the morning in Las Vegas, and it is still swinging here." His words rang true. The invitation he had written said that there would be a party to beat all parties at 2:30 in the morning at the Sands Lounge. Before that, he had contacted George Rhodes and Ernie Freeman and directed them to write "the best arrangements you've ever written! Tuck them under your arm and bring them here!" He was going to be backed by Buddy's incredible band and he wanted to make most of every second. Word was out that Buddy hadn't been very successful at the Aladdin Hotel, though the rumor spread that his band was something new, and that was enough for Las Vegas crowd, always on the lookout for new, fresh entertainment. The Sands lounge was so crowded that the waitresses couldn't get around to serve drinks.

The record, *The Sounds of '66*, was released on Frank Sinatra's Reprise label. It is a first-rate big band album, with both Sammy Davis Jr. and Buddy Rich at their peak. Buddy would say afterwards that this evening saved his band from oblivion after the debacle of the Aladdin opening. This collaboration with Davis would generate a longer engagement at another club, the Chez. It was at the Chez that Buddy Rich rehearsed a number that would become a trademark for the rest of his career. He had commissioned some arrangements from the man who was in charge of orchestrating big revue show numbers at the Dunes in Las Vegas, Bill Reddie. Buddy asked Stanley Kay to contact Reddie to request some spectacular charts that would make the band stand out. Reddie came back with a medley based on Leonard Bernstein's musical *West Side*

Story. Buddy knew the music well, but Reddie's new, exciting inter-pretation appealed to him instantly. This was no easy piece for the drums, given that Buddy Rich didn't read music, and it ran nearly ten minutes with many complex passages and varying time signatures. He dealt with the situation the same way he'd done with Shaw and Dorsey. "We rehearsed it with a different drummer while Buddy sat in the audience seats," said trumpeter Bobby Shew. "It took us a few hours to put it together after rehearsing the different sections. After we had it down, Buddy jumped up and played it through without a single mistake. He had memorized the whole thing. The guy had the most natural instincts."[2]

On July 1, 1966, marking time before the Chez opening, he was back at the Newport Jazz Festival, but not to perform as a part of a drum battle, and without the big band. Joe Morello, the popular, poll-winning drummer with Dave Brubeck, was there that year to perform with the Brubeck Quartet. Morello remembered that the quartet was considerably delayed arriving at their performance. "We finally got there and drove backstage," Morello recalled. "Buddy had set my drums up for me and he was going to play with the quartet if I didn't get there in time. But I got there in time, and he stood in the wings while we played."[3] Buddy himself played with Woody Herman's big band and Teddy Wilson's trio and quartet, reveling in it, since he considered Newport one of the finest festivals in the world.

On September 21, Buddy's new big band opened at the Chez. If the Sands had been crowded, it was nothing compared to the pandemonium at at the Chez. The valets that looked after the arriving cars had to park them as far away as Beverly Hills. The reviewers had praised Buddy's new band so much that everyone wanted to hear the band. "If you like music in the spirit of Count Basie and Woody Herman, you've got to see this,"[4] wrote the always-critical Leonard Feather. Generally, people were curious, especially those who knew Buddy only as a swing-era sideman with Dorsey, Shaw, and James. The performance was fantastic, and the stars were out in full force that night, as Tony Bennett, Connie Francis, and Judy Garland all came on stage as guest artists.

Bandleader Stan Kenton sat in the audience in a ringside seat, and was wild about the band, saying, "My first opportunity to hear it was the opening night at the new Club Chez in Hollywood. I sat in front of it and thrilled to the dynamic spirit projected from the musicians ignited by Buddy's drumming. A well-rehearsed organization with orchestrations that are fresh and new. They not only brought me, but the entire audience to its feet."[5] Talk show host Johnny Carson would become a dear friend of Buddy's and was, for years, a champion of the band and of Buddy Rich. "At least a dozen of the best drummers in the country were present," Carson recalled of the evening. "When Buddy finished his long solo in 'West Side Story,' I looked around me when he received his standing ovations. Several of the drummers were crying openly."[6]

After a later performance at the club, reporter Harvey Siders from *Downbeat* wanted to talk to Buddy. What he said explains much of Buddy's behavior and his attitude about playing. Siders opened the *Downbeat* story by asking Buddy, "Why did you leave the Harry James Band—you were probably the highest paid sideman in the business—for the headaches of fronting your own band?" "Cause we needed some good music in the business," Buddy replied. "Sure, I had a good-paying job for four and half years. It was beautiful. But, for four and half years I didn't play a goddamn thing. I sat up there; I went through the motions. Night after night, I knew what tunes I was going to play. I even knew what time we were going to play them. I had two solos in the band, and what the hell—that wasn't for me. It was security, all right. But what good is security if you're not happy, and especially if you know you can do better, be more creative, and let your personality come out? But if you're being held down, so to speak, in somebody else's band, what good is it taking home a heavy check every week? So, when the opportunity presented itself, I jumped at it."

Knowing Buddy's health history, Siders wanted to know, "How long can you hold up under this present rigorous routine, not in terms of popularity, but in terms of physical endurance?" Buddy replied, "I can't worry about that. I just take care of myself. I got no bad habits, and keep right on working. Any doctor will tell you that if you got a heart condition, you should keep active." Siders wouldn't let up. "But why do you drive yourself to the point of exhaustion?" he wanted to know. Buddy Rich told him, in no uncertain terms: "Man, cause I love it."[7]

At the Chez, the band recorded the LP *Buddy Rich: Swingin' New Big Band*. On the live recording, you can hear Buddy's characteristic solo ending on "West Side Story," which would become his trademark: a perfectly executed single-stroke roll that builds up in intensity and velocity to a point where anyone listening to it would believe that Buddy Rich was doing the physically impossible. The owners of the Chez wanted to extend the contract. Buddy was happy to oblige. The booking, according to Bobby Shew, was initially "for two weeks, but they held us over for two extra weeks. Celebrities jammed in regularly to see Buddy. Johnny Carson was, as you know, a huge fan of Buddy and came in and played with us one night. Judy Garland sang with us one night. Edie Adams bought out the entire club one night for a private party for her invited guests."[8] *Swingin' New Big Band* had good initial response. Richard "Dick" Bock, the general manager of the LP's releasing company, World Pacific, reported that 18,000 copies were shipped in the first weeks. Of the new band, an enthusiastic Bock said that "Rich's band is creating music that is as modern as today. We are not bringing back swing or bebop, we are going ahead."[9]

On November 11, Buddy Rich appeared as a guest on "The Tonight Show Starring Johnny Carson." Since Carson took over the program from Jack Paar in 1962, his show had gained more and more viewers. Buddy had met Carson a couple of times earlier, when he appeared as a guest on his show, but then he only played with the house band. Carson had seen Buddy much earlier, with the first time being at Larry Potter's Club in May of 1957. Through the years, Carson was fond of saying, "I remember that evening well. He had an act called 'That's Rich'. I remember it because it must have been the worst show I've ever seen in my whole life."[10] Despite the inauspicious beginning, Rich made a big impression on Carson, a talented amateur drummer himself. Carson was impressed with what he heard initially, and a few years later he got to attend one of Buddy's rehearsals. He never forgot the experience. "Once, in 1966, I got to sit and listen while the band rehearsed a very complex number called 'West Side Story.' It was 14 minutes long. After a while Buddy replaced the drummer who had played the song with sheet music in front of him. He played through the whole piece without missing a beat, a note or anything. It was completely incredible. How do you explain that?"[11]

When Buddy got the chance to perform on "The Tonight Show," he took advantage of the opportunity by performing two songs, "Apples" and the "West Side Story" medley. It was obvious from Carson's intro of Buddy that they had already become good friends. But what was so remarkable early on was that Johnny Carson, always known for bringing out the best in his guests, recognized Buddy's naturally quick wit, and didn't hesitate to use it humorously. Going forward, Buddy Rich was always introduced as "Mr. Humble," and Buddy Rich, courtesy of Johnny Carson, became much more than just a jazz drummer—he was now an entertainment personality.

The Basin Street East jazz club in New York City was the location of one of Buddy's classic blowups. Moving a new and hot big jazz band from Las Vegas to New York City to back up an English pop singer was described by some entertainment journalists as being something close to musical suicide. Buddy Rich, self-confident as always, was up for any challenge. As a result of the goings-on at Basin Street, the blaring headlines would follow thick and fast in the press in the coming weeks. It wasn't because Buddy had done something totally different. He had hired a female musician for the band for the first time in his life when he hired trumpeter Adelaide Robbins to replace Walter Battagello. Instead, it was an English singer who would make him see red.

Mary Isobel Catherine Bernadette O'Brien, better known as Dusty Springfield, had had many hits throughout the years. The latest, "You Don't Have to Say You Love Me," made it to the top of the hit parade in her home country of Great Britain, and reached fourth place in the United States. Her first two albums had sold well, and that was enough to convince some American promoters to bring her to the states. One of her first bookings was at Basin Street with Buddy Rich and his band. The band was the featured attraction, but the group also had to back up Springfield. It's important for a promoter to not only know the audience, but to know how the artists get along together, especially if the artists are going to perform on the same stage. Here, the collision was total. Evidently, Buddy wasn't overjoyed about Springfield being on the bill from the start. Prior to the start date, the promoters had tried to soften Buddy's aversion to her by showing him videos, but that didn't help. He just didn't think she could sing, and Buddy Rich had no time for people who had made it big with simple three-minute pop songs. But in the end,

Buddy felt, they would both get their place in the Basin Street spotlight, so what difference did it make if she couldn't sing?

The engagement started on November 3, 1966, and as soon as Buddy Rich saw the marquee above the Basin Street entrance, he became irritated. Springfield's name was in bigger letters than his, and the quarrel began there. A worker brought out a ladder to change the marquee, and before long Buddy Rich and Dusty Springfield could be seen standing outside the club and shouting at each other about who got top billing for the evening. Rehearsals were hell. Buddy didn't want to let Dusty rehearse with his band at all. With Dusty standing in the wings, Buddy loudly told his musicians not to make too much effort playing with her, so they wouldn't wear themselves out. When the shows got underway, everything became a parody of poor teamwork. First, a Mexican quintet performed, and then it was Buddy's band's turn. Buddy expanded his show for an extra hour while an irritated Dusty had to wait in the wings. Then he began to talk about all the celebrities in the audience for another hour and invited some of them on stage. Among others, Tony Bennett and Johnny Carson got to tell their favorite jokes. Time went by. Some in audience must have been getting bored. Others may have loved what was going on. When Buddy finally introduced her, two and a half hours after her scheduled time, he did it with the words, "It can't be easy to come on after my band. They say she's a good singer, but I've seen better!"

Dusty, of course, went up on stage extremely aggravated. She took the microphone and said, "We have three sexes in England: men, women and Buddy Rich." Now it was Buddy's turn to stand in the wings and get bugged, and Tony Bennett had to stop him from going back out on stage. Dusty struggled through every evening in tears, and just couldn't understand Buddy's attitude. The hostile atmosphere persisted for the entire three-week stand. Another evening he introduced her, "Now we're going to back up a third class singer." Another Rich witticism was, "She'll be singing 'Sunny,' so let's hope that it rains on the broad." Then there was, "She's third rate, just like all those black broads she favors."

One evening as a furious Dusty left the stage, she gave Buddy two middle fingers, and Buddy was livid. Both of them threatened to go to the musician's union, call the police, and sue each other, while their respective managers quarreled with each other. It was total chaos. Dusty demanded to rehearse more with the band so that she could run through two new songs, but Buddy refused. Dusty stormed into his dressing room with no fear, and found Buddy Rich with his feet up on the table. Buddy recounted, "She barged into my dressing room and started cursing me up and down and asking me who do I think I am and telling me what a stuck-up son of a bitch I am. Well, it happens this girl bugs me. She's got star eyes about herself. So I just sat there and smiled and looked at her. Joe Morgen, the press agent and an old, old friend, was with me. She started swinging at my head. I can't stand anybody putting their hands on me. I covered my head, and Morgen, who's a little guy, pinned her arms behind her back and said, 'Why don't you behave like a lady?' and hustled her out of the dressing room. When the door was shut the top blew off. My mind was red. I picked up a chair and smashed it to pieces against the wall."[12]

Dusty Springfield had a completely different version of what happened in the dressing room. In a TV show later in life she said, "Oh yes, Buddy was just incredibly arrogant, and it's a long story, but all I did was go to give him a good old Twenty Century Fox chorus girl slap, but I missed and got his toupé! And he never forgave me!"[13] According to Dusty, after she yelled at him in his dressing room, he is said to have answered, "You bloody broad, who the hell do you think you are?" and that's when she slapped him. Whatever happened, the result was that people came from all over to Basin Street to see the two go at it. Rumors of the two stars constantly fighting spread quickly on the street, and newspaper headlines read, "Rich and Springfield Fighting," and "Dusty Slams U.S. Star."

The final night of the run, Buddy didn't even want to introduce Dusty. One of the saxophonists went up to the mike and gave her a pair of red boxing gloves with a note that read: "You were brave enough to do what we didn't dare do." That was the musicians' way of saluting the singer who dared stand up to their tough bandleader. A few years later, Dusty Springfield was to appear on the "Sunday Night at The London Palladium" television show while Buddy Rich was also booked there. It is said that Buddy sent her a message to say he wanted to "bury the battleaxe." Dusty answered, "So do I—in the top of your head!"

Basin Street brouhaha behind them, on November 28, 1966, the band played at Lennie's on the Turnpike in West Peabody, Massachusetts. During the Lennie's date, the alto saxophonist, Gene Quill, suddenly disappeared, and nobody knew where he had gone. Buddy's management contacted trombonist Phil Wilson, who was working as a teacher at Berklee College of Music in Boston, who recommended a 21-year old by the name of Ernie Watts to fill in. He read music well and could surely sub in for Quill. Ernie accepted the offer, packed his horn and a suitcase and joined up with the band as fast as he could. "Lennie's on the Turnpike, that was my first gig with Buddy," said Watts. "I hadn't any chance to rehearse, just a binder with notes, a suit and a time to show up. It was just go straight out on stage and play."[14] The band never knew where Gene Quill went after his disappearance, but a few years later he showed up in a few house bands in Las Vegas, and ultimately in the house band of Atlantic City's Steel Pier.

The original engagement at the Chez was extended from two weeks to four, and there were those who thought the place should change its name to "Chez Rich." On one of the evenings, Duke Ellington sat in a ringside seat and listened to the whole concert from beginning to end, going up afterwards to Buddy and giving him a hug—and leaving him with a smile on his face for weeks. He had great respect for Duke. While at the Chez for this second stand, the album *Big Swing Face* was recorded live. The title was created by arranger Bill Potts, who thought that it was a good and fair caricature of Buddy. The album included a version of the Beatles' "Norwegian Wood," indicating Rich's recognition of The Beatles popularity. No, he didn't like them, least of all their drummer Ringo Starr, but he would later admit in an interview that the song he had chosen for his album was a good one. It remained in the book for years. It is worth noting that, in spite of Oliver Nelson having arranged two of the tracks on the album, his name was not included on the record jacket, because Buddy was upset with Nelson. During a band rehearsal, one of the musicians happened to say that he recognized one Nelson's charts from his days at music school. For Buddy, who only wanted to have new, fresh material that was exclusive to him, this was a slap in the face. He ordered the whole band to rip up the sheet music, and from then on, he would only keep Nelson's arrangement of Ellington's "In a Mellow Tone" in the book, since he loved the song.

Buddy was asked why he never had a vocalist in this edition of the band. "It's very simple why I won't get some young kid who sings half out of tune," was Buddy's blunt reply. "This is a jazz band. Singers bring down the pace. We're strong enough to hold audience without a singer. Without a singer, I don't have to apologize for being too loud. If you've got something going, people will know it. I like to feel my audience is intelligent enough to dig what we're doing. I have never prostituted myself by doing anything so commercial that people have loved me. If they care about my band, that's all that matters. I don't care if they love me. I've never tried to win a popularity poll as the sweetest man. As long as you come in to hear my band, that's important."[15]

Buddy Rich may never have sold himself commercially, but sometimes he played on some strange records. For some reason he appeared, though he can barely be heard, on Edie Adams's album *Edie Adams—Showtime on Broadway*.[16] Certainly, Adams was a big TV star with her own series, but the choice of songs on the album consisted more or less of sticky, sweet Broadway ballads and commercial music hall songs. Adams did visit many of the venues Buddy played, including the Aladdin, the Sands and the Chez, and she was a big fan of his, but all the music on the record went against what he stood for. Perhaps Buddy just needed a quick payday, given his constant trouble with the IRS.

In the case of vocalists, he made one exception. On his latest album, he had a singer: his daughter, Cathy—and it wasn't her idea. "It was the year when Sonny and Cher had a hit with 'The Beat Goes On,'" said Cathy. "One day we were driving around and suddenly the song came on the car radio. Daddy shouted. 'Why don't you do that song with my band?' Just like that! Everything was so easy to him. I said 'Okay.' The next evening we were at the Chez and the first person I see, at the table nearest the stage, is Judy Garland. I panicked. I rushed into the dressing room and told Daddy that I couldn't sing in front of her. So he went and got Judy and we talked for a few minutes. She was wonderful and said, 'Don't let anyone push you around! You're going to just go up and sing!' And I did." On the record, Buddy introduced her with these words: "My daughter is with us tonight. She's going to come up and sing 'The Beat Goes On.' And it's her first time in front of an audience. She's 12 and a half years old and drunk. Right there, that makes it a little tough!"[17] Cathy commented on it later. "Yeah, he says, 'She's 12 and a half years old and she's drunk,' which I probably should have been because it was so nerve-wracking for me. That's how he was. Spontaneous."[18] Cathy got good reviews. *High Fidelity* magazine wrote, "She performs with a wonderful innocent charm. Her talent is still at an early stage, but it is absolutely there. Her singing is grand and unaffected, and she has, if nothing else (she is Buddy Rich's daughter), an exquisite timing."[19]

Buddy was naturally proud every time Cathy stood behind the microphone, and thought things went so well with her that he had her join the band for the upcoming tour of England. Word got out to the U.K. about Buddy. Concerts in big halls and guest shots on popular television shows were awaiting him there. On March 31, 1967, the tour started in Croydon's Fairfield Hall in Surrey. The following 17 days were booked by promoter Harold Davison. He had seen Buddy's band one of the evenings on Basin Street and was extremely impressed. The same went for the audiences in England. The band received standing ovations everywhere. Perhaps the warm reception was the reason that he agreed to hold a drum clinic, during the day in the Empire Room in London, before the evening's gig there. Normally, he always said, "I'm not a drum teacher," but here he made one of his few exceptions.

Over 900 drummers crowded into the venue, and not one went away dissatisfied. For 90 minutes, Buddy entertained them. He demonstrated how to control the drum sticks, told funny anecdotes, and answered all the audience's questions. It put him in a good mood when he discovered that the English had the same sense of humor as he did. He started the show by saying, "In terms of questions, I'll only answer about what will happen tonight! If you want me to answer technical questions, wait until Roy Burns is back!" "Just play!" the audience shouted back. "Okay, what do you want to see? A single-stroke roll? Fast or medium?" He also defended his brisk use of the bass drum, saying, "It's the foundation of the whole band." "But bass players often think that it disturbs their playing!" shouted the audience again. "There are really only a half dozen good bassists in the world," was Buddy's quick reply. "And Ray Brown is all of them!"

Naturally, he was questioned about his favorite drummers. He answered with all the usual names: Chick Webb, Jo Jones, and Gene Krupa—but he was brutally honest about Gene. "Nobody has done more than him to place the jazz drummer in the center," he remarked of Krupa. "He is a fantastic showman, but what he has done the last ten years is insignificant. I can count up at least 20 drummers who have passed him." This clinic, on April 13, would be remembered as "The day when all the English drummers got to meet God without having to die."[20]

Buddy Rich was a huge success in England. There were several highlights. He was on the radio program "Hear Me Talkin' to Ya," and he appeared on the TV show "Late Night Line Up," where the interviewer asked him about if he had more songs by The Beatles (besides "Norwegian Wood") in his repertoire. He answered, "We have "Michelle" and "Yesterdays," all the songs that I think The Beatles wrote with a little more serious intent that the usual silly songs they've made."[21] (The name of The Beatles song is of course "Yesterday." "Yesterdays" is the standard written by Jerome Kern, but what did Buddy care?) He played two memorable nights at the famous Ronnie Scott's club in London, and as he flew home, he was sure that he had found another strong market for his band.

In the summer of 1967, Buddy's orchestra became the house band in a TV series called "Away We Go." According to certain sources, it was one of his booking agencies who fixed the job for him. That made sense, given the popularity the band was enjoying at the time, and television was the best exposure there was. Closer study reveals that it was his friend, singer and ex-Benny Goodman pianist Buddy Greco, who recommended that the producers hire his friend Buddy Rich as one of the cast members for "Away We Go," a summer replacement program for "The Jackie Gleason Show." Greco was fairly popular in 1967 and not without influence. "Things were going very well for me," Greco admitted. "I was doing movies, had hit records. I got a call from CBS. They wanted to do a series, and they asked 'Who would you like with you?' I said, 'You gotta give me my best friend, Buddy Rich,' and they said, 'We need a comic.'"[22] In the end, Buddy got the job as musical director and used his own touring band as the house group. Comic George Carlin, Greco, and Buddy Rich were the principal cast members, and as the season progressed, Buddy could be seen in 14 episodes where he got the chance to play, act, and demonstrate all his talents during peak viewing hours. As a complement to his appearances on Carson's show, this was perfect. A long lineup of stars made guest appearances on the program, including Richard Pryor, Sheila MacRae, Hal Frazier, and Rodney Dangerfield.

Rich also made a new album at this time, *The New One*, a recording that presented a self-confident drummer in top condition. The opening number was the title song to the "Away We Go" show, an up-tempo number in classic Las Vegas style. He even recorded Buddy Greco's "The Rotten Kid," which he also performed in the program. But the most remarkable track is still "Diabolis." On this ultra-complex chart, Buddy impressed listeners with his tremendous memory and musicality. Allyn Ferguson, who arranged "Diabolis," explained, "The song was rather difficult with many rhythm changes, and the first time Buddy heard the song was when he got to the studio. I had hired in another drummer who I knew read music well, and he got to play through it with Buddy listening. When we were done, Buddy just said, 'Okay, I want to try it out.' He sat down at the drums and played through the whole song perfectly. I couldn't believe my ears."[23]

The entire recording of *The New One* was completed at the same time as Buddy and the band were filming the TV series with Greco and Carlin. According to Ernie Watts, who was on the series and on the album, "'Away We Go' was 14 weeks of hard filming at the same time we were making an album. But we were right into it. Everything was just fun. Buddy was good, the band was good. Then you can't see any problems."[24] After these recordings, Buddy Rich was once again a guest artist at the Newport Jazz Festival, but this time with his entire band. He chose to perform his normal program and not, like most others, try out new material written expressly for the festival. This was a successful move, and when even Dizzy Gillespie spontaneously stepped up to join them as a guest, the cheering never ceased.

A tour with Frank Sinatra was next on the agenda, and that would mean 11 concerts performed over two weeks. The Sinatra tour meant that

Buddy had to sit and wait for a long time to come on, do a brief turn with the band that was climaxed by his solo on "West Side Story," and then, at times, sit and be friendly at one important dinner after another. This was not exactly Buddy's favorite way of spending an evening, and dancing to Sinatra's tune—however good friends they were—was not his cup of tea. Buddy also hated the tuxedos that the whole band had to wear. But he didn't say a word.

On September 30, 1967, Buddy Rich celebrated his 50th birthday. He was taking care of his health reasonably well. His heart had been healthy for five years, but he still ate junk food and meals at two in the morning. He had quit playing tennis, but still played golf—despite the fact that he found it more stressful than calming—and had also started to practice karate. At the time, Buddy admitted that he was "starting to put on some weight" and that he needed something for exercise. Of his initial interest in karate, he explained, "There was an instructor in Las Vegas, where I was working at the time, and we got to rapping about the prowess of the physical thing behind karate and then the philosophy of it. I started taking a few lessons from him, but it wasn't the kind of thing that I thought it would be. I went to Chicago next. I had some friends on the police department and I worked out at the Chicago Police Academy. After about a year, I went to New York and started studying under Aaron Banks. I was 47 by then."[25] Banks was a specialist in Asian martial arts. He had good contacts with Hollywood and was often seen on the film screen with different stars; it was important to him that the scenes looked as realistic as possible.

Banks had his own karate school, and when Buddy Rich came to him, he was very impressed. "I have had nearly 13,000 students over the years, and none of them have had the endurance or worked as hard as Buddy," said Banks. "I have never seen a person with such stamina. He always pushes himself over all the limits. He just refuses to stop." Buddy learned the philosophy behind karate and took lessons every week—time permitting—and got better and better. "Karate teaches you that temper doesn't prove anything," was Buddy's belief. "Verbal abuse can be tuned out. It's a matter of concentration. To use the striking force of karate against a defenseless person is like using a gun. You never hear of anybody in karate getting involved in a fight. He'll stay out unless contact is made against him. Then he'll take them out. I used to think of myself as a tough guy. Looking back now, I wonder what's so great about being a tough guy."[26]

The following year he made use of his new skills. He was relaxing by watching a little baseball with the students during a college date in Nashville, Tennessee. Someone noticed Buddy and started insulting him with personal attacks, racial abuse, and more. He looked around and saw all the people surrounding them, and he understood instantly that if he were to jump the guy, it could result in him being attacked by a throng of people. He recognized the guy who had been doing most of the shouting, so he called him over and said, "When you see your friend, you tell him he's one of the real lucky people in this town. Because if he had kept up, I would have taken both his eyes out. You deliver that message and if he comes tonight, to the concert, and I recognize him, it's all over." If that had happened a few years earlier, he wouldn't have considered the consequences. He would have hit first and asked later. That was what he had done in his childhood in Brooklyn. But since he had started practicing karate, he learned his limits and how he should avoid trouble.

Tenor and soprano saxophonist Pat LaBarbera had joined the band in October, 1967. He was the oldest of three brothers; Pat, John, and Joe were all active musicians and had studied at Berklee College of Music. They were young, talented, and already sought after, and it didn't take long until they were caught up in Buddy Rich's orbit in different ways. John was a fine arranger and Joe, a superb drummer. Both of their talents would be beneficial to Buddy later on. Pat arrived on the scene first. When Buddy's baritone saxophonist Bobby Keller gave notice, he recommended Pat LaBarbera for the bari chair. That was how it went in the band: when someone was moving on, or got fired by Buddy, there was always another, quickly recommended by someone, to replace them. On October 8, the band was to play with Sinatra at a charity gala at St. Paul's Auditorium in Minneapolis and then at a private party. Pat LaBarbera joined the band at this gig. "I met them at the airport on the way to the Sinatra gig in Minneapolis," LaBarbera recalled. "Two days later, I didn't get a wakeup call and overslept, and Jim Trimble, the band manager, called my room and said the whole band plus Buddy were waiting for me. I had all my stuff all over the room. I packed in five minutes and got on the bus. As I walked by Buddy, he said, 'Get yourself an alarm clock in the next town.' To this day, I have nightmares about trying to get all my stuff together and missing the bus."[27] Buddy was in in good spirits during this period, and agreed to hold another one of his few drum clinics, this time at Frank's Drum Shop in Chicago.

At the end of the year, the band was booked for a new Asian tour. It had been six years since Buddy Rich had more or less abandoned his sextet and gone home. On that tour, he was irritated by bad hotels, travelling, and just about everything else. Now he was going back with his whole orchestra, and at the very first concert, at Koseinenkin Hall in Japan, the musicians faced a different set of issues. Due to problems with customs, Buddy didn't have his drums and the band had no sheet music. He had to play the whole concert on borrowed drums, and the band had to play the entire show from memory. The performance, however, was a rousing success. Japanese reaction was unbelievable. After "West Side Story," the band got 11 curtain calls. On the closing night at the Tachikawa Military Civilian Club in Tokyo, Buddy brought a Japanese drummer onstage to play with him, and the Japanese audience was so overwhelmed with joy that Buddy threw his drumsticks high in the air, causing a delay in the concert. The year ended with Buddy Rich winning the *Downbeat* magazine's readers poll yet again. No one could challenge his claim to first place—and he couldn't have cared less.

Next on the agenda was return to the stage at the Sands, and Buddy didn't want to go back without having new material on hand. He turned to Bill Reddie again and asked him to produce another number as big and grand as "West Side Story." Reddie delivered again, and presented "Channel One Suite," a number based on a theme he had written for a Vegas revue show called "Viva le Girls." Buddy loved the number immediately; it was a difficult chart presented in three parts. As always, he had to learn it. The band had to play it with a drummer who could read the chart, and for this, Buddy now he called on Pat's younger brother, Joe LaBarbera. The experience remains etched in Joe's memory. "I had got a job at the Sands with an artist called Frankie Randall," Joe recalled. "All of a sudden one afternoon I was called to another room in the building. They wanted me to play a number called 'Channel One Suite' for Buddy Rich. He was going to sit in front of the orchestra and listen. It wasn't easy! The number was ten minutes long. I got the notes and I was very nervous. I was only 19 years old after all. When I was finished playing Buddy went up and played the number completely correctly right away! I had never seen anything like it!"[28] Around the same time the third brother, John came in on the trumpet. "I was contacted by Buddy's manager, Carl Ritchie, who asked me to come."[29] His stint as a musician with Buddy's band was short; he left in March the same year, but continued to write arrangements for Rich for years to come.

Given that the band was successful and because Buddy was so visible, rumors of how harsh and tough he was a bandleader began to spread. Some of the talented but young and unestablished musicians Buddy had hired at the time were probably prone to gossip. These musicians held Buddy in high respect, of course—he was one of the greats—but stories began to leak about Buddy's tirades against members of the band. The truth was that Buddy's fury was often just a show. He could yell at someone in front of all the other band members, and then afterwards call the same person into his dressing room and say that he shouldn't take it too seriously. Still, it was important to pay attention. If you were fired, you were often rehired after a couple of days. Ernie Watts remembers one occasion. "How I left Buddy? He fired me! We were playing a song called 'Alfie,' and I said to Buddy on stage that if we were going to play it that fast I didn't want to play it. He leaned over towards me and said, 'You've got two weeks' notice from now!' Later he wanted me to come back when he was going to record *Mercy, Mercy* at Caesar's Palace, but I couldn't. Art Pepper got the job instead."[30]

Bassist Ron Paley saw another side of Buddy. "I suppose one could say he was tough," Paley said. "He definitely let you know how he felt—at all times. But if you really watched him, and listened to what he said, and the way he said it, it became quite apparent that there was more to it than just being tough. He cared about the music immensely. I had never felt, and have never felt since, that kind of love of playing—like music was life itself."[31]

Buddy's image was also reinforced by the appearances he did with Johnny Carson. Regarding Buddy's temperament, Carson said, "This tough guy attitude, I think it evolved gradually. I don't think it was a conscious thing. I remember in the early 1940s, before we went into the service, he never ever swore in public. That was before we actually met, but we had mutual friends and they all verify the fact. I think the service changed him. It's an image now, the heavy, the tough guy. We always fool around in the show. But basically he is a very shy man."[32]

Joe LaBarbera observed Buddy closely. "After I had played for him there at the Sands, I saw Buddy backstage for a long time," LaBarbera explained. "For a whole month I watched him. I saw how Buddy yelled and shouted at the band, but, in some way, it felt calculated. Buddy was very conscious of his star status and he probably just wanted to show who was boss. I also saw Buddy's other side: Sometimes Buddy came home to dinner with me to my mother's. Afterwards she said that she had never had a nicer dinner guest."[33] Bobby Shew experienced yet another Buddy Rich, observing that "when his father showed up, Buddy was a different person. He became down right evil. He was spiteful, throwing chairs around and everything. Being around his father re-stimulated all that stuff from when he was growing up. Buddy always reacted to things from his past."[34]

Even if Buddy Rich was difficult to work with, musicians wanted to play in his band. Members came and went in turns, but there isn't a single existing interview where Buddy voiced concern about not getting people to play in his orchestra. If a musician could put experience playing with Buddy Rich in his CV, it carried immense weight in the music industry; it was like a psychological stamp of approval. Buddy's logic was simple: if you played well and to the best of your ability, he left you alone, but if he felt you were asleep on the job, you were told off immediately. You might even get fired on stage. If you didn't watch yourself, maybe he would lean towards you and shout, "Two weeks—from now!"

Buddy and the band returned to the Sands' main stage on January 2, 1968. He chose to save "Channel One Suite" for a bigger occasion, and that would come in the summer, when an engagement at Caesar's Palace in Vegas awaited them. But first, he received an offer from his recording company for an exciting and singularly unique musical collaboration.

Buddy was created to do exactly what he did: play the drums, sing, dance and entertain the world. His ability to play the kit as he did, in the style of the period, was unparalleled in my opinion. He took the "dance" style and rhythms of the '30s and '40s to new heights, together with his talent and evolution of the drum set, incorporating more ride cymbal work. He took and evolved the technical, musical, and showmanship aspects that Gene Krupa, Davey Tough, Baby Dodds, and Chick Webb started earlier to an incredibly high level of execution. His precision, musical feel, touch and humor on the kit, especially in a big band setting, struck a very deep chord with me at a very young age. He was, and still is, one of my most important and inspirational influences.

Dave Weckl

Buddy Rich. His name conjures images and memories of drumming wizardry, musical mastery, and excellence that went beyond mortal bounds with an arrogance that defied the gods of Talent. He cemented his place as part of that pillar of immortal greats who only come along every so often and define a generation, an epoch, an era. His drumming was so good and overpoweringly definitive that it almost ruined big band drumming for the rest of us mere mortals.

Peter Erskine

CHAPTER 16

Different
Drummer

Buddy at rehearsal, 1972.

255

Interest in combining Eastern and Western music was greatly increased when the Beatles, with George Harrison in the lead, traveled to India and composed new material largely inspired by sitar master Ravi Shankar. What the Beatles were doing was given a great deal of attention by the world, and that world included the recording industry, which was constantly on the lookout for what could be sold on the commercial market. World Pacific's Dick Bock spoke to *Billboard* about his company's view on developments in July, 1967. "We've turned down four bands," Bock told the trade magazine while Ravi Shankar's sitar album filtered through his office. "Bands are basically a jazz market product, but the company feels that the Buddy Rich band, as an example, is capable of reaching teenagers. Early sales of his second LP since joining the roster several months ago, *Big Swing Face*, have been as good as the local sales of his first WP package, *Swingin' New Big Band*. Rich's exposure on the 'Away We Go' summer series on CBS television is a plus factor for the label."[1]

Dick Bock had an idea. Given that the popularity of Ravi Shankar, who had been a part of the World Pacific family since the 1950s, was on the rise because of the Beatles connection, and Buddy's star was on the rise as well, why not come up with a recording that featured them both? Bock thought that if the pairing of Buddy with Sinatra helped Buddy reach a wider audience, a paring with Shankar could result in reaching not only a wider audience for them both, but a younger audience. Bock brought the concept to Buddy. According to Ernie Watts, "Bock had recorded a lot of Eastern music earlier. He presented the whole idea to Buddy, who liked it. Buddy was always open to all kinds of music."[2] First Rich and Shankar had to meet and see if they could work together.

In January 1968, they gathered in a rehearsal studio in California. Buddy brought some musicians from his band, and Shankar had with him (among others) India's most respected tabla player, Alla Rahka. Rahka was Shankar's right-hand man and was the first to play a solo concert on that instrument. "Every living thing is rhythm" was his motto, and that kind of attitude impressed Buddy Rich. Watts, who was on the sessions, agreed, saying, "Buddy respected Alla Rahka very highly. He thought he was extremely talented. For him, that was what made him decide to take on the project, more than that he wanted to follow the trend."

Pat LaBarbera, who was at the rehearsal, observed, "The rehearsal with Alla Rahka was to try charts that would work for both artists. I remember Shorty Rogers was there with a chart, and Alla Rahka had a young student protege with him who would sit next to him and tap out rhythms with one hand hitting his knee for downbeats and the other hand over the knee, palm down, catching the upbeats. He was basically decoding our 3/4 and 4/4 into something he could understand. I remember Dick Bock was there. I don't think it was recorded and I don't think the big band worked out because they opted for the small group."[3] On February 5, recordings began. Buddy Rich took only Paul Horn on the flute with him. With Alla Rahka came Shamim Ahmed on sitar, Taranath Rao on dholak, Nodu C. Mullick on tamboura and manjira, as well as Amiya Dasgupta on tamboura. Their joy of playing together those three days in the studio was evident throughout the session. Buddy's contribution is heard mostly on two of the five tracks. On the others, he played mostly on the dholak, a little hand drum, sitting with his legs crossed facing his Indian colleagues.

When the album *Rich a la Rahka* was released, it met with lukewarm reception. Only *Billboard* magazine had anything positive to say about it, writing, "Buddy Rich and his drums are a one- man rhythm section, laying down the beat, setting the pace, and delivering the music. With Alla Rahka on the tabla and Paul Horn on the flute, Rich and company explore the percussive soul in the material of Ravi Shankar, closing the gap between jazz and the beatless oriental swangings."[4] Taufiq Husain, Alla Rahka's son, loved it. "The first time I heard my father play with Buddy Rich I was thrilled," he enthused. "For me, tabla was everything. I didn't know any other instrument could be played so beautifully. Suddenly I heard this alien thing but something to which I was attracted. Buddy Rich was matching my father beat to beat."[5] In the end, the album didn't attract the general public, and it disappeared quickly into the edges of experimental music.

In the spring of 1968, Buddy took his whole band on another tour of England, this time with singer Tony Bennett, and they performed several large concerts at the Hammersmith Odeon, the Palladium Theatre and Royal Festival Hall. He was soon back home again, playing Lennie's on the Turnpike, where he was interviewed by Ernie Santosuosso from *The*

Boston Globe. It was a meeting with Rich that the reporter would never forget. What began as a quiet, pleasant conversation came to an abrupt halt when Buddy was asked how long he intended to keep banging on his drums. Agitated, Buddy quickly exclaimed, "Let's just get one thing straight. I don't bang on any drum. I neither hit nor kick them. A drummer plays his drums! We are musicians, just like Gene Krupa, Sid Catlett, Dave Tough and all the others. It's about time drummers got their due appreciation!"[6] Then he got up and walked out.

Caesar's Palace in Las Vegas was, at the time, the most glamorous hotel and casino in Nevada. Even the name commanded respect. With its garish furnishings inspired by the Roman era, the place was also a great tourist attraction, and if you performed there, it was deemed the height of success. On June 27, Buddy Rich and His Orchestra were booked in for a week's engagement. Buddy had made some changes in the band; Art Pepper came in on alto sax, Al Porcino on trumpet and Don Menza on tenor sax. These weren't just any musicians; they were talented, experienced players—Pepper and Porcino were already looked upon as jazz legends—and their playing raised the level of the band even higher. Buddy knew very well what sort of person lead trumpeter Porcino was. He was known everywhere for his powerful yet sure and calm way of playing, and Buddy remembered with pleasure the time they'd spent together in Dorsey's orchestra. At a rehearsal, Rich wanted to test Porcino, so he called out one fast number after the other; songs that were demanding for a lead trumpeter. Buddy sat laughing a little to himself behind the drums, but Al got through everything. During a break, he turned to Buddy and said with his slow, drawling voice, "Buddy, when are we going to play the hard songs?"[7] Al Porcino liked Buddy, but he said honestly in a later interview in life, "Buddy wasn't always so easy to get along with. He could boss people around like crazy. He wanted everything to be his style and it had to be just as he wanted it. The funny thing is that he was nearly always right."[8]

During the Ceasar's Palace run, Buddy's band was again backing singer Tony Bennett. Before Bennett came on stage, Buddy started with the Joe Zawinul song "Mercy, Mercy, Mercy," a perfect opening number, since it set the tone immediately that Buddy's band was contemporary. When he ended his portion of the show with "Channel One Suite," there was no end to the crowd's enthusiasm. With this wildly successful reception in Vegas, World Pacific's Dick Bock suggested that they should begin recording a new album featuring the band's new music. Everything was recorded in turn at United Studios, but surprisingly, the result didn't meet their expectations. Saxophonist Don Menza thought they could do better. "I talked to Buddy about it," Menza remembered. "I said. 'Hey man, the band is so hot now. What are you doing? You should record the band live now. You should do the album over again. What you do now puts the album away.' Sure enough, two days later, he comes to me and says, 'Tell the cats we're gonna record the whole album all over again, live at Ceasar's Palace.'"[9]

According to Dick Bock, "The final evening, the band played a late set for a specially invited audience. Celebrities from all of show biz were there. We started to play at three in the morning. The audience and band were so in tune with each other, and everything went so unbelievably well. Most of the songs were set on the first take."[10] Even Buddy Rich loved it. He remembered, "There were 400 persons there at three in the morning; actors, bartenders, dancers—everyone who worked in the area was there. For the afternoon performance the day afterwards, we invited the general public, and 800 came. What I liked best was that there were so many young people. They didn't just like the band; they also asked us musicians lots of intelligent questions. We were really accepted by the young people."[11] The album was titled *Mercy, Mercy* and was received positively. The cover was a nod to the youth market, with a happy Buddy Rich dressed in a Nehru jacket and posed in front of a wall decorated in flower-power style. Subsequent performances at Marty's on the Hill in Baldwin Hills, California were no less superb, and even the hard-to-please Leonard Feather was impressed. In his review in the *Los Angeles Times*, he praised all of Rich's arrangements, his ensemble and his soloists, and said that band's successes were based largely on "the 50-year-old child prodigy behind the drums."[12]

Despite all his musical success, Buddy's economic situation hadn't improved. Being true to his ideas and music was costly, and in August of that year, the newspapers blared that Buddy Rich was bankrupt. His creditors were demanding that he settle unpaid bills for hotels, transportation, medical expenses, clothes, lawyer's fees, liquor, toupees, jewels, rental vehicles, music arrangements, recording contract advances, and fees to the American Federation of Musicians. The IRS demanded the sum of $141,600. While there's no doubt that his agents and managers should have been more diligent about Buddy's finances—especially when it came to deducting tax payments—the truth was that Buddy Rich believed, quite simply, that since he worked hard nearly every night, he should be able to buy anything he wanted. What he needed was what every artist needed: a financial advisor who would keep on top of his tax payments and business expenses. No doubt that Norman Granz could have helped. The high wages Buddy received from Harry James hadn't made a dent in Buddy's debt, and manager Stanley Kay (who had taken over from Carl Ritchie) couldn't get things under control, either. But it wasn't easy for Stanley. Buddy was behind with his old payments, and the authorities had had enough.

On August 1, 1968, Buddy Rich was ordered to appear in court in Las Vegas, where he was declared bankrupt. The authorities seized his house and the Rich family moved to Mission Road in Palm Springs, California. It isn't hard to guess what Marie Rich thought about it all. Even if she loved her husband, her patience was stretched to the breaking point. She had always been used to Buddy looking out for their best interests, but their relationship was very strained, and there were notices in the papers that she had filed for divorce in July.[13] There was likely no truth to these rumors, and Buddy kept on playing at his usual intense pace, but he was in a foul mood.

In the fall of 1968, Buddy returned to England to film the first installment of a television concert series for BBC2 television called "Jazz at the Maltings." Buddy arrived in a taxi and got out angry as a bee. Pat LaBarbera explained that "Buddy was upset because they had told him that the gig was just outside of London, but it took at least three or four hours to get there."[14] On news film taken at the soundcheck, Buddy made no secret that he was very angry and irritated, but he agreed to an interview where he expressed his views on playing. "What turns me on? I get turned on by playing," he flatly admitted. "I have known for a couple of years that this is the most important time in my life. The fact is that every day is a challenge for me—the music is a challenge—because when I first organized this band, everyone said to me that a big band wouldn't have a chance because of the pop music that is being played, but I feel that there will always be a place for good music. So the challenge for me is to show all the young people that big bands are not dead .They are more alive than ever."[15] Briefly addressing his relationship with Marie, Buddy would only say, "Sometimes my wife gets a little upset when she thinks that I am away on tour a little too often. It actually isn't a problem, since I always ask her if she wants to come along. But she would rather stay home in Las Vegas. This is my job and it is what keeps me going." At the show that night, in a venue resembling an airplane hangar, Buddy played a wild solo in "West Side Story," sounding himself like a jet taking off.

A few days later, Buddy celebrated his 51st birthday by playing several days at Ronnie Scott's, and then the band travelled to Copenhagen, where he made the usual rounds of television shows and newspaper interviews. It wasn't the normally jovial Rich being seen in interviews of late. He was clearly depressed, and said that it was because the performances in England had been a little tougher than he had expected. Whether he was alluding to the long trip to Maltings or his tax problem, no one knew.

The entire spring 1969 was spent recording a new album called *Buddy and Soul*. Watts and Pepper had left the band, and the latter was replaced by Richie Cole, a 21-year-old alto saxophonist who was hired as quickly as Ernie Watts had been. "I was going to Berklee, and it was Phil Wilson who fixed me up with Buddy's band," Cole recalled. "I replaced Art Pepper on the alto sax. I didn't attend any rehearsal, but I was just told to show up at the next gig 'Be dressed in black and white, wear a clean shirt, and go for it!' were my instructions from Buddy. I was the youngest in the band when I joined up, and I just hung on and played from the very first day."[16] Cole's playing made an impact on Buddy and on the style of the band. According to Cole, "When I signed up, Buddy wanted the band to sound more like pop; more straight and direct. I don't think it was to follow the times, but rather that he just wanted to find out how it would sound. I am really glad that I could be part of the band and play with him just during that time." The fact was that Buddy liked Cole's playing so much that when the album was to be released a second time, he went along with calling it *Big Cole: Richie Cole with*

Buddy Rich and his Orchestra."[17] The young altoist, clearly being groomed for jazz stardom by the leader, played all the solos on half of the album's songs.

On February 21, Buddy Rich met Louie Bellson in a drum battle on "The Tonight Show Starring Johnny Carson." Buddy and Louie played "Only the Greatest," arranged by "Tonight Show" drummer Ed Shaughnessy. After every duel against Bellson, Buddy expressed great admiration for him. One could get the impression that he was still upset with Bellson due to his experiments with double bass drums, but it was simply not so. Buddy was very conscious of Bellson's talent and knowledge of the instrument, and his serious attitude about playing. Through the years, they became very good friends, although when Buddy was asked which drummers had inspired him most, he always answered Krupa, Sid Catlett, Jo Jones, and Chick Webb. On the other hand, Bellson gave the same answers when he was asked the same question.

It was clear that Buddy Rich's current band had an entirely different musical attitude from the orchestras he led in the 1940s, but one throwback to the old days was that he actually took on exactly the same leadership qualities as Tommy Dorsey. He didn't like it when someone decided to quit; only he should decide if someone should leave. He also changed his stance towards Dorsey. Earlier he said that Dorsey was the toughest leader he had ever worked for. Now, after Dorsey's tragic death in 1956, he had much kinder words to say about him. Buddy told Richie Cole that Dorsey "was the best trombone player I ever worked with." As for Buddy's leadership style, Cole believed, "It couldn't have been easy keeping tabs on 18 men. Buddy was tough, but he had to be, in my opinion. I got along with him easily because he knew that I understood that. I did as I was told, looked after myself, played the songs the way he wanted, and treated him with the respect I thought he deserved. It was really only when his music was at stake that he was tough. He set just as high demands on himself. During the two and a half years I was with him, the band only rehearsed twice. Then Buddy sat in front of us and listened when another drummer played all the new songs in one go, then he took over and played everything perfectly. Utterly incomparable."[18]

Buddy Rich was met by enormous respect everywhere, and not only from his own musicians. Indeed, some of the sources of this respect were unlikely. In September 1969, journalist Ralph Gleason, writing for *Rolling Stone* magazine, spent several afternoons with Miles Davis at the Plugged Nickel in Chicago. Buddy performed there one evening and Miles was there to check him out, watching every drumbeat Buddy played like a hawk. "Did you see how he led the band properly there?" Miles explained to Gleason. "And do you see what the devil did there? He beat on that little cymbal and got the whole band to swing!"[19]

In November, the band was back in England again—British audiences loved Buddy. This time, Marie and Cathy came along to attend Buddy's command performance for the Queen, which was to be held at the Palladium Theatre at the request of the monarchs themselves. Before the evening's show, all the artists had to practice curtsying and bowing for the queen backstage. The performers included Tom Jones, Herb Alpert and the Tijuana Brass, Cilla Black, Ginger Rogers, Shari Lewis, and Danny LaRue. Unfortunately, Buddy Rich was in trouble that night. "When I was to play, I suddenly got a terrible toothache," he remembered. "They sent for a dentist, who packed the tooth. I got a bag of ice and then I got busy. You can't let things like that take over. You just have to carry on."[20] Carry on he did. "West Side Story" brought the house down, and the audience had no idea of Buddy's pain, though Pat LaBarbera recalled that there was more than ice at work on Buddy's teeth, saying, "I remember that. Buddy had taken a pile of strong pills and played anyway!"[21]

The audience was filled with celebrities, and Britain's finest drummers were there en masse. Buddy was nervous, and joked on stage, "Seeing so many drummers all at once in a room is quite intimidating. I'm not easily frightened. The last time I was scared was when I read the review of my performance for your monarchy and noticed that I wasn't there! I don't want to speak ill of any critics, but when a reviewer gets all excited about Danny LaRue, I have to ask you to give it some extra thought!"[23] After the show it was time to meet the queen and bow nicely, but no one had told Buddy that there was a chance Her Majesty might actually speak with him. Unexpectedly, Queen Elizabeth said, "Mr. Rich, how do you do what you do?" Completely stunned, Buddy stammered, "Uh, just lucky, I guess."[22] When the queen had gone, he fretted to Marie, "Why did I say that? Where did it come from?" The line became a standing joke in the Rich family: "Just lucky, I guess?"

While in England, it was time for yet another television appearance, this one on "Talk of the Town." The rumor of his appearance on English television spread like wildfire, and on the actual show, the band swung like never before. "If Buddy noticed that there was at least one known drummer in the audience he always played extra well," recalled arranger John LaBarbera. "It always got him going." Singers Jon Hendricks and Annie Ross, of Lambert, Hendricks and Ross fame, were brought up from the audience to sit in, and the atmosphere in the studio was electric. Among the musical highlights of the appearance were Buddy's performance of Ravel's "Bolero" (played only on a snare drum) and an unparalleled and unbelievable extended solo on "West Side Story." Yes, he was certainly aware that the venue was filled with drummers.

Back in America, the band played five nights at the Cellar Door in Washington, D.C. Martha Sanders Gilmore wrote about it afterwards in *Downbeat* magazine. "His control of the drumsticks was so exceptional that he played a drum roll so quiet that you could have heard a pin drop, and then he built it up to an unbelievable crescendo. Rich stood up from the drums, lit a cigarette. It was wonderful to see how much he gave of himself to that discerning audience, but I was very worried about his heart that evening." It wasn't his heart that bothered him that evening; Buddy was beginning to have back problems. A month later, a different kind of problem arose in Rochester, New York. The police knocked on his hotel room door at the Midtown Towers. After entering, they searched the room from top to bottom and discovered a vial of the laxative Senokot. Believing that the vial contained a controlled substance, Buddy was charged with felonious possession of drugs and advised of his rights. Later, in court, the case was dismissed. Not long after, Buddy talked and laughed about the incident on "The Tonight Show."

On March 30, 1970 Buddy Rich and the band began work on another live Las Vegas recording. *Keep the Customer Satisfied* was recorded at the Tropicana, and the influence of alto saxophonist Richie Cole is evident throughout. *Keep the Customer Satisfied* was similar to the pop/rock rhythmic spirit evoked in the previous *Buddy and Soul*, with one hope being to maybe get a hit record out of it. In line with this quest, Buddy approached the great arranger Bill Holman about making an orchestration based on the music from the then-current hit film "Midnight Cowboy," which had been a huge success and received three Oscars that year. With the recording underway and the band busier than usual, his health began to give him trouble again. "During the recording of *Keep the Customer Satisfied*, my father was having severe back problems," Cathy Rich remembered. "The pain was so excruciating that between sets he would lie on the floor of his dressing room in the dark. When it was time to play, it took three men to carry him to the stage and place him behind his drums. But once the curtain went up, it was as if the pain disappeared. The audience never knew."[24] These problems would not go away.

Buddy signed a new contract with Willard Alexander's agency to manage his bookings. Given that Alexander was a veteran booker of big bands and a calming influence on Buddy who knew the business thoroughly, Buddy felt safe with him and may have even looked upon him as a father figure. Alexander thought Buddy should play more at universities and schools, given that Buddy had enjoyed his previous experiences on the college circuit. It felt as though he was giving something back—and the students loved him. His temperament suited them. The students loved Buddy's barbed exchanges like, "Do you want an extra number? Okay, but we don't play extra numbers. You have to listen to all the songs we played in the first set, but at another beat. I play whatever the hell I like with my band."

Economically, the band was doing quite well, but as usual, Rich still had the IRS after him. Stanley Kay worked like a madman to get his accounts in order, but it all seemed futile. The only thing that caught up with Buddy was the reality that however much tax he paid, the minus figures still kept growing. It was different for him on stage. When the lights were on, he had a kind of invincible, unbeatable, and immortal aura about him. It was remarkable that those around him had little or no idea about the physical pain he was in. Buddy was a restless soul, which may have been one way he coped with the pain. He simply didn't like performing in the same place for long. He always wanted to move on—one evening here, one evening there—and was happy as long as he got the band out on the road. One explanation for this restlessness—quite common among those in show business—is that Buddy Rich loved the feeling of anticipation. He knew very well that the audience out there, however big or small, expected a fabulous drum solo. Even if he never actually said he was the world's best drummer, he was marketed that way, and that didn't bother him, nor did the image as the hard, tough-as-nails bandleader who fired people on stage. The schtick worked well on the talk show circuit.

In August he was a guest with his band on the Philadelphia-based "Mike Douglas Show." Other guests were Mel Tormé and Artie Shaw. Shaw didn't know what he was in for when Mike Douglas first asked Buddy, "Do you know who is here? Artie Shaw. Wasn't he the one who got you your first job?" Buddy's reply was instantaneous. "Artie Shaw is a complete idiot!" said Buddy, pulling no punches. "I can't stand him and he can't stand me. If you are really intellectual you don't have to go around telling everyone. It will come out automatically. But he works on it. I did a radio show with him about a year ago, where he says he reads seven or eight books a day. I understand now that the books have one and a half pages per book and a lot of pictures. Artie Shaw is a great musician, but the attitude that he has taken the past few years, what jazz has done and what jazz was, as far as he was concerned, and his attitude about the kids who want his autograph, he brushes them off cause he has no time for them, he puts that all in the past and says that was never a part of his life. If that wasn't a part of his life, Artie Shaw wouldn't be here today on your show, or any other show, because that was the beginning of his career." During this commentary, Shaw stood in the wings waiting to be introduced.

On October 15, Buddy and the band started a new European tour that began in London, continued with a quick visit to Barcelona, Spain, and then headed to Sweden. In Sweden, Buddy took the opportunity to play a gig at a relatively small jazz club called Swing Inn. This time the reason was special. The promoter Bo Johnson, explained that "Buddy Rich never had any money. He didn't have money to pay the band. When Buddy was playing a few gigs with Sammy Davis Jr., he needed money, so I gave it to him. He paid me back by performing at my jazz club, Swing Inn, in the city of Malmö. It was a great concert. They performed at a real jazz club, which they loved. Buddy was in his best mood. He was larking about, bickering with the audience, imitating Sammy Davis Jr, singing and stepping. He even managed to get the two saxophonists, Andy Fusco and Steve Marcus, to sing-solo completely unprepared." Still, it was not an easy performance. Neither the drums nor the sheet music had arrived. The band had to play from memory, and Buddy performed on borrowed drums. Bo Johnson continued, "Neither notes or drums arrived in time. The first hour they had to play without notes and on a borrowed drumset. A drummer named Lasse Lindström lent his Yamaha set. On stage Buddy joked about it. 'My drums haven't come. I've had to borrow a Yamaha set. It should be called Hahaha set,' he joked. That maybe wasn't so nice towards Lindström."[25]

During his stay in Sweden, Buddy agreed to a long interview in the magazine *Orkesterjournalen*. He was open and honest. Whether he liked something or really detested things that were happening in society, he never hesitated to say straightaway what he felt. During the interview, he spoke freely about the war in Vietnam. "Unfortunately," he began, "it won't help how many people protest as long as Nixon has industry and the generals behind him. Then nobody can budge him. The war in Vietnam is criminal. Young guys are sent out to murder other young fellows who haven't even started to begin living." He also had strong feelings about conditions in the United States as well, saying, "Look at the slums at home. You can't believe it's true. In the richest country in the world, hell, over 20 million are living in misery. You can't understand it. Good God, people are literally hunted because they have long hair, because they are dressed differently. Freedom? Oh yes!" Moving on to President Nixon, Buddy wouldn't even consider performing for him. "We were invited to play for Nixon at the White House," said Buddy. "No thanks, nobody is going to come and say about me, 'See there goes someone who has shaken hands with Nixon!'"[26]

Buddy Rich took pride in his straight-ahead honesty and candor, and that aspect of his personality had nothing to do with trying to get more fans for the band. On live television, he didn't hesitate for a moment to say he liked smoking grass, that he didn't understand speed limits at all, and in comments that would later cause some controversy, that country and western music, as he called it, was "like rock music: all glitter, out of tune and full of no talents," adding that "country and western is music played with a funny hat." The tour then continued all around Europe, and ended with a two-week stay in England, his favorite country. At Ronnie Scott's he always felt right at home.

Back on American soil, on March 8, 1971, Muhammad Ali met Joe Frazier in what was billed as "The Match of the Century." The venue was Madison Square Garden, and both the boxers had been offered big money to fight for the title of heavyweight champion of the world. Celebrities were everywhere at the heavily-hyped match, with one of the more unique pieces of ballyhoo being that Frank Sinatra was on hand at ringside to take pictures for *Life* magazine. Few in Ali's camp thought that he would lose, so they had booked the New York Hilton to celebrate his victory. Buddy Rich and His Orchestra were playing a two-week engagement at the Royal Oak Hotel in Toronto, but Ali's offices flew the band in to the New York Hilton to play for the anticipated celebration party. Count Basie's band was also expected to perform, and naturally Buddy was in a state of exultation about that.

The match was a bloody one in which the tireless Joe Frazier prevailed after 15 rounds of ruthless boxing. The loss was Muhammad Ali's first as a professional boxer and no one expected a joyous celebration at the hotel—but it happened anyway. Free food and free drinks combined with great music meant that everyone who came along was in a partying mood. The orchestras dueled against each other. Drummer Jo Jones came by, sat in with Buddy's band, and Buddy got to play with Basie's. Though there was no success for Ali, the party itself was quite the event. A few years later, Rich and Ali met when boxing promoter Harold Conrad took Ali to a Buddy Rich concert in Philadelphia. Ali was so impressed that he said to the colorful Conrad, "I have to meet that man." They went to Rich's hotel, where upon being introduced to Buddy, Ali said, "Let me see your hands." Buddy held them out. "If my hands were as fast as yours," Ali said, "I would always be the master." Afterwards, Rich commented, "I was flattered. I thought he was the greatest."[27]

Another battle was ongoing in the music world, and in that stylistic clash, jazz was losing out. Jazz venues were disappearing while rock, in all its forms, was seemingly everywhere. The Woodstock Festival in August, 1969, an event of legendary proportions, was a high point for the half million people who crowded to see Janis Joplin and Jimi Hendrix for free. But rock, like jazz, was continuing to develop and evolve, and in some cases, the difference between rock and pop became thin. After the demise of The Beatles, the Rolling Stones and groups with tougher sounds (and some not without jazz influences, like Cream, Deep Purple, Black Sabbath, and Led Zeppelin) came to the forefront, as did the "art rock" or "progressive rock" of bands like Genesis and Yes. Many of these groups were beginning to fill stadiums, perhaps at the cost of jazz that had been played for years mainly in small clubs.

In the summer of 1971, Buddy Rich made one more appearance at the Newport Jazz Festival. Also on the Newport bill were the big bands of Stan Kenton and Duke Ellington. Exposure by way of big outdoor fests like Newport, plus the fact that Willard Alexander had seen to it that Rich was a frequent guest on TV shows—he appeared twice on "The David Frost Show" during this period, where he was introduced as "Mr. Black Belt in Karate," demonstrated his karate expertise by crushing wooden blocks, then sat in with Billy Taylor's house band—meant that, at least to Buddy, he was entitled to a better and longer recording contract. Buddy left his old record company Pacific Jazz and was signed for a three-album deal to one of the major labels, RCA Victor. Not long after the signing, the band began recording their first effort in RCA's own studios in New York.

During this time, Buddy hired more new, young musicians from Berklee. There was a good reason as to why so many came from the school, according to Pat LaBarbera, who explained, "Buddy donated his book to Berklee while we were playing Paul's Mall in Boston in the early 1970s. After that, many young players could study the charts, play them in ensembles and be ready for the call."[28] Rich further developed his association with the school a few years later, when the study of Buddy Rich's orchestrations would become part of the Berklee curriculum.

RCA's *Different Drummer* was released that fall, the start of a long-term publicity launch of the band. The record was released a month before Buddy was to tour in England for the sixth time. He went there with increasing back pain and a crack in his left foot caused by a karate lesson that had gone a little wrong. Marie and Cathy went with him again, and all three were also invited to Pat LaBarbera's wedding, which was to be held in London. The band taped the "Sounds for Saturday" television show for BBC, where Buddy can be seen playing a Fibes drum set, a drum company he endorsed for a very short period. From England, the band went on to Theatre Nationale Populaire in Paris, where Buddy Rich received standing ovations. After an 11 minute-plus solo on "West Side Story," the audience gave him three curtain calls, in spite of enormous back pains. They didn't want to let him leave the stage until he said, "Thank you, you are wonderful, we would like to do more but we have to make a plane flight."

Back in London, he took part in yet another drum battle. Buddy wasn't all that taken with these drum duels, but in this case he was enthusiastic, as the evening was dedicated to the deceased percussionist and journalist Frank King. The venue was Queen Elizabeth Hall and Buddy was to play with Louie Bellson and Kenny Clare. Together with a large orchestra conducted by Bobby Lamb and Ray Premru, King was saluted with enormous musical zest on behalf of drummers in all of London. It was preserved on the album, *Conversations: A Drum Spectacular*, which inexplicably has not yet seen the proper light of day on a commercial release. Then it was back to Ronnie Scott's, where the band was recorded live for the second RCA effort, *The Buddy Rich Band Very Alive at Ronnie Scott's*. As the jewel on the crown, Buddy again won the *Downbeat* poll as best drummer. In usual fashion, he didn't comment.

Everything would have been fine if it hadn't been for his back. The intense ache would never let up. He tried to ignore the electric flashes that felt like knives cutting into his lower back every time he sat down or got up from the drum set. Maybe it was the countless trips by bus, train and plane that had caused the problems, or perhaps just a sign of age, but somehow he managed to carry out performance after performance. The funny thing was that every time he began to play the ache disappeared. But ignoring pain in this way would turn out to be disastrous.

On January 7, 1972, Buddy Rich was performing at Brandi's Wharf in Philadelphia, a hospitable club that Buddy enjoyed and played frequently. The band was booked to play for three evenings, but on the very first night, several of the band members noticed that there was something wrong. They looked worriedly at Buddy, who looked strange and was grabbing at his back. Everyone was used to Buddy gritting his teeth and believed everything would sort itself out, but on this night, it was obvious that playing was agony to him. The week after the Brandi's shows, Buddy was taken to a hospital in Philadelphia to operate on two discs in his lower back that were out of place. He was now paying the price for sitting bent over a drum set for so many years. Unfortunately, something went wrong at the hospital. Cathy Rich explained, "He had two discs removed from his spine. The surgery was unsuccessful, and he lived the rest of his life with almost constant back pain. His schedule didn't change because of it, nor did his lifestyle."[29]

Buddy had to call in a replacement to sub during his convalescence. Gene Krupa was called, but had to beg off due to his own health problems. The choice was Louie Bellson, who hopped in for a couple of days, but then he had to return home again because his wife, Pearl Bailey, had had a heart attack. Buddy discussed it with his family and decided to go back to the band for the next performance. They could see that he was still in pain, but what could they do? Perhaps a telephone conversation played a role in Buddy's decision. According to Pat LaBarbera, "When Benny Goodman heard that Buddy had gone through a similar operation to his, he called him up and said that it was just as well that he put the band on the shelf for a year. That's how long it took to recover. Buddy didn't want to be like Goodman, and a month later he was back in the band. He modified the hi-hat so it would be easier to get it to open without having to exert his left foot too much."[30]

The ache didn't worry Rich, but he was more than unhappy when he received the news that RCA had condensed the sessions recorded live at Ronnie Scott's to a single album and retitled it *Rich in London*. There was more than enough material recorded at Scott's for a double album, which was reportedly RCA's original intent. Buddy was bugged, and began to wish he had never signed the contract. "They didn't care, man," said Buddy at the time, "and had the nerve to tell me I was overreacting. They violated my contract. Unless you were an Elvis Presley selling zillions of records, they didn't take any real personal interest in you. Just being recorded by them was supposed to be a big deal."[31]

Back problems or not, Buddy was constantly on the move. For the following three months he kept up a relentless tour pace of 20 one-nighters in different cities, plus appeared on "The Tonight Show" four times that year, "The Dick Cavett Show" three times, and "The Mike Douglas Show" once. For a musician with an injured back, he was unusually active. In August he recorded his third and final album for RCA—there was no contract extension—called *Stick It*. Buddy's 55th birthday was on September 30, 1972, and for once, he was off the road and could celebrate at home.

Buddy Rich's respect for Gene Krupa never ceased. Certainly, they had mutual respect for each other, and Buddy knew very well what Gene had done during his life for the development of the drums, and he could never praise it enough. Every time Krupa was a guest at one of his performances, Buddy was a different person. Trumpeter/arranger John LaBarbera remembered a particularly poignant scene at a performance in April that year. "Buddy took his bows, did his usual shtick with the audience, and came offstage, at first not noticing Gene," LaBarbera remembered. "When he saw him, the show business mask dropped and there, for a moment, was BR with his guard down. His expression communicated a whole lot of feelings. It was almost as if he said 'Sorry I made you wait, I didn't know you were here!' It was a touching moment that is hard to talk about. It showed how much feeling Buddy had for Gene, how much he cared about him."[32]

Of course he'd heard Gene say kind words about him in several interviews they'd done together, but he didn't really understand (at least at that time those early interviews were conducted) that his friend's words were so honest and direct from the heart. When Gene knew that he didn't have much time left, he told Roy Anderson, a Krupa friend and sometimes drummer, that he just wanted to "spend time with Buddy— just the two of us, no fans, no drums."[33] Anderson also saw that the walls of Krupa's basement recording studio were covered with photos of Buddy Rich—and no one else. Author Clarence Hintze also knew how Gene felt about Buddy. "I know that when Gene was being treated in the hospital, he always had a photo of Buddy Rich on the wall there," according to Hintze."[34]

Sadly, Gene Krupa had endured some tough times. He survived a heart attack in 1960 (around the same time that Buddy had his heart problems), then contracted emphysema seven years later (Gene was a very heavy cigarette smoker), and had back problems with pinched discs (a common complaint among drummers). He got divorced from his second wife, and that was also a blow, but it didn't end there. In January of 1973, he was diagnosed with benign leukemia. On top of everything else, there was a major fire in his beloved Yonkers, New York home, and he didn't have insurance to cover the loss. Buddy knew about all of this, and wanted to do something for his friend. He asked his manager, Stanley Kay, to organize a tribute evening for Gene. Buddy had deep feelings about this, said Cathy Rich. "My father had many philosophies," she explained, "but one was that you should give flowers to people while they are alive. He could never understand why people wait until someone dies to pay them tribute. He felt that you should let a person know how much they have meant to us all."[35]

On August 15, Buddy Rich helped bring together just about every living famous drummer to show their respect for the legendary Krupa. The memorable evening was held at Marsh's Restaurant, close to Central Park in New York City. Cathy Rich was there, and remembered, "During the evening, each person stood up and toasted Gene and everyone told what an influence he had on them. There was Joe Morello, Zutty Singleton, Roy Knapp, Papa Jo Jones, Cliff Leeman, Sonny Igoe, Henry Adler, Jerry Lewis, Frank Ippolito, and many more." Bobby Colomby, then the drummer for Blood, Sweat and Tears, represented the younger drummers. "Everyone was crying," Colomby remembered. "The only one in the whole room who looked good was Gene. He looked fantastic. Buddy doing that for his friend at such a personal level—it was the most unbelievable evening I've experienced in my whole life."[36]

At the end of the evening, Krupa gave a very moving speech to everyone who had come in his honor. He didn't feel that he was any genius behind the drums, he said. He ended by saying, "There is only one genius on our instrument and he is sitting there," and pointed at Buddy Rich. Gene Krupa died on October 16, 1973. The year before, he had been voted into *Downbeat* magazine's Hall of Fame via the readers, and on January 17 of the following year, there was a tribute to him held at New York City's Felt Forum, featuring music by Buddy Rich, Lionel Hampton, Louie Bellson, Roy Haynes, Dizzy Gillespie, Anita O'Day, Charlie Ventura, and many others. Gene Krupa was remembered that evening as a giant in jazz history, the man who brought drums to the forefront, made the drums a solo instrument, and ensured that drummers were given the the natural right to be called *musicians*.

After three weeks off at the beginning of the year 1973, Rich continued the everlasting touring that had become more intense the previous spring. The calendar was filled in with about 15 performances a month throughout the whole year. On February 6, he was a guest on "The Mike Douglas Show" during the day, and in the evening, performed a concert at Rochester Top of the Plaza in New York. The performance was filmed by three TV cameras for broadcast on Rochester public television. For the first time, the general public would have the chance to see the current Buddy Rich orchestra at work. A happy Rich introduced his band, dressed nattily in turtleneck sweaters, and played the strongest songs on his repertoire. He also talked for a long time with the audience, who were roaring with laughter at his jokes. If Buddy Rich hadn't been so good at the drums, he could easily have had a career as a standup comedian. The concert, still fondly remembered today by way of its commercial release on DVD, was called *Rich at the Top*.

In October, a new album was released, called *The Roar of '74*. Released by Groove Merchant, a small, New York-based company, the album indicated the future direction of the band. The new Groove Merchant deal guaranteed him the artistic freedom and control he craved. The album was positively received by the critics, with *Downbeat* summing up the reviews by writing, "The whole album is the result of good taste."[37] The month afterwards, on November 9, the band performed a memorable TV concert during an appearance at the Dorchester Hotel in London. Rich had been booked for a new tour in England, and it seemed as though he went there nearly every year. It was no doubt due to the fact that the local promoters noticed that he filled every club, theater or concert hall to the limits. But Buddy also said that he loved the British understanding of jazz music. At the performance in Dorchester, he had included another Beatles song on his repertoire, George Harrison's

"Something," where trumpeter Charlie Davis got to show off his skills. Buddy was in a good mood, bubbling with zest for playing. Ron Paley, the bassist, agreed, saying, "The concert at Dorchester was fantastic. Buddy was unbelievable. He had so many different sides as a person. He had a spark and an energy that showed both in his personality and his music. His chitchat with the audience between the numbers was so funny!"[38]

On the film footage of that date, a strong Buddy Rich is on view. He shouts out the choice of songs in the middle of the telecast. In fact, until Buddy called the tune, the musicians didn't know which songs they were going to play, not even on such occasions. John LaBarbera explained that "he was just calling the song numbers from a catalog. He always watched the audience to decide what would suit and them he kept a rhythm going on the hi-hat while he shouted out the song title. We never knew what he was going to choose."[39] For the whole concert, Buddy wore a picture of Donny Osmond on his jacket. This may have been a way of joking away his earlier statements in *Melody Maker* magazine, comments that even his close friends and most fanatic supporters had had trouble understanding. Buddy told *Melody Maker*, in no uncertain terms, "You are sick, Osmonds. I don't really understand how you can put a dwarf on the stage. You have no talent, Osmonds! No talent!" He tried to explain himself in several articles afterwards, saying that the statement was just meant as a joke. That was very unlike Buddy Rich. If he said something, he usually meant it.

Buddy read, with some interest, a 1970 *Downbeat* article where Cream's outspoken drummer, Ginger Baker, commented about his own ability playing double bass drums, and his words about Buddy's bass drum work. "Buddy Rich is a lunatic," the notorious Baker told *Downbeat*. "He considers himself the world's best drummer, but his feet are nowhere at all! He hasn't got any feet—he plays like a man with one foot. In most things he plays he's only got one foot going and that's playing four in a bar. He's kidding himself." Buddy got furious and invited Baker to play with his band. He said to Les Tomkins in *Jazz Professional*, 1971, "How would it be if I should ask Ginger Baker or Stu Martin, or any of your very hip drummers, to come out and play with my band some night—or Count Basie's or Woody Herman's? Do you think they're qualified to come up and sit in for about six minutes? Well, of course they aren't. But they're drummers, aren't they? And music is music. If they're so great, they ought to be able to do it." Baker never showed up. Ginger Baker must have been the only drummer in the world who didn't notice Buddy's incredibly fast feet. Having the last word in the matter, in the April, 1974 issue of *Downbeat*, Buddy said, "You know, I read Ginger Baker's remarks about me. That I'm not playing jazz, that I can't play drums. I accept that because it comes from a non-player."

Buddy didn't have much patience with artists who performed songs consisting of three chords with shrieking guitars, and was especially hard on rock drummers: "If you're not careful you may end up as a drummer in a rock band," he said in several interviews, as if that were the worst thing that could happen. Around this time, Buddy Rich also was being courted by various drum manufacturers who wanted him to use their particular product. A man showed up one day out of nowhere and wanted to show Buddy a new bass drum pedal. He said, "Mr. Rich, if you use this pedal you will be faster than anyone else in the world." Buddy replied, "Faster than who, for instance?"

Directly after England, the band travelled to Australia, which was a disappointment this time. Buddy thought the audiences were altogether too drunk at many places and didn't seem to care very much about the music that was being played. To top it off, one of his musicians had an accident. Trumpeter John Hoffman recalled that he was driving too fast and went off the road, rolled the car and broke several ribs. "Buddy was fair to me," he said. "He paid me full wages anyway. He just said, 'I've rolled a car myself,' smiled and walked away."[40] The last performance in Australia was in the Cabaret Room casino in Hobart, Tasmania. At 10:30 the next morning, the police knocked on Buddy's hotel room door. They searched the room and found a small amount of marijuana. Buddy was ordered to appear in court in February the following year, but he paid no attention to the summons at all. As he sat on the plane home, he read a newspaper story about how he had been apprehended with narcotics in his room. He smiled and sipped a glass of champagne.

CHAPTER 17

Buddy's Places

Mel Tormé, Ella Fitzgerald, and Buddy at Buddy's Place, circa 1974.

At the beginning of 1974, Buddy Rich was forced once again to realize that he still had great financial problems. The costs of keeping a big band on the road had shot up even more. His musicians wanted to be paid fairly—no one was in the business for charity—and a look at his calendar showed that the band was booked more and more at universities and schools, venues that Buddy enjoyed playing, but that could hardly afford exorbitant fees. This, combined with Buddy's generosity under some of these circumstances made his financial situation worse. (On several occasions, students came to his bus and said that they hadn't managed to raise the promised payment, to which Buddy answered, "Give what you've got to the boys in the band.")

He felt it was time for a change, and he decided he wanted to open, or at least "front," a club in New York geared strictly toward music, with no noisy, drunken, non-jazz fans allowed. Buddy didn't care where it was or whether there was a big band or a smaller ensemble on the stage. Good music was all that was important to him. This major career decision had all been preceded by a discussion with his manager, Stanley Kay, who was quite frank. "When we were losing money, I said, 'Buddy, I got a friend of mine, called Sam's Jazz Upstairs. I can talk to him. We can have a small band and you'll make some money, and we'll call it Buddy's Place.' He said, 'All right, get the band together.'"[1] The band members were informed of the new venture on the last night of a weeklong stand at Jimmy Ryan's on West 52nd Street in New York. The immediate plan was to install a small group at a club bearing Buddy's name. However well his big band had been received the past eight years, as an essential cost-cutting measure, cutting down to small group was the only option.

Buddy's Place opened on a Wednesday evening, April 10, 1974, on the corner of 64th Street and Second Avenue on Manhattan's East Side. The venue had earlier been comedian Jackie Kannon's watering hole called the Rat Fink Room, also said to be Robert Kennedy's favorite hangout. Stanley Kay made a deal with the owner that Buddy would lend his name to the club and play there several times a month. In his absence, the club would present nationally-known jazz names. The location was perfect, as Buddy's Place was situated in a neighborhood filled with cinemas, theaters, restaurants and shops.

On the eve of the opening, Rich said to a newspaper, "The whole idea of my club is to present the best music; not small or big band, not jazz, not labeled anything but first class entertainment. The only two forms of music in any field are good and bad. What happens in between is up to the taste of Middle America, which has no taste at all, whether in politics or music. We will not tolerate drunken people. If you can't behave, you have to leave the club."[2] It would soon become apparent that he meant what he said. At the premier, the celebrities were out in force, including Frank Sinatra, Tony Bennett, Johnny Carson, Artie Shaw, and Sy Oliver. Several radio stations were on hand to broadcast the opening live. Buddy Rich said that he thought it was time to offer the people of New York a little good music. He also looked at it as a good opportunity to spend time with his family for once. There was a lot of jamming that evening. Lionel Hampton played as guest with the sextet that Buddy had put together, made up of Sal Nistico on tenor sax, Sonny Fortune on alto sax, Jack Wilkins on guitar, Kenny Barron on piano, and Anthony Jackson on bass.

Good feelings were running high that night, until someone in the audience was a little too loud for Buddy's taste. Buddy went up to the microphone and said, "I'll pick up your check, but don't you ever come back here again!"[3] The band continued to play and someone else shouted, "Play it again!" Buddy's reply was, "You should have listened the first time, loudmouth!" This would happen several times while Buddy was playing, and he soon began to enforce a "quiet" rule, which meant no loud talking was allowed while he was playing. Offenders were shown the door, sometimes by Buddy himself. Stanley Kay was pulling his hair out, saying, "Buddy, you can't do this. It's a night club. People want to talk." "It's my club," responded Buddy. "I do what I want here. People come here to listen to me, not some loud-mouthed drunk bastard who is going to shout one thing or another. They can listen out on the street if they like."

Most likely Buddy had mixed feelings about having his own club. Granted, here he could play there as much as he liked and make his own rules, but the club also meant another kind of responsibility. Author John Minahan described a meeting with Buddy backstage. "Buddy Rich once told me that he was the loneliest man in the universe," Minahan wrote. "We were alone in his dressing room upstairs at Buddy's Place, his new club in New York, and he had just finished a frenzied session of slamming his fists into the two karate punching pads on the wall. When he said it, he was sweating and out of breath and one of his knuckles was bleeding." It's not hard to understand why Buddy Rich felt alone. It certainly had nothing to do with his family. Instead, it may have been a result of his having to constantly deliver on stage. It had become almost a psychological treadmill that was hard to stop. One evening he could do a solo that so fantastic, that no one believed he could ever top it. But the evening afterward, he was sitting there on stage with all the meters were reset to zero, and he had to start from the beginning again. The demands for new recordings also had to be fulfilled, though Buddy never liked recording, and during his whole career, there were only a few albums he was satisfied with. Buddy never explained or expounded upon the feelings he expressed to Minahan. Maybe all the thousands of hours warming up backstage, waiting to perform, made him suddenly ask himself whether it was all worthwhile. Somewhere within, however, he always found the strength to continue forward, perhaps because it was the only way he knew.

In May, the small band recorded the album *Very Live at Buddy's Place*, and the summer that followed he went on tour with his sextet. The bookings at Buddy's Place in the sextet's absence were really something, including top-name acts like Ike and Tina Turner, Stan Kenton, Lionel Hampton, Michel Legrand, Jimmie Walker, Clark Terry (who also recorded an album there), Dizzy Gillespie, Count Basie, and B.B. King. The club certainly looked like a success, but after the tour, as Buddy returned to the security that the club provided, it became clear that Buddy's Place was losing money. On November 23, Buddy's Place closed. Buddy's only comment on the situation was "We'll find a new place."

In 1975, Buddy Rich found himself topped by the 31-year-old Billy Cobham in the annual *Downbeat* magazine jazz poll, winning by over 300 votes. Buddy had to console himself with being voted into *Downbeat's* Jazz Hall of Fame by the magazine's readers. He was often asked how it felt to be chosen as best one year and then slide down the list the next. He waved the issue away by saying that the polls were just a measure of popularity with audiences, not who was best on their instrument. "And why compete?" Buddy believed. "Musicians should stick together. I got a call the other day that I had again been named to the *Playboy* Jazz Poll. That's great, but so what? Until I can walk into a building and visibly see that I am in a hall of fame, it doesn't make much of an impression on me. I've got other things to worry about. Things like why in the hell do I have to drive 55 miles an hour and where in the hell I'm going to get my next tank of gasoline."

Though most big-name rock drummers hadn't yet established themselves as individuals and star soloists during this period, a few were beginning to emerge. In addition to Ginger Baker, another was Carl Palmer from the group Emerson, Lake & Palmer, then together for five years. Palmer was already winning international polls in England, Japan and Germany, and actually won the then pop-dominated *Playboy* poll in 1977. It was just a matter of time before more rock drummers would begin dominating the polls. Palmer had gotten to know Buddy during Buddy's first tour of England in the mid-1960s. Buddy liked the young and ambitious drummer, and found a person who was as devoted to the instrument as he was (and played drums with the traditional grip!). Rich let him play as a guest with his band and they became close friends. It is easy to get the idea that Buddy Rich was uninterested in the new era's drummers because he didn't like the music, but this wasn't always the case. He liked Chicago, with drummer Danny Seraphine, and Blood, Sweat & Tears, with drummer Bobby Columby, for instance, and later would have kind words for Harvey Mason and Steve Gadd. Neither were rock drummers per se, but were versatile studio artists fluent in any genre.

Buddy generally detested rock drummers, who he believed were careless about technique and were more focused on the number of tom-toms they had in their kits.If an interviewer asked questions about rock, he would frequently suggest that rock drummers "learn the craft. Forget about pyro-techniques, spinning platforms and funny hats. Get the band you play with to swing or do something else." To *The New York Times* he said, "If this country were not so sold on gimmicks, musicians would not have to call a fully grown man Alice; the man who puts a boa constrictor around his neck makes a sexual act rather than a musical act."[4] At Buddy's Place, he was interviewed by cutting-edge filmmaker, broadcaster and journalist Efrom Allen, who asked Buddy, "What do you think about the rock business?" Buddy told Allen, "Well, you see, you call it rock business, not rock music. That's what it is: a business. I was living in Las Vegas ten years ago, and I think it was The Beatles first or second appearance in the country, and I took my daughter Cathy to see them at the Convention Hall in Las Vegas. I was destroyed by that. I couldn't believe what I heard. I heard nothing, because 10,000 kids were screaming the moment they approached on the stage and for the next twenty minutes—that was all they played. So I had no validation what The Beatles could do, but they did write good music later."[5]

His straightforwardness shone right through. This time he wasn't joking, as he had with the Donny Osmond misfire sometime back, especially when it came to his feelings about country and western music. The article that infuriated country and western fans came out on January 16, 1975. He was headed to the southern part of the country, as a part of a tour for his quartet that took him to Miami, Houston, Nashville and New Orleans. Bill Hance from the *Nashville Banner* wanted to do a story about Buddy before his arrival. Buddy didn't mince his words and told Hance, "Country music from Nashville appeals mainly to intellectuals with minds of four-year-olds. The quality and sound of country music is bad in most cases. You can take three people, put them in a studio, and they come out sounding like 33. It's just like rock music: all glitter, out of tune and full of no-talents."

These harsh comments started a debate that he hadn't reckoned with. Country lovers hit the roof, though in most of the interviews afterwards, he stood his ground, saying that the reason that music existed at all was because "people do whatever they can when they get hungry." Nashville was in an uproar, venues where the band was headed were getting bomb threats, and the press was against him everywhere he went. The common view was, "If Buddy Rich is so good, then why is he playing here?" The president of the Country Music Association, Jerry Bradley, stated, "When is Rich leaving town, and who invited him here in the first place? There are lot of four-year-olds with money that are buying country music, a lot more than jazz. My second love in music is jazz and my personal tastes have never included Buddy Rich."[6] Rich countered by saying, "If disc jockeys played more good music we would have more jazz hits. How can you know about jazz if it is never played? But sure, there is good country and western. Ray Charles plays in a league of his own. I used to think 'I Can't Stop Loving You' was an awful song until I heard Ray do it, or Count Basie. Good performers can deliver poor material, and vice versa." All of Buddy's comments made it to the national press, and though it would never damage his career—he would play in the southern parts of the country several times during the coming years—he continued to be associated with his infamous comments.

Stanley Kay and Buddy found a new location for Buddy's Place. Marty's Bum Steer, located on West 33rd Street, was owned by Martin Ross, a jazz-loving man who was willing to renovate his venue into Buddy's Place II. The club was twice as big as the previous Buddy's Place, and it was located right across from Madison Square Garden, with a capacity of nearly 400. Buddy decided once again to put his name out front, and for the opening put together a big band called Buddy Rich and the Big Band Machine. The club opened April 28, 1975, and, like the first grand opening, celebrities populated the room. Attendees included Willard Alexander, Mel Tormé, Ella Fitzgerald, Woody Herman, Stan Kenton, Benny Goodman, and Count Basie. Buddy Rich beamed with pleasure. About half an hour before the first show, his whole family arrived: father Robert with his new wife Louise, sisters Marge and Jo, brother Mickey and, of course, Marie and Cathy.

Buddy was excited that evening, and worked the room with high-strung pleasure. Singers Carmen McRae and comic Nipsey Russell were guests in the band. At this "new" Buddy's Place, the band dressed more casually, usually attired in fashionable sweaters. Granted, it was the fashion at the time, but what was more obvious than the band's garb was that they hadn't rehearsed enough. It sounded loose, and the hipper audience members noticed, since this wasn't what they were used to seeing or hearing from Buddy Rich's band. Nonetheless, the evening was a success, even if the reviews were more about the club than the music. Generally, the press was saying that Buddy's Place was "the place to go," gushing that Martin Ross had remodeled the place into a "Roman Coliseum," featuring a specially built loudspeaker system in connecting rooms that could be adapted to what was happening on stage and/or to make conversation easier. The prospects of the new Buddy's Place were generally excellent.

On May 23, saxophonist Steve Marcus, a young New Yorker and Berklee College of Music graduate, joined the band. Unlike other Berklee students, he had played with several well-known orchestras, including those of Stan Kenton and Woody Herman. Marcus became the group's foremost soloist, and would stay with the band until Buddy's death. After some time in the orchestra, Marcus had a clear picture of the band and his place in it, saying, "This band is a better milieu for a jazz musician. Buddy brings out the best in every musician, and it feels as though I do my best work here. He is so devoted to himself and his music. I have enormous respect for him."[7] Buddy Rich felt the same admiration for his young saxophonist, commenting, "Old Mr. Marcus is going to stay in my band until I understand what he is playing!"[8] The same spring the band recorded *Big Band Machine*, their second album for Groove Merchant. Buddy was already dissatisfied. "It was the same old story," a disappointed Buddy explained. "Poor promotion after being assured that it would be done properly. I'm fed up with record companies; I don't need that kind of aggravation. If or when we ever do sign with someone again, there'll have to be some definite guarantees."[9]

One of the bands booked to perform at the new Buddy's Place was Count Basie's. When the band settled in, Buddy visited his old friend in his dressing room, and a sensitive subject came up. Author John Minahan was privy to the conversation. Basie said, "I hear you're going to South Africa?" "Signed for a week in Johannesburg, starting August 4th, then a week in Cape Town and Durban," Buddy explained to Basie. "The whole band?" Basie inquired. "Oh, yeah," responded Buddy. "You got a black bass player. What's his name?" Basie asked. "Ben Brown. 21 years old. Dynamite," said Buddy. Basie lit his cigar slowly, turning it, smoke obscuring his face, then said, "South African government has to issue him a work permit." "No problem," answered Buddy. "They gave him a work permit?" asked Basie. "Not yet. Promoter says it's no problem," said Buddy. Basie inspected his cigar, turned it in his fingers, and then explained, "They'll give him a tourist visa, but you might have trouble on a work permit." After a brief silence, Buddy sat forward stiffly, shoulders hunched, and said, "If Brown doesn't work, nobody works. We made that as clear as you can make it, right from the beginning. I'll cancel the whole tour. I'll tell them to stick their tour up their ass. Nobody tells me who I can have in my band, here or there. Nobody tells me that." Basie glanced at him, smiled, saying, "You sure haven't changed any." "I'll never change on that issue. Not after all these years. You know that. The musicians come first, then the audience, then, maybe, the government— if there's anything left."[10]

On July 8, 1975, Buddy's booking agency told him that the South African government wouldn't give Brown anything more than a tourist visa. He was allowed to come along and listen, but not permitted to play with the band. Buddy Rich was told that he had to take along a white bassist. He was furious. In South Africa, the local promoter, Don Hughes, tried to placate the authorities without success. He issued a statement in the *Ottawa Citizen* on July 14 that read, "I have sent a second written plea for them to allow a black musician to perform, and I have been promised an answer within 48 hours. I have notified Mr. Rich of this by telephone, and he has answered that he will cancel the whole tour if they don't allow Brown to be part of it."[11] After another three days of angry phone calls back and forth, Buddy held a press conference on July 17 at Buddy's Place, where he said, "They said they would issue Ben Brown a tourist visa. They thought it would be good if I brought a white bass player and Ben, my bass player, could be a guest of the country. That was totally unacceptable to me. I don't want anybody telling me who I can have in my band here or there. I couldn't see myself changing that policy after all these years."[12]

Buddy cancelled the South African tour, and the news made headlines worldwide. The situation became extremely embarrassing for the South African government. The story emerged just as they were making attempts to show the world that they had changed with regards apartheid policy. Now, the government was exposed in headlines blaring that a black musician wasn't allowed to play in the country. They tried to blame the whole thing on Don Hughes, saying he didn't file the necessary papers properly, but nobody believed that explanation, least of all the South African press. The *Washington Afro-American Red Star* newspaper wrote, "We congratulate Buddy Rich, who, upon being notified of this, became 'outraged' and 'insane with anger' and cancelled the whole tour. It should be noted that the contract for Rich and his band to tour South Africa for three weeks had already been signed, and advance ticket sales had already reached $30,000. Thus, as Rich says, 'politics and stupidity won out over culture.'"[13] The following days, representatives for the government were invited to debate on the issue, but they refused. Things got even more out of hand afterwards, when the press tried to take advantage of Rich's stance to make a change.

In September of the same year, the monthly publication *Southern Africa* reported, "Jazz musician Buddy Rich recently announced cancellation of his planned tour of the white-ruled nation, because his black bass player was denied a visa. Observers believe the South African refusal was based on their opposition to racially mixed performances. An all-black American singing group, the Supremes, is expected to get visas for their upcoming tour without difficulty."[14] *Negro Digest* magazine, renamed *Black World* in 1970, was tougher on the issue and thought more should follow Buddy Rich's example. *Black World* wrote, "Last report says that the black singing group the Supremes had arranged to go there towards year's end, just as tennis pro Arthur Ashe, actress Eartha Kitt and singer Lovelace Watkins had done before them. Why are black entertainers so much less concerned about giving aid and comfort to the world's most racist regime than are some conscientious white entertainers?"[15] Cathy Rich summed up her father's actions afterward by saying, "He was campaigning against apartheid long before it became a cause célèbre. The money never mattered to him. It was always about staying true to your beliefs."[16]

Stanley Kay had a dream. He had always thought that there were no limits to what Buddy Rich could do; he'd been fascinated by him ever since he was a teenager. Kay approached Columbia Artists, a booking agency that had long specialized in handling the world's most renowned artists in classical music, and suggested to artists' representative Dennis Letzler that Buddy Rich should be given the opportunity to perform with a symphony orchestra. He said to Letzler, "He's like Toscanini! He would have no trouble with it! He can play 'West Side Story' as easy as anything, and then he can play a drum solo after the 'America' part." Letzler was sold on the idea and contacted Tommy Newsome, a superb orchestrator who also sat in the saxophone section of "The Tonight Show" orchestra, to write a special arrangement for it.

All Kay had to do was convince Buddy. Kay knew very well about Rich's aversion to symphony musicians. One of Buddy's typical arguments was that "to have everything written for you, it's not really creating. That's why I think symphony drummers are so limited. They're limited to exactly what was played a hundred years before them by a thousand other drummers. And, you know, I think the original recording of Ravel's *Bolero*, probably whoever played percussion on that will never have it played better. So, what do they do? They're simply following what was laid down in front and they play the same thing. So there's no great challenge in being a classical drummer."[17] Kay suspected that perhaps Buddy felt a little inferior to classical players, even if he never actually said so. But he had no doubts whatsoever that Buddy could play with a symphony orchestra. After carefully proposing what he had in mind, to his surprise, Buddy went along with it.

Newsome chart in hand, Kay got trumpeter Ross Konikoff, pianist Larry Novak, and bassist Ben Brown to prepare for Buddy Rich's first concert with a symphony orchestra. The performance, with the Milwaukee Symphony Orchestra, was held in Uhlein Hall on January 10, 1976. It was an unbelievable success, with Buddy receiving four standing ovations. Buddy was deeply moved by the experience, saying, "The score was totally different than the jazz arrangement that we play with the band, written for 105 musicians. To go in and play that for the first time was so thrilling that I almost lost control of what I was doing."[18] Ultimately, Buddy would play a total of 25 concerts with different symphony orchestras through 1986, including performances with the Milwaukee, Syracuse, Indianapolis, Halifax, Louisville, Tulsa, Cincinnati, Dallas, Little Rock, Long Beach, Detroit, Salt Lake City and Rochester Symphony Orchestras; the Royal Philharmonic Orchestra of London; and the Boston Pops.

During the coming years, an arrangement of "Strike up the Band" was added to the repertoire, and as time went on, Buddy learned to relax and enjoy this totally different way of playing. He was, ultimately, very positive about the whole experience, and told Larry King on the "Larry King Live" television show, "It's a completely different feeling all together. You are surrounded by horns, cellos and violins, bassoons and all the beautiful instruments. I got a kick out of it."[19] Cathy Rich confirmed that the admiration was mutual from the symphony orchestras. As Cathy recalled, "I remember one time at a symphony concert. After Dad finished, the conductor came off, and he was crying and said, 'I have seen Heifetz play. He is the greatest that will ever be at what he does. You are Heifetz on drums. I have never seen anything like this.' My father began crying. Everyone was crying."

Buddy's Place II closed its doors on January 3, 1976. The truth was that the audiences left the club, and it's difficult to figure out exactly why. It could hardly have been due to the entertainment, as Buddy's Place booked the finest performers. The food and drinks were superior, and reasonably priced. On the other hand, maybe Buddy Rich himself was the problem. Being the club's public figure wasn't really his bag, and when faced with the closing, he just shrugged his shoulders and said, "I just didn't have that kind of personality, mixing socially with customers just wasn't me."[20] This made a lot of sense. Every time anyone disturbed the musicians on stage, he was there, pointing finger at a noisy table as he toweled his face between numbers, shouting, "Hey you! This isn't the Metropole! Would you act like that if this was Segovia playing at Carnegie Hall? When I go to hear somebody, I don't want some broad screaming in my ear."[21] Martin Ross spoke out in the papers two days prior to the closing. "The people didn't care," Ross said to the press. "New Yorkers are interested in going out on weekends, but they don't care where. We were filled up half the weekends we were open. One night I asked the band to go out in the audience and fill things out. There were 14 people in the audience and 19 in the band!"[22]

There were musical problems during this period as well. The October preceding the club's demise, there was dissatisfaction among the band members about wages and long road trips, resulting in several members deciding to leave. Buddy and Stanley Kay reconstructed the Big Band Machine with a nearly completely new lineup. Steve Marcus was the only holdover from the old unit. Buddy was in even bigger need of a new record company. Since his refusal to extend with Groove Merchant, there had been an even greater shift in the music market. Disco had taken over, and a good deal of recorded music was being produced specifically for the dance market, which was substantial. What Buddy Rich thought about this hardly bears mentioning. Stanley Kay had good relations with a producer named Ken Glancy at RCA. Having released three Buddy Rich albums in years past, RCA was now offering him a new deal, which resulted in an effort called *Speak No Evil*, recorded February 25 and geared to the dancing public. Buddy would always regard it as the worst record he ever made, but he still played a couple of tracks from the record at his concerts, which would give daughter Cathy and Stan Getz's daughter, Beverly, the chance to sing some dance material with the band.

The reconstructed Buddy Rich Big Band, with Steve Marcus in tow, hit the road once more, and everything seemed back to normal. The band backed up Mel Tormé in May, and in June, Buddy was a guest on Carson's "Tonight Show." Then Buddy began to experience stomach pains. When the gang arrived in Wildwood, New Jersey at the beginning of August, he had such severe abdominal pain that he had to be taken to the hospital. Doctors found that he had acute kidney stones, and had to have an operation. The evening's performance had to be cancelled, but two days later, he was back on his drum stool. Resting just wasn't on his agenda. He was always on back the road as soon as it was possible— regardless of doctor's orders—and not long after the kidney operation, he reappeared on "The Mike Douglas Show" and "The Tonight Show," and performed at university after university.

On November 12, 1976, Robert Rich died in his bed in Brooklyn, New York, with his wife Louise by his side. Buddy Rich took his father's death very hard, said his sister Marge. "Despite everything that had gone on when he was a kid," Marge said, "the whippings and such, Brother loved Dad, and he kept telling himself that he could have done more for him, that he could have kept him alive longer somehow. Pop's passing hurt my brother for a long time."[23] Buddy really loved his father, but he seldom wanted to talk about his childhood, examine the past, or explore whether or not his father had been too hard on him when he was a little boy. Perhaps he was, but at the same time, it couldn't have been easy for Robert Rich. He knew he had an unusually talented boy and had to constantly find a balance between a traditional education for his son versus developing Buddy's obvious genius as a musician. Robert was also constantly aware that if anything were to happen to young Buddy, the family's source of income would disappear. For example, getting into a fight with other children could mean catastrophe. Every time Johnny

Carson, or anyone else Buddy trusted, tried to ask serious questions on the subject of his youth, he waved them off with comments like, "It feels like another world," or "It feels like we are talking about another person." Buddy hated the fact that the public knew he had been playing the drums since he was two, and was completely uninterested in discussing Traps the Drum Wonder.

On December 31, 1976, Buddy was back in the studio again, and as always, there were a lot of new faces, from Berklee and elsewhere, in the crew. Among the more prominent new members were pianist Barry Kiener, who Buddy would grow to like very much; trumpeter Dave Stahl; and tenor saxophonist Bob Mintzer, who would write several challenging arrangements for Buddy in the coming months. The new band was called Buddy Rich and the Killer Force. "Trumpeter Waymon Reed had to leave the band because of a prior commitment," remembered Dave Stahl. "He had work with Sarah Vaughn. Buddy didn't want to fill his chair immediately, so with Ross (Konikoff), Dean (Pratt) and myself, we carried the section. Buddy was so impressed with the powerful sound the three of us got that he started calling us his Killer Force. Somehow the name stuck for this period of the band."[24] The new RCA LP was called *Buddy Rich Plays and Plays and Plays*. The sound on the album was astounding; this was a modern band playing contemporary charts with a fresh sound.

A new European tour started on March 1, 1977, in Warsaw, Poland, followed by dates in West Germany, Denmark, Norway, Sweden and Finland. Cathy Rich accompanied the band on the entire tour together with singer Beverly Getz. Those who were a part of the tour offered some insight as to how life was on the road for Buddy Rich and his band. One of the first stops was Cologne on March 3. Bo Johnson, the production manager for Europe, frankly noted, "It could have ended in disaster. The tour bus with all the equipment was to be transported by a Polish driver down to Cologne, but the bus never came. Everyone was standing there waiting and waiting with growing irritation. Finally it arrived, and the reason for the delay was that the driver and one of his friends had been drinking vodka! Both of them had to have their stomachs pumped and were seriously ill!"[25]

A week later the band performed in the Swedish city of Borås, where they were reviewed by writer Lennart Blomberg. "A large part of the praise must go to Rich himself," Blomberg reported, "who I thought played more tastefully and with more feeling than earlier. He has always been technically driven, but at times the technique has dominated at the cost of the music. Remember the Jazz at the Philharmonic circus? Now he seems to have dampened the thrust significantly and plays more musically. In a duet with the brilliant pianist, Barry Kiener, he shows what can be done with only brushes; what playful elegance!"[26]

On March 18, the band performed in Helsinki, Finland, and on March 28, they were in the little Swedish city of Växjö. The venue was a school auditorium seating about 300 persons, and there Buddy's bad back acted up again. Johnson recalled that Buddy had to be helped to the drums, even for the soundcheck. It was a bit shaky at the start, but when he finally got settled, Buddy played as though there was nothing wrong. What he reacted to, on the other hand, was a man down at the mixer table with a little tape recorder. Buddy went straight down to him and said, "What are you doing? You can't record me without permission." "Excuse me, Mr. Rich, I am the piano tuner," the man explained to Buddy. "I am blind. I'm only going to have this for my own use." "Okay, that's alright then," Buddy said. Remembering this episode, Johnson said, "Buddy was upset, but he calmed down. I liked Buddy a lot. You could see that he made an effort to be the macho man he had a reputation of being. He fed his image, but was very fair. If there was something written in the contract, he wanted it. If it wasn't there, he didn't demand it. We organized a Porsche for him, for instance. If we hadn't, he would have made a fuss. But I liked him very much, I must say."[27]

After the gig there were the usual slightly depressed comments from the drummers in the audience who talked about selling their drums because they could never come close to what they had just seen and heard. Many of them sighed and couldn't believe their eyes. Cathy Rich said, "I heard this many times over the years; that many drummers wanted to burn their drum sets after they had heard Buddy play. But I can honestly say that every time my Dad heard that he was saddened. He wanted to be an inspiration to people, not the opposite."[28]

In the summer of 1977, the band went on a week-long tour of Japan, once again booked to play many colleges. Unfortunately, the band was poorly paid, but the audiences were extremely interested and listening carefully. Buddy loved this, but he couldn't keep quiet about the jazz critics who were writing negative things. Most of the time he didn't pay any attention to them, but sometimes he blew up—and it didn't matter if he knew the writer. If the person wrote something he thought was wrong, he reacted. At that time, he was very irritated with what the highly reputable, veteran critic Leonard Feather was writing. "Critics talk a lot of bullshit," Buddy commented about Feather. "Leonard Feather knows as much about jazz as I do about Polish. I never listen to critics. Nobody knows better than me what I am doing. If someone thinks I haven't played right, they can come up on stage and show the contrary. But it hasn't happened yet."

Feather, a person who was very knowledgeable about both composing and writing on music in general, and jazz in particular, gave Buddy a biting and lengthy published reply. "I have a few things to say to Buddy Rich," Feather started his diatribe. "His insults are insignificant when you consider the source. Rich is a great drummer and musician, but musically illiterate. I have forgotten more about music than what Rich will ever learn. I have written over 350 compositions, many recorded by some of the greatest artists in jazz history. If I let Buddy listen to some of those recordings without telling him who had written the music, I am quite sure that he would be impressed, but if I told him beforehand he would have such a preconceived notion that he wouldn't be able to accept the fact. Unfortunately, I am not as talented a practicing musician as he is, but I do have a lot of practical experience as a composer, arranger, lyricist and writer. So it depends what you compare with. Buddy Rich has never composed a line in his life. That is hardly remarkable if you know that Buddy Rich—despite all his years with Artie Shaw, Tommy Dorsey and his own big band—can't read music, isn't it? I have always known that. But what is even more important is that Rich, despite his musical ignorance, talks like this about nearly everyone else. He has a very short temper, he likes starting arguments and putting people down. But as soon as we meet he is always very friendly and he has never said these things to me personally. So, I would like to say to Buddy Rich: Sit down at a piano and write a melody that has some of the melodic qualities found in my compositions, but I know damned well you can't do it! And that's the truth!"[29]

Buddy Rich never replied, and in retrospect, Leonard Feather became to be regarded in some professional jazz circles as a self-serving blowhard. The reality was that Buddy could have cared less; he had just turned 60, and recorded three new albums. The first was with his own band, *Class of '78*, highlighted by Joe Zawinul's famous classic, "Birdland," which would become a staple in the Rich book. The second was an album that should have been recorded much earlier in his career: an album with Mel Tormé. This effort was a clear example of two world stars who were close friends for decades—actually so close that they never thought of working together. The situation bore resemblance to Buddy's relationship with Sinatra: although friends, they had never made a studio record outside of the Dorsey band. In the case of Buddy and Tormé, they'd appeared together as guests on television shows through the years singing each other's praises, yet neither of them had said, "Let's make a record together!"

In this case, it wasn't Buddy's fault. For all the times Buddy sat on the same talk show and said that he thought that Mel was the world's most underrated star, Tormé just laughed it off, no doubt slightly embarrassed. But it was clear that Mel's own admiration for Buddy held *him* back. Never was it the opposite—that Buddy would be jealous of Mel's tremendous musicality and singing voice. Whatever the personal dynamics, the album became reality on January 25, 1978, when Buddy and Mel recorded the fittingly-titled *Together Again for the First Time*. The text on the record jacket told of two close friends who knew how to rub each other the right way in love-hate fashion. Mel wrote about Buddy, "When Norman Schwarz suggested that I should record an album with Buddy Rich, I answered, 'What? Is he still alive?'" Buddy wrote about Mel, "You've got to give the man credit when you think that they had to do a tracheotomy on Mel to get anything out of him at all. The man doesn't realize that he has been dead since 1942!"

The third record release of this period saw Buddy as a guest of Lionel Hampton, who recorded this effort (among many others) on his own label. Featuring Steve Marcus on tenor and soprano sax, Gary Pribeck and Paul Moen on tenor saxes, Candido Camero on congas, Barry Kiener on piano, Tom Warrington on bass and Jon Hendricks on vocals, the resulting LP was called *Lionel Hampton Presents Buddy Rich*. All of Buddy's sessions with Hampton through the years are prime examples of irresistible, exciting, spontaneous live recordings. Hampton was a master of such things, and on the tracks themselves, you can hear his loud sighing when he gets carried away by the music.

Buddy Rich, in his own unique way, was a master of showmanship. He knew that a good band, good songs, good musicians, and good recordings were not enough, and was well aware that his talents as a tart-tongued, sometimes controversial interviewee kept the band going. He noticed that every time he said something controversial to a newspaper or on a TV show, there was more interest in booking his band. Therefore, he agreed to be interviewed often. On May 2, during an engagement at Jed's Place near Los Angeles, he spoke with reporter Alan Citron, later to become a *Los Angeles Times* staff writer. Before the performance, someone a radio station had said that Buddy Rich was "nothing but a sharp tongue." Rich opened up to Citron about the matter. "I was very upset," he told Citron in his rapid-fire style, "and if I see that man again I'll knock him on his head." Buddy admitted to the writer that his tongue may occasionally spew a bit of acid, but he said that he felt the DJ was trying to put him down. "I would characterize myself as honest," he explained to Citron, "but people are constantly misconstruing that emotion for arrogance." Buddy went on to say that he doesn't believe an artist's personality is any measure of his talent, and believes that the major key, more than ever, is how a musician is promoted.

Buddy continued, "In the 1960s, I saw a big change in the selling end of the business. It took a giant step backwards. Dignity went out the window. From Kiss to Miss, it's all commercialism. Our values are so insane lately. Who cares who Bianca Jagger is sleeping with? I don't. I don't even want to sleep with her." Alan Citron walked away from the interview believing that, as he wrote, "Buddy refuses to align himself with whatever renaissance may be taking place. If nothing else, it seems to make him all the more determined to remain a loner." Indeed, at the end of the interview, Buddy told Cintron, "I'm an alien," he claimed with a hint of bitterness in his gravelly voice. "I'm a part of a jazz world that died—a world that's no longer here. All of the good people have left."

In the summer of 1978, there was another tour of Europe, this time on the growing festival circuit. After a repeat performance at the Newport Jazz Festival, the band played at the Nice Jazz Festival in France, the North Sea Jazz Festival in Holland, the Montreux Jazz Festival in Switzerland, the Umbria Jazz Festival in Italy, the Royal Jazz Festival in England, and made yet another visit to Ronnie Scott's in London. Buddy also visited Sweden again. The Kristianstad Jazz Festival booked him for August 1, and promoter Lars Jernryd remembered in detail the uproar before the gig. "Buddy Rich had asked to be driven by limousine from his hotel in Copenhagen, Denmark," Jernryd recalled. "The band was going to travel by ordinary bus. One of the festival board members actually owned a limo, but when they were going to leave in the morning, it wouldn't start. The stopgap solution was an old Opel Kadett. When Buddy caught sight of the car, he went crazy. He was absolutely furious, and yelled and screamed all the way to the festival. To top it all off, the band's bus wouldn't start, either. The musicians had to push it to get it going. You can guess how ashamed we were.

"When Buddy got to the venue, he saw the recording bus from the Swedish broadcasting company. Then he became even angrier, if possible. I called his agent to ask how we could solve the problem and got the answer: 'Give Buddy a thousand dollars and there are no problems,' he told us. We did as he said, and the star calmed down. But it was a treacherous calmness. Buddy Rich wanted a special pizza of a kind that hadn't yet become as popular in Sweden as it is today. A woman from the organizing committee had to search the whole city looking for it. Finally she found something like what Rich had asked for, but when she gave him the pizza he threw it at the wall behind her. He shouldn't have done that. The woman became just as angry as he was, took him by the collar and shouted. "Who do you think you are, anyway? What the hell are you doing?" Buddy finally calmed down and carried out the concert as planned. I sat beside him on stage, and I couldn't believe my eyes. During his solo, I wept; I have never seen anything like it."[30]

★

In October, 1945, the 16-year-old Ed Shaughnessy managed to get into the Paramount Theater in New York. He was then a young drummer playing with greats like Bud Powell and Jack Teagarden on 52nd Street, and everything should have been tip top—but he had a problem. He was broke, and didn't even have the cash to buy a new pair of drumsticks. This became a fond memory for Shaughnessy, who remembered, "I told a friend about my predicament. He said, 'Walk over and see Buddy Rich. He's with the Dorsey band at the Paramount Theater. Say hello to Buddy for me. I'm an old friend of his.' I went over to the stage door and asked for him. He invited me up and I told him my story. I said, 'I am embarrassed by this, but your man told me to say hello. He thought you might be able to loan me a couple of sticks.' Buddy smiled and answered, 'Hey man, are you kidding? We've all been there.' He called the band boy. The guy came down and there were something like two dozen pair of drumsticks in the package. Buddy said, 'This will cool you for a while.' I will never forget it."[31]

Five years later, in May, 1950, Shaughnessy met Buddy Rich again, at Birdland in New York. He was then playing with the vibraphonist Terry Gibbs, whom Buddy knew very well, and on a break he went up to Buddy's table. It didn't go very well. Buddy Rich was there with his PR agent and just wanted to take it easy for an evening. The unsuspecting Shaughnessy asked Buddy what he thought of the music being played, and Buddy let him have it. He said that he honestly thought the compositions weren't very good. Shaughnessy asked Buddy, "Why are you here on your night off, if it's such worthless music?" The PR agent replied, "You can't talk to Buddy Rich like that!" Buddy told the agent to take a walk. Shaughnessy said to Buddy, "We may have to have bad feelings about this. I don't really care, because I can always buy your records." Buddy went into a fit of laughter and started banging the table. He loved it and said, "Kid, I think you and I are going to get along real good."

They did get along. Twenty-eight years later, on August 11, 1978, there was more on the line for Ed. Buddy Rich had been booked on "The Tonight Show," and Johnny Carson wanted to see Rich and Shaughnessy battle it out. The last "Tonight Show" drum duel had been with Louie Bellson, but Carson wanted to see what Shaughnessy could do against Buddy. Ed knew very well what he had to do, given that he, like so many other drummers, had followed Buddy through the years. In an interview he once commented that "you have to be a hell of a drummer yourself to appreciate Buddy Rich fully; not so much what he does, but how he does it. There's a great big heart inside that small body, and it comes through; a lot of soul there. The man is a giant for spirit."[32]

Now Ed Shaughnessy was sitting on a soundstage on live television in front of all the American people—and on his left side sat Buddy Rich, the man who could outplay any drummer. Before they went on, Ed said to Buddy, "Now don't do that left hand over-and-under on the floor tom and wipe me out!" Buddy replied, "Okay, but don't you do that East Indian stuff on me!" The number began, and both played their solos in turn. Ed thought he got eight really decent bars, but then Buddy did the funny "under-the-arm kettle drum thing" that he had promised not to do. Afterwards, Ed confronted him and asked, "What happened to our deal?" Buddy's answer was only, "Sorry, I got carried away."[33] They both laughed, and for Ed Shaughnessy, the performance became the high point of his musical life, as he wrote later in his autobiography.

A month later, Buddy Rich was to have his own career high point. On October 5, he was invited to the Berklee College of Music where he, Dizzy Gillespie, and Phil Woods received their honorary doctorate degrees in appreciation of their creativity in jazz. Buddy was filled with pride, and later said, "This was the high point of my life. I was very moved. Tears came. It was very difficult for me to be up there on the stage."[34] After the ceremony, he performed "Mercy, Mercy" with a Berklee student ensemble, and for the first time, he felt it was hard to play due to the gravity of the situation. Eleven days later yet another England tour began, which included the now-regular stops at Ronnie Scott's and Mike Parkinson's TV show. While there, Sammy Davis Jr. dropped by. It was a pleasant surprise. Buddy was always glad to see him; he felt an affinity with Sammy, as both had grown up on stage and knew what it meant to sacrifice a "normal life" in order to have a successful entertainment career. Since they were both in England and wanted to perform together, they decided to book a short tour, and a press conference in London was held to announce it. Though the public longed to see Sammy Davis and Buddy Rich on stage together, the dates never happened. This was likely for several reasons, including issues about billing and fees (though lifelong friends, Sammy and Buddy had enormous egos, and both were constantly cash poor), availability of both the stars and the venues, time constraints per necessary rehearsal time, and possibly because Buddy and Sammy overestimated their drawing power. Generally, the two entertainment giants were simply creatures of impulse and may have just not thought the whole thing out. Buddy continued on with his band (sans Sammy) to Sweden, to perform at the Concert House in Stockholm.

From January through April of 1979, Buddy Rich and the Killer Force Band were busy playing one-nighters across the U.S. and Canada, performing at theaters, clubs, concert houses and high schools. In May, the band returned to England for three more weeks, followed by a summer tour in the states. On August 6, 1979, Peter Lundin, the Swedish artist manager, stood waiting at London's Heathrow airport for Buddy, who was arriving from New York. The reason for his visit was that he had been booked to perform as guest with a Swedish big band at Gröna Lund, an amusement park in Stockholm. Peter Lundin recounted, "When Buddy finally arrived, I was slightly surprised. He had no baggage with him, only a briefcase with his arrangements—nothing else. We went and had dinner, but I felt he was keeping his distance. Suddenly he asked who was playing at Ronnie Scott's that evening. I checked the paper and saw that Dizzy Gillespie was playing, and right away Buddy wanted to go there."[35] We arrived after Dizzy had started playing, so on the break, Buddy went to visit Dizzy in his dressing room." The old friends caught up and laughed, improving Buddy's mood.

The next day the band flew to Stockholm for rehearsal with the Swedish musicians, which was to take place at Studio 4 in the Swedish National Broadcast Center. One of the musicians in the band was saxophonist Uffe Andersson, who remembered, "Buddy arrived with notes that you could hardly read. We had to sit and work it all out. After we had rehearsed with him, we decided to rehearse just the brass section for an extra day. The notes were extremely difficult and the pieces were very fast."[36] Friday's concert, on August 9, was jam-packed, and for the occasion, Buddy brought along two of his favorite guest soloists: Harry "Sweets" Edison and Eddie "Lockjaw" Davis. Buddy enjoyed himself, as did everyone on stage. When Peter Lundin was driving Buddy to the airport, Buddy told him, "I've got a cassette from the gig yesterday. Do you know what I'm going to do with it?" "No", answered Peter. "I'm going to take it to New York and play it for the boys in my band, and then I'm going to say, this is how my music should be played!"[37]

A few months later, Buddy appeared on "The Merv Griffin Show." This particular appearance became special to him, in that his great idol from his youth, Benny Goodman, was booked on the same program. For Buddy, it was a touching reunion. He described how he didn't really know what he was doing during the recording of "Rattle and Roll" in 1945. Benny sat beside him and smiled slightly, but didn't seem very amused. Buddy tried to lighten things up, musing, "When I played with Artie Shaw in 1939, Benny was my big idol." Buddy was doing his best to warm up to Goodman, but Goodman was a peculiar type of person. He never hung around with the musicians in his band, and if he should happen to eat dinner with them, he called everyone "Pops," because he couldn't remember their names. In one interview, he couldn't even remember that he'd played with Harry James. As he sat beside Buddy, many (including Griffin) expected that he would return Buddy's friendliness. Instead, Goodman said, "When Krupa left my band, Buddy wasn't my favorite drummer." Buddy looked at him, surprised, but quickly recovered, retorting, "And I still haven't gotten paid!"

In March, 1980, Buddy was once again back at Ronnie Scott's in London. While there, Buddy Rich and His Orchestra (the "Killer Force" moniker had been dropped) recorded a new album called *The Man from Planet Jazz*. In August that year, Traps the Drum Wonder would make a return appearance.

I was eleven years old when my seventh grade music teacher took me to see Buddy Rich and his Killer Force orchestra at the Forum in Binghamton, New York. It was the mid-'70s and I had just started playing drum set. I knew next to nothing about drummers from any genre of music and definitely nothing about jazz.

I remember this experience like it was yesterday: Buddy's band entered the stage before him, they were dressed in tuxedos. Buddy followed, wearing a black tee-shirt and black pants. Within one second of the band hitting the first downbeat I had an adrenalin rush more powerful than anything I can remember, I was awash in goose bumps and all the hair on my arms and neck stood on end; I'm sure my jaw hit the floor too. I had never heard anything like this in my life: powerful, exciting, dynamic, passionate, thrilling, creative, energized, burning and spectacular are some of the words (although inadequate) I would use to describe my perception of the music, Buddy, the band and the drums!

I had never heard jazz, let alone one of the world's greatest virtuosos, leading one of the most renowned big bands in history. The performance changed my life, or at a minimum immediately helped me find and focus my passion. When I got home I announced to my mother something like: "I just heard jazz and an amazing drummer named Buddy Rich. I'm not sure what he was doing, but that's what I want to do." So I did!

Buddy is the reason I play the drums. I was privileged to see him many times and was endlessly inspired; I still am.

Sherrie Maricle

CHAPTER 18

Life at Stake

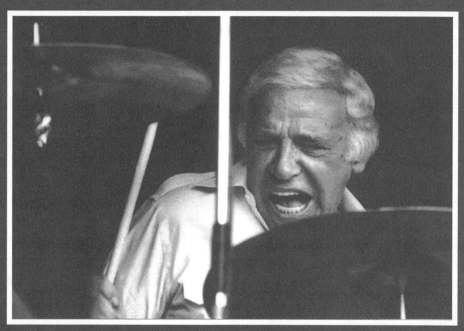

Buddy in Kalmar, Sweden (the author's hometown), 1984 .

In August 1980, Buddy received an offer from Jim Henson to appear on the "The Muppet Show" alongside Kermit the Frog, Miss Piggy and all the other Muppet characters who had become major figures in the TV world. The tapings would take place over a five-day period at ATV Studios in Birmingham, UK, where Henson's outfit was producing the programs. At first, Buddy hesitated to accept the offer. Cathy Rich convinced her father otherwise. "I was the one who convinced him to do it," Cathy said. "We got the script and the idea was, of course, that he was supposed to read it and learn it, but after a few days I never saw him touch it. The evening before the taping began I asked, 'Do you want to read through the script once together?' 'Good idea!' he shouted back."[1]

On the program, Buddy did a number reminiscent of the young Traps in the 1930 film *Sound Effects*. The television routine was similar to the Vitaphone routine, where he played on everything within reach, including chairs, tables, bottles, candlesticks, picture frames, stair railings, and a few Muppet heads (at one point quipping, "When I play at theater, I *play* the theater!"). He had some difficulty with his lines, largely because he didn't want to use his glasses, but he managed to get through everything. "I ad-libbed a lot of it," Buddy remembered. "I thought it turned out well, but being around those dummies was weird, man—enough to test your sanity, because after a while you start talking with and treating them as if they were human."[2]

Buddy sang a duet with Miss Piggy, "It's Not Easy Bein' Green." David Lucas, percussionist on the Asian tour, said, "Buddy really loved that song. The simple reason was he could relate the song to his own life. It was like singing 'It's Not Easy Being Me.'"[3] Buddy then played his unforgettable drum battle with the Muppet character Animal. The scene, which featured Ted Heath drummer Ronnie Verell performing Animal's parts, has become one of the most popular and memorable clips of Buddy. Buddy was deeply impressed by Verell and the entire Muppet program. "I felt like a Muppet myself," Buddy said of the show. "I was a like a kid playing with those guys, because that's how they made me feel. Singing the song was a knockout to me, and the silly karate thing with Miss Piggy was beautiful, I thought. The playing on the walls, chairs, and everything was a great idea of theirs. Then of course, the battle ending with Animal: to play opposite Ronnie Verell, one of my all time favorite drummers along with Kenny Clare, was a total gas to me. That week will go down as one of the most positive weeks in my career. I loved it and I thank them."[4]

In the beginning of October, 1980, Buddy performed a number of concerts together with his friend Mel Tormé. In spite of a recurrence of back problems and excruciating pain, he dragged himself to the drums every evening. The knowledge that there was an audience out there, some of whom who had perhaps travelled a very long way to see him, always gave him the keenest sense of responsibility; he couldn't cancel. He struggled through the tour as Tormé, who knew about Buddy's pain, became more and more concerned.

On October 15, the band recorded another album, simply called *The Buddy Rich Band* and released by MCA. As with many previous recordings, Buddy wasn't satisfied with the result. In fact, he hated it, and was very public about it. Pulling no punches, he said, "It's the worst thing that you could possibly listen to. I mean, it should be banned. It should be illegal. The recording is terrible, the band was terrible, the playing was bad, there were mistakes that the engineering let pass. I was away at the time the thing was released, or it never would have been released. What I have done in the past eight months that the album's been out is that every night, at every concert, I tell the audience that our new album is not to be believed, it's terrible, and please don't buy it. I'm saving myself the embarrassment of having people listen to it, and I'm also saving them the money that they would pay for a record that is not worth the price."[5] He said the same thing when he was a guest on "The Dick Cavett Show" later that year. What the people at MCA may have thought of these outbursts is anyone's guess.

On October 28, Buddy made a triumphant appearance on "The Tonight Show." After a breathtaking solo, he sat down on the guest sofa, let out a deep breath, and grimaced. "What have you done now?" Carson asked. "I've broken a toe," answered Buddy. "Fell in the pool yesterday." That, however, wasn't the truth. According to trumpeter Dave Stahl, "We played a gig near New York City. Buddy made his entrance at that rehearsal and immediately freaked out about the drums that were there for him. They had plastic heads and he was pissed. He slammed his foot into the drums in anger and was in pain, but he didn't let on that he was in pain. On the gig the next night we found out that Buddy had broken his foot while kicking the drums. He played with a cast on his foot and still tore it up."[6] Yet, a few nights later Buddy was guesting on the biggest talk show in the country, playing with incredible back pains and a broken toe—and laughing it all off.

Then there was rock music. If there was any music style that he disliked as much as country and western, it was rock'n'roll. It was as if he felt personally insulted every time it was mentioned. In August 1981, MTV began broadcasting, and to put it mildly, Buddy Rich wasn't a fan. Buddy spoke freely about this and other matters to journalist Les Tomkins for *Jazz Professional* magazine. Buddy trusted Tompkins, a respected jazz writer, and opened up to him about his thoughts on music, and his thoughts about himself. About rock music, Buddy told Tompkins, "So, what you're listening to is a cacophony of sound and noise, with no real, individual star up there playing. Everybody is playing everything. The drummers are banging everything in sight, the guitarist sounds like he's strangling 27 cats, and the vocalist is trying to figure out what the word 'hello' means. You've got all of this insanity going on, and there's nothing specific to cause you to say, 'Oh, that's really terrific.' You can only say, 'What the hell is going on?' Now, groups like Weather Report make sense to me, Chicago makes sense, so do Earth, Wind and Fire at times, and groups such as Tower of Power."[7]

Then Buddy got personal and opened up to Tompkins. "I don't hurt anybody. I don't go out and stick up a grocery store," Buddy told him. "I don't perform all kind of weird acts. If you were with me on a 24-hour basis, you'd find out that I'm very normal, depending on what normality is. I never drank. So I'm not the kind of guy that you see laid out on a bar or across the floor some place. You don't even hear about me getting messed up with women. You don't hear about escapades. I don't stand on the stage and take my clothes off. In those terms, I'm a very normal guy. I'm a married man. I have a daughter. I'm civilized in certain areas of my life. Hell-raising meant I liked a good time, and I wouldn't take any crap from anybody—but I wouldn't do that today either. So, if it means that you stand up to something—yes."[8]

Buddy Rich was regarded as a dinosaur in some rock circles. However, other rock groups had problems with the fact that when he played at the same festivals where they were performing, he rode roughshod over all the drummers with such fantastic solos that even they, just like some jazz drummers said over the years, felt like selling their drum sets the next day.

After performing at the 1981 Jacksonville Jazz Festival, he got a phone call from Frank Sinatra. At first, Buddy thought it was another tour in the making, but this was something entirely different. Sinatra had become informally responsible for handling the entertainment at the White House in Washington, D.C. In anticipation of a visit from Jordan's King Hussein and his wife, Queen Noor, President Ronald Reagan wanted Benny Goodman to play, and Sinatra had been asked to put it together. Backing Benny would be Bucky Pizzarelli on guitar, Hank Jones on piano and Milt Hinton on bass. At Frank Sinatra's request, Buddy Rich joined this quintet, even if he wasn't exactly jumping for joy. His attitude toward Goodman hadn't changed much since the incident on Merv Griffin's show two years prior, and he hated the idea of having to play in a suit, but he liked everyone else in the ensemble, so he said yes.

It was a cheeky Buddy Rich who arrived at the doors of the President's residence on November 2, saying, "Sinatra asked me to stop here and play for a while."[8] When he entered the East Wing and saw the portraits of George and Martha Washington, he commented, "Well, this was a very nice living room." He realized, however, that he had been reduced to the role of a sideman for Benny Goodman, and had to back him the entire evening. Buddy felt a little insulted by that, and the fact that he was seated next to the somewhat sullen and dull bandleader all evening definitely didn't help. After having played with Goodman on two occasions (in 1945 and 1979) where his idol didn't exactly express any mutual admiration, it was no surprise that this time he just wanted to "play and get the fuck out of there."

The performance itself went well, and the East Wing was really swinging. Guitarist Bucky Pizzarelli had a ball, exclaiming, "It was incredible. President Reagan was flipping out!"[9] Bassist Milt Hinton, who had seen and heard just about everyone throughout the years, was also impressed.

"We got on stage at the White House and I never heard Benny Goodman play more beautifully," Hinton remembered. "Although Buddy was known to be a difficult man, when Benny turned around and asked, 'Would you mind playing 'Sing Sing Sing?' Buddy answered, 'Anything you want, Benny!' He went into it just exactly the way Gene Krupa would have played it."[10] After Buddy saw how King Hussein was digging his drum solo, he thought the evening was actually okay. Later in the evening, however, he tried to sneak away from the whole spectacle, but was stopped by the security guards.

In January the following year, Buddy fulfilled a longtime dream by getting his own television show, where he would control the content and choose the guests. "Buddy Rich and Friends" was recorded over three days by PBS. An excited Buddy said, "It's something I wanted. I'd been told more than once, by people who supposedly knew what they were talking about, that the audience for jazz series was just too small. I never bought into that, and I feel we can prove them wrong."[11] His chosen guests were Gerry Mulligan, Mel Tormé, Woody Herman, Ray Charles, Anita O'Day, Stan Getz, Lionel Hampton and daughter Cathy. The show was recorded at the Statler Hilton in New York, and though the programs were impressive, the project couldn't get any sponsors and was never aired. Almost four decades after the show was filmed, after much litigation and a host of other issues, the programs were finally released commercially.

The 1980s offered a new opportunity for worldwide exposure, namely home video. Buddy was approached about recording the band for home video (with the promise of recording via the best possible audio and visual technology) but he was skeptical. He had never been satisfied with the drum sound on the albums he had recorded, and he also saw another danger. He told veteran music writer Eliot Tiegel that he "received three offers to videotape my band for video disc presentation, but I'm not sure I want to venture into the home market. A disc of one of my performances may kill my audience. They may not come out to see us if they have us on video disc."[12] He also explained to Tiegel the inner workings of how he deals with an audience. "I have to judge an audience within the first ten seconds I walk on stage," Buddy said. "I do it by looking at them. There's an anxiety, an anticipation, an involvement. You can tell by the response you get when you walk on the bandstand. If it's lackadaisical, then you know tonight we've got to work hard. If there's a great amount of cheering and love being shown, you know exactly what to do to please all these people. You can't take the time to walk out and think, 'I'll try this and if it doesn't work, I'll try this.' You have to know what will please them. That's the secret: Know your audience."

In 1982, Buddy received a tribute similar to the one Gene Krupa had been given. A retrospective tribute to Buddy Rich, part of the 1982 Kool Jazz Festival in New York City and organized by festival producer George Wein, jazz journalist Burt Korall and with assistance from Mel Tormé, was announced to take place at Carnegie Hall on June 27. Wein and all involved thought that such a tribute was deserved and overdue. During a "Tonight Show" guest spot, Buddy talked about the evening to Johnny Carson and admitted, "I'm really nervous about this. A little embarrassed too, but it will probably be fine." "You'll get over it," was Carson's quick retort. "Are you going to be humble and self-critical?" Taking the humorous bait, Buddy answered, "I'm going to be as sweet as only I can be." "You'll wreck the whole evening," said Carson. "I don't actually know how to handle this," said Buddy, turning serious. "They haven't told me everything, but the great Dizzy Gillespie will be there—I am really happy about that—and Zoot Sims, and lots more."

Mel Tormé was the master of ceremonies, and the show featured an all-star band made up of Buddy Rich alumni including Harry "Sweets" Edison, trombonist Eddie Bert, saxophonists Phil Woods and Zoot Sims, pianist John Bunch, bassist Bob Cranshaw, Dizzy Gillespie and "Papa" Jo Jones. Cathy sang "Razzamatazz," film clips from Buddy's time with Artie Shaw and Tommy Dorsey were shown, and the honoree himself performed several numbers, including his show piece, "West Side Story," to standing ovations. Finally, he was given a very special award from his friends at the Zildjian cymbal company. Buddy felt very proud and honored by the whole evening.

Soon Frank Sinatra came calling again, this time to perform with him for Americans in the Dominican Republic at an event in Altos de Chavon. The venue was a newly-opened amphitheater with a capacity of 5,000.

Also booked to perform on the same evening were Heart and Santana. Sinatra's conductor, Vincent Falcone Jr., wasn't prepared for what he saw upon his arrival. "When we landed," Falcone said," all we saw was poverty and dirt. I got out of the plane, went to the bus, feeling directly like I wanted to take a shower. There was dust, half-finished houses, rusty cars and children wandering around without shoes on their feet."[13] In spite of everything, Altos de Chavon was quite a pleasant oasis in the middle of the jungle, but from the hotel to the arena, the cast had to travel on a road so narrow that they were afraid that the bus would go off the road into a ravine at any moment. Once they arrived, there were television cameras all over the place, helicopters in the air and total surveillance in force. The heat was unbearable, and band members who normally would take most any "on the road" event in stride became increasingly irate. Irv Cottler, Sinatra's regular drummer, was even more salty than usual, jumping on Falcone about various things.

Falcone and Buddy, however, were fine. "Buddy and I got along great," Falcone reported, "and they were a good band, but they were young and intimidated by Sinatra. There was no reason for them to be, but it seemed to show. The lead alto sax player, Andy Fusco, a very good musician, was so intimidated that he threw up." The evening before the concert, Sinatra had invited them all to dinner at a large villa. Everyone was happy, until they were told that they all to play in tuxedos. That didn't thrill Buddy, but he did it for Frank's sake. Trumpeter Dave Stahl observed, "Buddy was extremely up for the gig because of Frank. He was nervous and really keyed up to do a hot job. He really wanted to impress Frank with the band and himself. This was kind of a reunion with Frank and it was very, very important to Buddy that things went well. He was so self-conscious and vain that he had his tux form fitted for the gig. He proudly showed it off to us."[14]

The concert on August 20 received rave reviews. Sinatra was in top form and so was Buddy Rich. The audience of all ages enjoyed it immensely, and it was simply a fantastic evening. The review in *Variety* was effusive: "The concert itself was an explosion, both literally and figuratively. In all instances, these two principals would provide sufficient fireworks by themselves."[15] Everyone who was there certainly agreed. Buddy had perhaps played his most technically complicated solo ever on "West Side

Story," but by the end of it Cathy, who sat in the audience, noticed that something wasn't right with her father. "I saw him sweating copiously," she recalled. "I could sense that there was something wrong. After the concert I ran to his dressing room. There he was, lying unconscious on the floor. I became hysterical. He had had a mild heart attack."[16] "Unfortunately the tux didn't allow any room for breathing," said Dave Stahl, "so the tux trapped in all the heat from his body and he really overheated, and being tight fitting, it meant more muscular stress for him. Put all that together and Buddy nearly took a left. Just how close to a heart attack it was, I don't really know, but he definitely hyper-ventilated and for a period of time after the gig he was out of it. It was terrible."[17]

One of the people who reacted quickly was tour leader Steve Peck, who immediately applied ice to Buddy's neck and wrists. Peck's presence of mind and his quick action helped avert what could have been certifiable disaster. Indeed, when the thermometers on stage where checked afterwards, they read an unbelievable 130°F! The natural heat in the air combined with the stage lights were the reason for the terrible heat, and playing under those circumstances had nearly cost Buddy Rich his life. At night, Cathy lay beside her sleeping father and watched him to make sure he was breathing. Upon waking the next morning, Buddy shouted, "Let's go to the beach!"[18] As always, he didn't take health warnings seriously.

After the traditional time off for Christmas and the New Year, the band gathered in New York for rehearsals in January of 1983. Concerts were booked in Tennessee, Oklahoma, Kansas, Arkansas, Indiana and Michigan. For the first long trip, Buddy bought along his favorite foods: chopped liver and apple pie. Despite doctors' warnings about changing his eating habits, he continued eating pasta, hot dogs and other fast food while on the road. Upon the band's January 28 arrival at the University of Michigan in Ann Arbor, Buddy was complaining to Steve Peck that he felt tired and weak, and was having trouble swallowing. He was driven to the hotel where he could rest, but at four in the morning, Peck was contacted by the hotel receptionist, who told him that Buddy had had a very serious heart attack.

Buddy was rushed to a hospital in Detroit, where x-rays revealed that that he had three blocked arteries and would require triple bypass surgery immediately. Soon it was discovered that he actually needed quadruple bypass surgery, but Rich wouldn't agree to it until his family was there. Marie, Cathy, sisters Jo and Marge, and brother Mickey flew to Detroit to support him, where Dr. Marvin Kirsch was waiting with his team. Four hours later, Buddy Rich woke up in the intensive care ward with the report that everything had gone well. They had taken a six-centimeter length of vein from his calf and sewn it into his heart. The doctors also claimed that they had saved him at the last minute.

The day after the operation, saxophonist Steve Marcus came to visit, and Buddy asked him, "Where are we Sunday?"[19] Although at first Buddy was in his normal routine of acting as though nothing had happened, soon reality set in. "When my brain started to clear, naturally, I thought about my career," Buddy admitted at the time. "I figured I was finished, and my whole active life had come to an end. A drummer with a busted arm is one thing. But a drummer, me, with a bum ticker mended with a quadruple bypass? That really scared the shit out of me. One doctor said I'd never play again. Two others said I'd have to lay off for a least a year. When I was discharged from the hospital I went to my home in Palm Springs. I was really depressed and in pain. I wondered whether I'd ever be able to cut it again."[20]

Cathy Rich was with her father throughout. "Two weeks after the surgery," Cathy remembered, "my mother flew him to California to recuperate at our home in Palm Springs. It was slow and very scary for all of us. I would lie awake at night listening for his breathing. Every time the sheets rustled, I would jump up and run into his room to make sure he was still alive. The recovery process was a mental one, as well. Depression set in. He thought he would never play again. The doctors told him he would have to rest for at least a year."[21] Buddy reflected on how hard the recovery process actually was. "I was in Palm Springs," he remembered. "I went to the house, and my daughter, my wife, and the two greatest nurses in the world took absolutely perfect care of me. The first visitor I had, who lives just around the corner, was Mr. Sinatra. I was supposed to get out of bed and walk a mile and I had all kinds of feelings about whether I wanted get out of bed ever again. It was a real depression—weird. And Frank came over and I went for my first walk, my first mile, with him."[22]

Buddy's lifelong friend Freddie Gruber helped him get back on his feet. They also walked a lot, and Buddy seemed to be recovering unusually quickly. As soon as he felt strong enough, Buddy contacted Bob Yeager, who owned the Professional Drum Shop in Hollywood, and asked him to fix up a drum set so he could see if he still had the strength to play. He did have the strength, and immediately began to think about returning to the stage. The next scheduled stop for the band was at Ronnie Scott's in London in March, but everyone around him strongly advised against even thinking about doing it. Frank Sinatra took him to his doctors, who agreed: "If you go to England, you probably won't come back." Buddy's mind, however, was made up. Freddie Gruber believed that Buddy "was up and around long before he really should have been. That tour was on his mind. He didn't want to cancel. Every day, he'd call and ask me to walk with him, to play on pillows, drums, whatever was around, so he'd be ready. As you well know, he was a stubborn cat."[23]

On March 24, 1983, Buddy took the stage at Ronnie Scott's in London, a mere 55 days after his heart attack. "Eight weeks after his surgery," Cathy Rich remembered, "he flew to New York to rehearse the band. He left for England with all of us protesting, threatening and crying. But he went, and it was one of his most triumphant tours. He had proven to himself that he could make it, and never looked back."[24] Was performing so soon after such a serious, life-threatening illness an act of courage or madness? It was possibly a little of each; it wasn't easy for him to get through these performances, but he enjoyed them. To the audience, he said, "It's so good to see you! It's good to see anyone!" He then opened the evening with the aptly-titled "Ya Gotta Try." On the break after the first set, he received a call from Sinatra, who scolded, "No 16-minute long drum solos!" Rich laughed and was so touched by his caring that he made it a point to tell the audience what an extremely nice person Sinatra was. Sinatra heard about this, and eventually sent Buddy a telegram that flatly stated, "If you don't stop saying all those nice things about me, you'll destroy my whole image! Love and take care of yourself, Frank."

On May 23, Buddy made another appearance on "The Tonight Show."

Johnny Carson couldn't believe that Buddy performed in England only eight weeks after a heart attack and major surgery. "I don't understand this," said an incredulous Carson. "How could you do that? Eight weeks later?" "I felt good!" Buddy responded. "As a matter of fact, I would have felt a lot worse if I would have stayed home feeling sorry for myself and going through all kind of bad things which I was going through for about five or six weeks. I had tried to play one time and didn't have any feeling in my hands, and I thought everything was all over for me. I really did. That's the truth." "What would you have done if the doctor had said you can't play anymore?" Carson asked him. "I would have got another doctor!" said Buddy.

Against all odds, the touring continued with the same intensity as earlier. Back in the U.S., he crisscrossed the country, visited Carson again in September, played at the Monterey Jazz festival, and (in October) recorded an LP called *The Magic of Buddy Rich*. Amidst all of this activity, not the slightest worry was voiced about his health. Not once that whole year—from the time he opened at Ronnie Scott's in London to being a return guest on both Merv Griffin's and Johnny Carson's shows—is there the least sign that the man who had been seconds from death was slowing down. On the contrary, Buddy Rich carried on as though nothing had happened.

In August, 1984, Buddy Rich was walking down a street in New York when he happened to pass by a record store. What he saw in the display window stopped him in his tracks. Frank Sinatra had recorded a new album. Buddy went into the store, studied the album jacket, and realized that Sinatra had collected a number of new, hungry musicians for this new effort, *L.A. is My Lady*, and that the drummer on many of the tracks was none other than Steve Gadd. For Buddy, this cast a pall over a series of upcoming concerts he was to perform with Sinatra; the seed of love vs. hate that had been sown between them in the 1940s was making itself felt again. Whether Rich and Sinatra ever had words about this is not known, but it is certain that Buddy was upset that he wasn't on the record—this would become clear later on.

During a five-night September stand at the Royal Albert Hall in England, Buddy received a phone call just before he was about to go on stage for the final concert. "I got a call to tell me that I was a grandfather," an excited Buddy Rich announced. "Cathy and her husband, Michael Lawyer, had had a little son, Nicholas, and I went out on the stage, dropped my drumsticks, tripped over the drums and did everything wrong the whole evening!" Overjoyed at the news, Buddy was nearly happier to have a grandson than he had been when Cathy was born, if that was possible. He said that his temperament changed after the birth of his grandson—but now and then the old temper still flared up.

In early October he was back in Sweden for four concerts in four days: Gävle, Västerås, Ödeshög and Stockholm. In Stockholm, Buddy opened up the concerts by playing "One O'Clock Jump" to honor Count Basie, who had died in April of that year. Swedish jazz promoter Bo Stenhammar had organized the tour. "You couldn't put anything over on that guy," said Stenhammar. "You had to be like a steel spring—on your toes the whole time! Once, when I was picking him up at Arlanda Airport, he opened his suitcase and shouted, 'I've been on tour with Sinatra for two months! I hate him!' Then he ripped up the finest, most expensive tuxedo I have ever seen, and threw it in a garbage can!"[25] Things didn't improve when he showed Buddy to his hotel room. To relax Buddy, Stenhammar had set up a stereo system in the room and thought a little Sinatra music (of all things) would be appreciated. Unfortunately, the record on the turntable was *L.A. is My Lady*. "He wasn't especially happy after that," said Stenhammar. "He complained about everything: the gravy shouldn't cover the beef; then he couldn't see if it was a good piece of meat. I tried to save money another time and booked a Volvo instead of a limousine. He sat in the back seat, stretched out his legs, and noticed that it wasn't a real limousine, and threatened to go straight home if I didn't get one within ten minutes. But I liked him anyway! He followed his contract exactly and didn't demand anything extra."

In the Swedish town of Ödeshög, the world famous concert pianist Peter Jablonski met up with Buddy Rich. The two had first met in the late 1970s, when Peter was only seven years old and drums were his main interest. At the time, Peter's father had asked Buddy if he would listen to his little son, because he was so good at the drums. Buddy agreed, and exclaimed, "Hell, you are nearly as good as I was at your age!" After applying to the Academy of Music in Stockholm, Jablonski was accepted as a drummer, though his degree was in piano. Now a full-fledged concert pianist traveling the world and filling concert halls with his performances, Ödeshög, greeted Buddy and remembered being shocked when Buddy took off his shirt. "He showed me the gigantic scar over his chest," Jablonski recalled. "The time before, when I met Buddy he was strong, powerful and full of energy. Now he looked very worn. There was such a difference. I couldn't believe it."[26]

After the performance in Stockholm, Rich was willing to be interviewed, as he did on every occasion in Sweden. This time he spoke at length about his love for jazz. "I love musicians like Dizzy and Miles," Buddy said with admiration. "They always dare to test new things, new styles." Regarding the art of drumming, Buddy told the interviewer he that he found it "so surprising that there are no courses about drumming traditions. Nowadays a name like Jo Jones has no worth; nobody knows him. I learned to understand jazz music and drummers from an early age, and it is a must for me to always be au jour with what's happening in the rest of the world. Casa Loma Orchestra was my first kick, and then more names just flowed in."

In the course of the interview, Buddy made it clear that his feelings about Frank Sinatra had changed, at least for the moment. He didn't like him, Buddy said—or any other singer, for that matter. The remark very much embodied the complex relationship between Sinatra and Rich; Buddy always had good things to say about his friend—heaping praises on him as a singer—on television programs and elsewhere, but it was evident that Buddy was still hurt from not getting to play on the new Sinatra record. Every time he met Frank, however, it appeared that they were the best of friends. Still, it seems strange that there isn't a single album they recorded together. Buddy ended the Swedish interview by saying, "If I have to stop playing, I'll wither away in two days. The music and touring make me strong and give me a zest for life. My soul gets what it needs, and everyone has to have a soul, you know."[27]

The tour continued to England and Scotland, and from there to Prague in Czechoslovakia, where he played a masterful solo on "West Side Story." At the age of 67, Buddy Rich was playing better than ever. Back in the States, the road dates continued, and he even conducted some drum clinics, including one at Seaford High School in New York on December 4, 1984.

Though it was said that Buddy mellowed personally when he became a grandfather, certain things did not change. If the musicians in the band didn't behave properly on stage and give their all, they could count on being shouted and screamed at on the bus. An errant player was still fired on stage, in front of the audience, from time to time. This was the usual image of Buddy Rich as a bandleader. Louie Bellson once said, "Buddy could walk into an empty room and start a quarrel."[28] While Bellson was surely poking fun, there is obviously some truth in the remark. The stories about Buddy Rich's temper are simply a part of the legend.

The truth is somewhat different. Everyone in his band knew very well that a verbal lashing could be expected if Buddy had his wife Marie, or anyone close to him, on the bus; at these times he wanted to show that he was the boss. It was as if he put on a mask. John LaBarbera said, "If there was a third person in the room, he had an audience and he would not be straight with you. He would not be totally honest with you if you asked a question. But when you were one on one, he would talk straight out." Bobby Shew, who played trumpet in Buddy's first band, described an incident that spoke volumes about Buddy's personality. "I remember one time he gave a horrific lecture to the band backstage," said Shew. "Then he turned to me and said, 'You, Shew, in my office right now.' His office was the dressing room. The guys in the band looked at each other, like, why is Buddy picking on Bobby? He didn't do anything. When we got inside, he shouted at me to close the door. When I did, he turned to me, softened up and said, 'How was I?' I said, man, Buddy, why do you do stuff like that? He said,' I like to keep them on their toes.'"[29]

Drummer Joe LaBarbera saw the same thing on another occasion, recalling, "We were sharing a dressing room, and when some of the boys from the band were going by to get to their dressing room, Buddy went completely wild and shouted at them. When they had gone, he turned to me and said, 'Don't pay any attention to that. I just wanted to show them who is the boss.'"[30] Trumpeter Eric Miyashiro joined the band in February of 1985, and he also got to feel the brunt of Buddy's temper. He remembered one incident in great detail. "One night, when he was in one of his moods," said Miyashiro. "Back in the bus, he started to walk through the bus yelling, 'What the fuck happened on that chart?' asking us one by one. Everyone kind of shrugged off his questions, saying, 'I don't know Buddy.' I had the traditional 'lead trumpet seat' in the very back of the bus, so I was the last one to face Buddy. When it came to my turn, I told him, 'You dropped a beat, Buddy.' He went through the roof, swearing and cussing as he stormed back to his seat. Things got real quiet on the ride to the hotel. I knew I was gone, through, done. But the next morning, when I got on the bus, there was Buddy, sitting in his seat with a big smile, 'Good morning Eric!' As I was walking to my back seat, confused as to what just had happened, I passed by Steve Marcus, and he said to me, 'Welcome to the band!' I found out later that Buddy liked a guy who stands on his own, especially the hot chair like the lead trumpet. He screamed at me countless of times after that, but each time was well justified, and I deserved it. He always treated me with respect, and I could feel his love as well."[31]

Pianist Lee Musiker joined the band in March, 1982. He always had his little cassette recorder with him, mostly to record his own solos so he could improve his playing. He thought that when Rich read the riot act to the band about one thing or another, he could listen carefully to any of Buddy's sage advice, and learn from it, which might be part of the scolding. Musiker explained, "To me, the impact of his speeches was purely professional, even though it was interpreted as funny by other people. But from my end, it was a revealing thing. I thought this was historical and I understood that it was educational. The intent of his screaming was really to shape the band, to demand everybody's best, and it was coming from a position of strength. He wanted people to play with the same intensity and honesty that he was playing."[32]

Musiker recorded Buddy Rich many times over the years until the inevitable happened. One day, trombonist Mike Davis asked Musiker for copy of the tape. He got it, and shortly after, Davis left Rich's band for Maynard Ferguson's group. He ended up in Woody Herman's band, and the tapes, with Buddy's ranting and raving on them, spread like wildfire among musicians all over. On the actual recording, the one who got the worst tongue-lashing on the bus was trombonist Dave Panichi. Buddy was upset by Panichi's beard one day, and the dressing down he received has become a part of internet history. This is just a part of Buddy's outburst: "You got two fucking weeks to make up your mind," Buddy shouted. "Do ya want that beard or do ya want a job? I will not have this shit! This is a band is not a Goddamn fucking House of David baseball team. It's the Buddy Rich Band—young people with faces! No more fucking beards. It's out! If you decide to do it you're through. Right now! This is the last time I make this announcement. No more fucking beards. I don't wanna see it. If ya got it, you're gonna shave it off. I'll treat ya just like they treat ya in the Marine Corps. This is the way I want my band to look. If ya don't like it, get out!"

Despite the outburst, Panichi wasn't at all frightened of Rich. He was a tough Australian who was used to much rougher treatment. "Being Australian," said Panichi, "you have a completely different relationship to authority figures than you do here. People here are much more sort of docile or obedient around authority figures. My own feeling was he couldn't get away with that shit with an Australian band. Someone would have popped him. As far as that shit is concerned, Buddy was like a really, really mild version of my father. My old man would never threaten to hit, he would just fucking haul off and whack you. So the thing with the threat shit is if you threaten somebody once and you don't do it, then it's an empty threat."[33] Dave Panichi got several dressing downs and was fired a few times, but just like all the others who were the victims of verbal threats, he was rehired and continued, voluntarily, to play with Buddy Rich for over a year more after this incident.[34]

In retrospect, after talking to many of the players who worked with Buddy Rich over the years, the truth was that if Buddy got bugged at someone, they probably deserved it. Ernie Watts summed things up nicely, saying, "When it came to music, Buddy always knew what he wanted. The only problem was if you didn't do the job. He always said, 'There are 24 hours in a day. You work for me for four of these. Be neat and tidy, wear your suit and play the music as well as you can.' Those who couldn't handle that had problems with Buddy. Then he got angry, and he was the kind that couldn't control his anger. He just got worse and worse because he wanted to explain, but didn't always manage to do it. I never saw him become angry or quarrel for no excuse. If he got angry there was always a reason."[35]

Was Buddy Rich's tough attitude towards his musicians really justified? In his eyes, he was protecting his name. If, for example, a trumpeter played badly, the audience wouldn't say "that trumpeter was not good." Instead they would think "Buddy Rich's trumpeter was not so good," or worse yet, "the Buddy Rich Band is no good." One thing is certain: after his failures with his earlier orchestras, Buddy wasn't taking any chances. Therefore, he consciously decided to follow Tommy Dorsey and Artie Shaw's style of leadership. As Shaw once said, "You have to present a kind of model for the men. You have to be the leader, meaning you've got to set the tone. You've got to do what you want the men in the band to do." That was exactly what Rich did; he gave 100 percent every evening and demanded the same of his musicians. But Buddy sometimes did go too far. Dave Panichi said, "One time when the band played at Disneyland, and the management had watched aghast as Rich started calling one of the trumpet players a motherfucker in front of a child-packed audience. They forced him to apologize, and Buddy was furious."[36]

Buddy Rich might have been a tough bandleader, but outwards he always defended his musicians. "This is the best band I've ever had," he often said. "I still have what I think is one of the best jazz bands ever, and I'm surrounded by people half my age, most of them, and they play with the authority and the sensitivity of kids that have been playing jazz all of their lives. Most of my guys are in their very early 20s and they are fantastic musicians, writers and players."[37]

On April 2, 1985, Buddy recorded another album, but this time in a completely different way. Three companies, independent of each other, worked together to film and record Buddy Rich and his band under the project name *Mr. Drums: Buddy Rich and his Band Live on King Street, San Francisco*. Mobile Fidelity Sound Lab, Pioneer Artists and One Pass Production (which was owned by the producer) joined forces to produce and release this effort. Rich was very excited about it, saying, "Not only has this production been a big educational piece for the industry, it has been a personal dream to me."[38] This statement is understandable, as there is is not a single interview where Buddy Rich voiced his satisfaction with the sound on any record he had made. Buddy was hopeful this project would finally be the one to capture it properly. Preparations were meticulous, and the existing film shows a very engaged and interested Rich who wanted to know where all the microphones would be placed and where all the cameras were. He rehearsed the band more carefully than usual, and before a specially invited audience, he performed all his most well-known numbers, including "West Side Story" and "Channel One Suite." In later interviews, he said he was satisfied with this recording.

Buddy's satisfaction may have had to do with the fact that, at long last, he was finally using a set of drums he liked. Having had various kinds of issues with all the brands of drums he endorsed over the years, including Slingerland, Ludwig, Rogers, and briefly Vox and Fibes, by this late period in his career, he finally found a set he was happy with. He returned to using the Slingerland brand, but this was a custom-refurbished set of Slingerland Radio Kings—the set's components were manufactured in the 1940 to 1944 period—brilliantly reworked and recovered by Eames drum shell company owner Joe MacSweeny and presented to Buddy in 1982. "Buddy was almost like a young kid getting his first drum," MacSweeny said at the time. Later on, Buddy said that the snare drum was the best that had ever been made.

In June there were several successful performances at the Playboy Jazz Festival at the Hollywood Bowl, and one more guest performance with The Royal Philharmonic Orchestra in London, where he took along his own quartet. The other guest soloists were Ella Fitzgerald and Oscar Peterson. In August, the band performed at the Chicago Jazz Festival, with Buddy looking unbelievably strong and sure of himself. He was feeling great, the band was playing great, more and more performances were booked, and a glance at his calendar would make you think that his booking agency was representing a young man. In January of 1986, Buddy Rich played 20 gigs in 20 days. In February, he did the same.

That month he also appeared at the Grammy Awards, where he was recognized for his musical endeavors over the years. After sitting and waiting for two hours, he finally went on stage to perform a short number with an all-star band consisting of Dizzy Gillespie, Jon Faddis, David

Sanborn, Gerry Mulligan, Gary Burton, Bobby Hutcherson, Kenny Burrell, Stanley Jordan and B.B. King. Rich wasn't happy with the result, saying at the time, "It was a drag. The producers had us sit around for almost two hours before we went on to play, which was ridiculous. Jazz is nothing but tokenism to them and it's a crime, wasting all that great, legitimate talent just doesn't make any sense." Afterwards, when he was back with his band, he told his trumpeter, Eric Miyashiro, "that the producer had arranged things so unmusically; he thought it was such a waste of all the stars up there. He also said his solo was cut short, so you can tell he was not happy."[39] The last comment could have been the real explanation for why Buddy was irritated. There was nothing in life that Buddy took more seriously than a drum solo.

The persistent touring continued in March with another 20 bookings for the month. In April, Buddy appeared on "The Regis Philbin Show," where the topics of conversation were a new diet and the news that he was going on a tour with Frank Sinatra and Ella Fitzgerald to the Soviet Union in September. For some reason, however, the tour never happened. For several years, the Carnation Garden stage at Disneyland was a regular touring stop for the band, as it was for the few remaining big bands on the road. Buddy played three sets every evening there, and the sometimes the audience danced to the band. Buddy didn't like the dancing, but he accepted it; he liked playing there and enjoyed performing so close to home. At Disneyland, his family could come and listen to him. On June 6, Cathy had her son Nicholas with her, and Buddy couldn't resist bringing him up on stage. A prouder granddad would be hard to find.

In the summer of 1986, Buddy went on a European tour with concerts in Denmark, Sweden, England, Italy, Germany, Holland and France. At nearly 69 years of age, he was touring more than ever, and he was happy and proud of his young band. In every interview he talked up his soloists, saying they "had a great future in jazz and several of them would surely become bandleaders themselves one day."[40] October saw the band embark on a two-week Caribbean Jazz Cruise aboard the SS Norway. On the cruise, he was pleased to meet and perform with many of his old jazz friends, including Dizzy Gillespie, Mel Lewis, Freddie Gruber, Milt Jackson, Joe Williams, and Mel Powell; and he made up with a musician with whom he had fallen out for some reason: saxophonist Flip Phillips, star of the JATP days.

Mel Powell recalled that "Buddy was playing superbly. He was relaxed, and not in a show business mood. He sounded sturdy but subtle. He didn't much want to take solos, and when I gave him the signal for four-bar exchanges, he barely agreed. His hair was whitish, but he had a Palm Springs tan, and there wasn't a wrinkle in his face. We had a kidding relationship, and when I asked him how he managed to keep so well, he said, 'By staying on the road.'"[41] Even Cathy was on the cruise with him, and she enjoyed every moment. "I spent two weeks with him," she remembered fondly, "and I am so incredibly happy for that today, that I had that time with him."[42]

In November, it was back to England for yet another tour. He felt so at home in Europe that he thought about the possibility of living there. "Yeah, if it wasn't for my family," Buddy said, "I could easily live over there. Believe me, I seriously considered doing just that more than once."[43] Once more, he returned Ronnie Scott's, playing five full-house evenings, with his friend Carl Palmer sitting in on drums to play the Ed Shaughnessy chart "Shawnee." From December 2 to7, Buddy and his band played at the Blue Note in Washington. The review in *The New York Times* was exceptional. "His virtuosity is still an essential element," the *Times* wrote, "both in the subtle skill of his rhythmic foundations and in the carefully constructed solo with which he ends each set."[44] Drum builder Joe MacSweeney, on hand representing *Modern Drummer* magazine, was also there, and wrote, "The performance... was typically strong. Buddy executed as no one can. More importantly, he supported his young band in a marvelous way."[45] It was, in fact, evident that in the past year, he was playing in a entirely different way. He seemed to enjoy playing a supporting role more than showing off and impressing an expectant audience. The final performance for the year was on December 10 at Orange High School in Pepper Pike, Ohio. As usual, his closing, extended drum solo was brilliant. Then the band went on holiday.

Somewhat reluctantly, Buddy allowed himself to be booked onto a television show on January 15, 1987, as a part of a tribute to Tommy

Dorsey. Despite all the years that had passed since Dorsey's death in 1956, Rich hadn't changed his opinion about the tough bandleader, but he still agreed to take part in what was called "Sentimental Swing: The Music of Tommy Dorsey." Mel Tormé was the master of ceremonies, and was to sing a few songs as well. At the rehearsals, Buddy appeared to be happy and enjoying playing Dorsey's songs again, and before a capacity crowd at the Hollywood Palladium, he delivered fantastic solos on both "Opus No. 1" and "Hawaiian War Chant" (the song that had been one of his great showpieces with Dorsey), and he even sang "Watcha Know Joe?" He seemed to be in incredibly good shape. Tormé ended the show by exclaiming, "Buddy Rich, one of a kind!"

A day or two later he visited his booking agency, the Willard Alexander Agency, to make plans for the rest of the year. There they discussed several things, including the availability of Phil Collins to produce the next Buddy Rich recording. Collins was, in fact, available, and a request was sent to him.[46] They also discussed whether Rich could truly handle as many university performances as he had done the previous year (to which he naturally answered yes), a tour of Japan, and more. Following the meeting, he met up with the band and informed them of what was being planned, then went home to the family's apartment in New York to rest up. He was feeling fine, but a little tired.

On January 26, Buddy went for a walk in New York. Suddenly, his left arm began to act strangely; it spun around, as though the arm had a life of its own. He had to hold it with his other arm to stop the involuntary movements. This was very frightening, but he went back to his apartment and tried to rest a little. Steve Marcus came by and got him to stop worrying and think about something else. They decided to go out and get a hot dog on 72nd Street. On the way back to his apartment, Buddy fell and hit the edge of the sidewalk. Freddie Gruber rushed over and drove Buddy to Mount Sinai hospital. Initially believing that he'd had a slight stroke, the doctors ran tests and discovered that Buddy had a brain tumor. His family was contacted, and they rushed to his side at the hospital. While this was happening, the band members were arriving in New York to prepare to depart on the newly-booked tour. "We flew to New York to start our next tour in January of 1987," trombonist Tom Garling remembered. "That same day, he had his first symptoms of the brain tumor. We were sent home the next day."[47]

None of the band members had noticed any sign that there was anything wrong at the last gig in Pepper Pike, Ohio, in December. Eric Miyashiro said, "He didn't show any sign of his illness, not a thing. He was real strong 'til the last gig. If anything, his back gave him trouble sometimes. He would be in pain, unable to move much, but as soon as he stepped on to the stage, he was Buddy Rich."[48] The family hadn't noticed anything either. "Neither my mother or I saw any sign at all that Buddy wasn't feeling well," said Cathy Rich. "That brain tumor came like a flash of lightning from nowhere."[49] As tests at the hospital continued for the next two and half weeks, Buddy's brother Mickey was sadly also in the same hospital having treatments for cancer. On February 14, Buddy was able to go home, only to have to return again. Marie Rich remembered, "He was home for ten days. At that point, he had eight seizures in one day, then eight more, and was rushed back to the hospital."[50] They performed a biopsy, which showed that Buddy Rich had not only one tumor, he had three, and that only a miracle could save him. The family was informed once again.

On March 6, it was decided to announce this information publicly to the press. Buddy's booking agent, Bill Monott, announced that an operation wasn't possible and that Buddy would undergo chemotherapy in an effort to reduce the size of the tumor. Major newspapers ran stories about Buddy's condition and how serious it was, and the word spread worldwide. But the week after, Buddy Rich made a decision. "You see, my family is a little uptight right now," Buddy said to Don Sweeny, a "Tonight Show" staffer who was alone with Buddy in his hospital room. "We just had a big talk with my doctor about this. The doctor says I have a tumor right here (he took a drumstick and pointed to the middle of his forehead). The doctor says I'm not in any condition to undergo an operation. Yet, if I don't have it taken care of soon, it could be all over. The family thinks I should leave it alone. If I do that, I will be like this for the rest of my life. That's no way I want to live. I am willing to take my chances with an operation."[51]

Though UCLA's Dr. Donald Becker had told him that an operation would not only be complex and dangerous, but that it could only *possibly* increase his chance of survival, he was still willing to take the risk. The operation was set for the following day, and Freddie Gruber was there. Recalling one of Buddy's most famous lines, Freddie said, "Just before the operation, when we were going down in the elevator, the doctors asked him if he was allergic to anything. Buddy answered, 'Only country and western music.'"[52] Four hours later, the hospital's press spokesman, Michael Burns, reported, "The surgeons consider the operation a success."[53]

On March 25, Buddy was allowed to go home again. During his recovery, several friends visited him, including Jerry Lewis, Nick Condos, Irv Cottler, Annie Ross, Jack Jones, and Terry Gibbs. Johnny Carson came by and joked, "You will get through this. You even survived Tommy Dorsey!" and "Now I've got a better left hand than you!" which lifted Buddy's spirits. His old friend Mel Tormé also spent time with Buddy, and they discussed the book Mel was working on about Buddy's life. For this biography, Buddy had great confidence in Tormé; they had known each other for years On April 1, Freddie Gruber visited with Armand Zildjian and Lennie DiMuzio. In running the Zildjian company, these men had produced cymbals for Buddy all his life, and they had become very close friends. Armand felt he needed to tell Buddy that, through him, he had got to experience the greatest musical moment in his life. It was a very emotional meeting and they left the room with tears in their eyes. During their visit, Freddie Gruber talked with Buddy about what he had learned during all his years in music and what he wanted his legacy to be. "Buddy often thought about all the young people and what he could leave behind him for them," Gruber said. "We had talked about making an instructional video and suddenly he shouted out, 'Never tell them what to play, only how to approach the instrument! Make sure you've heard what I said! Leave something for the young people!'"[54]

On April 2, 1987, Buddy was leaving the hospital after having gone through yet another treatment. He hardly made it home before he had another attack, and he was taken quickly back to the hospital. On the way, his blood pressure fell alarmingly, and only minutes after arrival at the hospital, Buddy Rich died of respiratory and cardiac failure. His wife Marie and daughter Cathy were by his side.

The funeral was emotional. Many of the important figures from Buddy's life were there: Frank Sinatra, Sammy Davis Jr, Artie Shaw, Georgie Auld, Hugh Hefner, Jerry Lewis, Mel Brooks, John LaBarbera, Angie Dickinson, Milton Berle, Edie Adams, Annie Ross; and drummers Ed Shaughnessy, Irv Cottler, Jake Hanna, Freddie Gruber and many more. All Buddy's family and relatives were there, except his brother Mickey, who was still fighting cancer and could not attend. Terry Gibbs, Al Viola, and Tom Warrington played some of Buddy's favorite songs, and among many speeches, it was perhaps Johnny Carson who said the most touching words: "Buddy was not afraid of dying. He was just afraid of living and not being able to play the drums."

Buddy Rich swings! I realize I am speaking about his drumming in the present tense, because his drumming is so great and timeless that it is, somehow, in the "now." In any event, Buddy's innate sense of swing was irresistible to me and most any other musician who ever heard him play. Second, his snare drum technique—i.e., his hands—were like Horowitz's or Paganini's hands: truly the hands of a master. Third, his language on the drumset, while rooted in swing, was incredibly modern and powerful, always perfect for the song he was playing. Even though he was a great soloist, Buddy was a band's drummer.

Peter Erskine

CHAPTER 19
Epilogue

A pensive BR, early 1970s.

At 2:27 p.m. on April 2, 1987, a life dedicated to finding the secret of perfection came to an end. Buddy Rich was a perfectionist who was always on the move and constantly searching, but he paid dearly for it.

One of his few close friends, Mel Tormé, was among the first to discover that things weren't right. They had just finished two of four planned concerts together in the beginning of October, 1980, when he was called to the band bus and found Buddy struggling with tremendous back pains. Band members had helped him with his clothes, and everyone around him had tried to brighten the atmosphere as much as possible. Mel stood in the doorway and found himself thinking, "Will he have to cancel a concert?" At the same time, Mel knew that his dear friend was as tough as nails, and had been brought up from the age of two to perform according to the old motto "the show must go on." The years and experiences toughened Buddy up, but even he admitted, "Those were hard days. Being on the road constantly then was much more difficult than it is today. There were few conveniences and if you weren't totally dedicated and didn't love it, you died."[1]

There was nothing to indicate that he would change on that night. If people had travelled a long way to see him, he wouldn't let them down. "It'll be alright! Open the curtains and let's get going!" That's the way it had always been. If he just got himself to the drums and clenched his teeth, the pains disappeared as though he pressed a secret button. He got through the concert, and as usual, played to his very limits. Through the years, more than one backstage visitor saw how this scenario played out. Swedish promoter Bo Johnson observed it several times on earlier tours. "Buddy always had terrible problems with his back," Johnson said. "Many times he had to be helped up to the drums, but once he was sitting there it was if the pain simply disappeared. It was completely inconceivable. I couldn't believe my eyes."[2] That October evening with Tormé was the same. "Help me to my drums and everything will be fine!" was Buddy's mantra.

In the beginning of 1983, Buddy Rich had a heart attack which nearly cost him his life. Anyone would have understood if he had chosen to slow down or even retire, but eight weeks later, he was back onstage at Ronnie Scott's in London. In his quest for the perfect drum solo, he not only stretched the boundaries, but broke them. The fact that he got through concerts with back pains, broken arms and toes, agonizing sciatica, kidney stone attacks, excruciating toothaches and even serious heart problems made his band members regard him as some sort of superhuman who could survive any difficulty as if he were another being. John LaBarbera said, "He was unique. Talk about extraterrestrial beings, I think he was planted here by a flying saucer or something. I think I sound like I am just spewing, but to have an association with someone that great, that doesn't happen very often in life, and this guy was just unique."[3]

Buddy Rich had many different sides that the public never knew about. These were the qualities that showed that deep inside he was a humble and sensitive person. It's been said that he cried through romantic movies. He could be childish, playful, and humorous. As a practical joke, he glued the piano keys together, and laughed so hard at the result that he nearly fell off his drum stool. He was sincere and helpful. Several people have spoken about the many times he helped friends who were in difficulty. There is the story of his roadie who had a terrible car accident and whose mother got financial help from Buddy for her son's hospitalization—without her son's knowledge. There's the story of the drummer colleague who hadn't enough money to buy drumsticks and received a dozen from Buddy for free. Someone else received a complete drum set. Another drumming colleague told of seeing a young Buddy give his last dollar to another when he didn't have money for food. There was the time when he saw a story on television about an elderly woman being treated unfairly—she couldn't afford electricity for her apartment—and Buddy immediately sent an anonymous contribution so she could get by. Finally, there were the hundreds of performances he held at universities and music schools for almost no payment, just because he loved to play for young people. These incidents were not rumors. Many times he asked the worried students, "How much did you get together? Okay, divvy it up among my musicians and let's get started."

It was only when it came to playing his music that the tough and demanding Rich put into force what he had learned from Artie Shaw and Tommy Dorsey. In countless interviews he tried to explain why he was so temperamental and why he reacted so strongly at times. "Where I sit,

I'm the coach, the quarterback, and I call the shots," he flatly stated. "If you miss that play, you've got to see me later. Nobody wants to do that, because I still have a temper, and I still want perfection from the people that work for me. That's why I hire them. They know if they blow it they'll hear from me right away. I call a guy a motherfucker while he is sitting on the bandstand not out of hate or anger, but out of disappointment, because I know the potential of the guy is great, and he's letting me down. But more importantly, he's letting himself down. He's letting his own talent down, and that's why I get mad."[4]

Music is where Buddy drew the line. If he got a bad review, he tackled it in his own way. He didn't want anyone in his band to be asleep on the job—that simply wasn't allowed. It was hard enough to lead a jazz big band in a world driven more and more towards, pop, rock and punk. If you played in the Buddy Rich Band, you were expected to give 100 percent, otherwise you would hear about it. Freddie Gruber was fond of saying, "Dizzy Gillespie once told me, your friend Bernard is crazy, it's not good enough for him to go out there and give 100 percent every night, he's got to give 120!"

There were people in Buddy's circle who learned to know the warning signs of his temper flaring up. Stanley Kay likely knew Buddy better than anyone, and explained, "Buddy had a temper that would simmer and simmer, and then explode. When I'd sit next to him at New York's Paramount Theater in the late 1940s, I could tell when the pot was boiling. Buddy always liked to put his left foot on one of the three legs of the hi-hat stand. Not the pedal; one of the three metal legs. After he'd play for a little he'd move to the pedal. I knew Buddy was getting into it when his foot wasn't on one of those legs. So I'd reach over and put his foot on the leg, which would make him laugh and settle him down."[5] Buddy's temperament drove him forward and aided his development as a musician. An extremely strong will to always do his best meant that he routinely warmed up for an hour or more. Many were the musicians who watched him sitting backstage slouched over a rubber practice pad, drumsticks rattling out the rhythms. Swedish promoter Bo Stenhammar watched Buddy warm up. "I booked Buddy Rich for the Stockholm Jazz & Blues Festival," Stenhammar remembered. "When I saw him there in the dressing room, I asked him, 'Why do you, the world's best drummer, need to warm up for so long?' He answered, 'That's why I'm the best.'"[6]

Buddy Rich himself often laughed it all off, and he had a fantastic knack of joking about things. Any performer risks getting a lousy review from time to time, but Buddy didn't care much about what the critics had to say. Only he knew how well or badly he played, and if a critic gave him a bad review, he was already chasing the ball. A typical comment in response to a bad write-up was, "I really don't give a damn about stupid critics. If they don't like something, they should be up there doing it better. If a critic said I was the greatest thing that ever happened to the drums, it wouldn't change my attitude one bit. The only critic I listen to is me. When I play badly, I'll be the first one to tell you, or when I play well—and it has nothing to do with being arrogant. It has only to do with knowing what you can do, and to deny that fact makes you a liar to begin with. False humility is the worst thing in the world."[7]

To many Buddy Rich was—and still is—the world's greatest drummer, and with that epithet applied to him, he couldn't simply sit down behind the skins and turn in a half-hearted performance. Buddy didn't like the title, and emphatically believed, "Nobody's the 'greatest' anything. All you can do is the best you can. I believe I'm as good as any drummer playing. I haven't heard all the drummers, but I wouldn't take a back seat."[8] His goal was never to be best in the world on his instrument, though he was on a constant quest to try and achieve the perfect solo. Buddy Rich never gave up on that point, and had a certain philosophy about his own playing. There was a depth and an idea behind nearly every stroke. After a fantastic solo, he once said, "Playing a drum solo is like telling a story. It has a beginning and a middle—and a bitch of a punchline. I try to play a drum solo constructed along a line. What comes out is what I feel. I am telling you about my wife and daughter, or the nice people I was with before I got on the stand. When Johnny Carson comes into the Riverboat, I try and play in that light, funny way he has. When Basie comes in, I play with love. Some nights, people tell me I've played vicious, and they're right. Maybe I've been thinking about thirty years of one-nighters, or maybe about what a drag it was in the Marines. But the next night I'll come to where I am playing and say, 'Sorry, little drums. I'll try to be tender tonight.'"[9]

In the end, do we know what drove Buddy Rich? Maybe Buddy revealed the answer to Thomas Cochran, a writer at *Modern Drummer* magazine, who once asked Buddy, "Is there anything you're still working on?" Buddy's answer was, "Yeah. Perfection." "How long do you plan to keep doing these one-nighters like this?" Cochran asked. "Until I find the secret of perfection," said Buddy.

There are many who thought he discovered the secret long ago.

Opening quote from Buddy from an interview with Les Tompkins, courtesy of the National Jazz Archive, England.

CHAPTER 1: FASCINATING RHYTHM

1. Robert Rich quoted in *The Torment of Buddy Rich*, Minahan, 2000, p110
2. Robert Rich quoted in *The Torment of Buddy Rich*, Minahan, 2000, p113
3. Free interpretation from *Vaudeville, Old and New: An Encyclopedia*, Cullen/Hackman/Donald, 2004
4. Robert Rich quoted in *The Torment of Buddy Rich*, Minahan, 2000, p115
5. Buddy Rich quoted in *Downbeat*, October 5, 1955
6. Buddy Rich quoted in *Super Drummer*, Balliett, 1968, p79
7. Confirmed by Cathy Rich in interview with the author, June 15, 2014
8. Review in *Variety*, June 23, 1922
9. Review in *Billboard*, July 1922
10. Robert Rich quoted in *The Torment of Buddy Rich*, Minahan, 2000, p115
11. Robert Rich quoted in *The Torment of Buddy Rich*, Minahan, 2000, p115
12. Gene Krupa, interview
13. Cathy Rich quoted in *Modern Drummer*, April 1991
14. Buddy Rich quoted in *Mister, I Am The Band*, Meriwether/Hintze, 1998, p7

CHAPTER 2: ENTER THE JAZZ SCENE

1. Review in *Variety*, April 30, 1930
2. Review in *Film Daily*, May 4, 1930
3. Review in *Motion Picture News*, May 10, 1930
4. Article in *Billboard*, May 31, 1930
5. Jo and Marge Rich quoted in *The Torment of Buddy Rich*, Minahan, 2000, p157/p159
6. George T. Simon quoted in *Drummin' Men*, Korall, 1990, p256
7. Buddy Rich quoted in *Traps The Drum Wonder*, Tormé, 1991, p30
8. Pauly Cohen interviewed by the author, May 18, 2014
9. Billie Holiday quoted in *Lady Sings the Blues*, Holiday/Duffy, 1971, p100
10. Dizzy Gillespie quoted in *52nd St.: The Street of Jazz*, Shaw, 1971, p11
11. Buddy Rich quoted in *Drummin' Men*, Korall, 1990, p257
12. Buddy Rich quoted in *Traps The Drum Wonder*, Tormé, 1991, p33
13. Buddy Rich quoted in *Drummin' Men, Korall*, 1990, p208
14. Woody Herman quoted in *Drummin' Men*, Korall, 1990, p259
15. Cathy Rich quoted in *Modern Drummer*, April 1991
16. Review in the *Chicago Daily News*, December 12, 1936
17. Review in *Variety*, April 14, 1937
18. Review in *Variety*, September 1, 1937
19. Buddy Rich quoted in *Traps The Drum Wonder*, Tormé, 1991, p32
20. Joe Marsala quoted in *52nd St.: The Street of Jazz*, Shaw, 1971, p142
21. John Popkin quoted in *52nd St.: The Street of Jazz*, Shaw, 1971, p142
22. Joe Marsala quoted in *Jam Session*, Shapiro/Hentoff, 1955, p150
23. Joe Marsala quoted in *52nd St.: The Street of Jazz*, Shaw, 1971, p142

CHAPTER 3: JOE MARSALA AND HIS CHICAGOANS

1. Buddy Rich quoted in *Super Drummer*, Balliett, 1968, p86
2. Stanley Kay later became Buddy Rich's backup drummer and manager
3. Stanley Kay quoted in *JazzWax*, June 25, 2010

4. Buddy Rich quoted in *Drummin' Men*, Korall, 1990, p261
5. Buddy Rich quoted in *Drummin' Men*, Korall, 1990, p263 54
6. Joe Marsala quoted in *Drummin' Men*, Korall, 1990, p262
7. Article by George Hoefer, "Buddy Rich: Portrait of a Man in Conflict," in *Downbeat*, June 9, 1960
8. Buddy Rich quoted in *The Drummers Time*, Mattingly, p53
9. Buddy Rich quoted in *Super Drummer*, Balliett, 1968, p88
10. Jim Chapin quoted in *Modern Drummer*, August 1987
11. Buddy Rich quoted in *Super Drummer*, Balliett, 1968, p88
12. Buddy Rich quoted in *Jazz Professional*, 1968
13. Buddy Rich quoted in *Mister, I Am The Band* Meriwether/Hintze, 1998, p10
14. *Wikipedia,* information on Vic Schoen, no other reference to the source
15. Maxene Andrews quoted in *The Andrews Sisters: A Biography and Career Record*, Nimmo, 2004, p74
16. Benny Goodman quoted in *Eddie Condon's Treasury of Jazz*, Condon, 1958, p247
17. Kolodin quoted on the album cover *The Famous 1938 Carnegie Hall Jazz Concert, Vol 2*, CL 815
18. Harry James quoted in *Eddie Condon's Treasury of Jazz*, Condon, 1958, p248
19. Buddy Rich quoted in *Drummin' Men*, Korall, 1990, p65
20. Bushkin quoted in *Come in and Hear the Truth: Jazz and Race on 52nd Street*, Burke, 2008, p144
21. Teddy Reig quoted in *Drummin' Men*, Korall, 1990, p263
22. Art Hodes quoted in *Hot Man:The Life of Art Hodes*, Hodes, p44
23. Teddy McRae quoted from *Oral History Files*, Institute of Jazz Studies, Rutgers University, Newark
24. Joe Marsala quoted in *Drummin' Men*, Korall, 1990, p262
25. National Jazz Archive, UK, *Dance Band Diaries*, Vol 9, 1938, p10
26. Stanley Kay quoted in *Drummin' Men*, Korall, 1990, p265
27. Freddie Gruber quoted in *Jazz Improv*, 2006, Vol. 6, No. 3, p132

CHAPTER 4: BUNNY BERIGAN AND HIS ORCHESTRA

1. Article, "Bunny Berigan," by Whitney Balliett in *The New Yorker*, August 11, 1982
2. Georgie Auld quoted in *Traps The Drum Wonder*, Tormé, 1991, p38
3. Johnny Blowers quoted in *Bunny Berigan: Elusive Legend of Jazz*, Dupuis, 1993, p178
4. Joe Dixon quoted in *Bunny Berigan: Elusive Legend of Jazz*, Dupuis, 1993, p168
5. Dick Wharton quoted in *Mr. Trumpet: The Trials, Tribulations, and Triumph of Bunny Berigan*, Zirpolo, 2011, p250
6. Dick Wharton quoted in *Mr. Trumpet: The Trials, Tribulations, and Triumph of Bunny Berigan*, Zirpolo, 2011, p251
7. Clyde Rounds quoted in *Mr. Trumpet: The Trials, Tribulations, and Triumph of Bunny Berigan*, Zirpolo, 2011, p252
8. Episode quoted in *The Torment of Buddy Rich*, Minahan, 2000, p151
9. Jack Sperling quoted in *Bunny Berigan: Elusive Legend of Jazz*, Dupuis, 1993, p99
10. Artie Shaw quoted in *Tommy Dorsey: Living in a Big Great Way*, Levinson, p120
11. Georgie Auld quoted in *Laughter from the Hip*, Feather/Tracy, 1979, p148
12. Bushkin in *The High Cost of Being Bunny Berigan*, Sudhalter, State of Wisconsin collection, p190
13. Berigan quoted in the article, "Bunny Berigan," Balliett in *The New Yorker*,

August 11, 1982

14. Ray Conniff quoted in *Mr. Trumpet: The Trials, Tribulations, and Triumph of Bunny Berigan*, Zirpolo, 2011, p267

15. Buddy Rich quoted in *Super Drummer*, Balliett, 1968, p93

16. Georgie Auld quoted in *The Lighter Side of Jazz*, Feather/Tracy, 1979, p72

17. Quote from *Swing, Swing, Swing: The Life and Times of Benny Goodman*, Griffin, 1991, p227

18. Haywood Henry quoted in *The World of Swing*, Dance, 1974

19. Stanley Kay quoted in *Drummin' Men*, Korall, 1990, p264

20. Buddy Rich quoted in *Crescendo* magazine, 1981

21. Harry Sweets Edison quoted in *Laughter From the Hip*, Feather/Tracy, 1979, p9

22. Georgie Auld quoted in *Laughter from the Hip*, Feather/Tracy, 1979, p73

23. Auld quoted in *Traps The Drum Wonder*, Tormé, 1991, p39

24. Rich quoted in the article "Rich and Tormé: Wild Repartee, Part II," *Downbeat*, Feb 23, 1978

25. Harry James quoted in *Trumpet Blues: The Life of Harry James*, Levinson, 1999, p27

26. Stanley Kay quoted in *JazzWax*, June 25, 2010

CHAPTER 5: ARTIE SHAW AND HIS ORCHESTRA

1. Artie Shaw quoted on the album cover *Melody and Madness*, Vol IV, 1984

2. Artie Shaw quoted in *The Trouble with Cinderella*, Shaw, 1952, p238

3. John Hammond quoted in *Non-Stop Flight*, White, 1998, p42

4. Bernie Privin quoted in *Non-Stop Flight*, White, 1998, p55

5. Artie Shaw quoted in the TV documentary "Quest for Perfection," BBC, 2003

6. Billie Holiday quoted in *Non-Stop Flight*, White, 1998, p43

7. Artie Shaw quoted in *Non-Stop Flight*, White, 1998, p52

8. Artie Shaw quoted on the album cover *Melody and Madness, Vol IV*, Anders R Öhman

9. Artie Shaw quoted in *Jazzen Går Vidare*, Lindgren, Stockholm, 1958

10. Artie Shaw quoted in *Off the Record: An Oral History of Popular Music*, Smith, 1989

11. Buddy Rich quoted in *Super Drummer*, Balliett, 1968, p93

12. Jay Corre quoted in *Mr. Trumpet: The Trials, Tribulations, and Triumph of Bunny Berigan*, Zirplo, p263

13. Georgie Auld quoted in *Traps The Drum Wonder*, Tormé, 1991, p40

14. Buddy Rich quoted in *Drummin' Men*, Korall, 1990, p265

15. Mike Zirpolo interviewed by the author, March 20, 2014

16. Shaw quoted in *Who is Artie Shaw, and Why is he Following Me?* Pacheco, Author House, 2005

17. Stanley Kay quoted in *Jazz Wax*, June 25, 2010

18. Buddy Rich quoted in *Drummin' Men*, Korall, 1990, p268

19. Artie Shaw quoted in *Profile: Artie Shaw*, Yanow, p102

20. Helen Forrest quoted in *I Had the Craziest Dream*, Forrest, 1982

21. George T Simon quoted in *Downbeat*, Feb, 1939

22. Buddy Rich quoted in *Drummin' Men*, Korall, 1990, p270

23. Artie Shaw quoted in *The Trouble with Cinderella*, Shaw, 1952, p339

24. Artie Shaw quoted in *Jam Session*, Shapiro/Hentoff, 1986, p384

CHAPTER 6: DRUMMER WITHOUT A BAND

1. Jerry Gray quoted in *Shavian Matters Revisited*, Zirpolo, 2010, p6

2. Georgie Auld quoted in *Traps The Drum Wonder*, Tormé, 1991, p44
3. Artie Shaw quoted in *The Trouble with Cinderella*, Shaw, 1952, p349
4. Artie Shaw quoted in the film *Time is All You've Got*, Bridge Film Productions, 1985
5. S. Sylvan Simon quoted in *Non-Stop Flight*, White, 1998, p64 .
6. Artie Shaw quoted in *Three Chords for Beauty's Sake*, Nolan, 2010, p127
7. Artie Shaw quoted in *Traps The Drum Wonder*, Tormé, 1991, p49
8. Helen Forrest quoted in *Three Chords for Beauty's Sake*, Nolan, 2010, p129
9. Artie Shaw quoted in the TV documentary "Quest for Perfection," BBC, 2003
10. Carmen Mastren quoted in *Drummin' Men*, Korall, 1990, p273
11. Buddy Rich quoted in *Drummin' Men*, Korall, 1990, p272
12. Buddy Rich quoted in *Mister, I Am The Band*, Meriwether/Hintze, 1998, p14
13. Buddy Rich quoted in *The Torment of Buddy Rich*, Minahan, 2000, p154
14. Buddy Rich quoted in *All or Nothing at All: A Life of Frank Sinatra*, Clarke, 1997, p46

CHAPTER 7: TOMMY DORSEY AND HIS ORCHESTRA
1. Sy Oliver quoted in *Drummin' Men*, Korall, 1990, p277
2. Buddy Rich quoted in *Jazz Professional*, 1982
3. Billy Cronk quoted in *All or Nothing at All: A Life of Frank Sinatra*, Clarke, 1997, p43
4. Gene Krupa quoted in *Metronome*, April, 1956
5. Harry James quoted in *Trumpet Blues: The Life of Harry James*, Levinson, 1999, p64
6. Frank Sinatra quoted in *All or Nothing at All: A Life of Frank Sinatra*, Clarke, 1997, p41
7. Harry James quoted in *Trumpet Blues: The Life of Harry James*, Levinson, 1999, p79
8. Tommy Dorsey quoted in *Traps The Drum Wonder*, Tormé, 1991, p53
9. Frank Sinatra quoted in *Tommy Dorsey: Living in a Great Big Way*, Levinson, 2005, p116
10. Frank Sinatra quoted in *Sinatra: Människan och Artisten*, Lahr, Stockholm, 1997
11. Tony Bennett quoted in *All the Things You Are: The Life of Tony Bennett*, Evanier, 2011, p38
12. Unknown band member quoted in *All or Nothing at All: A Life of Frank Sinatra*, Clarke, 1997, p48
13. Jack Egan quoted in *Drummin' Men*, Korall, 1990, p277
14. Film critic Frank S. Nugent in *The New York Times*, June 1939
15. Artie Shaw and Lana Turner quoted in *Three Chords for Beauty's Sake*, Nolan, 2010, p135
16. Hymie Schertzer quoted in *Drummin' Men*, Korall, 1990, p275
17. Tommy Dorsey quoted in *Eddie Condon's Treasury of Jazz*, Condon, 1958, p275
18. Buddy Rich quoted in *Traps The Drum Wonder*, Tormé, 1991, p53
19. Frank Sinatra quoted in *Traps The Drum Wonder*, Tormé, 1991, p54
20. Jo Stafford quoted in *Tommy Dorsey: Living in a Great Big Way*, Levinson, 2005, p147
21. Buddy Rich quoted in *Mister, I Am The Band*, Meriwether/Hintze, 1998, p19
22. Joe Bushkin quoted in *Jazz Anecdotes: Second Time Around*, Crow, 2005, p323
23. Buddy Rich quoted in the TV show "The Mike Douglas Show," Westinghouse, August 28, 1970
24. Buddy Rich quoted in the TV show "The Mike Douglas Show," Westinghouse, August 28, 1970
25. Jo Stafford quoted in *Frank: The Voice*, Kaplan, 2010, p117
26. Buddy Rich quoted in the TV show "Parkinson," BBC, July 5, 1986

27. Tommy Dorsey quoted in *All or Nothing at All: A Life of Frank Sinatra*, Clarke, 1997, p49
28. Article in *Downbeat*, September 1, 1940
29. Buddy Rich quoted in the TV show "The Mike Douglas Show," Westinghouse, August 28, 1970
30. Mince quoted in *His Way: The Unauthorized Biography of Frank Sinatra*, Kelley, 1986, p69
31. Review in *The New York Times*, March 20, 1941
32. Buddy Rich quoted in *Downbeat*, October 1940
33. Morris Diamond quoted in *Tommy Dorsey: Living in a Great Big Way*, Levinson, 2005, p138
34. Herb Caen quoted in *Tommy Dorsey: Living in a Great Big Way*, Levinson, 2005, p150
35. Sammy Davis Jr. quoted in the article "The Frank Sinatra I Know," in *Downbeat*, August 22, 1956
36. Frank Sinatra quoted in *All or Nothing at All: A Life of Frank Sinatra*, Clarke, 1997, p47

CHAPTER 8: LOVE AND WAR

1. President Roosevelt's "Infamy" speech to Congress on December 8, 1941.
2. Buddy Rich quoted in *The Torment of Buddy Rich*, Minahan, 2000, p159
3. Jo Rich quoted in *Traps The Drum Wonder*, Tormé, 1991, p74 154
4. Frank Sinatra quoted in *Frank: The Making of a Legend*, Kaplan, p22
5. Skitch Henderson quoted in *Sinatra: Människan och Artisten*, Lahr, 1997
6. Dorsey quoted in *All or Nothing at All:A Life of Frank Sinatra*, Clarke, 1997, p72–73
7. Buddy Rich quoted in *Traps The Drum Wonder*, Tormé, 1991, p81
8. Buddy Rich quoted in *Mister, I Am The Band*, Meriwether/Hintze, 1998, p20
9. Buddy Rich quoted in *Traps The Drum Wonder*, Tormé, 1991, p80
10. Buddy Rich quoted in *Super Drummer*, Balliett, 1968, p119
11. Military Police
12. Commanding Officer
13. Article in *Downbeat*, June 1, 1944
14. Buddy Rich quoted in the Swedish magazine *Orkesterjournalen*, December 1970 164
15. Deane Kincaide quoted in *We Don't Play Requests: A Musical Biography/Discography of Buddy Rich*, Meriwether/Hintze, 1984, p10
16. Buddy DeFranco quoted in *A Biography of Buddy DeFranco*, Zammarchi/Mas, 2002, p59
17. Al Porcino interviewed by the author, August 28, 2013
18. Dorsey quoted in September in the *Rain: The Life of Nelson Riddle*, Levinson, 2005, p48
19. DeFranco quoted in September in the *Rain: The Life of Nelson Riddle*, Levinson, 2005, p46
20. Jo Jones quoted in *Rifftide:The Life and Opinions of Papa Jo Jones*, Murray, 2011, p47
21. Count Basie quoted in *Good Morning Blues: The Autobiography of Count Basie*, Murray, 2002, p268
22. Buddy Rich quoted in *Drummin' Men*, Korall, 1990, p283 171
23. Buddy Rich quoted in *Crescendo*, June–July 1983, p24

24. Stanley Kay quoted in *JazzWax*, June 25, 2010
25. Buddy Rich quoted in *Jazz Professional*, July 1982
26. Article in *The Toledo Blade*, April 3, 1945
27. Breakup according to an article in *Cumberland Evening Times*, Nov 23, 1948
28. Article in *Bandleaders*, January 1946
29. Ed Shaughnessy quoted in *Downbeat*, April 12, 1973
30. Gene Lees quoted in *Singers and the Song*, Lees, 1987, p164
31. Alvin Stoller quoted in *Modern Drummer*, January 1990, p83
32. Buddy Rich quoted in *Super Drummer*, Balliett, 1968, p99

CHAPTER 9: BUDDY RICH AND HIS ORCHESTRA

1. Buddy Rich quoted in *Sinatra: His Way,* Kelley, 1987, p109
2. Eddie Finckel quoted in *Mister, I Am The Band*, Meriwether/Hintze, 1998, p26
3. Tony Scott quoted in *Downbeat*, October 17, 1956 182
4. Johnny Mandel quoted in *JazzWax* , October 22, 2008
5. Lester Young quoted in *Chicago Daily News*, December 1945
6. Buddy Rich quoted in *Mister, I Am The Band*, Meriwether/Hintze, 1998, p25
7. Benny Goodman quoted in *Traps The Drum Wonder*, Tormé, 1991, p91
8. Buddy Rich quoted in *Mister, I Am The Band*, Meriwether/Hintze, 1998, p28
9. Buddy Rich quoted in *Metronome*, October 1946
10. Based on an article in *The Times from San Mateo, California*, March 13, 1948
11. Stanley Kay quoted in *JazzWax*, June 25, 2010
12. Article in *The Morning Journal*, May 4, 1946
13. William F Ludwig II quoted in *The Making of a Drum Company*, Ludwig, 2001, p46
14. William F Ludwig II quoted in *The Making of a Drum Company*, Ludwig, 2001, p46
15. Review in the Swedish magazine *Orkesterjournalen*, November, 1946
16. The album *One Night Stand with the Battle of Dorseys* released on Joyce, no 1011
17. Walter Winchell in *The Evening Journal*, January 22, 1947
18. Louis Armstrong quoted in *JazzBar*, Condon, 1958, p166
19. Dave Tough quoted in *Jazzens historia*, Stearns, 1960, p154
20. Lennie Tristano quoted in *Jazzens historia*, Stearns, 1960, p159
21. Dizzy Gillespie quoted in *Jam Session*, Shapiro/Hentoff, 1986 p399
22. Buddy Rich quoted in *Metronome*, July, 1946
23. Dorian Leigh quoted in *The Independent*, July 14, 2008
24. Dorian Leigh quoted in *The Girl Who Had Everything*, Leigh/Hobe, 1980, p59
25. Leigh quoted in *Model: The Ugly Business of Beautiful Women*, Gross, Bantam Press, 1995, p72
26. Leigh quoted in *The Girl Who Had Everything*, Leigh/Hobe, 1980, p63 198
27. Buddy Rich quoted in the TV show "Parkinson," BBC, November 5, 1986
28. Buddy Rich quoted in *Traps The Drum Wonder*, Tormé, 1991, p95
29. Buddy Rich quoted in *Mister, I Am The Band*, Meriwether/Hintze, 1998, p32
30. Al Cohn quoted in *Mister, I Am The Band*, Meriwether/Hintze, 1998, p32
31. Buddy Rich quoted in *Mister, I Am The Band*, Meriwether/Hintze, 1998, p33

CHAPTER 10: STUBBORN GUY

1. Mickey Rich quoted in *Traps The Drum Wonder*, Tormé, 1991, p97
2. Sammy Davis Jr. quoted in the TV show "Parkinson," BBC, October 21, 1978 206
3. Buddy Rich quoted in *Jazz Professional*, 1968

4. Marge Rich quoted in *Traps The Drum Wonder*, Tormé, 1991, p146
5. Al Rose quoted in *I Remember Jazz: Six Decades Among the Great Jazzmen*, Rose, 1987, p224
6. Review by Bill Smith in *Billboard*, March 31, 1948
7. Pauly Cohen interviewed by the author, May 18, 2014
8. Terry Gibbs quoted in *Good Vibes*, Gibbs, 2003, p65
9. Interview with Stanley Kay in the video *Burning for Buddy*, DCI Music video, 1994
10. Terry Gibbs quoted in *Good Vibes*, Gibbs, 2003, p65
11. Marge Rich quoted in *Traps The Drum Wonder*, Tormé, 1991, p103
12. Hal McKusick interviewed by the author, September 21, 2011
13. Hal McKusick quoted in *JazzWax*, October 9, 2007 214
14. Terry Gibbs quoted in *Good Vibes*, Gibbs, 2003, p70
15. Jack Schiffman quoted in *Mister, I Am The Band*, Meriwether/Hintze, 1998, p34
16. Hal McKusick interviewed by the author, September 22, 2011
17. Terry Gibbs quoted in *Good Vibes*, Gibbs, 2003, p68
18. Article in *Downbeat*, January 14, 1949
19. Bellson interviewed by Anthony Brown, Archives center, National Museum of American History, October 20, 2005
20. Ted Fio Rito (1900–1971) was an American composer, bandleader and pianist
21. Louie Bellson quoted in *Downbeat*, unknown year
22. Louie Bellson quoted in *Drums & Drumming*, January-February, 1989
23. Hal McKusick interviewed by the author, September 22, 2011
24. Album title *Glen Gray and the Casa Loma Orchestra On the Air 1934*, Extreme Rarities LP
25. Article by Ted Warner in the Swedish magazine *Orkesterjournalen*, April 1949
26. Buddy Rich quoted in *Jazz Professional*, 1968
27. Buddy Rich quoted in *Super Drummer*, Balliett, 1968, p99

CHAPTER 11: JAZZ AT THE PHILHARMONIC

1. Granz quoted in the radio program "Out of the Norm: The Life of Norman Granz," BBC, 2003
2. Granz quoted in *The Sound of Surprise*, Balliett, 1959, p17
3. Granz quoted in *Norman Granz: The Man who used Jazz for Justice*, Hershorn, 2011, p117
4. Copy of the flyer in the author's possession.
5. Buck Clayton quoted in *Buck Claytons Jazz World*, Clayton/Elliott, 1986, p131
6. Buddy Rich quoted in *Mister, I Am The Band*, Meriwether/Hintze, 1998, p40
7. Review by Ted Warner in the Swedish magazine *Orkesterjournalen*, October 1949
8. Rich quoted in the radio program "Out of the Norm: The Life of Norman Granz," BBC, 2003
9. Granz quoted in the radio program "Out of the Norm, The Life of Norman Granz," BBC, 2003
10. Charlie Parker quoted on the album cover *Charlie Parker with Strings*
11. Lennie Tristano quoted in *Bird: The Life and Music of Charlie Parker*, Haddix, p124
12. Date is questioned in *Norman Granz: The Man who used Jazz for Justice*, Hershorn, 2011, p180
13. Norman Granz quoted on the album cover *Charlie Parker with Strings*
14. Buddy Rich quoted in *Downbeat*, December 16, 1949

15. John Karoly quoted in *Mister, I Am The Band*, Meriwether, 1998, p41
16. Max Harrison quoted in *Charlie Parker*, Harrison, 1960, p69
17. Roy Haynes quoted in *Charlie Parker: His Music and Life*, Woideck, 1996, p196
18. Article in *Billboard* by Hal Webman, September 9, 1950
19. O'Farrill quoted in *Swing to Bop: An Oral History of the Transition in Jazz in the 1940s*, Gitler, 1985, p293
20. Machito quoted in *Rhythm of Race*, D'Abreau, 2015, p162
21. Shirley Woolf quoted in *The Hungry Heart*, Baker/Chase, 1993, p294
22. Mel Tormé quoted in *Traps The Drum Wonder*, Tormé, 1991, p105
23. Zoot Sims quoted in *Mister, I Am The Band*, Meriwether, 1998, p42
24. Leo de Lyon interviewed in *Classic Television*, September 2012
25. Leo de Lyon quoted in *From Small Screen to Vinyl: A Guide to Television Stars who Made Records*, Leszczak, 2015, p89
26. Jonathan Haze in *Names You Never Remember, With Faces You Never Forgot*, Humphreys, 2006, p116
27. Review by Ted Warner in the Swedish magazine *Orkesterjournalen*, August 10, 1951
28. Chubby Jackson quoted on the album cover *Buddy Rich in Miami*, 1957
29. Marty Napoleon in *World of Gene Krupa: That Legendary Drummin' Man*, Klauber, 1990, p165
30. Buddy Rich quoted in *Mister, I Am The Band*, Meriwether, 1998, p44
31. Buddy Rich quoted in *From Birdland to Broadway: Scenes From a Jazz Life*, Crow, 1992, p39
32. Article by Dorothy Kilgallen in *The Toledo Blade*, December 15, 1948

CHAPTER 12: CROSSROADS

1. Gene Krupa quoted in *Drummin' Men*, Korall, 1990, p49
2. Lionel Hampton quoted in *Hamp: An Autobiography*, Hampton/Haskins, 1989, p70
3. John Hammond quoted in *Drummin' Men*, Korall, 1990, p70
4. Gene Krupa quoted in *Drummin' Men*, Korall, 1990, p71
5. Goodman quoted in *World of Gene Krupa: That Legendary Drummin' Man*, Klauber, 1990, p32
6. Stanley Kay quoted in *Jazz Improv*, Vol 6, no 3, 2006, p112
7. Buddy Rich to Mel Lewis in interview with Loren Schoenberg on Radio WKCR, 1982
8. Mel Lewis' story is verified in *The Making of a Drum Company*, Ludwig II, 2001, p48
9. Review by Hal Webman in *Downbeat*, Oct. 22, 1952
10. Stanley Kay quoted in *Jazz Improv*, Vol 6, no 3, 2006, p112
11. Buddy Rich in interview with Willis Conover for "Voice of America Radio," March/April 1956
12. Jack Egan quoted in *Drummin' Men*, Korall, 1990, p85
13. Lew McCreary quoted in *Trumpet Blues: The Life of Harry James*, Levinson, 1999, p182
14. Gene Krupa quoted in *The Torment of Buddy Rich*, Minahan, 2000, p128
15. Buddy Rich quoted in *Traps The Drum Wonder*, Tormé, 1991, p108
16. Marie Rich quoted in *Traps The Drum Wonder*, Tormé, 1991, p112
17. Marie Rich quoted in *The Torment of Buddy Rich*, Minahan, 2000, p128
18. Gillespie quoted in *Norman Granz: The Man who used Jazz for Justice*, Hershorn, 2011, p193
19. Jones quoted in *Norman Granz: The Man who used Jazz for Justice*, Hershorn,

2011, p192

20. Buddy Rich quoted in *Downbeat*, June 17, 1953
21. Review in *Billboard*, June 6, 1953
22. Norman Granz quoted in *Downbeat*, August 12, 1953
23. The album *Jam Session 3* was released on August 3, 1953
24. Oscar Peterson quoted in *The Will to Swing*, Lees, 1988, p117
25. Marie Rich quoted in *DrumTracks*, Vol 5, no 2
26. Cathy Rich quoted in *Jazz Improv*, 2006, Vol 6, no 3, p138
27. Buddy Rich quoted in *Downbeat*, December 1, 1954
28. Article in *The Argus*, July 19, 1954
29. Artie Shaw quoted in the TV documentary "Quest for Perfection," BBC, 2003
30. Article in *The Canberra Times*, July 20, 1954
31. Buddy Rich quoted in *Downbeat*, October 6, 1954
32. Buddy Rich quoted in *Downbeat*, December 1, 1954
33. Pauly Cohen interviewed by the author, May 18, 2014
34. John Frosk quoted in *Tommy Dorsey: Living in a Geat Big Way*, Levinson, 2005, p275
35. Pauly Cohen quoted in *Tommy Dorsey: Living in a Great Big Way*, Levinson, 2005, p264
36. Buddy Rich quoted in *Downbeat*, June 15, 1955
37. Buddy Rich quoted in *Mister, I Am The Band*, Meriwether, 1998, p51
38. Buddy Rich quoted in *Tommy Dorsey: Living in a Great Big Way*, Levinson, 2005, p275
39. Tommy Dorsey quoted in *Mister, I Am The Band*, Meriwether, 1998, p51

CHAPTER 13: DRUM BARBEQUE
1. Nat Hentoff, review in *Downbeat*, September 17, 1955
2. Buddy Rich quoted in the radio program "Voice of America," October 2, 1955
3. Buddy Rich quoted in *Downbeat*, October 5, 1955
4. Norman Granz quoted on the album cover *Buddy Rich Sings Johnny Mercer*, LP 283
5. Buddy Rich quoted in *Crescendo*, July, 1982
6. The album has the alternative title *Big Band Shout*
7. Buddy Rich quoted in *Downbeat*, Aptil 6, 1955
8. Buddy Rich quoted in *Jazz Journal*, interview with Stan Wolle, November, 1974
9. James Hill quoted in *Trumpet Blues: The Life of Harry James*, Levinson, 1999, p197
10. Buddy Rich quoted in *Mister, I Am The Band*, Meriwether, 1998, p57
11. Carl Ritchie quoted in *Downbeat*, June 27, 1957
12. Cathy Rich interviewed by the author, June 15, 2014
13. Buddy Rich quoted in *Mister, I Am The Band*, Meriwether, 1998, p57
14. Charles Middleton quoted on the album cover *Richcraft*
15. Review in *Billboard*, November 16, 1959
16. Kenny Clare quoted in *Crescendo*, May 1967
17. Buddy Rich quoted in *Downbeat*, October 1959
18. Review in *Variety*, October 14, 1959
19. Review in *Downbeat*, November 1959

CHAPTER 14: STRUGGLING ON THE ROAD
1. Buddy Rich quoted in *Mister, I Am The Band*, Meriwether, 1998, p60
2. Buddy Rich quoted in *Super Drummer*, Balliett, 1968, p105
3. Buddy Rich quoted in *Super Drummer*, Balliett, 1968, p111

4. Buddy Rich quoted in the TV show "The Mike Douglas Show," Westinghouse, 1967
5. Associated Booking Corporation
6. Buddy Rich quoted on the album cover *The Driver*, 1960
7. Buddy Rich quoted in *Downbeat*, October 27, 1960
8. Mike Mainieri interviewed by the author, July 1, 2013
9. Mike Mainieri quoted in *Downbeat*, December 1995
10. Mike Mainieri interviewed by the author, July 1, 2013
11. Buddy Rich quoted in *Santa Cruz Sentinel*, August 16, 1961
12. Congressional Record: Proceedings and Debates of the Congress, Vol 108, part 11
13. Buddy Rich quoted in *Super Drummer*, Balliett, 1968, p34
14. Buddy Rich quoted in *Spin*, October 1985
15. Joey Adams quoted in *On the Road for Uncle Sam*, Adams, 1963, p65
16. David Lucas interviewed by the author, November 25, 2017
17. David Lucas interviewed by the author, November 25, 2017
18. United States Information Service
19. Celeste Evans quoted in *Chicago Magic: A History of Stagecraft and Spectacle*, Witter, 2013
20. David Lucas interviewed by the author, November 25, 2017
21. Review from *The Times of Vietnam*, November 3, 1961
22. Sam Most quoted in *Los Angeles Times*, July 24, 1987
23. *On the Performance Front: US Theatre and Internationalism*, Canning, 2015
24. Mike Mainieri interviewed by the author, June 30, 2013
25. Congressional Record, tr 14356, July 20, 1962
26. David Lucas interviewed by the author, November 25, 2017
27. Article in *The Evening Standard from Union Town*, December 8, 1961
28. Buddy Rich quoted in *Mister, I Am The Band*, Meriwether, 1998, p63
29. Harry James quoted in *Trumpet Blues: The Life of Harry James, Levinson*, 1999, p220
30. Cathy Rich quoted in *Traps The Drum Wonder*, Tormé, 1991, p211
31. Cathy Rich quoted in *Modern Drummer*, April 1991
32. Buddy Rich quoted in *Traps The Drum Wonder*, Tormé, 1991, p120
33. Marie Rich quoted in *Jazz Improv*, Vol 6, no 3, 2006, p139
34. Review in *Downbeat*, August 12, 1965
35. Phil Wilson quoted in *Inside the Big Band Drum Chart*, Fidyk, 2015
36. Buddy Rich quoted in the TV show "Parkinsson," BBC, November 5, 1986
37. Buddy Rich quoted in an audio interview, August 28, 1986, unknown source

CHAPTER 15: SWINGING NEW BIG BAND

1. Buddy Rich quoted in the TV show "Parkinson," BBC, March 6, 1982
2. Bobby Shew quoted in *All That Jazz*, February 25, 2010
3. Joe Morello quoted in *Modern Drummer*, August 1987, p28
4. Review in the *Los Angeles Times*, September 23, 1966
5. Stan Kenton quoted on the album cover *Buddy Rich: Swinging New Big Band*, 1966
6. Johnny Carson quoted on the album cover *The New One*, LP Pacific Jazz records, 1967
7. Buddy Rich quoted in *Downbeat*, April 20, 1967
8. Bobby Shew quoted in *Jazz Improv*, Vol 6, no 3, 2006, p150
9. Dick Bock quoted in *Billboard*, December 10, 1966
10. Johnny Carson quoted in *The Torment of Buddy Rich*, Minahan, 2000, p144
11. Johnny Carson quoted on the album cover *Live on King Street*, 1985
12. Buddy Rich quoted in *Super Drummer*, Balliett, 1968, p114

13. Dusty Springfield in the TV show "Clive Andersson Talks Back," BBC, October 13, 1995
14. Ernie Watts interviewed by the author, April 22, 2017
15. Buddy Rich quoted in *Downbeat*, May 20, 1967
16. Columbia Special products, CSP131
17. Buddy Rich quoted on the album *Big Swing Face*, Sunset Records, SUN 5019
18. Cathy Rich quoted in *Jazz Improv*, Vol. 6, no 3, 2006, p138
19. Review in *High Fidelity*, October 1967
20. Article in *Crescendo*, May 1967
21. Buddy Rich quoted in the TV show "Late Night Line Up," BBC, April 6, 1967
22. Buddy Greco quoted in S*even Dirty Words: The Life and Crimes of George Carlin*, Sullivan, 2010
23. Allyn Ferguson quoted on the album cover *The New One*, CD Pacific Jazz Records , 1967
24. Ernie Watts interviewed by the author, April 22, 2017
25. Buddy Rich quoted in *Fighting Stars*, December 1973
26. Buddy Rich quoted in *The New York Times*, June 2, 1974
27. Pat LaBarbera interviewed by the author, January, 26, 2013
28. Joe LaBarbera interviewed by the author, February. 16, 2013
29. John LaBarbera interviewed by the author, October. 6, 2011
30. Ernie Watts interviewed by the author, April 22, 2017
31. Ron Paley interviewed by the author, February. 14, 2012
32. Johnny Carson quoted in *The Torment of Buddy Rich*, Minahan, 2000, p145
33. Joe LaBarbera interviewed by the author, February 16, 2013
34. Bobby Shew quoted in *All About Jazz*, February 25, 2010

CHAPTER 16: DIFFERENT DRUMMER

1. Dick Bock quoted in *Billboard*, July 29, 1967
2. Ernie Watts interviewed by the author, April 22, 2017
3. Pat LaBarbera interviewed by the author, March 23, 2013
4. Review in *Billboard*, June 8, 1969
5. Taufiq Husain quoted on the album cover *Rich a la Rahka*, CD BGO Records, 1968
6. Article in *The Boston Globe*, April 3, 1987
7. Al Porcino interviewed by the author, August 28, 2013
8. Al Porcino interviewed in *Jazz Wax*, September 9, 2011
9. Don Menza quoted in *Straight Life: The Story of Art Pepper*, Pepper, 1979, p383
10. Dick Bock quoted on the album cover *Mercy, Mercy,* World Pacific Jazz, LP ST20133
11. Buddy Rich quoted on the album cover *Mercy, Mercy,* World Pacific Jazz, LP ST20133
12. Review in the *Los Angeles Times*, July 16, 1968
13. Article in *The Indianapolis Star*, July 12, 1968
14. Pat LaBarbera interviewed by the author, January 27, 2013
15. Buddy Rich quoted in the TV show "Jazz at the Maltings," BBC2, September 25, 1968
16. Richie Cole interviewed by the author, April 25, 2017
17. The album *Big Cole: Richie Cole w/Buddy Rich and His Orchestra*, LIBK26P6133
18. Richie Cole interviewed by the author, April 25, 2017
19. Miles Davis quoted in *Rolling Stone*, December 1969
20. Buddy Rich quoted in the TV show "Parkinson," BBC, November 5, 1986
21. Pat LaBarbera interviewed by the author, January 27, 2013
22. Marie Rich quoted in *Jazz Improv*, Vol. 6, no 3, 2006, p140

23. Buddy Rich quoted in the TV show "Talk of the Town," BBC, November 23, 1969
24. Cathy Rich quoted in *Modern Drummer*, April 1991
25. Bo Johnson interviewed by the author, October 11, 2012
26. Buddy Rich quoted in the Swedish magazine *Orkesterjournalen*, December 1970
27. Buddy Rich quoted in *Spin*, October 1985
28. Pat LaBarbera interviewed by the author, January 26, 2013
29. Cathy Rich quoted in *Modern Drummer*, April 1991
30. Pat LaBarbera interviewed by the author, January 27, 2013
31. Buddy Rich quoted in *Mister, I Am The Band*, Meriwether/Hintze, 1998, p96
32. John LaBarbera quoted in *Drummin' Men*, Korall, 1990, p295
33. Roy Andersson's article in *Wappingers Falls*, Ohio, March 10, 1987
34. Clarence Hintze interviewed by the author, July 23, 2001
35. Cathy Rich quoted in *Modern Drummer*, April 1991
36. Bobby Colomby quoted in *Modern Drummer*, August 1987
37. Review in *Downbeat*, March 19, 1974
38. Ron Paley interviewed by the author, October 27, 2013
39. John LaBarbera interviewed by the author, Oct 6, 2011
40. John Hoffman quoted in the radio program "Jazz Radio on the Gold Coast," 94:1 FM

CHAPTER 17: BUDDY'S PLACES

1. Stanley Kay quoted in *Jazz Improv*, Vol. 6, no 3, 2006, p108
2. Buddy Rich quoted in *The Chicago Sun-Times*, 1974
3. Buddy Rich quoted in *We Don't Play Requests: A Musical Biography/Discography of Buddy Rich*, Meriwether/Hintze, 1984, p48
4. Buddy Rich quoted in *The New York Times*, June 2, 1974
5. Buddy Rich in interview with Efrom Allen at Buddy's Place, December 1974
6. Jerry Bradley quoted in *Mister, I Am The Band*, Meriwether/Hintze, 1998, p105
7. Steve Marcus quoted in an English flyer, 1978
8. Buddy Rich quoted at Dixie Queen, Stockholm, SVT, July 6, 1986
9. Buddy Rich quoted in *Mister, I Am The Band*, Meriwether/Hintze, 1998, p107
10. Conversation with Basie is quoted from *The Torment of Buddy Rich*, Minahan, 2000, p208.
11. Don Hughes quoted in *Ottawa Citizen*, July 14, 1975
12. Buddy Rich quoted in *The New York Times*, July 18, 1975
13. Article in the *Washington Afro-American Red Star*, July 29, 1975
14. Article in *Southern Africa*, Vol VIII, no 8, September 1975
15. Article in *Black World Negro Digest*, November 1975
16. Cathy Rich quoted in *Modern Drummer*, April 1991
17. Buddy Rich quoted in *Modern Drummer*, January 1977 402
18. Buddy Rich quoted in *Crescendo*, January 1979
19. Buddy Rich quoted in the TV show "Larry King Live," November 25, 1985
20. Buddy Rich quoted in *Mister, I Am The Band*, Meriwether/Hintze, 1998, p109
21. Buddy Rich quoted in *The New York Times*, June 2, 1974
22. Martin Ross quoted in *The Kansas City Times*, January 1, 1976
23. Marge Rich quoted in *Traps The Drum Wonder*, Tormé, 1991, p146
24. Dave Stahl quoted in *We Don't Play Requests: A Musical Biography/Discography of Buddy Rich*, Meriwether/Hintze, 1984, p53
25. Bo Johnson interviewed by the author, October 11, 2012
26. Review in the Swedish magazine *Orkesterjournalen*, April, 1977

27. Bo Johnson interviewed by the author, October 11, 2012
28. Cathy Rich interviewed by the author, June 15, 2014
29. Leonard Feather quoted in the Swedish magazine *Orkesterjournalen*, September, 1977
30. Lars Jernryd interviewed by the author, November 5, 2017.
31. Ed Shaughnessy quoted in *Drummin' Men*, Korall, 1990, p281
32. Ed Shaughnessy quoted in *Downbeat*, April 12, 1973
33. Ed Shaughnessy interviewed by the author, October 2, 2003
34. Buddy Rich quoted on "The Tonight Show Starring Johnny Carson," May 29, 1980
35. Peter Lundin interviewed by the author, March 3, 2014
36. Uffe Andersson interviewed by the author, March 5, 2014

CHAPTER 18: LIFE AT STAKE

1. Cathy Rich interviewed by the author, June 15, 2014
2. Buddy Rich quoted in *Mister, I Am The Band* Meriwether/Hintze, 1998, p121
3. David Lucas interviewed by the author, November 25, 2017
4. Buddy Rich quoted in *Jazz Professional*, 1981
5. Buddy Rich quoted in *Jazz Professional*, July 1982
6. Dave Stahl interviewed by the author, January 21, 2013
7. Buddy Rich quoted in *Jazz Professional*, 1981
8. Buddy Rich quoted in *Jazz Professional*, 1981
9. Bucky Pizzarelli quoted in *The Last Miles: The Music of Miles Davis 1980–1991*, Cole, 2005
10. Milt Hinton in interview with Joe Williams, May 31, 1995, for the *Jazz Archive of Hamilton*
11. Buddy Rich quoted in *Mister, I Am The Band*, Meriwether/Hintze, 1998, p122
12. Buddy Rich quoted in *Downbeat*, March 1982
13. Falcone Jr quoted in *Frankly, Just Between Us: My Life Conducting Frank Sinatra's Music*, Falcone, 2005, p95
14. Dave Stahl interviewed by the author, January 23, 2013
15. Review in *Variety*, August 25, 1982
16. Cathy Rich interviewed by the author, June 15, 2014
17. Dave Stahl interviewed by the author, January 23, 2013
18. Cathy Rich interviewed by the author, June 15, 2014
19. Buddy Rich quoted in *We Don't Play Requests: A Musical Biography/Discography of Buddy Rich*, Meriwether/Hintze, 1984, p59
20. Buddy Rich quoted in *Spin*, October, 1985
21. Cathy Rich quoted in *Modern Drummer*, April 1991
22. Buddy Rich quoted in the TV show "Larry King Live," November 25, 1985
23. Freddie Gruber quoted in *Drummin' Men*, Korall, 1990, p299
24. Cathy Rich quoted in *Modern Drummer*, April 1991
25. Bo Stenhammar interviewed by the author, September 6, 2013
26. Peter Jablonski interviewed by the author, April 20, 2017
27. Buddy Rich quoted in the Swedish magazine *Orkesterjournalen*, November, 1984
28. Louie Bellson in short comment to the author, November 17, 2003
29. Bobby Shew quoted in *All About Jazz*, February 25, 2010
30. Joe LaBarbera quoted in *Modern Drummer*, April 2002
31. Eric Miyashiro interviewed by the author, October 13, 2016
32. Lee Musiker quoted in *JazzTimes*, March 2002, p18
33. Dave Panichi quoted in *JazzTimes*, March 2002, p18

34. Dave Panichi quoted in *The Monthly*, July 2007
35. Ernie Watts interviewed by the author, April 22, 2017
36. Dave Panichi quoted in *The Monthly*, July 2007
37. Buddy Rich quoted in "Kups Show Talk" with Irv Kupcinet, Chicago TV, July 12, 1985
38. Buddy Rich quoted in *Mister, I Am The Band*, Meriwether/Hintze, 1998, p129
39. Eric Miyashiro interviewed by the author, October 13, 2016
40. Buddy Rich quoted in the TV concert at Dixie Queen, SVT, Stockholm, July 6, 1986
41. Mel Powell quoted in *The New Yorker*, June 15, 1987
42. Cathy Rich interviewed by the author, June 15, 2014
43. Buddy Rich quoted in *Mister, I Am The Band*, Meriwether/Hintze, 1998, p134
44. Review in *The New York Times*, December 8, 1986
45. Review in *Modern Drummer*, December 1986
46. Confirmed by Phil Collins in the DVD *A Salute to Buddy Rich*, Hudson Music, 1998
47. Tom Garling interviewed by the author, February 17, 2013
48. Eric Miyashiro interviewed by the author, October 13, 2016
49. Cathy Rich interviewed by the author, June 15, 2014
50. Marie Rich quoted in *Drummin' Men*, Korall, 1990, p301
51. Buddy Rich quoted in *Backstage at the Tonight Show: From Johnny Carson to Jay Leno*, Sweeny, 2006, p176
52. Freddie Gruber quoted in *Drummin' Men*, Korall, 1990, p301
53. Article in *The New York Times*, March 18, 1987
54. Freddie Gruber quoted in *Drummin' Men*, Korall, 1990, p302

EPILOGUE
1. Buddy Rich quoted in *Mister, I Am The Band*, Meriwether/Hintze, 1998, p7
2. Bo Johnson interviewed by the author, October 11, 2012
3. John LaBarbera interviewed by the author, October 6, 2011
4. Buddy Rich quoted in *Downbeat*, March 1982
5. Stanley Kay quoted in *JazzWax*, June 25, 2010
6. Bo Stenhammar interviewed by the author, September 6, 2013
7. Buddy Rich quoted in *International Herald Tribune*, July 3, 1986
8. Buddy Rich quoted in *The New York Times*, June 2, 1974
9. Buddy Rich quoted in *Super Drummer*, Balliett, 1968, p127

ACKNOWLEDGMENTS

Amanda, my daughter
You mean everything to me.

Cathy Rich
Thanks for answering all my questions and verifying some details around your father's childhood and his life in general.

Clarence Hintze
I am so grateful for all the Buddy Rich material you have sent through the years, and I really can't thank you enough. I am so sorry that you no longer are alive and could read the result of this book.

Walter Hern
We have known each other for a long time now and built our collections together. You have been a very big help for me, and I thank you for that.

Terry Wayland
You have sent me so many photos and articles that I don't think this book could have been written without your help.

The LaBarbera Brothers (Pat, Joe, and John)
You each told me many things about what it was like to play with Buddy Rich, or write charts for him, and I appreciate this so much.

Mike Mainieri
Thank you so much for telling me what really happened in Asia 1961.

Bruce Klauber
Who helped me in the editing process, and gave lots of important advice.

Torbjörn Ring
Who published and edited the original version of this book.

Jaruek Ruangjaroen
Who helped me with editing all the old photos in the original version of this book, and helped me analyzing the Asian sources.

Rob Wallis
My U.S. publisher at Hudson Music, it has been a pleasure to work with you.

A very big thank you to:
Greg Bauman, Reb Bilinski, Roger Berg, Louis Bernstein, Charley Braun, Dave Cooper, Per DyrnesliKristensen, Janne Ersson, Walt Heitner, Ron Hutchinson, Mike James, Peter Lanzarone, Leonard Maltin, Rien Moeliker, Janne Mårtensson, Geoffrey Nelson, Graham Sheridan, Shirley Shiffrin, Rex Strother, Paul Testa, Rob Wallis, Joseph Weinmeyer and Brian Wilson.

The publishers would like to thank Cathy and Marie Rich, Max Weinberg, Peter Erskine, Steve Smith, Bill Cobham, Dave Weckl and Sherrie Maricle for their support and contributions.

Last but not least, thanks to all the people I have interviewed and all of those who helped me through the years.

SOURCES
Books

Adams, Joey. *On the Road for Uncle Sam*. New York, NY: Bernard Geis Associated, 1963

Adler, Henry. *Buddy Rich – Interpretation of Snare Drum Rudiments*. New York, NY: Embassy Music Corp, 1942

Baker, JeanClaude, Chris Chase. *Josephine Baker: The Hungry Heart*. New York, NY: Cooper Square Press, 1993

Balliett, Whitney. *The Sound of Surprise*. Pelican Books, 1959

Balliett, Whitney. *Super Drummer*. Indianapolis, IN: The Bobbs–Merrill Co, 1968

Balliett, Whitney. *Goodbyes and Other Messages: A Journal of Jazz 1981–1990*. New York, NY: Oxford Univ Press, 1991

Cangany, Harry, Rick Van Horn. *The Great American Drums and the Companies That Made Them*. Cedar Grove, NJ: Modern Drummer, 1996

Canning M Charlotte. *On the Performance Front: US Theatre and Internationalism*, London: Palgrave Macmillan, 2015

Carr, Ian, Digby Fairweather, Brian Priestly. *The Rough Guide to Jazz*. London: Rough Guides Ltd, 2004

Clarke, Donald. *All or Nothing at All – A Life of Frank Sinatra*. London: Macmillan Publishers Ltd, 1997

Cohan, Jon. *Zildjian – A History of the Legendary Cymbal Makers*. Milwaukee, WI: Hal Leonard Corporation, 1999

Cole George. *The Last Miles – The Music of Miles Davis 1980–1991*. Ann Arbor, MI: University of Michigan Press, 2005

Condon, Eddie, Richard Gehman. *Eddie Condon's Jazzbar*. Stockholm, Sweden: Rabén & Sjögren, 1958

Cooper, Dave. *Buddy Rich – A Lifetime of Music*. Cooper, 1989

Clayton, Buck, Nancy Miller Elliott. *Buck Clayton's Jazz World*. London: The Macmillan Press Ltd, 1986

Crow, Bill. *From Birdland to Broadway; Scenes from a Jazz Life*. New York, NY: Oxford University Press, 1992

Crow, Bill. *Jazz Anecdotes: Second Time Around*. New York, NY: Oxford University Press, 2005

Cullen, Frank, Florence Hackman, Donald McNeilly. *Vaudeville, Old and New: An Encyclopedia*. New York, NY: Routledge, 2006

D'Abreau, Christina. *Rhythms of Race: Cuban Musicians and the Making of Latino New York City and Miami 1940–1960*. Chapell Hill, NC: University of North Carolina Press, 2015

Dance, Stanley. *The World of Count Basie*. New York, NY: Charles Scribners's Sons, 1985

DiMuzio, Lennie, Jim Coffin, Thèrése DiMuzo. *Tales from the Cymbal Bag*. Green Harbor, MA: Jump Back Baby Productions, 2010

Dupuis, Robert. *Bunny Berigan: Elusive Legend of Jazz*. Baton Rouge, LA: Louisiana State University Press, 1993

Falcone Jr, Vincent. *Frankly, Just between Us – My Life Conducting Frank Sinatra's Music*, Milwaukee, WI: Hal Leonard Corp, 2005

Feather, Leonard, Tracy Jack. *Laughter from The Hip*. New York, NY: DaCapo Press, 1979

Fidyk, Steve. *Inside the Big Band Drum Chart*. Pacific, MO: Mel Bay Publishing,2015

Fricdwald, Will. *Sinatra! The Song is You: A Singer's Art*. New York, NY: First Da Capo Press, 1997

Gibbs, Terry, Cary Ginell. *Good Vibes – A Life in Jazz*. Lanham, MD: The Scarecrow Press Inc, 2003

Gitler, Ira. S*wing to Bop: An Oral History of the Transition in Jazz in the 1940s*. New York, NY: Oxford Univ Press, 1985

Guiness Book of Records. Stockholm, Sweden: Forum, 1977 and 1979

Hampton, Lionel, James Haskins. *Hamp*. New York, NY: Amistad Press Inc, 1989

Harrison, Max. *Charlie Parker*. Stockholm, Sweden: Hörsta, 1960

Hershorn, Ted. *Norman Granz – The Man who used jazz for justice*. Berkeley, CA: University of California Press, 2011

Hodes, Art, Chadwick Hansen. *The Life of Art Hodes*. Urbana, IL: University of Illinois

Press, 1992

Humphreys, Justin. *Names you Never Remember, with Faces you Never Forgot*. Boalsburg, PA: Bear Manor Media, 2006

Keepnews, Orrin, Bill Grauer Jr. *People and Places from New Orleans to Modern Jazz*. New York, NY: Crown Publications Inc, 1955

Kelley Kitty. *His Way – The Unauthorized Biography of Frank Sinatra*. New York, NY: H.B. Productions Inc, 1986

Klauber, Bruce. *World of Gene Krupa: That Legendary Drummin' Man*. Ventura, CA: Pathfinder Publications, 1990

Korall, Burt. *Drummin' Men – The Heartbeat of Jazz – The Swing Years*. New York, NY: Schirmer Books, 1990

Lahr, John. *Sinatra – Människan och Artisten*. Stockholm, Sweden: Norstedts Förlag, 1997

Lees, Gene. *Oscar Peterson – The Will to Swing*. Toronto: Lester & Orpen Dennys Ltd., 1988

Leigh, Dorian, Laura Hobe. *The Girl who had Everything*. Garden City, NY: Doubleday & Company Inc, 1980

Levinson, Peter J. *Trumpet Blues – The Life of Harry James*. New York, NY: Oxford University Press Inc, 1999

Levinson, Peter J. *September in the Rain: The Life of Nelson Riddle*. Lanham, MD: First Taylor Trade Publications, 2005

Leszczak, Bob. *From Small Screen to Vinyl: A Guide to Television Stars who made Records*. Lanham, MD: Rowman & Littlefield, 2015

Lindgren, CarlErik. *Jazzen går Vidare*. Stockholm, Sweden: Nordiska Musikförlaget, 1958

Ludwig, William F II, Rob Cook. *The Making of a Drum Company*. Alma, MI: Rebeats Publications, 2001

McClellan, Lawrence Jr. T*he Later Swing Era, 1942 to 1955*. Westport, CT: Greenwood Press, 2004

Meath, Jason Killian. *Hollywood on the Potomac*. Charleston, SC: Arcadia Publishing, 2009

Meriwether, Doug, Clarence Hintze. *We Don't Play Requests*. Chicago, IL: KAR

Publications, 1984

Meriwether, Doug, Clarence Hintze. *Mister, I Am the Band*. North Bellmore, NY: National Drum Association Inc, 1998

Minahan, John. *The Torment of Buddy Rich*. San Jose, CA: Writers Showcase, 2000

Morgan, Alun, Raymond Horricks. *Modern Jazz*. Stockholm, Sweden: Bonniers, 1956

Murray, Albert, *Count Basie: Good Morning Blues: The Autobiography of Count Basie*. New York, NY: Random House, 1985

Murray, Albert, Jo Jones, Paul Devin. *Rifftide: The Life and Opinions of Papa Jo Jones*. Minneapolis, MN: University of Minnesota Press, 2011

Nesbitt, Jim, Buddy Rich. *Inside Buddy Rich*. Delevan, NY: Kendor Music, 1984

Nimmo, Harry. *The Andrews Sisters: A Biography and Career Record*. Jefferson, NC: McFarland & Company Publishers, 2004

Nolan, Tom. *Three Chords for Beauty's Sake: The Life of Artie Shaw*. New York, NY: WW Norton & Co Inc, 2010

Panassié, Hugues. *La Musique de Jazz et Le Swing*. Stockholm, Sweden: Forum,1945

Peterson, Oscar. *A Jazz Odyssey: My Life in Jazz*. New York, NY: Continuum, 2002

Schmidt, Paul William. *History of the Ludwig Drum Company*. Fullerton, CA: Centerstream Publishing, 1999

Shapiro, Nat, Nathan Hentoff. *Hear me Talkin' to Aa*. New York, NY: Rinehart & Company, 1955

Shaw, Arnold. 52nd Street: *The Street of Jazz*. New York, NY: Da Capo Press, 1971

Shaw, Artie. *The Trouble with Cinderella: An Outline of Identity*. Fithian Press, 1952

Stearns, Marshall. *The Story of Jazz*. New York, NY: Oxford University Press Inc, 1956

Stratemann, Klaus. *Buddy Rich and Gene Krupa: A Filmo-Discography*. Lübbecke, Germany: Uhle & Kleimann, 1980

Sullivan, James. *Seven Dirty Words: The Life and Crimes of George Carlin*. New York, NY: DaCapo Press, 2010

Tormé, Mel. *Traps, The Drum Wonder*. Alma, MI: Rebeats Publications, 1991 Troup, Stuart

Woody Herman. *The Woodchoppers Ball: The Autobiography of Woody Herman.* New York, NY: Limelight Editions, 1994

White, John. *Artie Shaw: Non-Stop Flight.* Hull, East Note, 1998

Woideck, Carl. *Charlie Parker: His Music and Life.* Ann Arbor, MI: University of Michigan, 1996

Zammarchi, Fabrice. Sylvie Mas. *A Life in the Golden Age of Jazz: A Biography of Buddy DeFranco.* Seattle, WA: Parkside Publications Inc, 2002

Zirpolo, Michael. *Mr. Trumpet: The Trials, Tribulations, and Triumphs of Bunny Berigan.* Lanham, MD: Scarecrow Press Inc, 2011

Newspaper Articles, Interviews and Reviews

Article in Variety, June 23, 1922; Article in *Billboard*, July 1922; Article in *The New York Times*, Sept 13, 1922; Article in *New York Tribune*, Sept 13, 1922; Review in *Variety*, Sept 15, 1922; Article in *Billboard*, March 28, 1924; Review in *Brisbane Courier*, June 30, 1925; Article in *Billboard*, Sept 19, 1925; Review in *Variety*, April 30, 1930; Review in *Motion Picture News*, May 10, 1930; Review in *Chicago Daily News*, Dec 12, 1936; Review in *Variety*, April 14, 1937; Article in *Variety*, Sept 1, 1937; Article in *The Morning Journal*, May 4, 1946; Article in *Metronome*, Oct 1946; Article in *The Times* from San Mateo, California, March 12, 1948; Article in *Billboard* about Buddy Rich with Josephine Baker, March 17, 1951; Interview with Buddy Rich in *Downbeat*, Oct 1959; Review in *Variety*, Oct 14, 1959; Review in *Downbeat*, Nov 1959; Article in *Downbeat* by George Hoefer: "Buddy Rich – Portrait of a Man in Conflict," June 9, 1960; Article in *Billboard*, Dec 10, 1966; Les Tomkins interview with Norman Granz in Jazz Professional, 1966–1967; Interview with Buddy Rich: "The Nouveau Rich," in *Downbeat*, April 20, 1967; Article in *The Indianapolis Star*, July 12, 1968; Article in *The Los Angeles Times*, July 16, 1968; "Les Tomkins meets Buddy Rich: At the Drum Clinic," Jazz Professional, 1968; "Les Tomkins meets Buddy Rich: One-Armed Drummer," *Jazz Professional*, 1968; "Les Tomkins meets Buddy Rich, Jack Parnell and Maynard Ferguson," *Jazz Professional*, 1970;"Les Tomkins interview with Harry James," 1970; "Les Tomkins meets Buddy Rich: Let's Honor the Living Greats," *Jazz Professional*, 1971; Interview with Buddy Rich about karate in *Fighting Stars*, Dec 1973; Interview with Buddy Rich in *Jazz Journal*, Nov 1974; Article in *Nashville Banner*, Jan 16, 1975; Interview with Buddy Rich by Frank Meyer, unknown newspaper, Feb 5, 1975; Article in *Ottawa Citizen*, July 14, 1975; Article in *The New York Times*, July 18, 1975; Article in *Washington Afro-American Red Star*, July 29, 1975; Article in *Southern Africa*, Vol. VIII, Number 8, Sept 1975; Article in *Black World Negro Digest*, Nov 1975; Review in *Downbeat*, "Buddy Rich at Mr. Kelly's in Chicago,"

1975; Interview with Buddy Rich in *Legends*, 1975–1977; Article in *Kansas City Times*, Jan 1, 1976; Jim Warchols interview with Buddy Rich in *Modern Drummer*, Jan 1977; Mel Tormé interview with Buddy Rich in *Downbeat*, Feb 1978; Review Buddy Rich at Granny's Dinner Playhouse, *Dallas Morning News*, Feb 14, 1978; "Les Tomkins meets Buddy Rich: Let Musicians be Heard as Individuals," *Jazz Professional*, 1980; Interview with Buddy Rich in *Modern Drummer*: Revisited, Dec 1980; Interview with Buddy Rich in UK Tour Program, 1981; Les Tomkins interview with Buddy Rich, July 1982; Buddy Rich interview in newspaper *Orkesterjournalen*, Sweden, 1984; Article in SPIN: "A Different Drummer" by Harold Conrad, Oct 1985; Article in *International Herald Tribune*, Mike Zwerin, July 3, 1986; Review of Buddy Rich at The Blue Note in *Modern Drummer*, Dec 1986; Review of Buddy Rich at The Blue Note in *The New York Times*, Dec 1986; Article in *The Los Angeles Times*: "Buddy Rich has Brain Tumor," March 6, 1987; Article in *The Los Angeles Times*: "Buddy Rich has Tumor Removed from Brain," March 17, 1987; Article in *The Los Angeles Times*: "Buddy Rich, Frenetic Jazz Drummer Dies," April 3, 1987; Article in *The Washington Post*: "Jazz Drummer Buddy Rich Dies," April 3, 1987; Article in *The Boston Globe*: "Buddy Rich – A Truly Different Drummer," April 3, 1987; Article in *Drums & Drumming*: "Rich vs Krupa and Other Classic Drum Battles," Nov 1990; Interview with Cathy Rich in *Modern Drummer*, April 1991; Article: "An Evening with Buddy," *Modern Drummer*, March 1999; Interview with Cathy Rich, The Jazz Zine, June 16, 1999; Article: "Behind the Famous Bus Tapes," *Jazz Times*, March 2002; Article in Jazz Times: "Artie Shaw on Artie Shaw," May 2002; Article in *Jazz Times*: "Norman Granz: Goodbye, My Friend," by Nat Hentoff, 2002; Interview with Freddie Gruber in *Jazz Improv* Magazine, number 3, 2006; Interview with Cathy Rich in *Jazz Improv* Magazine, number 3, 2006; Interview with Marie Rich in *Jazz Improv* Magazine, number 3, 2006; Interview with Dave Panichi in *The Monthly*, July 2007; Interview with Stanley Kay in *Jazz Wax*, June 25, 2010; Interview with Bobby Shew in All About Jazz, June 25, 2010.

Audio Interviews

Saturday Night Swing Session, April 12, 1947; Buddy Rich at Apollo Theatre, New York, Feb 14, 1952; Interview with Krupa and Rich at "Voice of America," March–April, 1956; Buddy Rich and Gene Krupa conversation at Mr Kelly's in Chicago, July 14, 1973; "Eyewitness News," Buddy Rich on Buddy's Place, Channel 7, April 10, 1974; Efrom Allen interview with Buddy Rich at Buddy's Place, Dec, 1974; Buddy Rich with Benny Goodman Quintet at The White House, Nov 2, 1981; Skitch Henderson Music Maker Show, Oct 8, 1983; Interview with Buddy Rich, Aug 28, 1986, unknown place; Steve Marcus' interview by Blaise Lantana, KJZZ, Oct 1, 2001; Ray Anthony interview with Buddy Rich's sisters Marge and Jo, unknown year; Chris Cortex' interview with Cathy Rich: I'm Talking Jazz, KCSMFM, May 16, 2004.

Archives

The State of Wisconsin Collection, USA; Library of Congress, Washington, D.C., USA; National Jazz Archive, UK; and Royal Library, Stockholm, Sweden.

Material from Buddy Rich Collectors, Relatives and Friends

Greg Bauman, Reb Bilinski, Roger Berg, Louis Bernstein, Charley Braun, Dave Cooper, Per DyrnesliKristensen, Janne Ersson, Walt Heitner, Walter Hern, Clarence Hintze, Ron Hutchinson, Mike James, Bruce Klauber, Peter Lanzarone, Leonard Maltin, Rien Moeliker, Janne Mårtensson, Geoffrey Nelson, Graham Sheridan, Shirley Shiffrin, Rex Strother, Paul Testa, Rob Wallis, Terry Wayland, Joseph Weinmeyer and Brian Wilson.

Author's Interviews

Ulf Andersson
Tenor saxophonist, played with Buddy Rich at Gröna Lund, Stockholm, 1979.
Pauly Cohen
Trumpeter, played with Buddy Rich in Tommy Dorsey's Orchestra 1954–1955.
Richie Cole
Alto saxophonist, played with Buddy Rich from January 1969 to July 1971.
Tom Garling
Trombonist, played with Buddy Rich from January to December 1986.
Clarence Hintze
Compiler of the discography in *Mister, I Am the Band* and friend of Buddy Rich.
Peter Jablonski
Acclaimed Swedish concert pianist and conductor.
Lars Jernryd
Swedish promoter for the Jazz Festival in Kristianstad, 1978.
Bo Johnson
Concert promoter and production manager at Buddy Rich's European tours 1976–1978.
Joe LaBarbera
Drummer, played with Buddy Rich in 1968.
John LaBarbera
Composer and arranger, worked with Buddy Rich 1968–1987.
Pat LaBarbera
Tenor saxophonist, clarinetist and flautist, played with Buddy Rich September 1967 to February 1974.
David Lucas
Percussionist on the Asian tour, and close friend to Buddy Rich.
Peter Lundin
Artist manager and TV producer for Buddy Rich in Stockholm, Sweden, 1979.

Mike Mainieri
Vibraphonist, played with Buddy Rich 1960–1962.
Sherrie Maricle
Drummer and leader for the DIVA Big Band and a close friend of Stanley Kay.
Hal McKusick
Alto saxophonist and clarinetist, played with Buddy Rich from July to November 1948.
Eric Miyashiro
Trumpeter, played with Buddy Rich from February 1985 to December 1986.
Ron Paley
Electric bassist, played with Buddy Rich from October 1973 to February 1974.
Al Porcino
Lead trumpeter, played with Buddy Rich in Tommy Dorsey's Orchestra, 1944, and in Buddy's band, 1968.
Cathy Rich
Buddy Rich's daughter.
Ed Shaughnessy
Drummer on "The Tonight Show Starring Johnny Carson" and friend of Buddy Rich.
Dave Stahl
Trumpeter, played with Buddy Rich 1976–1982.
Bo Stenhammar
Swedish promotor for The Swedish Jazz & Blues Festival in Stockholm, 1986.
Ernie Watts
Alto, tenor and soprano saxophonist, played with Buddy Rich from October 1966 to March 1968.
Mike Zirpolo
Author of the book *Mr. Trumpet: The Trials, Tribulations, and Triumphs of Bunny Berigan.*

Filmography

BUDDY TRAPS IN SOUND EFFECTS

Release January 24, 1930. Vitaphone short. Warner Bros. Director: Murray Rooth. Starring Buddy Traps – Marvel drummer. 10 min black and white short movie, sound disc. Conversation with the store proprietor and drumming on various objects. Medley: "That Wonderful Boyfriend of Mine," "Am I Blue," "That Wonderful Boyfriend of Mine" (repeated), "If You Were Mine," "Bashful Baby" vocal & tap by Buddy Traps, "Stars and Stripes Forever." Only the audio portion and still photographs survive. Film footage undiscovered thus far.

ARTIE SHAW'S CLASS IN SWING

Release September 8, 1939 Paramount Pictures. Director:Leslie Roush. Starring Artie

Shaw and His Orchestra. 9 min black & white. "Paramount Headliner: short featuring Shaw performing the "I Have Eyes," Nightmare," "Shoot the Likker to Me John Boy" and "Table d'Hote" with Buddy Rich on drums. This is a pseudo-educational short movie trying to explain the sections and mechanisms of a swing band. All tracks are occasionally overdubbed by an unknown narrator's commentary.

DANCING CO-ED

Release September 26, 1939 MGM. Director: S. Sylvan Simon. Starring Lana Turner, Richard Carlson, Anne Rutherford, Artie Shaw and His Orchestra 80 min, black and white. Based on the Beatrice Lille autobiography "Every Other Inch a lady". LanaTurner (19 years old at the time) stars in this lighthearted musical comedy as Patty Marlow, a dancer fighting her way up the show business ladder. Famous hoofer Freddie Tobin (Lee Bowman) is about to start work on a new movie when his dance partner becomes pregnant and drops out of the project. Press agent Joe Drews (Roscoe Karns) dreams up a publicity stunt to find Freddie's new co-star: He'll stage a contest on college campuses to find a dancer among the student body. Buddy Rich with Artie Shaw and His Orchestra.

ARTIE SHAW AND HIS ORCHESTRA IN SYMPHONY OF SWING

Release December 30, 1939 Vitaphone short. Director: Joseph Henabery. StarringArtie Shaw and His Orchestra 10 min, black & white. This music short features the Shaw band with Buddy Rich, Helen Forrest and Tony Pastor, performing "Alone Together," "Deep Purple," "Jeepers Creepers," and "Lady Be Good."

LAS VEGAS NIGHTS

Release March 28, 1941. Paramount. Director: Ralph Murphy. Starring Phil Regan, Bert Wheeler, Constance Moore, Virginia Dale. Time 86 minutes, black and white. For his first feature-film appearance in two years, comedian Bert Wheeler (of Wheeler & Woolsey fame) teamed up with bandleader Phil Regan. The story focuses on a quartet of vaudevillians-- Regan, Wheeler, Moore, and Dale--who show up in Vegas with nary a cent between them. Even Bert Wheeler admitted that "Las Vegas Nights' was a bomb, noting, "A picture like that can come back and haunt you." Still, it holds some historical value as the film that introduced Frank Sinatra, appearing as the uncredited vocalist for the Tommy Dorsey and His Orchestra. Buddy Rich plays with Tommy Dorsey Orchestra.

ROAD TO ZANZIBAR

Release April 11, 1941. Paramount Pictures. Director: Victor Schertzinger Starring Bob Hope, Bing Crosby and Dorothy Lamour. Time 91 min, black and white. Hope and Crosby flee a South African carnival when their sideshow causes a fire. After several similar escapades, they've finally saved enough to return to the USA, when Chuck spends it all on a "lost" diamond mine. Before long, a pair of attractive con-women have tricked our heroes into financing a comic safari, featuring numerous burlesque jungle adventures. Buddy Rich plays on the opening soundtrack with Tommy Dorsey and His Orchestra on the song "You Lucky People, You." It's probably Buddy Rich playing tom toms in the jungle scene.

SHIP AHOY
Release April 23, 1942. MGM. Director Edvard N. Buzzel Starring Eleanor Powell, Red Skelton, Virginia O'Brien Time 112 min, black and white. In this musical, tap dancer Tallulah Winters (Eleanor Powell) and Tommy Dorsey's orchestra are traveling to Puerto Rico on an ocean liner to perform at their next gig. However, when Tallulah gets mixed up in a spy plot, she draws writer Merton K. Kibble (Red Skelton) into the confusion for a few laughs. This film features a number of songs, including "On Moonlight Bay," "Last Call for Love," and "Ship Ahoy." Buddy Rich with Tommy Dorsey and His Orchestra featuring Frank Sinatra.

HOW'S ABOUT IT
Release February 3, 1943.Universal. Director: Erle C. Kenton Starring The Andrews Sisters, Louis DaPron, Walter Catlett, Robert Paige, Bob Scheerer. Time 60 min, black and white. The Andrews Sisters play elevator operators who work in an office building containing a music publishing business. The girls, all aspiring singers, hope to get a break while working there. Songs include "Don't Mind the Rain," "Take It and Git," "East of the Rockies," "Going Up," and "Here Comes the Navy." Buddy Rich appears as an orchestra leader, performing with an uncredited studio orchestra.

PRESENTING LILY MARS
Release May 6, 1943. MGM. Director: Norman Taurog. Starring Judy Garland, Van Heflin, Richard Carlson Time 105, min black and white A Booth Tarkington novel was the source for this Judy Garland musical. Garland plays a small-town girl with big- city ambitions. She heads to Broadway hoping for stardom, but after a series of disappointments, the best she can manage is an understudy job. Garland sings a lot, and whenever she does, the picture soars. Other musical acts include the orchestras of Bob Crosby and Tommy Dorsey. Buddy Rich plays with Tommy Dorsey and His Orchestra on soundtrack only.

DUBARRY WAS A LADY
Release August 13, 1943. MGM. Director: Roy del Ruth. Starring Lucille Ball, Gene Kelly, Red Skelton. Time 101 min, color. Two talented redheads cavort through the court of King Louis XV in one of MGM's lightest and frothiest musical concoctions. Adapted from a Cole Porter Broadway show but missing most of its best songs, it's still a treat to see Tommy Dorsey and His Orchestra in powdered wigs. Buddy Rich with

Tommy Dorsey and His Orchestra.

GIRL CRAZY
Release November 26, 1943. MGM. Director: Norman Taurog Starring Judy Garland, Mickey Rooney, Guy Kibbee. Time 100 min, color. A wealthy New Yorker, fed up with his son's romantic escapades, ships the budding playboy to a men's-only southwestern university. There, the would be Romeo falls for the pretty but uninterested dean's granddaughter and saves the school from financial ruin. This eighth pairing of Rooney and Garland includes many classic Gershwin songs such as "I Got Rhythm," "Fascinating Rhythm,"and "Embraceable You." This is the second screen version of the 1930 Broadway musical comedy. Buddy Rich plays with Tommy Dorsey and His Orchestra only on the soundtrack.

PHANTOM LADY
Release January 28, 1944. Universal.Director: Robert Siodmak Starring Franchot Tone, Ella Raines, Alan Curtis, Fay Helm. Time 87 min, black and white. Robert Siodmak's shadowy, expressionistic film noir is a brilliant visual adaptation of the haunted nightmare world of Cornell Woolrich (writing as William Irish). Most haunting of all the images in the film is the orgasmic drum solo Cliff plays while being seduced by Carol, who will stop at nothing to save the man she loves. Buddy Rich plays the 40 second drum solo on soundtrack only.

BROADWAY RHYTHM
Release April 13, 1944. MGM. Director: Roy del Ruth. Starring George Murphy, Charles Winninger, Gloria de Haven, Ginny Simms. Time 112 min, color. A veteran producer searches for a star for his new show, and the girl of his dreams, a beautiful Hollywood movie celebrity, proves to be more than he can handle. She rejects his offer and chooses to star in a musical his father is producing instead. Buddy Rich with Tommy Dorsey and His Orchestra on soundtrack only.

THRILL OF A ROMANCE
Release May 22, 1945. MGM. Director: Richard Thorpe. Starring Esther Williams, Van Johnson, Spring Byington. Time 104 min, color. This aquatic musical is set at a mountain resort in the Sierra Nevadas where a heroic Army Air Corpsman has come for a vacation. There he falls in love with the lovely swimming instructor, who is unfortunately newly married to a rather stodgy businessman. The mayhem begins when her new husband is called to Washington on urgent business. Songs include "Please Don't Say No," "Say Maybe," "I Should Care," "Lonely Night," "Vive L'Amour," "Schubert's Serenade," and "The Thrill of a Romance." Buddy Rich with Tommy Dorsey and His Orchestra.

EARL CARROL'S SKETCHBOOK

Release July 30, 1946. Republic Pictures. Director: Albert Rogell. Starring Constance Moore, William Marshall, Bill Goodwin. Time 90min, black and white. Though Republic had decided to forego plans for an annual film edition of "Earl Carroll's Vanities," their reciprocal deal with the Broadway impresario was still very much in effect in 1946: Hence the creation of the musical extravaganza "Earl Carroll Sketchbook." The plot involves a serious composer named Tyler Brice (William Marshall) who "sells out" to write radio commercials. Artistically redeemed by heroine Pamela Thayer, Brice decides to lend his talents as composer and singer, to producer Earl Carroll's newest nightclub revue. The film revives Harold Arlen and Ted Koehler's "I've Got a Right to Sing the Blues." Retitled "Hats Off to Rhythm" for television broadcast. Buddy Rich appears as a bandleader with his orchestra, though it's doubtful that Buddy is playing on the soundtrack.

THE GREAT MORGAN

Release 1946. MGM. Director: Nat Perrin. Starring Frank Morgan, Leon Ames, Carlos Ramirez, Eleanor Powell, Virginia O'Brian. Time 57 min, black and white. Buddy Rich appears with Tommy Dorsey Orchestra. Unusual MGM outing, in that it is a compilation film built around a slight plot line, with a running time of less than 60 minutes. Produced for overseas markets and features Fran Morgan (the Wizard in "The Wizard of Oz"). Morgan, playing himself, is given a chance to put together his own movie, and he does so by combining several unrelated comedic and musical short subjects with his own short film. In 1980, a print was found, and the film was subsequently released to the American home video market.

BUDDY RICH AND HIS ORCHESTRA

Release November 23, 1948. Universal International Studios. Director:Will Cowan. Starring Buddy Rich, Lois DaPron, Mello-Larks, Terry Gibbs.14:54 min, black and white. Buddy Rich plays drums, sings and taps. Gene Krupa also did a film short like this with the same director, released same year and by the same movie company.

THRILLS OF MUSIC

Release January 20, 1949. Columbia Pictures. Director:Henry Foster. Starring Buddy Rich, Steve Condos, Betty Bonney. 10 min, black & white. Buddy Rich performs "Kicks with Sticks," "Great Head,"("Woody'n You"), Condos-Rich tap dance, "A Man could be a Wonderful Thing" (Buddy and Bonney vocal duet). From Columbia's "Thrills of Music" series.

HARRY JAMES AND HIS MUSIC MAKERS

Release May 08, 1953. Universal International. Director: Will Cowan. StarringGale Robbins, Allen and Ashton (dancers), Harry James and His Orchestra. 14:25 min, black and white. Note: "Brave Bulls: and "Trumpet Blues and Cantabile" also used in Leonard Feather's "Feather on Jazz" series.

MELODIES BY MARTIN

Release December 28, 1955. Universal Pictures. Director:Will Cowan. Starring Freddie Martin and His Orchestra with guest Buddy Rich. 16 min, black and white. Jitterbug Routine, " Do Do Do" by Ira and George Gershwin; "A Man;" "Somebody Stole My Gal" by Leo Wood.

VISIT TO A SMALL PLANET

Release February 4, 1960. Paramount. Director: Norman Taurog. Starring Jerry Lewis, Joan Blackman, Fred Clark, John Williams. 90 min, black and white. Not Jerry's best. When a space alien's fascination with Earthlings gets the better of him, he breaks one of his planet's laws and speeds off to visit earth. Once there the alien (Jerry Lewis) encounters a nice family who kindly take him in. In exchange for having them teach him about human ways, he uses his many fantastic powers to help them. Buddy Rich's Sextet has an amusing cameo.